The Ethics of Artificial Int Education

The Ethics of Artificial Intelligence in Education identifies and confronts key ethical issues generated over years of AI research, development, and deployment in learning contexts. Adaptive, automated, and data-driven education systems are increasingly being implemented in universities, schools, and corporate training worldwide, but the ethical consequences of engaging with these technologies remain unexplored. Featuring expert perspectives from inside and outside the AIED scholarly community, this book provides AI researchers, learning scientists, educational technologists, and others with questions, frameworks, guidelines, policies, and regulations to ensure the positive impact of artificial intelligence in learning.

Wayne Holmes teaches Learning Sciences and Innovation in the Faculty of Education and Society at University College London, UK, and is Consultant on AI and Education for the International Research Centre for Artificial Intelligence (IRCAI), UNESCO, and The Council of Europe.

Kaśka Porayska-Pomsta is Professor of Artificial Intelligence in Education at the Department of Culture Communication and Media in the Faculty of Education and Society at University College London, UK.

The Ethics of Artificial Intelligence in Education

Practices, Challenges, and Debates

Edited by
Wayne Holmes and
Kaśka Porayska-Pomsta

Routledge
Taylor & Francis Group

NEW YORK AND LONDON

Cover image: Paweł Kuczyński

First published 2023
by Routledge
605 Third Avenue, New York, NY 10158

and by Routledge
4 Park Square, Milton Park, Abingdon, Oxon OX14 4RN

Routledge is an imprint of the Taylor & Francis Group, an informa business

© 2023 Taylor & Francis

Library of Congress Cataloging-in-Publication Data
Names: Holmes, Wayne, 1959- editor. | Porayska-Pomsta, Kaśka, editor.
Title: The ethics of artificial intelligence in education : practices, challenges,
and debates / edited by Wayne Holmes and Kaśka Porayska-Pomsta.
Description: New York, NY : Routledge, 2022. | Includes bibliographical
references and index.
Identifiers: LCCN 2022011875 (print) | LCCN 2022011876 (ebook) |
ISBN 9780367349714 (hardback) | ISBN 9780367349721 (paperback) |
ISBN 9780429329067 (ebook)
Subjects: LCSH: Artificial intelligence–Educational applications–Moral and
ethical aspects.
Classification: LCC LB1028.43 .E75 2022 (print) |
LCC LB1028.43 (ebook) | DDC 371.33/4--dc23/eng/20220316
LC record available at https://lccn.loc.gov/2022011875
LC ebook record available at https://lccn.loc.gov/2022011876

ISBN: 978-0-367-34971-4 (hbk)
ISBN: 978-0-367-34972-1 (pbk)
ISBN: 978-0-429-32906-7 (ebk)

DOI: 10.4324/9780429329067

Typeset in Baskerville
by Taylor & Francis Books

Contents

PART 2
Introduction to Part II 147
KAŚKA PORAYSKA-POMSTA AND WAYNE HOLMES

Illustrations

Figures

Tables

Acknowledgements

The editors would like to thank all the contributing authors (for the excellence of their writing, their kind support, and their persistence in these challenging times), our publisher Dan Schwartz (for his faith in us, his unerring support, and his extraordinary patience), Dr Duygu Bektik (without whom this book would never have been started), and Paweł Kuczyński (for allowing us to include his thought-provoking art). We would also like to thank Gabriela Ramos and Professor Neil Selwyn for their inspirational forewords.

Wayne would also like to thank Tracey (for always being there), Cate (for always being interested), and Oliver (for always being critical), as well as his friends and colleagues at the UCL Knowledge Lab (especially Allison, Andrea, Caroline, Charlotte, Eileen, Fatiha, Jen, Kaśka, and Manolis); UNESCO (especially Fengchun, Fideliz, Glen, Juan David, Maksim, Michela, Xianglei, and Yara); the International Research Centre for AI (especially Colin, Davor, Gasper, John, Marko, Mihejala, Mitja, and Monika); and all his other friends and colleagues over many years (especially Doug, Maya, Mike, Paco, Rebecca, Shuling, and Stamatina). Wayne would like to dedicate this book to every student around the world who already has, or who will someday, engage with an AIED system. Hopefully, this book will help that experience genuinely benefit your present and future lives.

Kaśka would also like to thank Professor Richard Noss (UCL Knowledge Lab) for his uncompromising questioning of her about the assumptions within AI for Education and the presumed beneficence of AIED technologies; all of her collaborators (academic, industrial, teachers and learners) and students throughout the decades, too numerous to list but whose contributions helped shape her research; Keith Anderson (Google Deep Mind) for his blunt interrogation of her research from the AI engineering perspective and for all the morning coffees; and Michael and Jo Anderson for constantly challenging her views through their periodic frustrations about the AI-fuelled world, the rigidity of schooling, and the conventionality of social expectations. Kaśka would like to dedicate this book to her life-long inspiration – her father, Professor Józef Porayski-Pomsta.

Foreword 1

AI is already powering numerous algorithmic applications in education. Intelligent tutoring systems facilitating smart assistance; personalized learning systems promoting students' learning; and automated systems to support teachers in assessing what students know are but a few examples. They also influence the learning ecosystem through a wide array of social networks, blogs, gaming platforms, and mobile applications that seamlessly merge within the learning processes. As we reluctantly enter the third year of the COVID-19 pandemic, AI technologies in education continue to empower students and parents, schools and teachers, professors, and institutions around the world, fostering content, processes, and learning outcomes with the aim to mitigate learning losses and support up-skilling.

While the benefits of AI technologies for education are acknowledged, and for good reasons, to maximize their benefits we need ethical frameworks to avoid the drawbacks of such general-purpose technologies. For instance, current AI applications in education are devoid of the voices of around 2.9 billion individuals who are still offline. This skews representativeness within the virtual world significantly, making it risky to extrapolate the gained insights and apply the same directly to real-world complex scenarios, especially when the unrepresented are impacted. Further caution should be drawn, acknowledging the pervasive nature of AI technologies that impact (positively or adversely) learners beyond the classroom walls. Indiscriminate applications of AI in education risk perpetuating or exacerbating existing systemic biases and discrimination, augmenting the inequalities that disadvantaged and marginalized groups suffer from and amplifying racism, sexism, xenophobia, and other forms of injustice.

The world needs principles and ethical criteria to ensure that transformative technologies serve human goals, and not the other way around. This is the call that UNESCO has heard loud and clear from its Member States, asking to ensure AI develops solutions that are fair, accountable, transparent, and that it counters bias, strengthens autonomy and agency, and combats non-discrimination. All this includes AI-powered education. To move towards AI technologies that are ethical 'by design', on 23 November 2021, 193 UNESCO Member States adopted the historic 'Recommendation on the Ethics of AI' to fulfil these exact demands. The Recommendation builds on key societal values and principles, and its remit encompasses a wide array of policy areas, including education and research, where it stresses the need for technological intervention(s) to be implemented in a way that fully contributes to respect human rights and foster inclusion and diversity.

This book contributes importantly to inform and sensibilize readers towards encoding ethics in the AI used in education, at times challenging the status quo as well as current pedagogical and technological practices. Putting ethics at the core of AI in education means preventing harmful assumptions being repeated and outcomes distorted. The book acknowledges that important ethical questions remain unasked and unanswered, and calls on researchers, developers, and corporations to address the gaps. This is the gap that the implementation of the UNESCO's 'Recommendation on the Ethics of AI' in education, labour, health, and many other domains aims to address. The Recommendation takes a strong stance on how we can ensure full respect for human rights with concrete proposals on data governance, privacy, manipulation, discrimination, and biases. It notes that implementing even the latest privacy-preserving concepts, such as differential privacy or federated learning, without contextual assessment will not deliver as they should.

The Recommendation specifically underlines the need for a multi-stakeholder construct around data governance and ownership, and pushes for the adoption of a 'digital commons' approach to encourage companies to share the data they collect with other stakeholders, as appropriate, for the benefit of research, innovation, or the public. The Recommendation stresses on going beyond cognitive competency development, and developing critical and creative thinking, teamwork, communication, socio-emotional and AI ethics skills within learners – especially in countries where there are notable gaps in these skills – to promote informed decision-making. It further emphasizes the need to enhance the interoperability of tools, datasets, and interfaces of systems hosting data to foster the creation of collaborative platforms to share quality data in trusted and secured spaces.

AI is key for our future, and for the future of education. If we develop, implement, and deploy it in an ethical manner, AI will help make our future brighter, our children smarter through education, and our societies more inclusive and resilient.

Gabriela Ramos,
Assistant Director-General for Social and Human Sciences, UNESCO

Foreword 2

AI, education, and ethics – starting a conversation

Regardless of how 'inter-disciplinary' this field might appear to the casual observer, academic discussions of AI remain beset by intellectual schisms and fundamentally different beliefs. On one hand, those working on AI design and development understandably feel that only they have adequate understanding (let alone direct experience) of the technical complexities and underpinning computational theory involved. From this perspective, it can seem that AI innovation has begun to attract unwarranted scrutiny from 'uncredentialled commentators' and 'non-experts' who peddle "a curious 'counter-hype' of critical stances towards AI" (Galanos 2019, p.421).

In contrast, we see mounting frustration among critics working in the humanities, arts, and social sciences who consider themselves more attuned to the complex social contexts within which AI technologies are implemented. From this perspective, then, it might be reasoned that "the AI community suffers from not seeing how its work fits into a long history of science being used to legitimize violence against marginalized people, and to stratify and separate people" (Chelsea Barabas, cited in Van Noorden 2020, p.358).

All told, a distinct sense of 'them and us' continues to pervade academic discussions of AI, especially as AI tools move out of R&D phases and into 'real-world' contexts. This inevitably provokes distinctly different claims and counter-claims – all rooted in very specific approaches to making sense of what 'AI' is, and contrasting understandings of how AI technologies become part of everyday life.

On one hand, these very different outlooks reflect distinct differences in ontology – in other words, how one sees the existence of the social world. As might be expected, there are plenty of computer science researchers and AI developers who immerse themselves in the immediate challenges of improving the functionality of "technologies in use today" (Krafft et al. 2020, p.72). This leads to pragmatic expectations that AI technologies can function in social settings in ways that are broadly quantifiable, calculable, and capable of operating effectively given the correct inputs (Wajcman 2019).

In contrast, there are many others who feel that these assumptions do not extend to the complex social contexts within which AI technologies are now being implemented. From this point of view, any 'real-world' implementation of AI is severely compromised by the 'problem-solving mindset' that prevails within the computer sciences (Berendt 2019). As such, we are seeing growing calls to imbue AI development with a heightened sense of the social, political, and cultural dimensions of this work.

So, where does this leave our own specific interest in AI and education? Is education simply another domain in which AI experts and their critics are destined to continue talking at cross-purposes? While it might be argued that these different mindsets and belief systems are defining elements of what it means to work in 'STEM' (science, technology, engineering, and mathematics) as distinct to 'HASS' (humanities, arts, and social sciences), there is clearly a need for increased dialogue and mutual understanding – especially as AI systems and processes begin to pervade mainstream education systems and settings.

Thus, while educational AI will undoubtedly continue to be a hotbed of technically focused problem-solving, we need to take seriously Bettina Berendt's point about the dangers of seeing AI in purely computational terms. The recent push for more discussion of 'AI ethics' is one such response to this predicament – perhaps offering common ground on which different academic factions involved in the educational implementation of AI can meet.

AI ethics: a conversational starting point

This book is a good opportunity to bring about such cross-disciplinary encounters and conversations. As many of its chapters illustrate, considerable progress has already been made in crafting a sense of what AI ethics might look like with regard to education. For example, there are burgeoning discussions of educational AI in terms of privacy, explicability, respect for human autonomy, and so on. This has translated into emerging debates over how educational issues fit with broader discussions of 'fairness, accountability and transparency', 'trustworthy AI', 'humane AI', and so on.

That said, this book also reminds us that these are not discussions that can be wrapped up quickly, or perhaps ever addressed to everyone's complete satisfaction. The coming-together of AI, education, and ethics immediately raises tricky questions and confronting ideas. In short, AI ethics is not a topic that can be entered into half-heartedly!

Indeed, unlike many other discussions around AI, talk of 'AI ethics' will quickly push many of us into unfamiliar and unsettling territory. When applied to a real-life setting such as education, questions of ethics are inherently normative – concerned with developing shared principles of "how we should live and what we morally ought to do" (Driver 2005, p.31). These are complex questions of what should be considered 'good' or 'bad' conduct, what constitutes 'right' or 'wrong' behaviour, and similar value judgements. These are tricky negotiations over what we think should (and should not) be done, what is collectively acceptable … and what is not.

So, this book needs to be read as a starting point for a number of different conversations around education and AI that hopefully will evolve over the next few years. Nothing that is written here will provide a definitive guide to how anyone might be able to best 'do' ethics. Instead, this book should provoke more questions than it will provide answers, and raise more contentions than conclusions. It is perhaps best to approach these chapters in a spirit of problem-raising rather than problem-solving. To get things going, then, here are three preliminary sets of contentions …

i. AI ethics are not clearly defined and easily 'fixed'

Despite everything I have just written, it might still seem tempting to hope that AI ethics is something that can be neatly bundled up and dealt with – ideally in a similar manner to how matters of 'ethics' are actioned in domains such as medicine, journalism, and business. This might be described as a matter of applied ethics – that is, identifying how to practically apply moral questions and normative judgements to the development and application of AI in education.

There are certainly many people in the AI community pursuing this line of thought – framing ethical issues in terms of technical challenges that can be addressed through better design and development of AI. This mindset is evident in current enthusiasms for notions such as 'privacy by design', or addressing complex issues of social bias and discrimination through 'correcting' statistical bias, under-representation, and variance in datasets.

At first glance, such efforts might well seem to be an effective pragmatic way to address a tricky problem. Yet, the moral conundrums and challenges that underpin AI ethics in education are obviously not wholly reducible to sets of discrete procedural challenges that can be codified and then 'solved' through better design and programming. As Brent Mittelstadt (2019, p.505) puts it, "the risk is that complex, difficult ethical debates will be oversimplified to make the concepts at hand computable and implementable in a straightforward but conceptually shallow manner".

As such, when talking about AI ethics and education we need to remain sceptical of 'technical fixes' that convey promises of being able to engineer achievable 'ethical' action. We need to remain vigilant for surface-level responses that slip into corporate obfuscation and 'ethics-washing' (Wagner 2018). This has certainly proven the case with Big Tech efforts to set up ethics frameworks and ethics boards to no great effect (other than as an attempt to avoid regulation). Instead, as Mittelstadt (2019, p.505) concludes:

> Ethics is not meant to be easy or formulaic. Intractable principled disagreements should be expected and welcomed, as they reflect both serious ethical consideration and diversity of thought. They do not represent failure, and do not need to be 'solved'. Ethics is a process, not a destination.

ii. AI ethics are not an intuitive matter of doing 'good'

Of course, this framing of ethics as a 'process' of ongoing moral reflection runs the risk of pushing some folk to disengage completely from any sort of grounded, systematic approach to engaging with AI ethics. Oftentimes, this sees discussions descend into the presumption that AI ethics might be best tackled through personal intuition and/or individual commitments to working out how one's own work with AI might be aligned with 'good' outcomes. This inevitably leads to efforts that are underpinned by flimsy and unarticulated political assumptions about what 'AI for good' might constitute (let alone the question of whether an unproblematic 'good' might be achievable at all).

At best, this approach falls into what Ben Green (2018) describes as a non-politicised "know it when you see it" approach to deciding what constitutes fair/humane/good AI and data science. In terms of discussions around AI and education, this can result in crude equivalencies such as 'Poverty=Bad' or 'Staying enrolled on a university course=Good'.

Of course, deciding what constitutes 'good' involves complex normative judgements, which ideally need to be worked out through sustained dialogue amongst all those implicated in any particular technology use. Crucially, this dialogue should be driven by a strong guiding political philosophy. The lack of such a systematic approach and grounding principles means that any identified ethical 'goods' can become dangerous oversimplifications of politically complex and long-contested issues. This form of 'AI ethics' therefore runs the risk of what Green (2018, p.2) describes as blithely "wading into hotly contested political territory" and resulting in contestable (perhaps regressive) actions.

iii. Conversations around AI ethics need to be inclusive and far-reaching

Both of these approaches (the over-codified and the over-vague) relate to a third important point of contention. In short, we need to call out the tendency for discussions of AI ethics to be driven by already privileged and dominant voices. Talk of AI ethics rarely originates from the people and groups who are most disadvantaged by AI. Instead, discussion of AI ethics to date has been something of a closed shop – dominated by those who are already invested in (and advantaged by) AI.

This leads to narrow and unimaginative discussions about what AI ought to be. For example, as Kate Crawford (2021) observes, discussions tend to focus on idealised ethical ends for AI, rather than more messy questions over the actual means through which AI might be applied in an ethical manner. This also leads to a limited set of ideas about how AI should be overseen and how key protagonists might be held accountable. For example, we continue to see prominent calls for industry 'self-regulation' that hold little weight in the face of Big Tech actors for whom multi-million dollar fines are accepted as minor collateral damage. As such, AI ethics codes and guidelines are rarely reinforced by effective mechanisms to ensure that companies and/or their employees actually adhere to stated principles or else are held accountable for any transgressions.

We also need to call out the tendency for AI ethics to be discussed almost exclusively in terms of European and North American understandings of ethics – thereby overlooking philosophical traditions from non-Western contexts. There is much to learn from viewing AI development through the lenses of Buddhist ethics, moral thinking in the Chinese/Daoist tradition, views on ethics from Persian, African, and Indian thought. Similarly, framing AI through Indigenous knowledges opens up numerous different ways of thinking about how AI and education might come together (or not).

Above all, discussions of AI ethics need to steer well clear of any belief that these are novel issues and concerns that are best dealt with by 'AI experts'. Instead, when talking about 'AI ethics in education' we are primarily talking about educational ethics and societal ethics – issues and debates that have engaged diverse groups and communities for centuries. The implementation of AI in education is inevitably entangled with long-standing ethical and political dimensions of educational professions, processes, and practice. In short, "AI ethics is effectively a microcosm of the political and ethical challenges faced in society" (Mittelstadt 2019, p.505).

Conclusions

All told, 'AI ethics' is a useful starting-point (rather than obvious end-point) from which to: (i) advance the commitment that many AI developers have to making better products, as well as (ii) address the serious concerns that critics are now raising around AI and education. This book's interrogation of AI ethics should be seen as an opening gambit that will hopefully lead on to more complex conversations. As argued earlier, AI ethics is not something that can be wrapped up quickly, or ever satisfactorily decided upon and concluded. Engaging with ethics is a morally reflective process that needs to be ongoing.

Crucially, these conversations around AI, education, and ethics should be framed by explicit sets of values, and ready to embrace the politics of negotiating between competing perspectives, goals, and agendas. Indeed, many of the most critical issues surrounding the (mis)use of AI in education are profoundly political in nature, and entangled with broader issues of power, disadvantage, and marginalisation (see Verdegem 2021). The forms of AI that are beginning to pervade education, and the infrastructures they are embedded in, all "skew strongly toward the centralisation of power" (Crawford 2021, p.223). As such, it could be argued that AI can never be engineered to be completely 'fair' or 'democratised'.

As such, I hope that this book (and others that follow) act as a catalyst for collective discussions of how the educational AI community is co-engaged in political action that has varying impacts on different groups of people in various educational contexts. This might not sound like an attractive proposition for any technically minded innovator looking to develop spectacular 'AI solutions' capable of transforming education. Instead, pursuing educational AI along more ethical lines requires considerable time and effort, and a considerable amount of deliberation, debate, dialogue, and consensus building. All of this implies replacing ambitions of 'scaling up' with a commitment to slowing down. This book takes a useful initial step in the right direction.

Neil Selwyn,
Monash University, Melbourne

References

Berendt, B. (2019). AI for the common good? *Paladyn: Journal of Behavioural Robotics*, 10(1), 44–65.

Crawford, K. (2021). *Atlas of AI*. Yale University Press.

Driver, J. (2005). Normative ethics. In Jackson, F. and Smith, M. (eds) *The Oxford handbook of contemporary philosophy*. Oxford University Press (pp.31–62).

Galanos, V. (2019). Exploring expanding expertise. *Technology Analysis & Strategic Management*, 31(4), 421–432.

Green, B. (2018). Data science as political action: grounding data science in a politics of justice. *Journal of Social Computing*, 2(3), 249–265, https://arxiv.org/pdf/1811.03435.

Krafft, P., Young, M., Katell, M., Huang, K. and Bugingo, G. (2020). Defining AI in policy versus practice. In *Proceedings of the AAAI/ACM conference on AI, ethics, and society* (pp. 72–78).

Mittelstadt, B. (2019). Principles alone cannot guarantee ethical AI. *Nature Machine Intelligence*, 1(11), 501–507.

Van Noorden, R. (2020). The ethical questions that haunt facial-recognition research. *Nature*, 20 November, www.nature.com/articles/d41586-020-03187-3.

Verdegem, P. (2021). *AI for everyone?* University of Westminster Press.

Wagner, B. (2018). Ethics as an escape from regulation. In Bayamlioglu, E. et al. (eds) *Being profiled* (pp. 84–89). Amsterdam University Press.

Wajcman, J. (2019). The digital architecture of time management. *Science, Technology and Human Values*, 44(2), 315–337.

Contributors

Ivana Bartoletti is the Global Data Privacy Officer at Wipro, the leading international information technology, consulting, and business process services company. She is an internationally recognised thought leader in the fields of privacy, data protection, and responsible technology, and has many years of experience working for large organisations in privacy policy, strategy, and programmes related to digital transformation, cloud, and automation. A sought-after subject expert, Bartoletti is interviewed frequently in the mainstream media and speaks at many international events. The Cyber Security Awards named her Woman of the Year (2019). As a Visiting Policy Fellow at the University of Oxford, her research focuses on how to advance the global sharing of information in the context of privacy, security, data protection, and human rights. Bartoletti is co-editor of *The AI Book* (Wiley, 2020), a handbook for investors, entrepreneurs, and fintech visionaries, and author of *An Artificial Revolution: On Power, Politics and AI* (Indigo Press, 2020). She is also founder of the influential 'Women Leading in AI' network (https://womenleadinginai.org).

Su Lin Blodgett is a postdoctoral researcher in the Fairness, Accountability, Transparency, and Ethics (FATE) group at Microsoft Research Montréal. Her research focuses on the social implications of natural language processing technologies (NLP), and on using NLP approaches to examine language variation and change (i.e., computational sociolinguistics). She completed her PhD in computer science at the University of Massachusetts Amherst.

Benedict du Boulay is Emeritus Professor of Artificial Intelligence in the School of Engineering and Informatics at the University of Sussex, UK, and Visiting Professor at University College London. He has two main research areas. The first is the psychology of programming, where his main work has been in the area of novices learning programming and the development of tools to assist that process. The second is the application of AIED. Here he is particularly interested in issues around modelling and developing students' metacognition and motivation. He was President of the International Society for Artificial Intelligence in Education (2015–2017) and is an Associate Editor of its *International Journal of Artificial Intelligence in Education*. He has edited/written 12 books and written some 190 papers (including 58 journal papers) in the areas indicated above.

Lionel Brossi is a Professor at the Institute of Communication and Image of the University of Chile (ICEI) and a Director of the Artificial intelligence and Society Hub (IA+SIC). He is a Faculty Associate at the Berkman Klein Center for Internet and Society at Harvard University and a member of the Millennium Nucleus to Improve the Mental Health of Adolescents and Youths, IMHAY (https://www.imhay.org). As a member of the Youth and Media team, he supports ongoing research and application efforts in the field of AI and inclusion, and the study of youth digital skills, digital social innovation, and internet content gaps in Latin America. He actively participates in working committees, expert groups, and consultancies for international organisations, and leads cross-cutting regional and international research projects on the intersection of youth, technologies, education, wellbeing, and human rights.

Ana María Castillo is Assistant Professor at the Institute of Communication and Image of the University of Chile (ICEI) and a Director of the Artificial intelligence and Society Hub (IA+SIC). In the latter role, she works on the intersection of emergent technologies and social justice, the study of digital skills and the impact of algorithmic technologies on traditionally marginalised communities, and in Latin America with special focus on human rights. Castillo holds a PhD in Communication and Journalism, a Master's degree in Communication, and a degree in Journalism and Social Communication.

Sandra Cortesi is a Fellow and Director of Youth and Media at the Berkman Klein Center for Internet and Society at Harvard University. She is responsible for coordinating the Youth and Media policy, research, and educational initiatives, and leads the collaboration between the Berkman Klein Center and UNICEF. At Youth and Media, Sandra works closely with talented young people and lead researchers in the field as they look into innovative ways to approach social challenges in the digital world. Her work focuses on topics such as inequitable access, information quality, risks to safety and privacy, skills and digital literacy, and spaces for participation, civic engagement, and innovation.

Ezekiel Dixon-Román is Associate Professor in the School of Social Policy and Practice at the University of Pennsylvania. His research seeks to make cultural and critical theoretical interventions toward rethinking and reconceptualising the technologies and practices of quantification as mediums and agencies of systems of socio-political relations whereby race and other assemblages of difference are by-products. He is the author of *Inheriting Possibility: Social Reproduction and Quantification in Education* (University of Minnesota Press, 2017), recipient of the 2018 Outstanding Book Award from the American Educational Research Association. He co-edited "The computational turn in education research: Critical and creative perspectives on the digital data deluge" (*Research in Education*, 2017) and is currently working on a book project that examines the haunting formations of the transparent subject in algorithmic governance and the potential for transformative technopolitical systems.

Shayan Doroudi is Assistant Professor at the Irvine School of Education and (by courtesy) the Department of Informatics at the University of California. His research is at the intersection of the learning sciences, educational technology, and educational data science. He is particularly interested in the foundations of learning about learning and the design of socio-technical systems that improve learning. Doroudi received his BS in Computer Science from the California Institute of Technology and his MS and PhD in Computer Science from Carnegie Mellon University.

Alison Fox is co-convenor of the Professional and Digital Learning research group in the Institute of Educational Technology at the Open University, UK. After training as a secondary school science teacher, Fox moved into initial teacher training and research about beginning teachers. Over the last 20 years she has been involved in research projects related to professional learning, professional networking, and, most recently, how the use of social media relates to both. Her expertise in research ethics has been developed in relation to international and multidisciplinary research settings. She was involved in the review and revision of the British Educational Research Association ethical guidelines (4th edition, 2018) and contributed to the development of the Association for Learning Technology's Framework for Ethical Learning Technology (2021), and she is Deputy Chair of the Open University's Human Research Ethics Committee.

Wayne Holmes (PhD, University of Oxford) is a learning sciences and innovation researcher who teaches at University College London. He is a consultant researcher on AI and education for UNESCO, a member of the Executive and Education Scientific Committee for the International Research Centre for Artificial Intelligence (IRCAI) under the auspices of UNESCO, and lead expert for AI and education for The Council of Europe. Holmes's research takes a critical studies approach to the connections between AI and education. His recent publications include *Artificial Intelligence in Education: Promises and Implications for Teaching and Learning* (2019), *Ethics of AI in Education: Towards a Community-Wide Framework* (2021), and, for UNESCO, *AI and Education: Guidance for Policy-Makers* (2021).

Kenneth Holstein is Assistant Professor of Human–Computer Interaction at Carnegie Mellon University, USA, where he directs the Co-Augmentation, Learning, and AI (CoALA) Lab. His research interests lie at the intersection of human–computer interaction, AI, design, and cognitive science, focusing on the design, development, and real-world evaluation of human–AI collaborative systems that combine the strengths of human and AI judgement and mitigate their respective limitations.

Iris Howley is Assistant Professor of Computer Science at Williams College, USA, leading the Human AI Interaction Lab (HAILab) in applying methods from the learning sciences and human–computer interaction to the design and evaluation of AI systems. Her undergraduate team's work places the needs and goals of people and communities at the centre of the development of AI systems, with a particular focus on empowering everyday users of complex algorithmic systems to adaptively interrogate those technologies.

René F. Kizilcec is Assistant Professor of Information Science and Founding Director of the Future of Learning Lab at Cornell University, USA. He studies the use and impact of technology in formal and informal learning environments and scalable interventions to broaden participation and reduce achievement gaps in education. Kizilcec received a BA in Philosophy and Economics from University College London, and an MSc in Statistics and PhD in Communication from Stanford University, USA.

Hansol Lee is a PhD student in Education Data Science at the Stanford Graduate School of Education, USA. She graduated from Cornell University with a BA and MS in Computer Science, where she collaborated with Cornell Engineering Undergraduate Admissions to introduce a machine learning system to support the admissions process. Her current research interests include leveraging data science to support human decision-making and exploring issues around algorithmic fairness in education.

Michael Madaio is a postdoctoral researcher in Microsoft Research's Fairness, Accountability, Transparency, and Ethics (FATE) group. His work focuses on human-centred approaches to responsible AI through research with AI practitioners and people impacted by AI systems. He completed his PhD in Human–Computer Interaction from Carnegie Mellon University, where he was a fellow in the Institute for Education Sciences' Program for Interdisciplinary Education Research.

Elijah Mayfield is a strategic advisor to GSV Ventures, the leading venture capital firm investing in education technology globally. Previously he was Vice President of New Technologies at Turnitin, managing machine learning and NLP research for educational products used by more than 30 million students, and CEO at LightSide Labs, which he founded with support from the Gates Foundation, the College Board, and the US Department of Education. He received his PhD in Language Technologies from Carnegie Mellon University, and has served as adjunct faculty at the University of Pennsylvania School of Social Policy and Practice. Mayfield has received awards – including a Siebel Scholarship, an IBM PhD Fellowship, and Forbes 30 under 30 in Education – and has co-authored more than 40 peer-reviewed publications on language technologies, education technology, and human–computer interaction.

Darakhshan Mir is Assistant Professor of Computer Science at Bucknell University, USA. Her research is focused on studying socio-technical interventions and frameworks that are in active conversation with the values of fairness, justice, transparency, and privacy in an increasingly data-driven world, and on questions of justice, diversity, access, and ethics in the overall computing curriculum. One of her ongoing projects with colleagues and undergraduate students involves studying the impact of algorithmic decision-making in the lives of incarcerated individuals in Pennsylvania.

Kaśka Porayska-Pomsta is Professor (Chair) of Artificial Intelligence in Education in the Faculty of Education and Society, UCL Knowledge Lab, at University College London. Her research focuses on developing AI systems for education, and evaluating fundamental questions about how AI can be designed to support human learning and development. She has extensive experience of working with diverse users of AI, including neuro-diverse learners and learners at risk of social exclusion, as well as a range of educational practitioners. Her work bridges AI theory and engineering, human neuro-psychology, and education, and is embedded in front-line practices. She actively contributes to UK policy on AI and ethics. She recently completed her three-year service as Departmental Head of Research at the UCL Institute of Education; she is also a member of the management committee for the Centre for Educational Neuroscience, member of the Executive Board, and a co-chair of the Inclusion working group of the International Society for AI in Education.

Evan Peck is Associate Professor of Computer Science at Bucknell University, USA. His research sits at the intersection of human–computer interaction and information visualisation, and considers how data tools and representations can empower more diverse communities to engage with data. Peck's work integrating social responsibility into CS1 (computer science) courses has been adopted by both higher and secondary education instructors (https://ethica lcs.github.io), and he broadly advocates for undergraduate research and teaching. Peck believes in *student-centred everything*.

Nathalie A. Smuha is a researcher in the Faculty of Law and Criminology at the Katholieke Universiteit Leuven, Belgium, where she examines ethical and legal questions around AI and other new technologies. Her research focuses particularly on AI's impact on human rights, democracy, and the rule of law. Smuha acts as a scientific expert on AI for the Council of Europe, and is a member of the OECD's Network of Experts in AI (ONE AI). Previously, she worked as a lawyer in an international law firm and at the European Commission (DG Connect), where she coordinated the work of the High-Level Expert Group on Artificial Intelligence and contributed to EU policy-making in the field of AI. Smuha holds degrees in Law and Philosophy from the KU Leuven, and an LLM from the University of Chicago School of Law. She is also a qualified attorney at the New York Bar.

Jutta Treviranus is the Director of the Inclusive Design Research Centre (IDRC) and professor in the faculty of Design at OCAD University in Toronto (http://idrc.ocadu.ca). Treviranus established the IDRC in 1993 as the nexus of a growing global community that proactively works to ensure that our digitally transformed and globally connected society is designed inclusively. She also founded an innovative graduate program in inclusive design at OCAD University. Treviranus is credited with developing an inclusive design methodology that has been adopted by large enterprise companies, as well as public sector organizations internationally. Among her work in accessibility standards she chaired the Authoring Tool Accessibility Working Group of the W3C Web Accessibility Initiative. Since 2013, Treviranus has raised awareness of the implications of AI decision systems for people with disabilities.

Introduction

Artificial Intelligence (AI) seems to be rarely out of the news. It has also quietly entered classrooms, with 'intelligent', 'adaptive', and 'personalised' Artificial Intelligence in Education (AIED) systems increasingly being deployed in schools and universities around the world. In fact, Big Tech (Amazon, Apple, Facebook, and Google) is investing millions of dollars developing AIED products and associated ecosystems, with the overall AIED market predicted to reach \$21 billion by 2028.[1]

For over 40 years, the AIED research community's work has been mostly under the public radar. Although there have been 22 International AIED Conferences and 31 volumes of the *International Journal of AIED*, and despite commercial AI-driven education products beginning to emerge more than 20 years ago (with a notable early example being MATHia from Carnegie Learning),[2] broader conversations about AIED, beyond the research community, have begun only recently. This is especially true of discussions centred on the ethics of AIED:

> It is only relatively recently with "adaptive products" hitting the mainstream that AIED has found itself being touched by the broader public spotlight. Until then, it was an academic community, with such a small user base that nobody was asking ethics questions.
>
> (Buckingham Shum, cited in Holmes et al., 2021)

In fact, the discussions about the application of Artificial Intelligence in educational contexts that have started to take place, and the increasing public awareness, have probably been prompted more by the debates centred on Artificial Intelligence in general, which themselves have been driven by the advances in machine learning (itself made possible by the arrival, over the past decades, of sufficiently powerful computers and huge amounts of data). Successes such as an AI system beating the world's leading player of Go (2017),[3] applications such as neural network-based automatic language translation (2016),[4] and warnings such as the possible impact of AI on jobs (2013)[5] have kept Artificial Intelligence prominently in the media and increasingly in the public eye.

DOI: 10.4324/9780429329067-1

There has also been a growing narrative centred on the ethics of AI. In fact, the ethics of Artificial Intelligence in general has received a great deal of attention, by researchers (e.g. Boddington, 2017; Whittaker et al., 2018; Winfield & Jirotka, 2018) and more widely (e.g. the UK's House of Lords,[6] the World Economic Forum,[7] and the OECD).[8] Numerous institutes for AI ethics have been set up – such as the Ada Lovelace Institute,[9] the AI Ethics Initiative,[10] the AI Ethics Lab,[11] AI Now,[12] and DeepMind Ethics and Society[13] – and now even an Ethics of AI massive open online course (MOOC).[14] There have also been numerous controversies related to the extent to which Big Tech companies were genuine in their investment in ethics – a commitment seemingly contracted by actions such as Google's decision to remove research activists like Timnit Gebru from its ethical AI teams (a characterisation that Google disputes) (Hao, 2020).

In 2019, Jobin and colleagues (Jobin et al., 2019) identified as many as 84 sets of principles for ethical AI, such as the Asilomar AI principles,[15] the Montreal Declaration of Responsible AI,[16] and the IEEE General Principles[17] (again to name just a few). There have been many more since, including notably UNESCO's 'Recommendation on the Ethics of AI', which was adopted by 193 countries in November 2021. This global framework defines common values and principles with the aim of guiding the construction of the necessary legal infrastructure, and to ensure the healthy development and implementation of AI. In short, the Recommendation aims both to realise the advantages that AI might bring to society and reduce the risks it entails. It aims to ensure that the application of AI promotes human rights and contributes to the achievement of the UN Sustainable Development Goals, addressing issues around transparency, accountability, and privacy. It includes specific chapters on gender, data governance, education, culture, labour, healthcare, and the economy:

> This Recommendation addresses ethical issues related to AI. It approaches AI ethics as a systematic normative reflection, based on a holistic and evolving framework of interdependent values, principles and actions that can guide societies in dealing responsibly with the known and unknown impacts of AI technologies on human beings, societies, and the environment and ecosystems, and offers them a basis to accept or reject AI technologies. Rather than equating ethics to law, human rights, or a normative add-on to technologies, it considers ethics as a dynamic basis for the normative evaluation and guidance of AI technologies, referring to human dignity, well-being and the prevention of harm as a compass and rooted in the ethics of science and technology.[18]

However all of that – the growing public awareness of AI and the debates about the ethics of AI – concerns AI in general. For AI in Education, it was probably not until 2019 that we saw much public engagement, with UNESCO's flagship Mobile Learning Week conference of that year being devoted to Artificial

Intelligence (Holmes, Chakroun et al., 2019). In its early years, AIED research focused on the development of cognitive tutors (e.g. Anderson et al., 1995), which was soon extended to include approaches such as dialogue-based tutoring systems (e.g. Graesser et al., 1999), exploratory learning environments (e.g. Biswas et al., 2004), automatic writing evaluation (e.g. Foltz et al., 1999), AI-supported collaborative learning (e.g. Diziol et al., 2010), automatic forum monitoring (e.g. Goel et al., 2016), and much more besides. This rich history of enquiry has involved the development of countless AIED tools that have been used by hundreds of thousands of students worldwide, and are likely to impact on many more.

The year 2019 also saw the publication of *Artificial Intelligence in Education: Promise and Implications for Teaching and Learning.* (Holmes, Bialik et al., 2019), which was aimed towards educators, and *Should Robots Replace Teachers?* (Selwyn, 2019), aimed towards social science researchers. In 2019 the *Beijing Consensus on Artificial Intelligence and Education* (UNESCO, 2019) was also adopted, and it aimed towards policymakers. Since then, there has been a plethora of publications, such as the OECD's "Trustworthy Artificial Intelligence in Education" (2020), UNESCO's *Artificial Intelligence and Education: Guidance for Policy-makers* (Miao & Holmes, 2021), and UNICEF's "Policy Guidance on AI for Children" (2021), which considers wider implications of AI for children that extend beyond the application of AI in educational contexts. In addition, the European Commission's Joint Research Centre (JRC) has further developed its DigComp initiative to include the AI competencies that might be desirable for the citizens of Europe to acquire,[19] while the Council of Europe is exploring the connections between AI and education and the core values of human rights, democracy, and the rule of law.[20]

In the meantime, with AIED now out of the lab, there has been an explosion of commercial AIED products emerging around the world (or at least commercial products that claim they are grounded in AI). Many of those products have multi-million dollar funding, and most of them are examples of the so-called 'intelligent tutoring systems'. Interestingly, these products appear to be unquestionably welcomed with open arms by education policymakers around the world, despite their uncertain implications for children and their developing minds, and with negligible evidence for the products' educational efficacy being available. The global COVID-19 pandemic appears to have helped these organisations' profit-lines, as educators around the world scrambled for anything that would help them deliver teaching online (Williamson, 2021). In fact, educational technology (whether truly AI or not) has increasingly become part of the mainstream machinery of education, and is thus contributing to setting the tone for how education itself may be developed in the coming years.

Accordingly, like AI in general, AIED raises far-reaching ethical questions with important implications for students, educators, parents, and other stakeholders. For example, what happens if a child is subjected to a biased set of algorithms that impact negatively and incorrectly on their school progress? While to date there have been sporadic attempts to put AI ethics at the forefront of AIED practices (Aiken & Epstein, 2000; Holmes et al., 2021; Holmes, Bektik, et al., 2018), it remains the case that most AIED work has occurred without any serious engagement with the potential ethical consequences of using AI technologies to support teaching and learning. In fact, around the world, no framework has been devised, no guidelines have been provided, no policies have been developed, and no regulations have been enacted to address the specific ethical issues raised by the use of AI in education. Indeed, an understanding of what these issues are exactly is only emerging. This is not to suggest that AIED researchers, developers, and corporations have so far acted unethically, but rather to acknowledge that important ethical questions remain unasked and unanswered. Nonetheless, this is a gap that a UNESCO project, 'Artificial Intelligence and the Futures of Learning' – launched in September 2021 and focused on applying the organisation's 'Recommendation on the Ethics of AI' to the domain of education – aims to address.[21]

The ethics of AIED: practices, challenges, and debates

This book, *The Ethics of Artificial Intelligence in Education: Practices, Challenges, and Debates*, aims to stimulate the necessary discussion for addressing the many questions that arise in the context of the ethics of AI in Education. It identifies key ethical issues for AIED while also discussing some misconceptions around AIED and its nuances, and exploring ways in which the multiple challenges identified might be addressed. Importantly, to help establish a robust foundation for meaningful ethical reflection, the book is divided into two parts that offer independent perspectives – sometimes complementary, sometimes in opposition – from outside and inside the AIED research community.

Part I presents reflections from a range of disciplines outside of AIED, by authors who engage with the ethical concerns for individuals, the education system, and society more broadly that arise from the increasing introduction of AI into and beyond classrooms. As such, Part I offers an outside perspective which is characterised by broad concerns related to people's relationship with technology (sometimes much more broadly understood than the special case of AI technologies). Many of these views, while providing context-specific insights into the ethics of AI in educational applications, align with the discussions and reflections on the ethics of AI available across different contexts of applications.

Part II offers detailed explorations of AIED through socio-technological, engineering, design, and pedagogical lenses. The contributions in this part explicitly bridge AI theory and engineering, human–computer interaction, philosophy, social sciences, psychology, and educational practice. They aim, first, to map the state of the art in the ethics of AIED and, second, to identify practical approaches to ensure these ethics are embedded in the culture of the AIED community and in the designs and deployment of its technologies. As such Part II offers an insight not only into the description of the general problems related to AI applications in education but, importantly, actionable contributions to an emerging mindset and *modus operandi* for ethical AIED by design.

The book concludes with a reflection on the nature and purpose of AIED in the broader context of both Artificial Intelligence in general and the socio-economic system of which the educational system forms an integral part. These reflections aim to highlight prominent questions about what AIED is and what makes it a special case of technology and a discipline of inquiry. Based on all the contributions in this book, it offers a bird's-eye view of the possible landscape, potential blind-spots, and pathways available towards ethical AIED that is both aware of its own contribution to the broader socio-technological context and is able to raise awareness of risks and take action towards their mitigation or elimination.

What do we mean by Artificial Intelligence?

Like many texts on AI, and because AI in Education is often equated with applications that are in fact not AI, we begin with our working definition of AI and its application in education. For this we use UNICEF's definition, which in turn clarifies (for those of us who are not computer scientists) the OECD's definition that has been accepted by member countries around the world.

> AI refers to machine-based systems that can, given a set of human-defined objectives, make predictions, recommendations, or decisions that influence real or virtual environments. AI systems interact with us and act on our environment, either directly or indirectly. Often, they appear to operate autonomously, and can adapt their behaviour by learning about the context.
> (UNICEF, 2021, p. 16)

It is important to note that this definition does not depend on data (although it does accommodate data-driven AI techniques such as artificial neural networks and deep learning), and therefore includes rule-based or symbolic AI and any new paradigm of AI that might emerge in future years (cf. Marcus, 2020). It is also important to note the central position of humans in this definition and the phrase "*appear* to operate autonomously", given the critical role of humans at all stages of the AI development pipeline. In addition, on reflection, it is self-evident how this definition might be adopted and extended for the application of AIED.

With that in mind, we continue by setting out to establish a foundation for the ethics of AI applied in educational contexts, in two steps: first, by briefly introducing the philosophical foundations of ethics; second, by discussing extant work on the ethics of AI in general. A parallel aim of establishing this foundation is to highlight that the ethics of AI, and hence of AIED, is more complex and nuanced than simply 'being good'.

What counts as an ethical approach?

While it is almost certainly the case that all members of the AIED research community are motivated by ethical concerns (Holmes et al., 2021), AIED's self-image of being good begs the question: what does 'being good' actually mean? Are there immutable, universal ethical principles that should guide individual and collective behaviour; or does what constitutes being good depend on one's individual socio-political perspective, as evidenced by recent history in both the USA and the UK? Such questions are inevitably complex and remain open despite more than 2000 years of ethics discourse. Nonetheless, instead of proposing a set of common-sense but somewhat random principles, any attempt to develop robust and actionable principles that ensure AIED research and practice is 'good' ought to be grounded in core concepts from moral philosophy. Naturally, given the long history of ethical debate, that is easier said than done. Which ethical concepts from the history of moral philosophy should be prioritised, and how can they be used to disentangle and shed light on ethical questions raised in the context of AIED in order to rationalise, defend, and recommend 'good' actions? Here, we adopt one of the simpler, albeit still complex, normative ethics models, which comprises three approaches: deontology, consequentialism, and virtue ethics. Each of these comes in multiple variants, comprises multiple components, and has been debated for millennia – yet for present purposes, while we cannot engage with the details, it remains helpful to consider their contrasting orientations.

To begin with, deontology emphasises universal human rights and obligations (Kant, 1785). Actions are intrinsically and universally good or bad, and we have a moral obligation to undertake good actions and avoid bad actions, whatever the consequences may be. Meanwhile, every individual has equal value – whatever their gender, ethnicity, sexuality, and so on – simply because we are rational beings. Accordingly, everyone is entitled to respect and dignity, which means that we should treat other people as we would want to be treated by them. More recently, deontological obligations have been reconceptualised prima facie as duties (Ross, 1930), some of which are frequently quoted in the AI ethics literature as beneficence (doing good), non-maleficence (not causing harm), justice (ensuring people receive that which they deserve), and fidelity (honesty and keeping promises).

The second ethical approach in the simplified model under discussion is consequentialism, of which utilitarianism is probably the best-known variant (Mill, 1863). Consequentialism is orthogonal in orientation to deontology, with the outcomes or consequences of any action taking precedence over any prima facie duties or individual rights. The most moral actions are those that result in the greatest good for the greatest number of people, which depends on calculating the potential consequences of each possible action and choosing the one that best maximises benefit and minimises harm. However, this begs the question of how we define 'benefit'. For example, decisions about which AI tools to develop for education depend on whether the purpose of education is conceived as being for knowledge building, socialisation, or self-actualisation. As will be touched upon throughout this book, despite their foundational importance for what AIED systems we design and deploy in real-world contexts, these high-level considerations are seldom examined or addressed within AIED or more broadly in the educational technology research and industry.

Finally, virtue ethics is transversal, focusing as it does on the moral characteristics or virtues of people (Aristotle, n.d. c300 BCE), rather than the moral principles or consequences of actions. For virtue ethics, acting ethically becomes acting as a virtuous person would act, which means determining what a virtuous person would do in any given situation. Example virtues include honesty, courage, compassion, generosity, fidelity, integrity, fairness, self-control, and prudence. The understanding is that anyone who has developed such virtues will be naturally disposed to act in ways that are ethical.

The moral philosophy model just outlined can be considered the backbone of the current thinking on the ethics of AI. In this context, questions remain about whether AI can be designed to adhere to human moral principles, how those principles can be actioned in the specific designs of AI technologies, and what happens if those principles are flouted (including who or what should be held responsible). While human principles provide high-level aspirations for all AI stakeholders (engineers, designers, policymakers, technology businesses, and users), the way that they are being addressed from within the different disciplinary perspectives can sometimes be difficult to reconcile. In a bid to bridge different disciplinary takes on the ethics of AI, we next introduce some general AI principles, and align these different perspectives with the three moral philosophical approaches reviewed. Understanding this general AI ethics landscape is necessary for situating the ethics of AIED within the wider AI field, and for AIED to draw from this body of relevant work.

The 5P framework

The deontological and consequentialist approaches constitute the basis for a 'unified framework of five principles for AI in society' (henceforth, the 5P framework) proposed by Floridi and Cowls (2019). The 5P framework consolidates six of the most prominent proposals for ethical AI: the Asilomar AI principles (2017), the Montreal Declaration of Responsible AI (2017), and the IEEE General Principles (2017), noted above, plus the European Group on Ethics in Science and New Technologies (EGE) principles for Ethical AI (2018),[22] the UK House of Lords AI code (2018),[23] and the Tenets of the Partnership on AI (2018).[24]

The 5P framework is conceived as an overarching, high-level starting point of reference for considering the moral prerogatives for AI researchers that cut across different AI subdomains. The aim of the framework is to ensure inclusivity and dignity of heterogeneous groups of AI users, and to link its principles to the consequences of them being adhered to or violated (i.e. to good or bad consequences). Specifically, the 5P framework relies on four principles derived from bioethics, a domain that is considered to align with digital technologies such as AI in the way that it addresses questions around new forms of agents, users, and environments (Floridi, 2013). Four principles draw on the simplified ethical model outlined above: (i) beneficence ('do good' for human wellbeing, dignity and for the planet); (ii) non-maleficence ('do no harm' by avoiding over-reliance, over-use, or misuse of AI technologies in order to preserve personal privacy of users and prevent use for harmful purposes); (iii) autonomy (achieving and pre-serving a balance between artificial and human autonomy, which ultimately promotes the latter, and which does not impair human freedom of choice and decision-making, especially as it relates to delegating decisions to AI); and (iv) justice (seek and preserve justice, prevent any forms of discrimination, and foster diversity, including the way in which AI is used to enhance human decision-making). The fifth principle – (v) explicability – accounts for the changing roles of the users, which, depending on the circumstances, may demand different degrees of intelligibility from the AI technologies (i.e. transparency with respect to the ways in which such technologies work and on what they base their decisions) and accountability, relating to who is responsible for the ways in which they work. This explicability principle is considered an enabler for applying the first four principles, insofar as it gives access to how a given AI technology allows the user to exercise their autonomy and to be audited with respect to any potential benefits and harms. All five principles are considered necessary to support trustworthy and responsible AI designs and deployment.

The 5P framework aims for universality, domain-independence, and as a basis for a dialogue between engineering and social scientific perspectives on AI. However, this comes at the price of a lack of concreteness. In short, there remains a paucity of guidelines for how those principles might be actioned in specific AI designs and application contexts. A substantial part of the problem lies in the relativistic nature of the concepts involved, which tend to depend on: socio-cultural norms, which are in themselves subject to change over time (e.g. the concept of justice is perpetually evolving based on our growing knowledge and changing practices); the circumstances and needs of individuals (e.g. the concept of individual fairness is deeply rooted in the situational and subjective realities of individuals); and the context (e.g. the tension between multiple conflicting interests, expectations, and needs of different stakeholders, such as climate change, which may lead to different interpretations of the beneficent nature of AI).

A second part of the problem lies in the fact that the domains in which AI is applied by definition differ from one another, and raise ethical issues specific to them. Although there may be common issues and overlaps (Andrade, 2019), discussions around, for example, the ethics of AI in healthcare and the ethics of AI in autonomous vehicles must consider issues specific to those domains (e.g. patient choice in healthcare, and assigning responsibility for crashes in autonomous vehicles). The same is true for AI applied in education, to which we return later.

A third part of the problem lies in the fact that AI is neither a single application – even in a single domain, such as education, there is a plethora of approaches and specific tools (Holmes, Bialik, et al., 2019) – nor a simple process. Every AI application or tool, and every part of the AI development pipeline, raises specific issues, all of which need to be considered carefully and addressed. Cramer and colleagues (2019) propose a seven-step machine learning pipeline illustrating the complexity, involving: (i) task definition (identifying and specifying the problem an AI system is designed to address, e.g. to help predict student attainment); (ii) data construction (selecting a data source, acquiring data, pre-processing and labelling data); (iii) model definition (the selection of specific AI approach and of the objective function); (iv) training process (training the model on data); (v) evaluation process (validating the model on additional data); (vi) deployment (when the system leaves the lab); and (vii) feedback on how the system fares in the wild. However, it might be suggested that even those steps are concerned only with *doing things ethically*, rather than *doing ethical things* (Holmes et al., 2021), and that a wider perspective needs to be adopted asking the foundational question: what is the purpose of the AIED (Holmes, Anastopoulou, et al., 2018; Kay, 2012)? For example, is it to prepare students to pass examinations or to help them self-actualise? Is it to address issues identified in computer science departments or problems identified by educators in classrooms worldwide? Is it to replace teacher functions or to empower teachers? There are many other such questions; but only once the purpose(s) is/are decided do we have sufficient context against which to consider the more detailed issues.

As it is not possible to cover all the complexity encapsulated in the 5P framework, or the problems just discussed, next we focus briefly on three illustrative ethical concerns that relate to the non-maleficence principle and that have been widely debated: bias, harm, and fairness (for a more detailed discussion see Porayska-Pomsta et al., in press).

Bias in AI has long been the subject of research (Crawford, 2013), revealing many overlapping definitions (a simple one being 'a tendency to discriminate in favour of certain things or people over others') and requiring AI developers to examine when and how bias emerges in AI systems, and how to mitigate or eliminate it. Inevitably, what bias is in practice is itself complex (for example, in certain circumstances, bias may be positive or negative); and in any case different types of bias do not always align, such that addressing one type of bias may not render a system ethically 'better'. To begin with, we might distinguish between moral or legal bias and statistical bias (Danks & London, 2017). Moral bias refers to a deviation from moral principles related to, for example, people's autonomy and rights, while legal bias refers to undue prejudice that violates written legal norms (e.g. employment discrimination based on gender, race, or disability). Statistical bias, on the other hand, creates AI models that do not accurately represent the population that they aim to represent. An example of statistical bias with serious consequences was embedded in the infamous algorithm developed by Amazon to recruit engineers, which turned out to fundamentally discriminate against women and was subsequently abandoned (Dastin, 2018).

Bias may be introduced at most of the machine learning development pipeline steps described by Cramer and colleagues. For example, data bias might be introduced at the source, during data sampling (as was the case with the Amazon recruitment tool), during data cleaning or labelling, or in the choice of algorithm. Further illustrating the complexity, Suresh and Guttag (2019) identify seven categories of data bias, including: historic bias – bias that is deeply embedded in historic, cultural, and social stereotypes, such as gendering of nouns describing professions (e.g. female nurse vs male doctor) Bolukbasi et al. (2016); representational bias (in which some of the population is under-represented or over-represented); measurement bias (labels are proxies for the often complex and abstract constructs, and are thus inevitably oversimplifications); aggregation bias (e.g. when a model that is derived from data of neuro-typical learners is used to model neuro-divergent students); and deployment bias (when the task that the model is supposed to solve is different from the task for which it is being used).

In turn, bias may be the cause of diverse forms of *harm*, of which again there are multiple types. Barocas and colleagues (2017) identify two overarching categories of harm: harms of allocation (i.e. opportunities or resources withheld from some groups); and harms of representation (i.e. ways, usually stereotypical and negative, in which some groups may be misrepresented). An infamous education example of a harm of allocation was the A-level grading scandal in the UK in 2020, in which high-achieving students in schools in poor socio-economic communities were graded as lower achieving because of the grade average of their schools (Kolkman, 2020). Meanwhile, harms of representation do not occur in single transactions. Instead they are ingrained within cultural and institutional contexts: they are long-term processes that impact people's beliefs and attitudes; they are diffused across time; they are historical and socio-cultural contexts; and they often lie at the root of allocative harms. Barocas et al. (2017) specify several subtypes of harms of representation that need to be considered, including: stereotyping (e.g. gender stereotyping); recognition – where particular groups, such as people of colour, are invisible to the algorithm (Guynn, 2015); and ex-nomination – in which the majority demographic becomes accepted as a norm and where any deviation from this norm becomes apparent.

Finally, questions about algorithmic bias cannot be separated from the questions about what constitutes fairness (see Chapter 7 in this volume, by Kizilcec and Lee, and Narayanan, 2018). As discussed in Porayska-Pomsta et al. (in press), fairness in the context of technology concerns what and whose values are embedded in the technology, who is excluded as a result, and whether this is justified in the eyes of the law, in the light of moral principles, or in the eyes of the individuals who may be affected. In this context, there is an inevitable tension between the social scientific and computational sciences conceptions of fairness: attempting to quantify a complex, context- and perspective-dependent notion of fairness in terms of mathematical formulae is considered by social scientists at least non-trivial if not entirely doomed to failure. To paraphrase Narayanan (2018), fairness cannot be equated with the number 0.78 (or any other number for that matter), however hard computer scientists might try. In other words, seeking a single definition of fairness may be a futile undertaking because fairness is a socio-culturally, institutionally, situationally, politically, and subjectively determined construct (Barocas et al., 2017; Narayanan, 2018). The challenges are highlighted when we consider two dimensions of fairness. The first is individual fairness vs group fairness (i.e. the outcomes for individuals or for groups who share some identity criteria – what may be considered fair for one group may be deemed unfair for another group, or completely unfair to specific individuals). The second dimension is outcomes fairness (equity of results, which is a consequentialist lens) vs process fairness (equity of treatment, a deontological lens).

The ethics of Artificial Intelligence in Education

Our brief foray into the nuances of ethical AI principles and issues of concern, despite the various examples, highlights the urgent need to contextualise *high-level* ethical principles in order to develop *actionable* principles and best practices that might be implemented effectively and for the common good. The point here is that AIED is neither a basic science (interested solely in theory) nor an applied science (interested solely in application); instead AIED sits in what Stokes (1996) calls Pasteur's quadrant: it is interested both in designing interventions to improve (educational) outcomes and in developing fundamental theory (about teaching and learning). In other words, AIED is a *design science* that is intertwined with real front-line systems, increasingly affects the very culture of education as well as learners' cognitive and socio-emotional development, and makes fundamental efforts to understand how humans learn and develop.

The shift from research labs to real-world – and usually commercial – applications, accelerated by the COVID-19 pandemic, means that AIED is fast becoming a tool that sets the tone for how educational policies are enacted worldwide. Accordingly, it is increasingly important for AIED researchers and developers to stand back, to think about how their technologies are imposing on or contributing to the system, to consider what type of world they are helping to create, piece by piece, with "small acts of technology-based automation" (Selwyn et al., 2021, p. 1). If the research or development fits or serves the current system, despite the fact – and knowing that – it is broken, while understanding that AI has the capacity to amplify, reinforce, and perpetuate poor pedagogic practices – is this ethical? To give an example, at a recent International Conference of AI in Education some researchers considered the question of 'how' to make an e-proctoring system 'fairer' by refining how it worked, without any consideration of the ethical consequences by definition (e.g. raising issues centred on mental health) of any e-proctoring system (Logan, 2021). A type of question that a critical AIED practitioner may want to ask is: why is there a focus on addressing the ongoing demands of the current system, such as enabling online examinations using AI-driven tools (e.g. e-proctoring), rather than using the power and potential of AI to develop innovative approaches – in this example – for assessment and accreditation?

Although still in their early stages, ethical AIED research and practices already point to the education context as a useful setting for examining the impact of AI applications for individuals and society at the psychological, neuro-cognitive, affective, social, and economic levels. More than this, they demonstrate in concrete and practical terms a known adage in the philosophical, historical, and future-facing discourses about human relationships with technology throughout history: namely that as we create technology to enhance our innate abilities and quality of life, technology (whatever it may be) changes us in return, in ways that are inevitable but that also remain ill-understood (Harari, 2018; Kelly, 2011; Kurzweil, 2006; Russell, 2019).

A key take-home message from those discourses relates to the complexity of the socio-technical context that defines our dependency on technological innovation and reflects the web of multiple and often conflicting interests, the balance of which at any given point determines what technologies take root in our societies, how they are being designed, exploited, and promoted (and by whom), and indeed whether such technologies are used always with best intentions and to best effects. Questions related to what might constitute effects (for better or worse) of our reliance on technology have been contemplated to some extent in the context of the philosophy of technology (Bostrom & Sandberg, 2009), where they have been linked to the human evolutionary processes, and in psychology, where costs and benefits of specific types of technological enhancements – such as the use of cameras to remember lived experiences, scheduling systems to remember appointments, or GPS navigators to help people navigate through geographical terrains – have been explored with respect to human cognitive capacities, including on working memory and spatial navigation competencies (Hejtmánek et al., 2018).

However, little exploration of whether, how, or why technology – and especially AI technologies – may fundamentally change the way that people think and behave (broadly speaking, human psychology) has been done within the AIED context beyond evaluations of the effects of the specific pedagogical designs of the AIED systems they use on students' domain-specific problem-solving skills. To begin such an investigation, it is critical first to be clear about how we define: (i) AI as representing a special case of technology, by virtue of its explicit aim to interact autonomously and adaptively with and change the human environment and human action therein; and (ii) the specificities of educational interventions as encapsulated in the particular pedagogies employed by AIED systems, also purposefully aiming to change learners' thinking and behaviour.

There is also the need for AIED researchers to 'step outside the bubble' of the academic discipline. While, within the bubble, developers demonstrably work hard to ensure their AIED tool is unbiased, harmless, and fair (as illustrated by the e-proctoring example above), the question from outside the bubble is whether the use of the AIED in that particular context or to achieve that particular ambition is itself ethical. In short:

> The educational contexts which AIED technologies aspire to enhance highlight the need to differentiate between doing ethical things and doing

things ethically, to understand and to make pedagogical choices that are ethical, to account for the ever-present possibility of unintended consequences, along with many other considerations.

(Holmes et al., 2021)

As we noted earlier, the first step of the AI development cycle is task definition. However, rarely do AIED researchers question the selection of the task – because it is mostly assumed that the aim is to help students learn. However, in whose terms, and with what consequences? For example, all too frequently there is talk of AIED systems being developed and implemented to 'improve efficiency' (i.e. improving education from the perspective of some policymakers and economists) rather than enabling learners to develop their own potential or to self-actualise (for which the financial benefits are not so easily identified or quantified). Similarly, all too often (especially in the commercial space) there are claims that AIED tools are 'as effective' as or 'more effective' than a human teacher (Ahmad et al., 2020; VanLehn, 2011), usually without any reference to the fundamentally social nature of learning, and with only limited supportive evidence drawn from limited situations. Nonetheless, this claim is particularly attractive for policymakers in contexts where there are insufficient experienced or qualified teachers necessary to provide all learners with the quality education that is their human right. The argument goes that, because there are insufficient teachers, surely AIED tools can effectively fill the void. However, while current cohorts might benefit from being given access to an AIED tool (no mean feat in the rural contexts for which this is often proposed), this techno-solutionism addresses the symptoms (today's learners not receiving a quality education) rather than the cause (the lack of experienced or qualified teachers). The problem is just kicked down the road: what happens when the tools break down or need replacing? In short, where are the AIED tools designed specifically to support teachers, rather than to replace their functions, to enable them to become good or even super teachers?

As we noted, there are multiple ways in which AI is being applied in educational contexts. The most common applications include the so-called intelligent tutoring systems, dialogue-based tutoring systems, exploratory learning environments, automatic writing evaluation, learning network orchestrators, language learning, chatbots, the smart curation of learning materials, and AI to support learners with disabilities (Holmes, Bialik, et al., 2019). And, as we have seen, it is unlikely that any one set of ethical principles will be appropriate for each of these applications. Further, as we have noted above and discussed elsewhere, the domains in which AI is applied by definition differ from one another, and raise ethical issues beyond those centred on data (Williamson, 2020) and algorithms (Kearns & Roth, 2020) and specific to those domains:

The ethics of AI raises a variety of complex issues centred on data (e.g. consent and data privacy) and how that data is analysed (e.g., transparency and trust). However, it is also clear that the ethics of AIED cannot be reduced to questions about data and computational approaches alone.

In other words, investigating the ethics of AIED data and computations is necessary but not sufficient. Given that, by definition, AIED is the application of AI techniques and processes in education, the ethics of AIED also as noted earlier needs to account for the ethics of education ... . Yet, while the ethics of education has been the focus of debate and research for more than 2000 years, it is mostly unacknowledged and unaccounted for by the wider AIED community.

(Holmes et al., 2021)

In education, as discussed in the following chapters, pertinent ethical questions include: the accuracy and validity of assessments; the impact on human development and cognition; what constitutes useful knowledge; power relations between teachers and their students; teacher and student agency; and choice of pedagogy (with instructionism all too often being prioritised over constructivism).

At the International Conference for AIED held in 2018 we organised the first ethics of AIED workshop, in which we hypothesised a 'strawman' draft framework, as shown in Figure 0.1 (Holmes, Bektik, et al., 2018). In this framework, data, algorithms, and education constitute the foundational level, while at the overlaps a second level comprises the ethics of data in AI (cf. the 5P framework, Floridi & Cowls, 2019), the ethics of data in education (cf. Ferguson et al., 2016), and the ethics of models and algorithms applied in educational contexts, the last of which remains the least developed area of research. There is also the central intersection: the *unknown unknowns* (indicated by the question mark in Figure 0.1) – the ethical issues raised by AIED that have yet to be even identified, involving interactions between AI systems and human cognition at the individual level. This framework was proposed as a

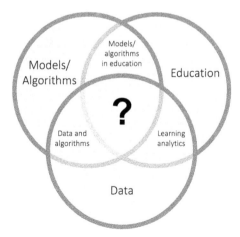

Figure 0.1 'Strawman' draft framework for the ethics of AIED

first step in the necessary conversation, and remains open to being enhanced and calibrated by insights from all the emergent work in this area, much of which is explored throughout the following chapters.

Starting point

This, then, is the starting point for this book: the complex relationships between ethics, data, algorithms, models, education, human development, and cognition. Accordingly, with AI increasingly being used in educational contexts, what ethical questions should AIED researchers, developers, and companies – along with policymakers, educators, students, parents, and society more generally – be asking? We conclude this introduction by offering a few suggestions that the following chapters begin to address:

- How does the transient nature of student goals, interests, and emotions impact on the ethics of AIED?
- What are the ethical consequences of encouraging students to work independently with AI-supported software (rather than with teachers or in collaborative groups)?
- How can K12 students give genuine informed consent for their involvement with AIED tools?
- What are the AIED ethical obligations of private organisations (developers of AIED products) and public authorities (schools and universities involved in AIED research)?
- How might schools, students, and teachers opt out of, or challenge, how they are represented in large datasets?
- What are the ethical implications of not being able to interrogate easily how some AIED decisions are made (e.g. using multi-level neural networks)?
- How do we ensure that the ethics of AIED is not just about stopping researchers and developers from 'doing harm'? Instead, what proactive, protective, and facilitative set of foundational guidance, within which to ground AIED research and development, is needed?
- What distinguishes the use of automated systems being used to identify and respond to student emotions from what good human teachers do all the time?
- How do we know what the application of AIED is genuinely capable of (how do we get beyond the hype) and how it might best be used?
- What does an AI system need to be capable of before we can allow it to make decisions (e.g. is it enough to show that an AI essay-grading tool reaches the same conclusions as human markers, or do we use this opportunity to question the human markers)?
- What is gained and what is lost when an AI tool takes over a human teacher's functions (and will it really save teacher time)?
- When we call for more personalised learning, do we mean efficient pathways to homogenised outputs or enabling each individual learner to develop their individual potential and to self-actualise? Are these ethical choices?

- What is the role of individualised systems in classrooms, which are by definition social spaces, or should they only be used outside of classrooms?
- What are the ethical implications of the choice of pedagogy adopted by many AI educational tools?
- What evidence do we need about, for example, the efficacy of AIED systems before we can make robust ethical choices with respect to where and when to use them?
- What are the ethical consequences of the typically solution-based approaches to AIED, rather than problem-based approaches?
- Where is the ethical line drawn between monitoring students for their learning or safety and unacceptable surveillance?
- Which AI technologies and what contexts, if any, have no place in education (e.g. face recognition)?
- What are the ethical (and systemic) consequences of implementing AI tools in classrooms where there are insufficient experienced or qualified teachers?
- How do we prepare for the ethical implications of future possible AI tools in education?

Notes

1 https://tinyurl.com/AIED-market-prediction.
2 https://www.carnegielearning.com/.
3 https://www.bbc.co.uk/news/technology-40042581.
4 https://alexmoltzau.medium.com/the-history-of-google-translate-fcbe9de3c10e.
5 https://www.oxfordmartin.ox.ac.uk/downloads/academic/The_Future_of_Employment.pdf.
6 https://publications.parliament.uk/pa/ld201719/ldselect/ldai/100/100.pdf.
7 https://www.weforum.org/agenda/2016/10/top-10-ethical-issues-in-artificial-intelligence.
8 https://oecd.ai/en/ai-principles.
9 https://www.adalovelaceinstitute.org.
10 https://aiethicsinitiative.org.
11 http://aiethicslab.com.
12 https://ainowinstitute.org.
13 https://deepmind.com/applied/deepmind-ethics-society.
14 https://ethics-of-ai.mooc.fi.
15 https://futureoflife.org/ai-principles/.
16 https://www.montrealdeclaration-responsibleai.com/.
17 https://ethicsinaction.ieee.org/#series.
18 https://tinyurl.com/UNESCO-AI-ethics-principles.
19 https://data.europa.eu/doi/10.2760/115376.
20 https://tinyurl.com/CoE-AIED.
21 https://en.unesco.org/themes/ict-education/ai-futures-learning.
22 https://publications.europa.eu/en/publication-detail/-/publication/dfebe62e-4ce9-11e8-be1d-01aa75ed71a1/language-en/format-PDF/source-78120382.
23 https://publications.parliament.uk/pa/ld201719/ldselect/ldai/100/10002.htm.
24 https://partnershiponai.org/about/.

References

Ahmad, K., Qadir, J., Al-Fuqaha, A., Iqbal, W., El-Hassan, A., Benhaddou, D., & Ayyash, M. (2020). Artificial intelligence in education: A panoramic review. EdArXiv. doi:10.35542/osf.io/zvu2n.

Aiken, R. M., & Epstein, R. G. (2000). Ethical guidelines for AI in education: Starting a conversation. *International Journal of Artificial Intelligence in Education*, 11, 163–176.

Anderson, J. R., Corbett, A. T., Koedinger, K. R., & Pelletier, R. (1995). Cognitive tutors: Lessons learned. *Journal of the Learning Sciences*, 4(2), 167–207.

Andrade, G. (2019). Medical ethics and the trolley problem. *Journal of Medical Ethics and History of Medicine*, 12, 3.

Aristotle. (n.d.). *The Nicomachean Ethics*.

Barocas, S., Crawford, K., Shapiro, A., & Wallach, H. (2017). *The problem with bias: Allocative versus representational harms in machine learning*. SIGCIS Conference. http://m eetings.sigcis.org/uploads/6/3/6/8/6368912/program.pdf.

Biswas, G., Leelawong, K., Belynne, K., Viswanath, K., Schwartz, D., & Davis, J. (2004). *Developing learning by teaching environments that support self-regulated learning*. International Conference on Intelligent Tutoring Systems, 730–740.

Boddington, P. (2017). *Towards a Code of Ethics for Artificial Intelligence Research*. Springer.

Bolukbasi, T., Chang, K.-W., Zou, J. Y., Saligrama, V., & Kalai, A. T. (2016). Man is to computer programmer as woman is to homemaker? Debiasing word embeddings. *Advances in Neural Information Processing Systems*, 29, 4349–4357.

Bostrom, N., & Sandberg, A. (2009). The wisdom of nature: An evolutionary heuristic for human enhancement. In J. Savulescu & N. Bostrom (Eds.), *Human Enhancement* (pp. 375–416). Oxford University Press.

Cramer, H., Wortman Vaughan, J., & Holstein, K. (2019). *Challenges of incorporating algorithmic 'fairness' into practice*. ACM Conference on Fairness, Accountability, and Transparency (FAT* 2019).

Crawford, K. (2013, April 1). The hidden biases in big data. *Harvard Business Review*. https://hbr.org/2013/04/the-hidden-biases-in-big-data.

Danks, D., & London, A. J. (2017). Algorithmic bias in autonomous systems. *IJCAI*, 17, 4691–4697.

Dastin, J. (2018). Amazon scraps secret AI recruiting tool that showed bias against women. *Reuters*. https://www.reuters.com/article/us-amazon-com-jobs-automa tion-insight-idUSKCN1MK08G.

Diziol, D., Walker, E., Rummel, N., & Koedinger, K. R. (2010). Using intelligent tutor technology to implement adaptive support for student collaboration. *Educational Psychology Review*, 22(1), 89–102. doi:10.1007/s10648-009-9116-9.

Ferguson, R., Brasher, A., Clow, D., Cooper, A., Hillaire, G., Mittelmeier, J., Rienties, B., Ullmann, T., & Vuorikari, R. (2016). Research evidence on the use of learning analytics: implications for education policy. http://oro.open.ac.uk/48173/.

Floridi, L. (2013). *The Ethics of Information*. Oxford University Press.

Floridi, L., & Cowls, J. (2019). A unified framework of five principles for AI in society. *Harvard Data Science Review*, 1(1). https://doi.org/10.1162/99608f92.8cd550d1.

Foltz, P. W., Laham, D., & Landauer, T. K. (1999). Automated essay scoring: applications to educational technology. In B. Collis & R. Oliver (Eds.), *Proceedings of ED-MEDIA 1999: World Conference on Educational Multimedia, Hypermedia and Telecommunications* (pp. 939–944). AACE. https://www.learntechlib.org/p/6607/.

Goel, A., Anderson, T., Belknap, J., Creeden, B., Hancock, W., Kumble, M., Salunke, S., Sheneman, B., Shetty, A., & Wiltgen, B. (2016). Using Watson for constructing cognitive assistants. http://www.cogsys.org/papers/ACS2016/Papers/Goel_et.al-ACS-2016.pdf.

Graesser, A. C., Wiemer-Hastings, K., Wiemer-Hastings, P., Kreuz, R., Group, T. R., & others. (1999). AutoTutor: A simulation of a human tutor. *Cognitive Systems Research*, 1(1), 35–51.

Guynn, J. (2015). Google photos labeled black people "gorillas." *USA Today*. https://www.usatoday.com/story/tech/2015/07/01/google-apologizes-after-photos-identi fy-black-people-as-gorillas/29567465/.

Hao, K. (2020). We read the paper that forced Timnit Gebru out of Google: Here's what it says. *MIT Technology Review*. https://www.technologyreview.com/2020/12/04/1013294/google-ai-ethics-research-paper-forced-out-timnit-gebru/.

Harari, Y. N. (2018). *21 Lessons for the 21st Century*. Random House.

Hejtmánek, L., Oravcová, I., Motýl, J., Horáček, J., & Fajnerová, I. (2018). Spatial knowledge impairment after GPS guided navigation: Eye-tracking study in a virtual town. *International Journal of Human-Computer Studies*, 116, 15–24.

Holmes, W., Anastopoulou, S., Schaumburg, H., & Mavrikis, M. (2018). *Technology-enhanced Personalised Learning: Untangling the Evidence*. Robert Bosch Stiftung. https://www.bosch-stiftung.de/sites/default/files/publications/pdf/2018-08/Study_Techno logy-enhanced%20Personalised%20Learning.pdf.

Holmes, W., Bektik, D., Whitelock, D., & Woolf, B. P. (2018). Ethics in AIED: Who cares? In C. Penstein Rosé, R. Martínez-Maldonado, H. U. Hoppe, R. Luckin, M. Mavrikis, K. Porayska-Pomsta, B. McLaren, & B. du Boulay (Eds.), *Artificial Intelligence in Education Part II: 19th International Conference, AIED* (pp. 551–553). Springer.

Holmes, W., Bialik, M., & Fadel, C. (2019). *Artificial Intelligence in Education: Promises and Implications for Teaching and Learning*. Center for Curriculum Redesign.

Holmes, W., Chakroun, B., Miao, F., Mendes, V., Domiter, A., Fan, H., Kharkova, I., Orr, D., Jermol, M., Issroff, K., Park, J., Holmes, K., Crompton, Helen, Portales, P., Orlic, D., Rodriguez, S., Kaur, A., & Assouline, N. (2019). *Artificial Intelligence for Sustainable Development Synthesis Report: Mobile Learning Week 2019*. UNESCO. https://unesdoc.unesco.org/ark:/48223/pf0000370308.

Holmes, W., Porayska-Pomsta, K., Holstein, Ken, Sutherland, E., Baker, T., Buckingham Shum, S., Santos, O. C., Rodrigo, M. M. T., Cukorova, M., Bittencourt, I. I., & Koedinger, K. (2021). Ethics of AI in education: Towards a community-wide framework. *International Journal of Artificial Intelligence in Education*. doi:10.1007/s40593-021-00239-1.

Jobin, A., Ienca, M., & Vayena, E. (2019). Artificial Intelligence: The global landscape of ethics guidelines. *Nature Machine Intelligence*, 1(9), 389–399. doi:10.1038/s42256-019-0088-2.

Kant, I. (1785). *Grundlegung zur Metaphysik der Sitten/Groundwork of the Metaphysic of Morals*. Hartknoch.

Kay, J. (2012). AI and education: Grand challenges. *IEEE Intelligent Systems*, 27(5), 66–69. doi:10.1109/MIS.2012.92.

Kearns, M., & Roth, A. (2020). *The Ethical Algorithm: The Science of Socially Aware Algorithm Design*. Oxford University Press.

Kelly, K. (2011). *What Technology Wants* (Illustrated edition). Penguin Random House.

Kolkman, D. (2020, August 26). "F**k the algorithm"? What the world can learn from the UK's A-level grading fiasco. *LSE Impact of Social Sciences*. https://blogs.lse.ac.uk/

impactofsocialsciences/2020/08/26/fk-the-algorithm-what-the-world-can-learn-from
-the-uks-a-level-grading-fiasco/.

Kurzweil, R. (2006). *The Singularity Is Near: When Humans Transcend Biology*. Duckworth.

Logan, C. (2021). Toward abolishing online proctoring: Counter-narratives, deep
change, and pedagogies of educational dignity. *Journal of Interactive Technology and
Pedagogy*. https://jitp.commons.gc.cuny.edu/?p.

Marcus, G. (2020). The next decade in AI: Four steps towards robust artificial intelligence. ArXiv:2002.06177 [Cs]. http://arxiv.org/abs/2002.06177.

Miao, F., & Holmes, W. (2021). *AI and Education: Guidance for Policy-Makers*. UNESCO.
https://unesdoc.unesco.org/ark:/48223/pf0000376709.

Mill, J. S. (1863). *Utilitarianism*. Parker, Son and Bourn.

Narayanan, A. (2018, March 1). *Tutorial: 21 fairness definitions and their politics*. Tutorial at
the FACCT Conference. https://www.youtube.com/watch?v=jIXIuYdnyyk.

OECD. (2020). *Trustworthy AI in Education: Promises and Challenges*. OECD. http://www.
oecd.org/education/trustworthy-artificial-intelligence-in-education.pdf.

Porayska-Pomsta, K., Holmes, W., & Nemorin, S. (in press). The ethics of AI in education. In B. Du Boulay (Ed.), *Handbook of Artificial Intelligence in Education*.

Ross, W. D. (1930). *The Right and the Good*. Clarendon.

Russell, S. (2019). *Human Compatible: Artificial Intelligence and the Problem of Control*. Penguin.

Selwyn, N. (2019). *Should Robots Replace Teachers? AI and the Future of Education (Digital
Futures)*. Polity.

Selwyn, N., Hillman, T., Bergviken Rensfeldt, A., & Perrotta, C. (2021). Digital technologies and the automation of education: Key questions and concerns. *Postdigital
Science and Education*. doi:10.1007/s42438-021-00263-3.

Stokes, D. E. (1996). *Pasteur's Quadrant: Basic Science and Technological Innovation*. Brookings
Institution.

Suresh, H., & Guttag, J. V. (2019). A framework for understanding unintended consequences of machine learning. ArXiv:1901.10002, 2.

UNESCO. (2019). *Beijing Consensus on Artificial Intelligence and Education*. https://unesdoc.
unesco.org/ark:/48223/pf0000368303.

UNICEF. (2021). *Policy Guidance on AI for Children*. https://www.unicef.org/globalin
sight/media/2356/file/UNICEF-Global-Insight-policy-guidance-AI-children-2.
0-2021.pdf.pdf.

VanLehn, K. (2011). The relative effectiveness of human tutoring, intelligent tutoring
systems, and other tutoring systems. *Educational Psychologist*, 46(4), 197–221.
doi:10.1080/00461520.2011.611369.

Whittaker, M., Crawford, K., Dobbe, R., Fried, G., Kaziunas, E., Mathur, V.,
MyersWest, S., Richardson, R., Schultz, J., & Schwartz, O. (2018). *AI Now Report
2018*. AI Now Institute.

Williamson, B. (2020). Datafication of education. In H. Beetham & R. Sharpe (Eds.),
Rethinking Pedagogy for a Digital Age (pp. 212–226). Routledge. doi:10.4324/
9781351252805-14.

Williamson, B. (2021). Education technology seizes a pandemic opening. *Current History*,
120(822), 15–20. doi:10.1525/curh.2021.120.822.15.

Winfield, A. F. T., & Jirotka, M. (2018). Ethical governance is essential to building
trust in robotics and artificial intelligence systems. *Philosophical Transactions of the Royal
Society A*, 376(2133), 20180085. doi:10.1098/rsta.2018.0085.

Part I

Introduction to Part I

Wayne Holmes and Kaśka Porayska-Pomsta

With the application of AI in educational contexts recently emerging from the research labs, the potential benefits and implications of AIED for learners, teachers, and wider society are increasingly becoming part of a wider debate, involving perspectives from outside the AIED research community. These perspectives represent an important part of the growing ethics of the AIED landscape, and offer independent voices from within the social sciences and policymaking that have the power to influence the future directions of AIED research and frontline practices. Accordingly, Part I of this book presents reflections by authors from a range of disciplines outside of the community of AIED researchers, who engage with the ethical concerns for individuals, the education system, and society more broadly that arise from the increasing introduction of AI into and beyond classrooms.

Part I opens with Chapter 1, 'Learning to learn differently', by Jutta Treviranus. She begins with the observation that AI technologies typically depend on large homogeneous datasets in which, by definition, outliers and minorities are underrepresented. This, despite best intentions, inevitably exacerbates inequities and automates disparities, with students in the tails of the normal distribution being further disadvantaged. She also critically engages with some central claims made for the application of AIED – such as its role in 'personalisation', which she points out actually involves leading all students towards 'perfected conformance' – which she suggests can effectively obscure critical problems in our education systems. She concludes by arguing for applying a Wabi-sabi aesthetic to the design of education – an approach which, contrary to machine logic, celebrates 'the imperfect, impermanent, and incomplete', thus emphasising and valuing the rich diversity of humanity.

In Chapter 2, 'Educational research and Artificial Intelligence in education: Identifying ethical challenges', Alison Fox shifts the focus to how to build ethics into the research for and about AIED. She begins by grounding the discussion in the CERD ethical appraisal framework – which builds upon consequentialist, ecological, relational, and deontological ethical thinking – and by emphasising a context-specific approach to ethical justification. These are then used to construct a framework for key considerations, which include: the ethics of data sources and their long-term curation, to whom AIED

DOI: 10.4324/9780429329067-2

researchers are beholden; avoiding harm and minimising risk (such as, building on Chapter 1, the risk of normalisation through data cleansing); showing respect and duty of care; the need for transparency and choice for genuine consent; and legal, moral, methodological, and ethical obligations. She concludes with a call for an ethics by design approach in which researchers need to be sensitive to both the positive and negative potential consequences of their research, and to be prepared to consider alternative options.

Chapter 3, 'AI in education: An opportunity riddled with challenges', by Ivana Bartoletti, explores the potential of AI to support the education system's fundamental role of improving equal opportunity and social mobility. It queries whether AI can act as a 'springboard' for opportunity or whether it inevitably compromises mobility by eroding human agency and perpetuating existing economic and cultural divides. Bartoletti continues by exploring six key areas fraught with risks for the implementation of AIED: that it might scale up poor pedagogic ideas; the negative impact of detecting student emotions; the ethics of nudging; the erosion of human agency; encroachments on privacy; and the teaching of AI. She continues by re-emphasising that technology is never neutral – it always reflects cultural, social, and political norms – and concludes with a call for an ethics framework that includes, at the very least, principles centred on purpose, impact, justice and fairness, and human values.

In Chapter 4, 'Student-centred requirements for the ethics of AI in education', Lionel Brossi, Ana María Castillo, and Sandra Cortesi call for the 'student voice' to be at the centre of discussions on the development, design, deployment, and regulation of AIED. Drawing on UNESCO's *Beijing Consensus on Artificial Intelligence and Education* (2019), in which they identify some limitations, they argue that the adult voices that usually dominate narratives around AI effectively shut out most young people, minimising their engagement in discussions that are all too often central to their future lives. The same is also true for people from other marginalised communities, such as developing countries and rural areas, as well as, all too often, women and girls and people with disabilities. In conclusion, the authors draw together their many threads by discussing HabLatam, an innovative Latin American research initiative on youth and digital technologies that demonstrates one effective way in which the student voice can be properly heard.

Completing Part I is Chapter 5, 'Pitfalls and pathways for Trustworthy Artificial Intelligence in education', by Nathalie Smuha. In it she discusses the ethical challenges posed by the use of AIED in terms of the seven requirements for Trustworthy AI identified in the Ethics Guidelines of the European Commission's High-Level Expert Group on AI: respect for human agency and oversight, technical robustness and safety, privacy and data governance, transparency, diversity, non-discrimination and fairness, societal and environmental wellbeing, and accountability. Smuha continues by pointing out that the use of AIED is itself complex, with multiple technologies collecting different types of data, and having different purposes and different impacts on teachers and students, such that no one-size-fits-all approach can be adopted. This is further complicated by, for example, the asymmetries of power and information that exist in all educational relationships, and the range of stakeholders (students, parents, teachers, schools, policymakers) whose needs all ought to be carefully considered. A key conclusion is that, before implementing any AI solution in an educational context, we should first better understand whether the identified need needs to be solved, and whether AI is the best tool for so doing.

1 Learning to learn differently

Jutta Treviranus

Introduction

Artificial Intelligence has often been sold as a "power tool" (Falk, 2020) to more effectively and accurately filter large data sets, recognize patterns, search for desired items, and make decisions at scale. Like all power tools, AI can provide great efficiency and productivity; but it can also do great harm if not applied safely and ethically. AI is said to be the most disruptive and transformative technical innovation of our time (Girasa, 2020). To date, AI's disruption has primarily been in accelerating, amplifying, and automating existing patterns and processes, not in forging new ones. Unlike other power tools, once launched, we abdicate decisions and understanding to Artificial Intelligence. This implies that we must carefully consider the trajectory we set for Artificial Intelligence before we hand over the controls of education.

Awareness of the powerful influence of machine learning on our human trajectory is evidenced in the abundance of dystopian and utopian imaginings and projections (Simut, 2017). While making manifest our worst fears and best hopes, these narratives have distracted us from the subtle and pervasive ways in which machine learning has entered our daily lives. On the dystopian side of the decision ledger, the use of AI to accelerate, automate, and make more efficient the trends toward greater disparity, technological progress at the cost of biosphere destruction, and the brutal security systems needed to guard these trajectories is far more likely and threatening than the projections of AI robots eclipsing human intelligence and dominating humans. On the utopian side, even if AI fulfils all the optimistic promises, we should heed Marshall McLuhan (1994) when he warned that every augmentation is also an amputation, and the accompanying insight that first we shape our tools and then our tools shape us.

AI in education, more than in any other application, has far-reaching consequences. Education is an entrée and leverage point that has an impact on every aspect of our society. This impact is not limited to the present; it has even greater influence on our future. The decision to unleash the "power tools" of AI on formative minds must be made with great care. This decision is made riskier because what is being proposed is that we hand over decisions and judgement to a technology we may not fully control, and whose reasoning

DOI: 10.4324/9780429329067-3

is opaque or beyond our understanding. Educators are entrusted with the awesome responsibility of making decisions on behalf of future generations. With respect to deploying Artificial Intelligence, our ability to make an informed decision lags well behind the current and future implications of the decision, meaning that in many cases we are asked to trust an entity we do not own or govern with the most private thoughts and actions of our students and educators. This could render them exposed and vulnerable to as yet unknown influences in perpetuity.

As I write this chapter much of the world is attempting to recover from a global pandemic, and there is an outcry against the cruelty and injustice of systemic racial discrimination. We are poised at a pivotal point in history. Education is facing a discontinuity as many schools are adjusting to a "new normal." For better or worse, our formal institutions of education have been impervious to change. However, there is a general consensus that returning to what was considered normal before the disruption is not an option (Harris, 2020). As the world is struggling to right itself, many technology companies are exploiting the crisis to further their own interests, hopefully without malice or bad intent. Most remaining attitudinal barriers to computer-mediated, online education have been breached. Constraints are at their weakest, and desperation can lead to rash, improvident decisions.

Complex Adaptive System in Flux

There is no denying that the reality faced by today's students differs from the reality of the designers of our existing formal education systems. With the exponential rise of technological disruptions and associated practices, worldwide population growth, globalization, and climate effects the present and future reality can be seen as an entangled, complex, adaptive system in accelerating flux (Meadows, 2008). The broad adoption of Artificial Intelligence systems plays a pivotal role in current and anticipated discontinuities students will encounter in their lives. In addition to potentially disrupting the teaching professions Artificial Intelligence, automation, and smart systems have put into question the future of work, the viability of many existing professions, and the associated educational preparation (McKinsey & Manyika, 2017).

The discontinuity caused by the COVID-19 pandemic may offer an opportunity to reconsider not only how and when we deploy Artificial Intelligence to optimize and automate processes within education, but the course and design of education itself. Is it preparing students to thrive in this uncertain future? Once deployed in a competitive system, Artificial Intelligence is self-reinforcing. It will be harder to change course. Is this the best course to accelerate? Where are we taking our students? The pandemic has made this reckoning clearer by revealing our human weaknesses and the cracks in our social systems.

As the technology we are adopting is intelligence, and one of the intended skills we are augmenting and delegating is decision-making, this may be one of the last critical moments to consider these decisions and how we wish to be represented in delegated decisions. The current interruption of the status quo by the pandemic may provide an opportunity to pause to consider how we wish to teach and learn, and how these decisions affect our survival. Before we fully unleash the power tools of AI in education, we should ask: what do we wish to automate, accelerate, and optimize? What are we willing to amputate? How will this shape us individually and collectively as learners, and as educators?

Stuck on Local Optima

Despite the yearnful calls to "return to normal" during the pandemic, there is a global sense that existing patterns must change to navigate out of inevitable threats to human civilization. Among these accelerating threats are the risks of biosphere collapse, increasingly virulent health risks, rising disparity, socio-political polarization, and human-wrought terror (Rushkoff, 2020).

Current AI systems (including learning analytics, natural language processing, and pattern recognition systems that enable voice recognition, face recognition, and many other functions) rely on large amounts of data to detect likely patterns. Data, by its very nature, is about the past. Large data patterns only exist for majorities or large groups and the contexts of those who are not excluded (Mau, 2019). AI that relies on Big Data analytics and optimization is thereby destined to replicate, automate, and amplify dominant discriminatory patterns of the past. This will amplify the disparities and push toward ever more vulnerable monocultures.

Viewed from the standpoint of complexity modelling, the state of our current and future reality can be seen as a complex, unstable, mountainous terrain with a rising sea level (Figure 1.1). Safety and the key to our survival can be found on the highest, largest peaks, or the "global optima." However, we are heading up a lower peak that is threatened with submersion, or the "local optima." One of the lessons regarding navigating complex adaptive terrains is that a fixation on optimization will likely lead to being stuck on the local optima rather than the global optima needed to escape the crisis (Taleb, 2012). To climb down from our current local hill, we need to reverse course and search widely for the next promising ascent. Finding the global optima requires a diversification of perspectives, a willingness to fail or reverse optimization to find new paths, a willingness to abandon current strategies and try new ones, and the imperative to collaborate across differences. We also need to work together and maintain cohesion, to share insights generously, including our failures and successes.

An added complexity is that we are not just travellers over a static terrain. Our actions influence the shape of the terrain, especially the steepness of the slopes and how difficult it is for the full diversity of our ecosystem, needed for survival, to ascend to safety. One of the most powerful determinants of the state of that ascent to safety is education.

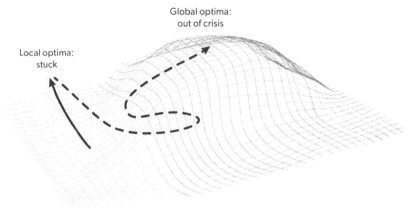

Figure 1.1 Complex terrain with local and global optima

The educational AI power tools we have deployed so far – from intelligent tutoring systems to automated grading systems, plagiarism-detection tools, and remote proctoring systems – all optimize the path to the dead-end of the local optima. Combined with the extractive AI-powered platforms awaiting graduates, and the rising cost of higher education, we have also made the ascent to the tip much steeper and precarious.

Who are the Stress Testers and Innovators?

In searching for the global optima out of our crises, we are poised at a paradox. The people best equipped to see the flaws and find alternative paths out of the crisis are the very people we have marginalized, disenfranchised, and excluded from the decision table. This means that, as a society, our vulnerabilities and also the innovative approaches that might resolve this crisis are overlooked. Both we and the tools we design are less able to handle diversity, complexity, and uncertainty at a time when we need this ability the most. One thing we are certain of, as underlined by the pandemic, is that the positive and negative impacts of any decisions will not be evenly distributed (Blundell et al., 2020). However, the pandemic has made it evident that "none of us are safe until all of us are safe" (UN, 2020).

This applies beyond our vulnerability to a tiny virus that is 10 million times smaller than humans but has nonetheless found and is able to exploit our human weaknesses. A dangerous habit we have passed on in the shaping of our tools is the propensity to reduce complexity and diversity, and to think categorically (Mau, 2019). Because we are in a time when truth is under threat and disinformation is rampant, we defend truth by reducing it to that which can be measured and is true for the majority, or what we label "hard science." Our view of science and evidence are inextricably linked to the truth of the statistical average or majority, or those who have no lived experience of the margins or exclusion. The power tools we have deployed in education threaten to exacerbate this pattern, during this crisis and the many crises to follow. We are not preparing students to operate in a complex adaptive terrain. We are not preparing them to thrive in their future.

This paradox can be illustrated by plotting data regarding human needs (Treviranus, 2018b). To accurately reflect the many variables our human needs occupy requires plotting unconstrained multi-parametric data on a three-dimensional multivariate scatterplot. When we do this, a common pattern that emerges with any naturally occurring population is what resembles a three-dimensional starburst, or what I have called a "human starburst." As in normal distributions, the centre is occupied by approximately 80% of the needs, taking up 20% of the space. The remaining 20% of the needs occupy the periphery or the remaining 80% of the space. The needs in the middle are close together, meaning they are similar. As the needs are distanced from the centre, they are also distanced from each other, meaning they are more different (Figure 1.2). Our systems – whether they are markets that look for economies of scale, research that looks for statistical power, systems of employment that look for replaceable workers, politics that depend upon a majority, or media that rely on popularity – are all designed for the central 80% that occupy 20% of the terrain. This has led to vicious cycles of increasing disparity. Artificial Intelligence is dependent on Big Data, and is therefore biased toward the central 80%, reinforcing this vicious cycle in all the domains it is applied.

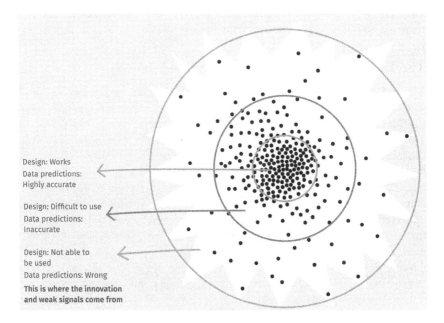

Figure 1.2 Human starburst: A multivariate scatter plot of diverse needs

This self-reinforcing pattern has also led to dangerous oversights and destructive, perseverative decision patterns that exclude the very individuals that have the insights we need. The individuals that are most aware of crises to come, are most vulnerable to the current risks, have the greatest motivation to find alternative paths, and have the least attachment to current failing strategies are the people at the outer edges of the human scatterplot or the bottom of the hierarchy or the current sub-optimal hill. Transformative innovation is not discovered by those who are complacent, comfortable, and invested in the status quo; it is discovered by addressing challenges at the edges of the human starburst. Weak signals and crises to come are not within the focus of those intent on climbing the current hill; they are felt by those left vulnerable at the devalued jagged edges (Treviranus, 2020).

This insight undergirds the theory and practice of inclusive design (as it is applied at the Inclusive Design Research Centre in Toronto, Canada) (Treviranus, 2018b). The centre is committed to proactively intervening in emerging sociotechnical practices to ensure that everyone can participate in benefitting from the opportunities and in addressing the risks. The centre is guided by an evolving framework that lays out three dimensions of inclusive design: design with the understanding that everyone is unique, and in doing this support individuals in understanding and valuing their own differences; ensure that the process of design is inclusive, with decision power given to people that feel the greatest impact of the design decision, including those who can't use or have difficulty with current designs, in part by continuously seeking the perspectives that are missing; and understand that you are intervening in a complex adaptive system in flux – no design decision is made in isolation, iteratively strive for benefit for all.

The Dangers of Old Patterns Amplified

The trajectory of the local optima we are stuck on was set before Artificial Intelligence entered the scene. The conventions adopted during industrialization and entrenched in our systems of formal education prime us against the transformative changes needed to reach the global optima out of this existential crisis. Among these conventions are our notions of averages and norms in our measurement of human performance; the association of quantified measurement and statistical power as the favoured forms of evidence, truth, and knowledge; our obsession with competition and associated flawed ideas of survival of the fittest as a competition between the strong and the weak, rather than adaptation; the formulas we have applied for quick wins, easy profit, and market dominance; and the sorting, classifying, and filtering embedded in all our practices. Each of these foundational notions primes us to reduce or deny diversity, variability, and complexity. These notions are built into our technical tools and are at the foundations of our current machine learning systems (Mau, 2019). It is these notions that are being amplified and automated by current AI tools (Rushkoff, 2020).

Ursula Franklin (1999) framed technology as more than the machines, gadgets, or electronic transmitters. She argued that technology is a comprehensive system that includes methods, procedures, organization, and, most of all, a mindset. She saw technology as practice, how things are socially and morally done. She distinguished the holistic technologies of creative artisans from the prescriptive technologies of factories and large enterprises, which discourage critical thinking and civic engagement. Holistic technologies give agency to the creator in the whole process of creation. Prescriptive technologies require a division of labour, and demand a culture of compliance while distancing the worker from the creative process, concentrating power and wealth, and fragmenting knowledge. Education, like our global economies, has trended toward prescriptive technologies before the deployment of Artificial Intelligence. The peak of education is greater specialization and a disdain for the more holistic view. Rigour, standardization, and what is seen as "quality" in education all trend toward the prescriptive standard. Artificial Intelligence is optimizing and making more efficient the patterns begun by quantification, metrics, statistics, and data analytics in education and other systems (Mau, 2019).

We have many early warning signs of the destructive influence of the power tools of AI on our society. The dystopian and utopian imaginings of the role of Artificial Intelligence may be wildly unrealistic when taken literally, but the warnings and promises they contain are already manifest in subtle, pervasive, and hidden ways (O'Neil, 2016). Our global competition and push for technological progress to avoid economic collapse compels us to push for ever more innovative digital technologies to accelerate the trajectories established in the prior era (Rushkoff, 2020).

The sense that the course of our sociotechnical progress may not be in the right direction has been growing for some time among those tasked with leading the way and those in the thick of the crowd. In 2001 Cass Sunstein, who was later to become the CIO of the Obama administration, warned of the negative effects of media personalization and echo-chambers, reducing our exposure to dissonant views. I worried about the exacerbation of this effect in popularity optimization systems in social media and search engine optimization in my paper "The Value of the Unpopular" (Treviranus & Hockema, 2009). Early technology pioneers such as Jaron Lanier (2013) and Sherry Turkle (2011) have reversed their enthusiasm and warned about the destructive impact of current sociotechnical systems. Tech giants such as Elon Musk (Holley, 2018) and the most brilliant minds such as Stephen Hawking have warned of the danger of human extinction if the current course is followed to its end (Rincon, 2018). The evidence of abuse of power and influence through these systems broke through to the public consciousness and resulted in what was termed the "techlash" (Heaven, 2018). However, while even the most ardent view of the positive impact of technical progress was tarnished, the concerns have been largely sublimated, especially while our economy moved online during the pandemic. Our societal dependence on the tools has already become irresistibly entrenched.

Each iteration of technical progress brings new levels of opportunity and threat. There is a growing awareness of the negative influence of our data technologies on our politics and economy. Shoshana Zuboff (2019) describes the pervasive and exploitative impact data surveillance has on our economy: leading to rising economic disparity and concentration of power. She illustrates how the collection and commodification of personal data in the context of a profit-making motive, coined as "surveillance capitalism," threatens human liberty, autonomy, equity, and well-being. The associated mass surveillance or a surveillance state, fictionalized in George Orwell's iconic 1949 novel *Nineteen Eighty-Four*, is currently manifest in mutated forms and operationalized through the extractive technologies and associated practices described by Zuboff, and assisted by a citizenry bartering personal data and privacy for convenience or essential services.

Even enthusiasts of the entrepreneurial innovation mindset have come to realize the destruction wrought by AI's amplification and acceleration. The business strategist and economist Roger Martin, in his recent book (2020), warns about the dangers of an overemphasis on efficiency, exacerbated by technical systems that create a feedback loop that speeds the rise of some at the expense of the rest. He recognizes and describes how this leads to dangerous, divisive levels of economic disparity.

These phenomena noted in markets, news media, social media, enterprise companies, and practices of governments result in monocultures and rising inequity, with the associated lack of adaptability and resilience. Our education practices follow the same pattern. Implementation of Artificial Intelligence amplifies and optimizes these patterns. However, the change resistance of our education systems and the disruption brought about by the pandemic may mean that there is still an opportunity to pause and consider how AI will shape our future generations

AI Ethics Movement and Disability

The emerging flaws and risks of Artificial Intelligence have triggered an AI ethics movement. Scholars and authors such as Cathy O'Neil (2016), Virginia Eubanks (2018), and Safiya Noble (2018) have cogently described the impact of AI bias in our social systems and critical decisions. Powered by social justice efforts there is a nascent public understanding of the problem of biased representation in data, algorithmic bias brought about by flawed and incomplete data, human bias influencing the design of machine learning, and the overreach of AI-guided or determined decisions. Well-known examples include: automated systems that do not recognize dark skin; classification systems that apply derogatory labels; and chat bots that repeat racist and sexist utterances learned from social media. Even if not the subject of negative AI bias, many people are concerned about the erosion of privacy brought about by data surveillance systems, and political targeting that polarize electorates through strategically distributed disinformation. This has produced privacy protections, AI ethics guidance, and tests to detect bias in existing machine learning models (Trewin et al., 2019).

Unfortunately, the problems at the very edges of our human scatterplot go deeper than these measures. Current social justice approaches may even intensify the problems at the edges. The AI ethics solutions are largely dependent on comparative metrics regarding the treatment of bounded justice-seeking identity groupings. There is a push for more equitable representation of groups that have faced discrimination in data sets used to train machine learning systems. Decision systems are tested for bias by comparing decisions regarding the overall population with decisions for a specific bounded justice-seeking group.

From a data perspective, one factor that exists at the edges of all these groupings is disability. People experiencing disabilities do not fit any bounded groupings such as racial genetic origin, language, skin colour, gender, or sex. As far as data is concerned, the only common element across people with disabilities is sufficient difference from the average that systems don't work for you (Gupta & Treviranus, 2020). At the jagged edge of human data sets, representation is not possible; many people belong to a grouping of one; or, worse, their disability is episodic and variable, so whatever representation there is will be fleeting.

There is no clear, bounded set of characteristics when it comes to disability. Diagnostic categorization offers very few functional benefits, and risks further excluding people who don't fit or who straddle the categories. For example, knowing a student is blind does not tell you whether they are Braille literate, how much residual vision they have or use, whether they once had sight and formed spatial models from the time they had sight, or any of the many other relevant characteristics of the person. As a result, most assumptions that come with disability categorization are flawed. To fully capture the relevant needs of all individuals that experience disabilities would require an unrealistically large number of representative groupings. For many people with disabilities, no one else can adequately represent their unique needs. People with disabilities are therefore the outliers or tiny minorities in any population data set. Even if full proportional representation can be achieved, the data of the outliers and tiny minorities will be overwhelmed by the majority or average in systems trained on population data. This is an issue with all decisions based on data averages for a population.

For students and teachers who are small minorities or outliers, this sets up a vicious cycle. They do not match the models the AI systems have been trained on or are designed to replicate and reward. This makes interaction with the systems more difficult. This means that there will be less data regarding pathways to success used by these students and teachers. The more the system is adopted, the more difficult and excluded these small minorities and outliers will be.

It can be said that persons experiencing disabilities are the most disadvantaged by the current design of Artificial Intelligence, but also the group with the most compelling applications. At the same time, people with disabilities have the most to gain from technical innovation. They are frequently the technical pioneers that experiment at the bleeding edge, before the early adopters of new disruptive systems (Jacobs, 1996). The majority of the technical innovations we take for granted were initiated in an attempt to address the challenges of disability, from email to telecommunications, to optical character recognition, text to speech and speech to text, to smart home systems. There is a saying that for most people technology makes things more convenient; for people with disabilities, it makes things possible. This also means that the possibility is dependent on technology. If the technology ceases to work, the person may no longer be able to speak, write, move, or breathe.

Disabled people are also some of the most vulnerable to the abuses and misuses of data. Current privacy protections, which resort to de-identification at source, fail to protect people with disabilities (Gupta & Treviranus, 2020). If you are highly unique you can be re-identified. If you are the only person in a neighbourhood to order a colostomy bag, if you are the only student in the school requiring a sign language interpreter, if you are the only teacher with a specialized wheelchair, you can be re-identified. Most people with disabilities must barter their privacy for essential services. The act of requesting an exception, or something not usually provided, identifies you whether or not you provide your name, address, your government identification number, or whether or not your face is recognized. Data privacy for people that are outliers is often an unrealistic luxury that can't be protected by de-identification at source.

At this time there is no privacy protection strategy that works for individuals that are highly unique. We have overemphasized securing the data at the expense of ensuring that, if and when there is a data breach, we can prevent its abuse and misuse. Locking data away also hampers its utility. Differential privacy, a strategy to test privacy protections, requires the removal of data that is needed to serve the needs of the individual who is highly unique. While it may afford privacy protection, it reduces representation of unique needs. At the same time, people with disabilities are often treated paternalistically or infantilized. They are not afforded the "dignity of risk." Systems are lacking that offer self-determination of the acceptable level of risk as a matter of informed personal choice and agency.

As a result of these challenges and opportunities, people with disabilities often inadvertently act as stress testers: they provide the early warning signs of the flaws of new systems. The flaws and risks in automated decision-making based on machine learning are significant. So are the opportunities if we use this disruption to transcend old patterns. However, even AI with full proportional representation, the removal of all data gaps, and the eradication of algorithmic bias will not steer us to the global optima unless we more fundamentally change the patterns we are optimizing, accelerating, and automating.

AI's Promises for Education

AI has already made significant incursions into education, ushered in by promises to address several difficult challenges that are symptoms of our current education system design. These promises have included helping struggling students; helping to find suitable resources from a plethora of content; relieving teachers from more mundane or routine tasks so they can focus on teaching; automating testing and grading; acting as assistive technologies and translators for students facing accessibility barriers; and optimizing educational administration and planning.

To address the issue of unequal performance and the plight of students struggling to keep up with their peers of the same age, we have deployed machine learning, in the form of intelligent tutors, to personalize instruction. Holmes et al. (2018) provide a comprehensive and thoughtful guide to forms of computer-aided personalization. However, most personalization systems are deployed to corral all students to the same destination. Personalization is most often applied to customize the pace of learning, the time each student spends on any one lesson until it is mastered. In fewer instances, instructional tutors offer a personalized path of learning to the same destination, using more tailored learning approaches or motivation tools. Rather than supporting students in differentiating themselves and orchestrating their unique skills and knowledge with those of other learners, AI is deployed to support greater conformance to a norm. Not only do the tools shape standardized learners, learners are often pitted against each other to motivate performance in leader boards and simplistic gamification strategies. Any difference from the statistical optima is mechanistically eliminated and reward is attached to perfected conformance.

Digital systems, the Web, social media, and apps have led to an explosion of content that overwhelms curation, organization, sorting, and filtering. This offers a potential wealth of resources for educators, students, and researchers alike, if you sort and find the resource that meets your needs. AI systems have become better and better at pattern matching and searching. Rather than spending time sorting through a mass of unsuitable content, AI-assisted search can locate the perfect match far faster and more accurately – sometimes before we have fully articulated what we want. However, this is done at the expense of serendipity, finding the unexpected, and being offered novel alternatives. The chosen material is also affected by a popularity echo-chamber. The most popular receives more attention, is highlighted and given priority of place, and thereby receives more attention. This pattern plays out at the expense of the less popular, resulting in widening oversights. This feeds into the confirmation bias of researchers, and shields learners from multi-perspectival views. This also contributes to the creation of educational content hierarchies and monopolies.

The most widely accepted justification for AI in education is that it will relieve teachers from the more mundane, routine tasks so they can focus on teaching (Holmes et al., 2019). Among these mundane tasks are tracking attendance, monitoring student task completion, grading, and preparing reports. Some systems even prepare standard messages to be sent to students, maintain schedules, prompt, and remind teachers of errands. The risks in doing this is that these functions become automated, and we fail to question whether they are necessary or beneficial.

Students with disabilities who require alternative access means often present the most compelling opportunities of AI in education.

(World Institute on Disability, 2019; Treviranus, 2018a)

Text-to-speech and screen-reading systems make it possible for a blind student or teacher to read. Image recognition identifies images that can't be seen. Speech-to-text, gesture recognition, and disambiguation aids in writing when students lack the dexterity to use a keyboard or write. Captioning supports students who are Deaf or who have hearing loss. AI can translate from one language to another for a language learner, and it can help a student with dyslexia to correct spelling and grammar errors. The primary flaw in these systems is that they are trained on large data sets that are biased toward the average. This means that the students who differ the most from the average – who have the most anomalous speech, the least controlled gestures, the most unusual spelling errors, who are also often the students that need the assistance the most – have the greatest difficulty with the recognition systems.

Each of these applications of AI obscures the foundational problems in our current formal education systems. Like the plaster obscuring the cracks in the foundation, AI assists in denying they exist. The more we invest in the AI systems in education, the less motivated we are to make fundamental changes. Without fundamental changes, AI will amplify existing patterns of discrimination and disparity. The promise we are given is that AI will do what educators are expected to do currently – more efficiently, vigilantly, thoroughly, and effectively. Data-guided optimization consolidates and intensifies existing patterns and increases the bias toward the majority.

Disrupting Employment and the Future of Work

The primary short-term risk of AI to capture the public consciousness is the fear that it will supplant jobs currently fulfilled by humans. Looking at the many positions replaced by automation and the business-to-business advertising promising further replacement by automation, this fear is not unfounded. For example, McKinsey Global Institute (2017) estimates that half of today's work will be automated by 2055. The prescriptive technologies and the hierarchical and extractive forms of labour Ursula Franklin critiqued have primed the labour market for this disruption. Work has been segmented into formulaic chunks that can be fulfilled by machines. Systemization and fragmentation have pervaded almost all sectors, from manual labour to surgery. The mindset and procedures standardized in human resources processes that produce prescriptive job descriptions that detail measurable units of work and seek replaceable workers contribute to this trajectory. Quality control, standardized measurement, and certification efforts to regulate professions and trades have further ushered in this accelerated trajectory. The data gathered through work surveillance extracts the data needed to teach machines to replace humans. In a parallel trajectory, machines are gaining mastery of even highly complex, intellectual, and social tasks such as writing and customer service. This human labour disruption will have an impact not only on workers but also on the entire system of wealth distribution and the public tax base upon which public education and essential services rely. To ameliorate this socio-economic system collapse, it has been proposed that robots be taxed (Porter, 2019).

Our formal education systems appear to be unwitting contributors to a future of unemployment for graduates, without offering the utopian alternative of a meaningful and productive life free from labour. Given our design decisions regarding education, we are turning our children into assets that serve the machine, to ultimately be replaced by the machine.

The story of Uber, the "ride-sharing" app, is an apt, simplified anecdote to illustrate a larger, more complex sociotechnical pattern (Scholz, 2017). Uber created an extractive platform whereby the producers of value, the drivers, did not share in the governance or profit. They were merely parts of a large machine. Work surveillance systems, which shape their performance and conformance to a desired norm, pit them against each other for ratings, and optimize their efficiency. Any deviation from optimal performance – such as helping a passenger in need, failing to accept a ride, or taking time to speak to family members – degrades performance, ranking, and rewards. The data used to shape and optimize their performance is largely hidden from them to the point that drivers were prompted to keep shadow records. Customers are complicit in shaping the system, ranking drivers, and being ranked themselves. They are attracted by lowered costs of transportation. The larger purpose however is to gather data to feed a machine learning system to ultimately replace drivers with automated vehicles. The entire enterprise is made palatable by appealing to the values of sharing transportation and reduced car traffic.

Our education systems appear to be unaware participants in a similar strategy at a much larger scale. This goes beyond the industrialized forms of education that have been entrenched in our culture for over a century, to current prioritization of certain forms of education and the computer-mediated systems we have deployed. When politicians justify public investment in the geopolitical race toward national dominance in AI innovation, they argue that the AI industry will not reduce jobs for humans (Government of Canada, 2018). They reason that the jobs lost to automation will be replaced by jobs in data science and AI-related fields. This justifies and bolsters the focus on science, technology, engineering, and mathematics (STEM) in education over subjects that will not serve this purpose. Nation states invest in data science education to compete in the global race, diverting funds from other forms of education. Asking the simple question "What can people do that machines won't be able to do in the foreseeable future?" shows that our educational practices seem primed to turn our kids into replaceable machines without preparing them for the roles unique to humans.

Valorizing the Formulaic

In high school and college, when we offer choices in terms of learning directions, we valorize the formulaic topics such as STEM and promote standardization as a sign of quality. This has been a pattern for many decades but has been intensified to bolster performance in the AI race. This not only benefits the advance of AI but also primes students to be replaced. STEM topics are also the first topics to be mastered by machines. If we can express the formula, we can teach the machines the formula. If we can precisely document the process and steps, we can instruct the machines to follow the process more efficiently and precisely. What won't be replaced in the foreseeable future is the unexpected, uncertain, non-formulaic, non-linear work that requires continuous human judgement and creativity. These are all the topics we generally discourage students from pursuing. Support for a liberal arts education has declined significantly (Zakaria, 2015). A career in the arts is generally discouraged.

Equality is Not Equity

Paradoxically, the battle for diversity and inclusion appears to be playing into the same strategy. Human difference is our greatest asset and the key to our survival. Our "diversity, equity, and inclusion" (DEI) efforts fight for equal treatment for under-served, protected groups (Bellamy et al., 2019). To this end we are measuring equity through performance in standardized tests. I fear that we may have unintentionally sacrificed student diversity in the struggle for equality.

Our DEI efforts fight to include excluded groups of students in systems not made for them, that are not constructed to meet their needs, thereby setting them up for a much harder time, if not failure. Even if we still have the misguided goal of getting everyone to the same place, people start out from different places and need different paths and different ways of getting there. A better approach would be to create an education system that can leverage, value, and reward the diversity of perspectives and help each student reach their unique potential. This will compel us, as a society, to cover much more ground, reduce oversights, and build more choices into our systems.

We need to show students how to differentiate themselves. The conventional, complacent, established patterns are usually the first to go extinct when our world is disrupted. It doesn't make sense to fight to become just like the average, at the cost of abandoning or suppressing our uniqueness.

Conformant, Rule-bound, Competitive, and Divisive

Our formal education systems still "socialize" inconvenient human variability out of our students. We shape them to be conformant and rule-bound. They are taught to defer to authority without question and perform their role within the established hierarchy. We also teach them to see their peers as competition rather than as collaborators or team members. We mislabel collaboration and resourcefulness as cheating, because of the outdated notion that our students' minds are made to store information, and not for independent thought, critical analysis, and creative teamwork.

Machines are rule-bound (unless they break down). Our students need to be more. We fail to help students develop a moral compass and hone their human and humane judgement. They are not given the dignity of risk; nor are they taught the incredible learning value of failure and mistakes.

By removing human difference and variability we also put our collective survival at risk. Our educational trajectory and rewards implicitly teach students to see the world as something to be exploited, rather than as a connected, single organism. We fail to teach them that they have a collective responsibility and individually unique role in ensuring the survival of this precarious miracle that is our world.

Our Metrics Society

Of all the educational practices that contribute to replacement by machines, assessment and grading are the most effective. Looking retrospectively, it would seem that we have architected the trajectory of educational assessment and certification to serve this ultimate agenda of human replacement. Like Uber, the rationale for the mechanization of learning has appealed to altruistic senses and irreproachable ideals. Motivated by such values as quality, rigour, evidence, and excellence – which demand standardization, measurement, and competition – and even equality, which is a measurable alternative to diversity and equity, we have created a system that extracts the necessary data for optimization, pushes students toward learning that can be mechanized, and discourages any deviation from the favoured standard. Learning diversity is offered as segregated academic disciplines with their own microcosm of standardization, competitive hierarchies, and accompanying high-stakes assessments. This pattern is bolstered by economic austerity, which demands efficiency. Standardized tests favour and optimize performance in the formulaic subjects that can be captured in metrics. The feedback loop of reduced investment in the commons reinforces this pattern as education seeks to attract investment by commercial interests and to supply the private sector with necessary workers.

The education company Singularity University has been a popular leader in this strategy, and has been bolstered by tech giants and many aspiring political administrations seeking participation and leadership in technical progress (Boenig-Liptsin & Hurlbut, 2016). The company's name refers to a phenomenon called "the singularity" – a hypothetical point in time at which machine intelligence surpasses human intelligence, and technological growth becomes uncontrollable and irreversible. The private university is focused on "exponentially accelerating technologies." It promotes the view that technology will solve the world's greatest problems; we just need to exponentially accelerate its progress and the proliferation of successful technical start-ups.

While enterprises such as Singularity University are seen as transformative departures from traditional education, in many ways our formal education systems have been primed to participate in this strategy to progress toward "the singularity." Our systems of assessment, rewards, marking, and grading promote the notion that all students need to be ranked on a single scale and all students in a cohort need to reach the same learning outcomes. We have indoctrinated them so well that the goal most students articulate by the time they reach university is "to get the best grades." A more pervasive and entrenched form of work surveillance than evident in extractive platforms like Uber has not only been normalized but has become the primary focus of many formal education systems. It has become internalized by students, parents, and teachers alike. When I recently asked a class of undergraduates what their primary goal was, they responded that they wanted to get good grades, and the most ambitious aspired to the top mark in their class. When I asked a group of teachers how they knew whether a student was a good student who would do well in life, the majority cited good grades. However, we know that grades are not a reliable indicator of success in life (Baird, 1985), or even an accurate indicator of the ability to retain and apply knowledge. They cause a great deal of anxiety and fear of failure (Kohn, 2011). They discourage risk taking, constructive critique, critical thinking, independent exploration, and any inclination to diverge from the specified direction of learning – all the skills that machines are less likely to replace (Andrade & Valtcheva, 2009). Anything standardized and easily measured can be replaced and optimized by machines. We are corralling the amazing diversity of students that enter formal education toward the same redundant endpoints.

Tests, assessment, marks, ranking, and grading are no longer just tools for measuring and tracking success; they have come to represent success itself at all the nested levels of education. Through ever more ubiquitous aggregation, analysis, and rewards and promotions tied to test results, these results have come to signal the success and status of students, teachers, schools, school boards, states, and nations. Through public, private, and philanthropic funding tied to quantified evidence, test results have become the prerequisites of success and survival for educational institutions (Ostrander, 2015). Even the economic survival of nations is tied to test results, as national economic aid is contingent upon measures such as the OECD's Programme for International Student Assessment (PISA) scores (Addey & Sellar, 2018). Testing, and the data surveillance and measurement that feed the assessment ecosystem, begins at infancy and continues throughout the lifespan of education and beyond.

Like Uber drivers, students are often not privy to the data that is used to optimize their performance. Standardized tests and the educational practices that serve them remove agency from students, teachers, and communities. Teachers teach to the test. Schools promote teachers that optimize marks. Deviation from the prescribed pattern is discouraged. Students that learn differently are seen as liabilities. Multiple strategies are used to exclude them from the measures, including segregation or refusal of admission. Students are discouraged from pursuing their own passions. Teachers are discouraged from using their discretion to vary the curriculum. School boards are discouraged from honouring diverse local cultures.

The assessment ecosystem not only serves to produce replaceable workers capable of building the systems that will replace them; the favoured forms of assessments, tests, marks, and grading are ideal processes to automate and optimize as well. Computer-mediated tests and assessment have been prevalent and accepted for many decades (Wise & Plake, 1989). The pandemic has accelerated the incursion of mechanization and AI systems into education. Proctoring systems for supervising students taking tests remotely during the pandemic are prime examples (Harwell, 2020). Rather than implementing systems that enable learners to either assess their own learning – enabling students to produce convincing evidence of their learning or creating learning assessments that are impervious to cheating – AI-based remote proctoring systems have proliferated. The systems are intended to prevent and flag cheating during assessments, including high-stakes assessments, and millions of dollars have been spent by thousands of universities to implement these systems. The students submit to remote surveillance and elaborate protocols to prove that they are not receiving assistance and don't have access to digital or physical sources of information. Any deviation from the norm causes the student to be flagged as a potential cheat. This could include "suspicious" gaze patterns; non-standard equipment, such as assistive technologies used by persons with disabilities; the inadvertent presence of any other person in crowded homes; background noises or utterances; or any interruptions while taking the tests, including technical glitches. Students with disabilities whose actions, affects, and behaviours are different from the norm are most vulnerable to flagging. The steps required to satisfy the system detract from performance in the skills and knowledge to be tested, and exclude students with disabilities who could otherwise complete the test. Indeed, students have urinated at their desk and wept with stress.

Rather than heeding the lessons of the pandemic by addressing the exposed flaws in our education system, we have used smart technologies to reinforce discriminatory mindsets. Our educational approaches to the pandemic have provided painful examples of the risks of unleashing AI to optimize current educational practices. The unacknowledged outcome appears to be to produce graduates for whom surveillance is normalized, and who can provide intelligence and data to ultimately replace themselves.

Before We Unleash AI

The pandemic has provided a disruption in the status quo, a departure from the seemingly inevitable determined trajectory. Before we return to a pre-pandemic "normal" and deploy our AI power tools to help students and educators "catch up" and compensate for time lost, let's give some sober thought to how "normal" has served us through this crisis. In considering billionaires and front-line workers, what have we learned about how we value and reward skills and what is truly important? In considering our attempts to organize and collaborate to slow the spread of the virus, what collective learning gaps has this forced hiatus revealed? When we witness the popular belief in disinformation and the increased tribalism it engenders, what have we learned about how well schools have prepared a populace for critical thinking, navigating uncertainty, respectful debate, and collaboration?

To find the global optima out of this and the next crisis we need to diversify skills and knowledge, encourage diverse perspectives, and avoid oversights to detect the weak signals of crises to come. This requires a diversity of areas of inquiry and scholarship. However, throughout the most formative years of education we are focused on creating standardized students that are carefully measured copies of each other, ranked and sorted on a single scale. This trend continues throughout most of post-secondary education. How can we nurture and capitalize on students' inherent differences to produce the diversity of knowledge and skills? How can we leverage this diversity to provide choices to weather this and the next unexpected crisis?

What would happen if we taught students to assess their own learning and compete with themselves (Andrade & Valtcheva, 2009)? What if we nurtured internal motivation to gain knowledge, skills, and mastery? How would this serve students during times of disruption?

One of the concerns expressed during the pandemic is the threatened extinction of endangered knowledge due to the accelerated loss of more vulnerable generations (Hall & Tandon, 2017). This includes indigenous and other minority languages when the last remaining speakers die. It includes survival skills honed by generations who lived through prior crises. At the same time young parents are struggling to work and act as tutors for their children. Generational fragmentation and loneliness are on the rise. While our formal education systems may not be to blame, they have played a pivotal role.

Why do we need to sort and segregate students by age? Do we all mature according to a tightly prescribed formula? Why do we make it so hard for students that take their time maturing or for students that mature too quickly? What would happen if we mixed the ages, and even brought in the many generations to help each other learn? Isn't one of the best ways to learn something by teaching it?

In this race, is the notion of a finish line, or school completion, even realistic given that the world is changing so fast? Is there an expiry date for learning? Shouldn't learning be life-long (Medel-Añonuevo et al., 2001)?

Are the subjects students need to learn really like many stacks of bricks, one brick on top of the next in an unerring sequence, each stack or course segregated from the other stacks (Durand & Downes, 2009)? Are the problems and projects students need to tackle when they finally graduate so rigorously organized? How will they solve the gnarly, messy problems they will inevitably encounter? Why can't we engage their hungry minds in tackling authentic problems so they can practise early and often (Barrett, 2010)? What harm will we do by mashing up the subjects and learning the undiscovered relationships between the disciplines and how they can support each other (Jacobs, 1989)? Might the resulting whole be greater than the parts and better suited to real life?

Do students really need to spend their many hours at school and home producing disposable assignments, exercises that only the student and the teacher review and that ultimately end up in the trash (Wiley & Hilton, 2018)? Can we engage their still eager minds in authentic assignments, with real measures of success, and the opportunity to feel authentically valued and relevant (Lombardi, 2007)?

Do we need to lock up and guard knowledge? Why do we value private wealth over collective learning? Why can't we adopt ways to credit production and innovation while contributing to the common (Feldstein et al., 2012; Caswell et al., 2008)? Why do we add economic burden to our students, their families, and our schools (Nusbaum et al., 2020)? Can we create structures that engage students in producing knowledge and sharing the knowledge they create through open learning practices?

Do we really want to discourage depending on each other by classifying it as cheating? Can we create systems of reward that encourage collaboration and teamwork (and not only when it is to beat another team) (McInnerney & Roberts, 2009)?

Most importantly, why is this a race with winners and losers when we know that we ultimately all lose if we leave people behind and vulnerable? Could it be a collective journey of discovery and learning through trial and error, of optimizing each student's unique potential, and learning to orchestrate the vast potential of differentiated rather than standardized skills?

As far as handing educational decisions and formative minds over to AI, let's remember that anything that AI can teach AI can automate. If the progress of Artificial Intelligence is inevitable, our education systems should be preparing students to excel in the uniquely human skills that cannot be replicated, are not formulaic, and defy metrics.

Conclusion

Rushkoff, in his recent book *Team Human*, argues that "the stuff that makes our thinking and behaviour messy, confusing, or anomalous is both our greatest strength and our greatest defence against the deadening certainty of machine logic." I have argued for the application of the Wabi-sabi aesthetic in the design of education (Treviranus, 2010). Wabi-sabi celebrates the value of the imperfect, impermanent, and incomplete. The imperfect invites participation, the impermanent supports culture change, and the incomplete welcomes a diversification of contributions. Each serves to nurture diverse individual potential. The Canadian songwriter Leonard Cohen wrote: "There is a crack, a crack in everything; That's how the light gets in." This pandemic has offered a crack in the trajectory we are accelerating and automating through AI. The people at the edges of our human scatterplot that are far from the optimal norm, they are most affected by the cracks in our seemingly perfect plan. They provide the options, lived experience, and resourcefulness we need. The diversity, inconvenient differences, deviation from the norm, dissonance or non-compliance that has been characterized as an issue to be addressed by educational strategies is actually our greatest human asset. It is the key to collectively finding our global optima and co-creating a fulfilling role for humanity in whatever future we construct.

References

Addey, C. & Sellar, S. (2018). Why do countries participate in PISA? Understanding the role of international large-scale assessments in global education policy. In Verger, A., Novelli, M. & Altinyelken, H. (eds), *Global education policy and international development: New agendas, issues and policies* (pp. 97–118). Bloomsbury.

Andrade, H. & Valtcheva, A. (2009). Promoting learning and achievement through self-assessment. *Theory into Practice*, 48(1), 12–19.

Baird, L. L. (1985). Do grades and tests predict adult accomplishment? *Research in Higher Education*, 23(1), 3–85.

Barrett, T. (2010). The problem-based learning process as finding and being in flow. *Innovations in Education and Teaching International*, 47(2), 165–174.

Bellamy, R. K., Dey, K., Hind, M., Hoffman, S. C., Houde, S., Kannan, K., … & Nagar, S. (2019). AI Fairness 360: An extensible toolkit for detecting and mitigating algorithmic bias. *IBM Journal of Research and Development*, 63(4–5). https://arxiv.org/abs/1810.01943.

Blundell, R., Costa Dias, M., Joyce, R. & Xu, X. (2020). COVID-19 and inequalities. *Fiscal Studies*, 41(2), 291–319.

Boenig-Liptsin, M. & Hurlbut, J. B. (2016). Technologies of transcendence at Singularity University. In Hurlbut, J. B., & Tirosh-Samuelson, H. (eds), *Perfecting human futures: Transhuman visions and technological imaginations* (pp. 239–267). Springer.

Caswell, T., Henson, S., Jensen, M. & Wiley, D. (2008). Open content and open educational resources: Enabling universal education. *International Review of Research in Open and Distributed Learning*, 9(1).

Durand, G. & Downes, S. (2009, July). Toward simple learning design 2.0. In *2009 4th international conference on computer science & education* (pp. 894–897). IEEE.

Eubanks, V. (2018). *Automating inequality: How high-tech tools profile, police, and punish the poor.* St. Martin's Press.

Falk, K. 2020. Artificial intelligence: HR's new power tool. Retrieved at: https://www.bencfitnews.com/opinion/artificial-intelligence-hrs-new-power-tool, December 31, 2020.

Feldstein, A., Martin, M., Hudson, A., Warren, K., Hilton III, J. & Wiley, D. (2012). Open textbooks and increased student access and outcomes. *European Journal of Open, Distance and E-Learning*, 15(2).

Franklin, U. (1999). *The real world of technology.* House of Anansi.

Girasa R. (2020). *Artificial intelligence as a disruptive technology: Economic transformation and government regulation.* Palgrave Macmillan,.

Government of Canada (2018). Prime Minister announces investment in artificial intelligence to create over 16,000 jobs for Canadians. Retrieved at: https://pm.gc.ca/en/news/news-releases/2018/12/06/prime-minister-announces-investment-artificial-intelligence-create August 1, 2020.

Gupta, A. & Treviranus, J. (2020). Inclusive designed artificial intelligence. In Schaffers, H. Vartianen, M. & Bus, J. (eds), *Digital innovation and societal change*. River Publishers.

Hall, B. L. & Tandon, R. (2017). Decolonization of knowledge, epistemicide, participatory research and higher education. *Research for All*, 1(1), 6–19.

Harris, A. (2020). *COVID-19: School leadership in crisis?*Journal of Professional Capital and Community, 5(3–4), 321–326.

Harwell, D. (2020). Cheating-detection companies made millions during the pandemic: Now students are fighting back. *Washington Post*. Retrieved at: https://www.washing tonpost.com/technology/2020/11/12/test-monitoring-student-revolt/.

Heaven, D. (2018). Techlash. *New Scientist*, 237(3164), 28–31.

Holley, P. (2018). Elon Musk's nightmarish warning: AI could become "an immortal dictator from which we would never escape". *Washington Post*. Retrieved at: https://www.washingtonpost.com/news/innovations/wp/2018/04/06/elon-musks-nightma rish-warning-ai-could-become-an-immortal-dictator-from-which-we-would-never-es cape/ August 1, 2020.

Holmes, W., Anastopoulou, S., Schaumburg, H. & Mavrikis, M. (2018). *Technology-enhanced personalised learning: Untangling the evidence*. Robert Bosch Stiftung.

Holmes, W., Bialik, M. & Fadel, C. (2019). *Artificial intelligence in education*. Center for Curriculum Redesign.

Jacobs, H. H. (1989). *Interdisciplinary curriculum: Design and implementation*. Association for Supervision and Curriculum Development.

Jacobs, S. (1996). Fueling the creation of new electronic curbcuts. Center for an Accessible Society. Retrieved at: http://www.accessiblesociety.org/topics/technol ogy/eleccurbcut.htm. August 1, 2020.

Kohn, A. (2011). The case against grades. *Educational Leadership*, 69(3), 28–33.

Lanier, J. (2013). *Who owns the future?*Simon & Schuster.

Lombardi, M. M. (2007). Authentic learning for the 21st century: An overview. *Educause Learning Initiative*, 1, 1–12.

Martin, R. (2020). *When more is not better: Overcoming America's obsession with economic efficiency*. Harvard Business Review Press.

Mau, S. (2019). *The metric society: On the quantification of the social*. Wiley.

McInnerney, J. M. & Roberts, T. S. (2009). Collaborative and cooperative learning. In *Encyclopedia of distance learning*, 2nd Edition (pp. 319–326). IGI Global.

McKinsey & Manyika, J. (2017). Technology, jobs, and the future of work. McKinsey Insights.

McKinsey Global Institute. (2017). *A future that works: Automation, employment, and productivity*. https://www.mckinsey.com/~/media/mckinsey/featured%20insights/ Digital%20Disruption/Harnessing%20automation%20for%20a%20future%20tha t%20works/MGI-A-future-that-works-Executive-summary.ashx.

McLuhan, Marshall. (1994). *Understanding media: The extensions of man*. MIT Press.

Meadows, D. H. (2008). *Thinking in systems: A primer*. Chelsea Green.

Medel-Añonuevo, C., Ohsako, T. & Mauch, W. (2001). Revisiting lifelong learning for the 21st century. Retrieved at: https://uil.unesco.org/lifelong-learning/revisiting-li felong-learning-21st-century.

Noble, S. U. (2018). *Algorithms of oppression: How search engines reinforce racism*. New York University Press.

Nusbaum, A. T., Cuttler, C. & Swindell, S. (2020). Open educational resources as a tool for educational equity: evidence from an introductory psychology class. *Frontiers in Education*, 4, doi:10.3389/feduc.2019.00152.

O'Neil, C. (2016). *Weapons of math destruction: How big data increases inequality and threatens democracy*. Crown Books.

Ostrander, R. R. (2015). School funding: Inequality in district funding and the disparate impact on urban and migrant school children. *Brigham Young University Education and Law Journal*, 1, 271–295.

Porter, E. (2019). Don't fight the robots. Tax them. *New York Times*. Retrieved at: https://www.nytimes.com/2019/02/23/sunday-review/tax-artificial-intelligence.html, August 1, 2020.

Rincon, P (2018). Stephen Hawking's warnings: What he predicted for the future. Retrieved at: https://www.bbc.com/news/science-environment-43408961 August 1, 2020.

Rushkoff, D. (2020). *Team human*. Ledizioni.

Scholz, T. (2017). *Uberworked and underpaid: How workers are disrupting the digital economy*. Wiley.

Simut, A. (2017). Contemporary representations of artificial intelligence in science fiction films, visual arts, and literature: A short introduction. *Ekphrasis: Images, Cinema, Theory, Media*, 17(1), 5–8.

Sunstein, C. (2001). *Echo chambers*. Princeton University Press.

Taleb, N. N. (2012). *Antifragile: Things that gain from disorder* (Vol. 3). Random House.

Treviranus, J. (2010). The value of imperfection: The Wabi-Sabi principle in aesthetics and learning, *Open ED Proceedings*, Barcelona, November.

Treviranus, J. (2018a). Learning differences and digital equity in the classroom. In Voogt, J., Knezek, G., Christensen, R. & Lai, K. W. (eds), *Second handbook of information technology in primary and secondary education* (pp. 1025–1046). Springer.

Treviranus, J. (2018b). *The three dimensions of inclusive design: A design framework for a digitally transformed and complexly connected society* (Doctoral dissertation, University College Dublin).

Treviranus, J. (2020). It's time to drop "Darwinism" and listen to Darwin and his successors on Human Evolution. Retrieved at: https://medium.com/@jutta.trevira/its-time-to-drop-darwinism-and-listen-to-darwin-and-his-successors-on-human-evolution-19239068e8dc, August 1, 2020.

Treviranus, J. & Hockema, S. (2009). *The value of the unpopular: Counteracting the popularity echo-chamber on the Web*, IEEE Toronto International Conference Science and Technology for Humanity (TIC-STH), Toronto, 26–27 Sept 2009.

Trewin, S., Basson, S., Muller, M., Branham, S., Treviranus, J., Gruen, D., Hebert, D., Lyckowski, N. & Manser, E. (2019). Considerations for AI fairness for people with disabilities. *AI Matters*, 5(3), 40–63.

Turkle, S. (2011). *Alone together*. Basic Books.

UN. (2020). None of us is safe until we all are, says UN chief at EU push to end COVID-19 pandemic. Retrieved at: https://news.un.org/en/story/2020/05/1063132, August 1, 2020.

Wiley, D. & HiltonIII, J. L. (2018). Defining OER-enabled pedagogy. *International Review of Research in Open and Distributed Learning*, 19(4).

Wise, S. L. & Plake, B. S. (1989). Research on the effects of administering tests via computers. *Educational Measurement: Issues and Practice*, 8(3), 5–10.

World Institute on Disability. (2019). AI and accessibility (July 2019). Retrieved at: https://wid.org/2019/06/12/ai-and-accessibility/, June 23, 2019.

Zakaria, F. (2015). *In defense of a liberal education*. Norton.

Zuboff, S. (2019). *The age of surveillance capitalism: The fight for a human future at the new frontier of power*. Public Affairs.

2 Educational research and AIED

Identifying ethical challenges

Alison Fox

Introduction

Artificial intelligence (AI) is accepted as including the development and application of machine learning (ML) technologies, with ML referring to models built and trained with the purpose of better recognising patterns, clusters, and structures in processing large amounts of data by models to learn to cluster and/or recognise patterns (Alpaydin, 2016; Russell & Norvig, 2009). AI and ML are here discussed in relation to research focused on understanding how to effectively deploy these 'intelligent', 'adaptive,' and potentially 'personalised' systems for educational benefit – that is, AIED research.

Reference is made to the ethical guidelines from the British Educational Research Association (BERA, 2018) and the Association of Internet Researchers (AoIR) (franzke et al., 2020) and, in particular, to the 'AI and ML Internet Research Ethics Guidelines', a companion to the main AoIR documentation (Bechmann & Zevenbergen, 2020). The points raised also align with other codes of ethics (e.g. ARC et al., 2018; AERA, 2011). The chapter supports and illustrates one of the key principles of the AoIR guidance, that of *ethical pluralism*. As Bechmann and Zevenbergen argue, this is not a case of accepting relativist arguments that any ethical principles might be accepted, but rather to support context-specific approaches to ethical justification (for example, re: fairness, Kroll et al., 2016; privacy, Nissenbaum, 2011; justice, Hoffmann & Jonas, 2016; and respect for individuals, Hongladarom, 2017). This acknowledges that 'an essential virtue of this approach is precisely that it acknowledges the legitimacy of specific local norms, practices, etc., while nonetheless conjoining these across significant differences with more encompassing and shared norms, values' (franzke et al. 2020, p. 6).

There are four traditions of ethical thinking (Flinders, 1992; Seedhouse, 1998) which have been brought together into the CERD framework for appraising educational research: consequential, ecological, relational, and deontological (Stutchbury & Fox, 2009, Fox & Mitchell, 2019). This is used to underpin the organisation of this chapter: to help appreciate the interconnections between these lenses for ethical thinking and to allow researchers to appreciate how different issues can be both highlighted and interpreted

DOI: 10.4324/9780429329067-4

differently. This offers a practical way to embrace and apply ethical pluralism to appraisal of any educational research. As mentioned, the CERD framework has four dimensions. First, *consequential* ethical thinking highlights the value of evaluating beneficence against assessment of risk. This relies, second, on an application of *ecological* ethical thinking to identify the full range of those affected by, in addition to those immediately involved in, a study in this field. Such analysis leads attention to, third, *relational* ethical thinking which involves decisions as to how to show respect to the range of humans involved with AIED and its research. Indeed, there are also calls to include the machines and algorithms in this demonstration of respect, given their creation by and interplay with humans. As has already been explicated in this book, this includes designers and developers as well as users (young people and adult learners, educators, and parents responsible for young people), sponsors, and educational leaders. As will be debated, this arguably also includes all of us, citizens and political leaders, as part of wider society. One of the particular issues in AIED research is that, given the uncertainties surrounding AIED, researchers need to consider what can and can't be promised to those involved and affected; and hence both collaboration and transparency are advocated. This relates to applying the fourth and final dimension of the CERD framework – *deontological* ethical thinking, which makes explicit the range of obligations to which educational researchers engaging in AIED research need to attend. Re-imagination of participation, consent, anonymity, and researcher obligation are covered.

Issues raised extend discussions elsewhere in this book in relation to AIED by focusing on applications of ethical thinking to educational research of, for, and about AIED, rather than the AI developments themselves. *Why* and *what* questions are linked to the need to identify and maximise the benefits of a study, balanced against minimising harm – considered as issues *to avoid* (consequential thinking). Identification of stakeholders in AIED research, around questions of *to whom* to apply ethical thinking, leads to examination of how *to show* respect (relational thinking). Finally, AIED researcher obligations or *musts are* detailed (deontological thinking). The case is presented that identifying the appropriate obligations and how to enact these is best navigated by a holistic and ongoing AIED study to ensure that pluralistic and not universal ethical ways of researching are accommodated for study and context-specific defensible research. The chapter concludes by summarising the key ethical challenges for AIED research and directions for future action.

The why: Anticipated benefits

Designing and conducting studies that maximise the positive consequences while anticipating and striving to minimise any potential negative consequences (aligned to the consequential strand of utilitarian ethical thinking) is useful in evaluating the following key questions:

Why is the research being undertaken?

Why should it be considered legitimate and worthwhile?

What are its anticipated benefits and for whom?

How will the design need to be adapted to offset benefits for certain groups against any negative consequences or harm which might result?

To apply consequential ethical thinking is to go beyond a simple risk analysis and then harm–benefit evaluation, to commit to a holistic appraisal of the plans for research with a flexibility that embraces considering alternatives, listening to others, and being prepared to be responsive.

Legitimacy

Researchers have responsibilities to explain the warrant for their research to those who might be affected by AI. In part such transparency compensates for, and respects, the lack of transparency inherent in elements of AI models (to be discussed further later). In explaining their work, researchers can be explicit about what they can and cannot control, for example, in terms of the inclusion and characteristics of technical features and data flows included for the training and operation of the models, and which affect the data collected for any one study (franzke et al., 2020). In the AI environments which form the focus for AIED research, where human participants are indirectly positioned, this responsibility is particularly acute and places as much responsibility on the AI designers as the researchers collecting data. This needs particular checks and balances to be in place when the researcher and designer are one and the same, such that they are particularly attuned to and critically reflexive of the influence of the agendas and biases they bring – the human choices being made, in the otherwise potentially hidden processes underpinning AI, to be documented. Such justification of legitimacy goes beyond documenting how legal obligations such as data protection – e.g. the Data Protection Act, 2018 or the European General Data Protection Regulations (GDPR) (2018) – are being met to allow for moral evaluation, including meeting human rights, showing respect, and upholding democratic values (Bechmann & Bowker, 2019). Such legitimation should be justified socially and economically as well as legally (franzke et al., 2020). Having agreed that the warrant for both the AIED tools/systems and the associated research are justified, there is a joint responsibility between AIED designers, developers, and researchers to communicate this rationale clearly and accessibly. This calls for a partnership approach to AIED research in order to justify it: its focus, its intentions, its conduct, and its dissemination.

Evaluating alternative methodologies and scope of research

One way of justifying a particular piece of research to those potentially affected is to explain why AI as part of the design is better than alternative methodologies (franzke et al., 2020). This involves open-mindedness when thinking about possible research designs, and serious consideration of alternatives that value both quantitative and qualitative data generation, especially given that the former usually dominates AIED research. Researchers need to make clear the scope of the research and explain to what extent it aims to test hypotheses and/or explore the complexities of the AI's interaction in its social setting. Bond et al. (2019), in their analysis of 50 years of educational technology research publications, note warnings made to educational technology-focused researchers to overcome their tendency to rely on data science and computational methods as insufficient to generating a rich understanding of individuals' experiences, practices, and learning (Veletsianos et al., 2015).

Planning for AIED research to have beneficence

An article contributing to the launch of the Department of Artificial Intelligence in Education at the University of Sydney's School of Information Technologies summarised the changing claims of beneficence for AIED research (Kay, 2012). Kay reflects on how the earliest AIED researchers aimed to generate evidence that would lead to the design and provision of personalised teaching systems to benefit individual learners. Certain aspects of learning were thought likely to lend themselves to the easier replacement of teachers by intelligent tutors, with evidence claimed of success in very early quasi-experimental studies – for example, of geometry (Wertheimer, 1990), algebra (Anderson et al., 1995), and computer programming (Anderson et al., 1989). Working towards an understanding of how learners can be supported in self-regulated learning through engagement with AIED systems has been a key focus for empirical studies (e.g. Azevedo & Hadwin, 2005; Biswas et al., 2004). Ethical beneficence was argued to be central to the earliest AIED research, as demonstrated through a 'care' for the learner, by making an understanding of them and meeting their needs central to the research design (e.g. Self, 1999). This still featured as a concern a decade later (Leeds University Business School, 2010). Initial intentions were to develop an understanding of how 'expert' human teachers enhance the learning of learners, particularly in one-to-one teaching situations, and then applying this knowledge to digital learning environments. The aims were to 'make computationally precise and explicit forms of educational, psychological and social knowledge' explicit (Self, 1999, p. 1), with such models hoped to make AIED's greatest contribution to education (Cumming & McDougal, 2000). Such research has now broadened to recognise that AIED is part of a broader learning context, with different roles for educators and others influencing a learner's experience, including families and out of school learning support. Research about increasingly comprehensive learner models now 'aims to gain the benefits of computer supported collaborative learning, taking account of and exploiting the context of the learner' (Kay, 2012, p. 67).

Kay asserts that AIED research is driven by educational problems which are to be solved through models of human learning and learner characteristics in conjunction with technical knowledge about how to apply these through AI tools to create AIED systems. AIED research hence can play a role in evaluating the effectiveness in solving the original problems. This driver for AIED to make a difference has been used in how learners are educated about its potential to benefit society (e.g. Eaton, 2017; Sintov et al., 2017). While the benefits of such research should affect learners engaging with the AIED environment, wider benefits for other educators and the general AIED community should also arise through increased knowledge of models of human cognition, theories of affect, AI tools and techniques, and the systems within which AIED can be set.

In the first decade of the 20th century, AIED models are said to have been making the following four key contributions to education (Underwood & Luckin, 2011a), as:

a   scientific tools for greater understanding or prediction of a certain aspect of education;
b   components of a learning environment that responds to user needs;
c   guides for the design of more effective learning environments;
d   open resources for learners and educators to learn from and develop.

The following key themes were identified in the same period for AIED research (Underwood & Luckin, 2011b): agents, collaborative learning, dialogue systems, narrative and games, pedagogic strategies, authoring tools, evaluation, learner modelling, hypermedia, and web-based systems.

The what: Sources of data

One of the outputs of the decision-making about the design and approach to AIED research is identifying what data will be needed and from whom/where. ML in particular is a data-rich environment for AIED research, but does not always make this identification straightforward. The intersection of models (training, test, and live), data, and the surrounding contexts (human and social) defines a complex decision space that not only the AIED models but also the AIED researchers need to learn about, act upon, evaluate, and adjust. This involves selection of data and awareness of what can be claimed as a result of its generation, collection, and analysis.

Challenges for the ethical generation and use of training data

One aspect of data generation, and use, in AI and ML contexts relates to recognising biases and discrimination. While deliberate discrimination is regulated against, there have been calls for governance to extend to AI model use (Bechmann & Bowker, 2019). The speed at which processing takes place challenges the practicalities of such governance but should not be used as an excuse for researchers to avoid recognising and mitigating for discrimination. Biases are associated with the processes of masking and redlining while running algorithms which have been challenged to discriminate on gender, race, and minority characteristic grounds (Baldwin, 2016). The responsibility is not only on researchers. Designers too should be challenged to balance their prioritisation of creating effective and fast models and processes with that of high ethical standards. This will involve spending development budgets on balancing tests and transparent audit trails documenting ethical practices (Bechmann & Bowker, 2019; Kroll et al., 2016). Baldwin (2016) argues that AI developers could show their duty of care when training models by using large, socially diverse datasets for fairer representation of diversity in the population. Further, these datasets should be made open-source in a space where researchers and developers can work together towards demonstrating democratic and inclusive values.

While the training models might sometimes use novel datasets, there can be a tendency to use existing data repositories. In these cases too, AIED developers and researchers should be evaluating the basis for the outcomes of such systems as valid and ethical for reuse. While openness of datasets implies options for reuse, the basis and extent of this openness should not be assumed. Questions need to be asked about whether there is consent for reuse, recognising that there is now a change of context for which the data will be used in the planned research (Nissenbaum, 2001, 2009). This causes researchers to interrogate whether there has been transparency about the data generation, which, as discussed above, is also needed to evaluate the partiality and biases of human labelling and categorisation inherent in the models (Baldwin, 2016).

Researchers are increasingly encouraged to make their data available for further use. Clear advice in ethical guidance (e.g. BERA, 2018, item 9 and 69; ESRC, 2015, p. 39) is that prior thought should have been given as to how participants providing the original data were informed about these intentions. This is not straightforward for researchers in fast-moving fields such as AIED; for example if neither the models nor the research had been envisaged when the original datasets were gathered. AIED researchers can and should be attentive to the broader advice about data reuse to inform ethical decision-making. As data moves beyond the original purposes of their collection into secondary repositories data ownership is important to consider. One option is that, once de-identified and disaggregated, the original providers of the data are asked to hand over their ownership to new owners, to act in proxy for them, in ongoing decisions about their data use (BERA 2018, item 14). The ownership could relate to the original research team asking for permission to reuse the data themselves, or for them to take the role of custodians for making it more public or 'open'. In either case this requires consultation with the original data owners about how their data would be processed and stored (and for how long), explaining the ways in which their privacy will remain protected, and any risks from identification in the future minimised.

Despite the growth in de-identification techniques open to researchers, the norm that secondary datasets will be anonymised is itself under threat from sponsors, as recognised by BERA's guidelines (item 44). Hence, responsibilities for transparency about future possible uses are even more important when gaining consent. Recognising that it is often difficult, if not unfeasible, to re-contact the data owners, item 15 of BERA's latest guidelines states that researchers need to offer an audit trail of their efforts to ascertain ownership and clarify consent for reuse. The bottom line is that researchers should not assume that existing datasets, which appear to be open to the public, are necessarily available without question for research, especially when reuse permissions are unspecified. The legal basis for reusing the dataset needs to be examined alongside moral considerations, in particular whether the data's subjects (anonymised or not) could conceivably object to the new use of their data.

Educational datasets, as a result of the integration of technology into learning support, became key sites for learning analytics in the 2010s (Bond et al., 2019), planned to have the following benefits:

- deepening understanding of student learning within digital learning programmes (e.g. Jesus Rodriguez-Triana et al., 2015);
- informing learning design through examining connections with measurements of student success (e.g. Toetenel & Rienties, 2016);
- informing the design of assessment tools (Bennett et al., 2017);
- evidence-based pedagogic reform (e.g. Ellis, 2013; Nix & Wyllie, 2011; Whitworth & Wright, 2015);
- direct support to students (e.g. Daley et al., 2016; González-Marcos et al., 2016).

While learning analytics might not have originally been seen as part of the field of AIED, as the datasets become aggregated to create profiles and are used in ML scenarios, data use has migrated beyond its initial uses. This therefore raises the issues outlined above about how transparent educators, learning designers, and AIED researchers need to be in gaining properly informed consent and maintaining privacy (e.g. Pardo & Siemens, 2014). There is a particular responsibility to consider whether those considered by age to be minors (i.e. most school children) are involved in data provision. The advice is not specific to AIED research; but, given the challenges already outlined, there are additional considerations for those unable to give legal consent (e.g. in the UK children under the age of 18). Children and young people are able and, especially given the 1989 United Nations Convention on the Rights of the Child, have a right to be consulted and offer their assent.[1] Researchers should therefore negotiate how to gain both assent from the learners themselves and the required consent from their legal parents/guardians. This is new territory for AIED researchers, one that others have been learning how to deal with in other cyber-research such as social media sites (e.g. Hudson & Bruckmann, 2004; Robards, 2013). Gaining consent is particularly challenging in AI due to the disconnect between data providers and researchers. Users are decoupled from the systems into which their data feeds, and hence into AI research (Luger & Rodden, 2013; Hong et al., 2009). If identifiable and contactable, a further issue is that the willingness of children and young people to participate may differ from the views of their parents/guardians. A stance on their rights to ownership and control over the onward use of data relating to them will need to be navigated.

Within-institutional research might lead to an increased risk that individuals could be recognised by their peers and those who hold responsibility for them as educators. However, this could be militated against by guaranteeing that data will not be transferred beyond the institution and will be used only to inform its own learning provision. Whether or not this trust is warranted, individuals might feel an increased sense of safety and motivation to provide data. In contrast, when studying on open courses the converse is likely. Individuals are able to participate with control over their student identifiers but without the safety net of closed use of their data. In both cases rights to privacy and to be invited to consent to provide data should be offered. Recognition that the most vulnerable are likely to be those least active digitally and therefore likely to be the least aware of how to protect their privacy rights (Lewis et al., 2008).

Methodological questions specific to AI and ML research should also be considered as part of the warrant made for its ethical conduct. Researchers need to be aware of the limitations of knowledge derived from datasets used to model individual and collective behaviour. This awareness should affect claims made about the generalisability of the study's findings and/or the applicability of the predictors identified (franzke et al., 2020). This self-awareness is an important aspect of appraising the likely beneficence of the study. With limitations to transparency within existing datasets (to be discussed later in terms of discrimination and bias), morally careful, non-normative AI systems are called for. These should attempt to offer greater inclusivity and reduce the vulnerability by exclusion of certain data providers (Prinsloo & Slade, 2016). This involves researchers not only generating new datasets but also new adaptive, deep-learning modelling systems that allow machines to be taught ambiguity, queerness, and identity fluidity (Baldwin, 2016).

The responsibilities: To whom AIED researchers are beholden

There has been explication in this book as to a wide range of those who might be directly involved in as well as indirectly affected by AIED research. One way of thinking ethically about the range of humans to whom AIED researchers can be considered responsible is to employ ecological metaphors of webs of interlinked relationships (Flinders, 1992). Ecological ethical thinking allows us to recognise the roles of parents, facilitators, and teachers as well as learners, their co-learners, and the communities in which they learn (Kay, 2012). Responsibilities for AI designers and developers have also been alluded to.

If benefits are also to be reaped for those beyond the immediate users of the AIED interface, then AIED developers and researchers in all the related fields are also part of the ecological web associated with any particular AI system under investigation.

In terms of direct participants in AIED research, the previous section referred to sources of data and data ownership from those who might be termed 'learners, 'students' or 'course participants' (depending on the educational environment) and from 'educators', 'teachers', 'lecturers', 'academics' or 'supervisors'. An analysis of open learning courses has identified a further network of collaborators in online educational provision, consisting of: 'learning designers, non-academics, the technical people, multimedia developers, educational technologists, massive open online course (MOOC) team developers, technology specialists, digital learning team members, the University, the MOOC organiser' (Papathoma, 2019, p. 89), as well as tutors and mentors who work directly in support of student learning. Ethically, the rights of all of these should be considered by AIED researchers, and responsibilities towards them clarified. In terms of AI specifically there needs to be explicit recognition of the dependence on third parties.

A dependence on third parties

The AIED sector is a competitive one, as companies spin out from innovative systems. Hence, patent law and proprietary rights over algorithms are used to protect innovations (Bechmann & Bowker, 2019). These are third-party companies whose rights should be considered. However, the competitive free market, which trades goods at prices determined by the market, puts additional pressure on the rights to privacy of those providing the data that is the basis of the product. In the digital market not confined to AIED but encompassing AI, ML, and social networking tools more widely, this book has noted how AIED goods as datasets hold personal and social data. In this free market, there is economic pressure for openness about such data to guide purchase decisions. As a result, the normative practice in modern society has become that, when we engage in online activities as individuals, we are expected to (and indeed do on a large scale) agree to provide such data as part of a social contract: 'part of the price of online exchange' (Nissenbaum, 2011, p. 34). This has become something we have to take or leave, with little room for freedom to choose (Nissenbaum, 2011). This has implications for those who are particularly vulnerable in relation to power imbalances: for example, if a teacher directs their students to use a tool, what does that mean for individual students? This question has a particular significance in terms of responsibilities for all involved, if the tool uses ML. However, rather than building trust in the products on sale, data gathering, aggregation, profiling, and dissemination has been increasingly proven to be opaque to either those about whom the data relates and/or to the buyers in the market (Data Protection News, 2019, 2020a, 2020b, 2020c). AIED research falls into a wider societal expectation of needing to be ethically transparent to all those who are both involved and in a position to judge it as ethically sound. Third parties involved in AIED research need to be held accountable to ensure their compliance with commitments made by researchers, for which clear data sharing agreements need to be in place. As Zenenbergen and colleagues predict, 'trust in the research sector will diminish when data subjects find their data to be re-identified in some way, when they had given consent after having been promised a rigorous de-identification process' (2013, p. 32); and they advocate that, in line with UK Information Commissioner's Office advice (2014), Privacy Impact Assessment should be a central part of research design.

Sociotechnical context

AIED research also needs to recognise the socio-technical as well as the social context for its conduct. As well as humans, there are increasingly autonomous agents involved. Human-created bots and algorithms are explicitly and increasingly trained to develop actions and behaviours beyond those they were initiated to exhibit. Our responsibilities to, as well as for, these non-human actors in AI and AIED research are new aspects of ecological ethical thinking.

A meta-analysis of 309 studies between 1992 and 2017 into the classroom introduction of what have been termed 'social robots' – i.e. those who assist learners as tutors or peer learners – concluded that they had the potential 'to become part of the educational infrastructure … with the potential to deliver a learning experience tailored to the learner, supporting and challenging students in ways unavailable in current resource-limited educational environments' (Belpaeme et al., 2018, p. 7). This includes non-human actors as part of the ecological web or network of any learning environment, something already explored in the social world by actor network theorists such as Latour (2004). In making explicit the contribution of intelligent systems to educational provision AIED has gone beyond thinking about autonomous agents as mirroring or replacing humans, to thinking of them as forming part of possible assemblages between humans and non-humans. This has been termed a 'posthumanist' approach to education (Edwards, 2010; Bayne, 2015). No longer seeing a distinction between learners and educators, learning is not viewed as learning facts but rather as developing understandings together. This allows for a creative coming-together of both to explore collectively identified 'matters of concern' (Latour, 2004). This intention has been exemplified through the deliberate design of 'productive play' (e.g. Bayne, 2015, p. 460) into a teacher bot used in a higher education open course to help human learners explore with the bot the potential and challenges of AIED through direct experience. This study found the bots largely accepted by the adult learners, in keeping with the views of learners interacting with social bots in school classroom interactions (Belpaeme et al., 2018). However, parents and teaching staff are more cautious about whether they want education to be delegated to machines, calling for a careful social analysis of what might be lost (Kennedy et al., 2016).

If we reimagine the socio-material boundaries between codes, machines, and humans, AIED need not be viewed as replacing teachers or as compensating for any deficit in their efficacy, but instead as a way of viewing both at once rather than as a dualism (Pickering, 2005; Bayne, 2015). However, it has been suggested that, if there is a future in which both humans and machines are tasked with learning together, 'attention needs to be given to the ways learning itself is theorised, modelled, encoded, and exchanged between students and [these] progressively more "intelligent", "affective", and interventionist educational technologies' (Knox et al., 2020, p. 42). This will require interdisciplinary work to challenge what is currently being measured as proxies for learning, performance, and behaviour management into exploring how AIED can contribute to what society needs and wants from educational provision. Reimagining the role of machines and algorithms in this way, as an integral part of our research, challenges us to include them in our ethical deliberations. This has been argued, from reflections on high-frequency trading, that:

> even if we do not all agree that non-human entities like algorithms … have the same level of agency as humans, we must address and evaluate them as if they do at the epistemological level, since the outcomes of their actions, functions, or calculations have serious impact.
>
> (Hayles, 2015 cited in Markham et al., 2018, p. 2)

The responsibilities: To avoid harm and minimise risk

In offering a risk assessment of the potential harms introduced by AIED against the potential benefits (negative versus positive consequences) in a consequentialist analysis of any AIED research, both risks that can and cannot be anticipated should be accepted. Both should be militated against, with ethically principled contingency plans in place for the latter situations should they arise. Such analysis should be undertaken from the earliest stage of research planning, include evaluation of the potential for all identified participant and stakeholder groups, and conducted to apply an ethic of respect that is built into the design of the study (BERA, 2018). This is something researchers in the field call 'ethics by design' (d'Aquin et al., 2018; Dignum, 2018; Greene et al., 2019) – the building in of ethical thinking for the entire research journey, including beyond project (or downstream) researcher responsibilities and beyond meeting initial 'getting started' approvals. Integrating ethical evaluation of AI developments, alongside the technical, is starting to inform education about AI with even young learners (e.g. Ali et al., 2019). There is also the need to inform the ethical review committees associated with institutions providing approval for AIED research. This relates to this kind of cyberspace research making data providers vulnerable (Prinsloo & Slade, 2016), and hence posing the highest level of risk to privacy, data reliability, and consent (Haigh & Jones, 2007).

Recognition of risks to privacy

As outlined above, open-source datasets generate data that can be processed through ML models; and, while these are likely to have been de-identified and not contain explicit personal data, AoIR guidance advocates that it is still possible to breach the privacy of the original owners of the data (Bechmann & Zevenbergen, 2020). This is due to dataset aggregation, which results in creating 'proxies' for human subjects and their behavioural patterns, of which the original data providers will be unaware when published. Any such breach of confidentiality through aggregation increases the vulnerability of those providing data (Prinsloo & Slade, 2016).

Awareness of biases and errors in the training of models

A second risk, particularly when open-source datasets are used for AI model training, is that researchers rely on the documentation available to help understand the basis on which these were created. The principles underpinning the decisions made in developing the models should be made explicit (Bechmann & Zevenbergen, 2020), placing obligations on those generating the datasets to make their decision-making transparent for ethical appraisal. Bechmann and Bowker (2019, p. 7) present an analytical framework that exposes how even 'seemingly mundane classification processes carry potential discriminatory consequences in a type of *hyperdiscrimination*' – from defining the task and outcome variables through the selection of what is considered data, model selection, data preparation, and model training and deployment.

Accuracy claims should be questioned by researchers relying on data generated from ML models and both false positives and omissions considered. Differences in the accuracy of predictions based on ML approaches have been noted, for example, in predicting student drop-out rates (e.g. Kotsiantis et al., 2003) and educational test analysis (e.g. El-Alfy & Abdel-Aal, 2008).

The risk of normalisation through data cleaning

In identifying inaccurate and incomplete data records and either replacing or removing them, a process of data cleaning is used to gain structural consistently and ensure data is processable in an AI model. The decisions made about this are important to report for others using the dataset to appreciate the rigour of the cleaning processes and the resulting validity of the model. Ethically, it is important to consider how this process could introduce biases into a model as outliers are removed and data 'normalised'. It is possible that minority representations are cleaned out of a dataset such that it no longer reflects the population it claims to represent (Bechmann & Zevenbergen, 2020) – not accurately reflecting intersecting gender, race, class, and power relations (Lupton, 2018). Researchers should recognise that they need to respect how the data providers themselves self-identify, aware that in digital activity they can show agency in how to identify through identity, roles, and gender that might appear to contradict other personal data held on the same individual.

Accepting unintended consequences

Markham's (2020) model for ethical impact assessment of internet research identifies different times, scales, and forms of unintended side effects. In terms of timing, these can become apparent during research, for example provoked during prototype testing or, less obviously, occurring later after the research ends. In terms of scale, these could be limited to those involved with the project itself or, by interacting with other datasets and the intervention of third parties, have ripple effects at broader cultural or societal levels. Markham cites examples of where ethical concern should be focused. This should consider how users might be caused to feel by engaging with the AIED intervention, or when they realise that their data has been transferred from one context to another and/or is being used for purposes for which they have not given explicit consent.

The responsibilities: To show respect and ethics of care

According to BERA, respect and trust should be key underpinning principles of all educational research. Its ethical guidelines argue that respect should be shown by researchers to:

- person;
- knowledge;
- democratic values;
- the quality of educational research;
- academic freedom

(2018, p. 5)

Trust needs to be developed and maintained between researchers and the researched. Trust also needs to be built between users of AI and the AI systems. To do so, autonomous or intelligent AIED systems need to be designed in such a way that is considered trustworthy. This will involve:

- the actions of people behind the design of every AIED intervention;
- respect for the knowledge being generated by and with non-human actors;
- democratic values being woven into the design of the AIED systems;
- methodological transparency and critique of limitations to the generalisability of the research as part of AIED's claims to make contributions beneficial.

AIED researchers should be afforded the trust that, as long as they remain open-minded to alternative research designs and apply the above principles to their research, they should be welcomed into academia.

What has yet to be explored, but which might derive from AIED research if it continues to take ethically and philosophically reflective directions, is considering how respect can be shown for the increasingly autonomous systems themselves. Recognition of non-human actors shows recognition of the power invested in that system, mindful of whether it is exercised for good or ill.

Practically, respect can be shown through demonstrating care for all those identified through ecological ethical thinking. An ethics of care is often considered a type of virtue ethics, on which researchers base their behaviours. It has been associated with the writing and research of psychologist Carol Gilligan (1982) and a feminist perspective, later adopted into educational research (Flinders, 1992). An ethics of care offers an emotional, affective alternative to other rational, logical strands of ethical tradition. This will allow partiality to be recognised and dynamic situations to be embraced to focus fundamentally on developing relationships. Given the challenges to the rationality of AI systems design and the dominance of quantitative research, there is a strong argument that AIED researchers should consider relationality as part of their holistic ethical appraisal. The following points offer concrete aspects to these considerations.

Data sources and identity

How researchers talk about the sources of data on which their research is based is a good starting point for determining their relational positionality. This involves researchers reflecting on their use of language for those providing the data needed for their AIED research. Four possibilities are considered. The first, and common in educational research more generally (e.g. BERA, 2018), is that those providing data are considered 'participants' who have been invited to 'participate', agreeing to offer their data voluntarily, willingly, and knowingly. Second, however, they might be considered as data 'subjects' on which it is assumed research is being conducted. It would be important that this second identification does not confer less attention by researchers to pursuing their right to provide data as voluntary. A third possibility is that the providers of data also in some cases hold additional roles, such as 'interface testers, piece workers, volunteers, or end users' (Markham, 2020, p. 76). In the case of AIED interventions the present volume shows how this might involve educational designers, learning technologists, tutors, and learners, some of whom might also be students or tutors. In these cases of dual or multiple intersecting roles, tensions in data providers' rights and researchers' responsibilities to them is needed. A fourth, more abstract, possibility is that data providers are considered as 'digital signals, user profile, or data points' (Markham, 2020, p. 76). It is most likely in these cases, once the human identity of the providers has been removed, that data providers are most at risk of researchers not paying full attention to their rights as humans involved in the research. Identification of and by data providers is something ethical review committees should be alert to, to ensure that respect is being shown for the humans involved in and affected by the research.

Returning to privacy as a right

Privacy should be about the right to control data about oneself. International legislation clarifying such rights have been appearing since the late 1990s. Examples include European Parliament Directive 97/66/EC regulating information processing in electronic communications;[2] Canada's Model Code for the Protection of Personal Information;[3] Australia's *National Privacy Principles* (Australian Government, 2006); and *Consumer Data Privacy in a Networked World* in the USA (White House, 2012). Revisions are constantly being made in response to technological and social changes. For example, in 2012 a new article was added to the earlier European e-Privacy directive (EU, 2002) covering the transparency of consent related to the storage of cookies and comprehensive revision (Cheverie, 2012). This became the European General Data Protection Regulations (EC, 2018). The exercising of this right within AI research requires consent to be re-imagined by researchers to accommodate how clear information can be provided by them as consent seekers and how they can support the consent giver in exercising agency and showing a voluntary, tangible signal of consent. This should require an ability to withdraw consent (Luger & Rodden, 2013). Data providers should not be left vulnerable by being unaware of how public or private what they provide will become (Prinsloo & Slade, 2016). Digital spaces, especially in AIED systems – which learners might assume are being developed for the improvement of learning experiences – might feel safe and lead learners to disclose more than they would if they had been more fully aware of where and how their data might be used in the future. However this form of disinhibition has been associated with all aspects of cyberspace in which inhabitants can feel absorbed in a digital persona that allows identity, social role, and even gender to be fluid (Suler, 2004). Nissenbaum also cautions that considerations of privacy should not be limited to the digital world, 'because much of what happens online is thickly integrated with social life writ large (and vice versa), solving the privacy problem online requires a fully integrated approach' (2011, p. 45).

Group privacy and power dynamics

It has been argued that ethics of care starts by recognising and militating against how individuals become embedded in relationships with uneven power relations through their participation in research (Suomela et al., 2019). This recognises in an AIED context that neither technology nor research involved with technology is neutral in terms of power (Bechmann & Zevenbergen, 2020). This involves researchers disclosing potential power structures within AI systems (e.g. Bechmann & Bowker, 2019; Crawford et al., 2016; Sandvig et al., 2016) as well as those power imbalances caused by the inequalities in who instigates and who receives AIED interventions (e.g. boyd & Crawford, 2012; Crawford & Calo, 2016; Crawford et al., 2016). These are important considerations given their potential to influence what society values and the directions society takes as a result. In AIED contexts the power imbalance between educators/researchers and learners needs to be recognised, as it would in other educational research situations (e.g. BERA, 2018, item 19), as well as the inherent challenges of researcher positionality in relation to the learners that might limit the potential agency of learners invited to participate in research. There are potential dangers, particularly in the learning environments generating learning analytic data, of learner surveillance about which learners might feel uninformed (Slade & Prinsloo, 2013). While surveillance in itself is not necessarily harmful, as it can have a protective function through monitoring processes, it does increase data provider vulnerability (Prinsloo & Slade, 2016). Learners have been found to change their behaviours once they become aware of such data use (e.g. Dawson, 2006); this also affects educators and the relationship between educators and learners (e.g. Knox, 2010).

Legal and regulatory checks and balances are in place to minimise the misuse of power with relation to data, but the security these offer around the world differs (e.g. Knapp & VandeCreek, 2007). AoIR advice is that researchers should be open to real possibilities that their methods and models may be misused by others, especially if this reveals personal and/or sensitive data that could be used directly or indirectly against groups or individuals (Bechmann & Zevenbergen, 2020). Researchers themselves need to build in ways to mitigate such risks and potential for harm from their use of AI systems in research. This requires them to imagine possible negative consequences of procedures within the design, and identify possible third-party users who might access the data and misuse it due to having decision-making power in cultures and contexts where this would increase vulnerabilities.

A further issue, again not specific to AIED research, is that data is often interactional, involving more than one data subject. Even if some data subjects give consent, they are in danger of consenting by default on behalf of the others with whom they interact. Interaction data belonging to several data subjects (or none) at the same time scales the number of consents needed exponentially per data unit (franzke et al., 2020).

There are also risks (and responsibilities) once knowledge is generated and inferred from the models in terms of how this knowledge is used and whether it shifts power balances with regard to specific communities. This includes possible impacts of the increased use of predictive algorithms in ways that affect how others behave towards them, and hence their experience.

Consent requires transparency and choice

It has been outlined already how gaining informed consent from all data subjects for AIED research is challenging, and sometimes even unfeasible (franzke et al., 2020; BERA, 2018). As well as negotiating transfer of ownership as stewards of data for its reuse, proxy consent should also be explored, for example, from a representative or institutional ethics committee on behalf of the potential participants (franzke et al., 2020).

Even when consent is sought, it is arguable that it should be fully informed as the understanding of appreciating risk in relation to the onward use of data provided is difficult to explain to those beyond the field, due to both the complexity of the models and the difficulties of foreseeing onward use of the data, models, and findings once released into society (Bechmann, 2014; Nissenbaum, 2011; Solove, 2004). As all citizens will already be familiar, privacy policies for providing personal data have become long, complex, difficult to comprehend, and, in response to constant revisions of legislation and changes in practice, are often revised. Update notifications requiring a user to sign off as having read the lengthy, amended terms and conditions (T&Cs) of tools are now part of modern experiences of technology. So keen are we to continue using the tool or application that we do not pay attention to the detail, in order to proceed. As a consequence, data providers are asked to re-read T&Cs and re-consent on a regular basis. As a researcher producing such documentation, as we try to meet our legislative and ethical responsibilities, we cannot be confident such policies are being read, understood, and considered rationally before potential data providers offer consent (Bakos et al., 2009; Plaut & Bartlett, 2007). Luger and Rodden ask researchers to reflect on their personal experiences and familiarity with clicking 'I accept' when engaging with a digital service. They pose that 'we have agreed 'in the moment', to a specific transaction, and that moment is almost immediately forgotten. But is this momentary agreement a fair reflection of the on-going use of our data?' (2013, p. 529). This leads to users showing 'digital promiscuity' (Payne, 2014) by freely providing personal information without challenging the basis on which it is being used. This has led to AI and AIED researchers being in danger of effectively providing 'notice' of their intentions to use learner data, rather than in reality inviting consent. As Nissenbaum (2011) asserts, this is not only unfair to those affected but also is missing an opportunity to check that the social and political spheres into which technology activity is transgressing are interrogated morally, critically, and, most of all, transparently.

The obligations: Legal, moral, methodological, and ethical

This chapter leads to the final dimension of the CERD framework, that of deontological ethical thinking. Traditionally, this is built on the argument that judgements cannot wholly be made on the consequences of actions, but instead need to be based on agreed ethical standards, which can be considered as obligations or 'duties'. Deontology comes from the Greek root *deontos*, meaning necessity or obligation (Flinders, 1992). Immanuel Kant is most strongly associated with this tradition and what he termed 'categorical imperatives'. His imperative that we should treat others not solely as a means but as ends in themselves is perhaps particularly pertinent to our discussions here about the role of others in AIED research.

Dataset accountability

This chapter has called for transparency about all stages of methodological and ethical decision-making as a responsibility for AIED researchers to apply to their research. Transparency is based on the assumption that 'truth is correspondence to, or with, a fact' (David, 2015, n.p.) and explanations of complex, dynamic, and adaptive systems would offer greater clarity and accountability. A critical and open-minded analysis of how the system is working has been described as holding up a mirror to it (Christensen & Cheney, 2015), useful as an explicit basis for ethical decision-making. Christensen and Cheney draw our attention to how transparency is not only aiming to see into situations to gain insights but also to see through them, ignoring the 'glass', to gain deeper insights. While we have experience of transparency, translucence, and opacity in relation to materials such as glass, we are arguably less enlightened about social and socio-technical systems. The extent to which AIED researchers can claim transparency about ever-developing intelligent and autonomous systems needs to be recognised as an aspiration rather than necessarily being achievable (Annany & Crawford, 2018). This contrasts with claims that big data analysis is the way forward in generating 'truths' (e.g. Anderson, 2008; McAfee & Brynjolfsson, 2012). To strive towards these ideals and recognise that within these systems there is only an '*aura* of truth, objectivity, and accuracy' (boyd & Crawford, 2012, p. 663; emphasis added), researchers need to avoid the temptation to ignore the filter through which we are observing them (Hansen & Flyverbom, 2014). This will require attention to the influence of biases and assumptions as well as recognising unintended consequences.

Allowing for reproducibility and replicability

A further aspect of transparency relates to a researcher's accountability in offering an audit trail that allows readers to evaluate the quality of the research, and other researchers to replicate the studies. This relates to the earlier decisions about what can be shared, in terms of ensuring consent is in place and privacy preserved, if in an ideal world the training data, the model, and test prediction results are to be made available for scrutiny. One way forward is for publishers to support researchers in gaining the balance between safely and adequately documenting AI research. The 2019 Neural Information Processing Systems (NeurIPS) conference for example required ML researchers to complete a 'reproducibility checklist' in support of their dissemination.[4]

Researcher downstream responsibility

Researcher obligations are not met only by completing projects and producing written reports. While meeting responsibilities to the immediate project stakeholders, there are longer-term responsibilities for downstream ethical effects.

This is especially important to consider in the field of AIED research as there is unpredictability, related to the running of adaptive algorithms and ongoing aggregation of datasets and analytical systems, beyond that originally envisaged. The models created are likely to influence others, and the outputs are likely to be used beyond the immediate control of the researchers. Such planning should also include imagining consequences for data providers of erroneous identifications, labelling, or categorisations (franzke et al., 2020). It should also consider the potential for the outputs (datasets and models) to be used for profiling and targeting commercially and politically as well as through malicious misuse, beyond the control of the immediate researchers. Others can use the published research methods and models for new purposes other than intended, and this function creep might itself cause unintended consequences (franzke et al., 2020).

While there are legal checks and balances in place which limit the exertion of power over the use of data, it must be accepted that these differ across national contexts, and there is more potential for misuse in some contexts than others (Knapp & VandeCreek, 2007). To be able to foresee issues that might arise requires a researcher to have cultural sensitivity to the local norms, values, and legal regulations that might affect those providing data, as well as a technical and political understanding of how the data might be used beyond their own project plans by third parties. Consultation with others is needed to identify who might be interested in using the methodologies and datasets as well as anticipating their agendas and methods. It is not only the researchers who need to be alert to these possibilities, but also those approving applications. Researchers should, in dialogue with ethical review committees and other stakeholders relevant to a specific project, find ways to mitigate such potential risks and harms.

Returning to consequential thinking risk needs to be balanced against the intended benefits of the research through knowledge production, with the outcomes of such deliberations made explicit through Privacy Impact Assessments (Zevenbergen et al., 2013). It must be accepted that there are limits to what a researcher can prevent through design (Markham et al., 2018), and hence for what they can be held responsible in terms of hypothetical reuse of their data, methods, and findings. Society also has a place in supporting, holding accountable, and governing the onward use of AI innovations (e.g. Leese, 2017); and hence public engagement and education are needed as part of the remit of the AIED research community. Only an educated public can demand checks and balances to be in place, and be prepared to call out unclear and questionable developments in ways that will drive consumer demand and funder agendas.

Post-research data governance

When signing off a project, researchers are usually responsible for secure data archiving and model storage that matches their commitments to those providing data for their future access, deployment, and development. In relation to AI data, institutional and national data repository owners need to be aware of how best to assist researchers in post-research data governance. As outlined earlier in the chapter, different sensitivities require different precautions ensuring that anonymisation (assuming it is possible) and aggregation are performed carefully, and that data destruction is carried out as planned. Despite all such preparation, dataset holders and researchers need to be prepared to manage unknown futures for reuse. Repositories need to have mechanisms in place a) to be alerted to issues arising, b) containment policies to be able to alert researchers who, in turn, should c) know their obligations to respond. For example, if sensitive information is disclosed by a third party unexpectedly, researchers must alert those who provided data so they are aware and can take precautions if they see fit (franzke et al., 2020). Archivists need to know how to contact researchers, who in turn should know how to contact data providers. Such policies and protocols need to have thought about whether compensation will be offered in such situations, and how this will be funded and managed.

Conclusions

This chapter has debated how ethics might be built into the design, conduct, and completion of AIED research (d'Aquin et al., 2018). This will involve researchers being open-minded, collaborative, prepared to challenge assumptions, sensitive to recognising both the potential positive and negative consequences of research, and prepared to consider alternative solutions. In these ways, ethical pluralism can be demonstrated, accepting that there are no right or wrong ways to proceed, but rather that any project needs to be contextually situated (Bechmann & Zevenbergen, 2020). The chapter has explained how a comprehensive analysis can be undertaken through the application of four traditions of ethical thinking: consequential, ecological, relational, and deontological (Stutchbury & Fox, 2009). In doing so, the fast-moving and complex context of AIED research can be recognised, and normative views challenged and militated against regarding:

- the openness of datasets;
- obligations for transparent research practice;
- claiming inclusivity;
- respecting rights to data ownership and privacy.

Consequentially – A key issue in relation to the contributions AIED research can claim relates to transparency. This is not something that can be claimed without deep examination of the origins of datasets, the workings of algorithms and models, and the way these systems play out in the context of both the immediate educational setting and, more broadly, in society. Important aspects of this examination include an interrogation of the nature of the consent provided for data use, claims about inclusivity, and anticipated issues relating to onward use. This involves researchers both generating and using

AI systems to recognise the importance of context to any one project. Once this contextual integrity is lost, data providers have an increased level of vulnerability which can lead to misinterpretation, misuse, and discrimination (Prinsloo & Slade, 2016).

Ecologically – Collaboration in ethical reflexivity about the implications of AIED research which exposes data providers to vulnerabilities (Haigh & Jones, 2007; Prinsloo & Slade, 2016) needs to be interdisciplinary, including educational technologists, learning designers, and AI developers working with researchers and their ethical review committees towards practical understandings of the risks and how to mitigate them.

Relationally – Respect in AIED research includes embracing the view that an AI system is part of a human–non-human actor assemblage. While not replacing educators, intelligent systems can work together in new creative collectives. However, not all in society are confident about moving into this post-human view of education (Bayne, 2015; Kennedy et al., 2016). This is a situation to be recognised by AIED researchers. Indeed, attitudes to, hopes and fears about, and suggestions for the future of education would be worthwhile topics for further AIED research, as would how respect should be shown to increasingly autonomous systems.

Deontologically – In terms of obligations, researchers need to think about the ownership of data and of models not only at the point of generation but also imagining how this ownership can be respected given the iterative nature of data use in models within projects and in their onward use post-project. Researchers need to think about their role in curating data beyond the completion of their project to deal with any downstream issues which arise (BERA, 2018), and be clear in communicating how they will act to uphold data providers' rights into the future. This will involve containment policies, ensuring continuing access to the data providers, and may involve continued liaison with archival repositories (franzke et al., 2020).

Notes

1 https://downloads.unicef.org.uk/wp-content/uploads/2010/05/UNCRC_united_nations_convention_on_the_rights_of_the_child.pdf?_adal_sd=www.unicef.
2 http://www.legislation.gov.uk/european/directive/1997/0066.
3 https://www.uwo.ca/vpfinance/legalcounsel/privacy/Mode%20Code.pdf.
4 https://www.cs.mcgill.ca/~jpineau/ReproducibilityChecklist.pdf.

References

AERA (2011). *AERA Code of Ethics*. https://www.aera.net/Portals/38/docs/About_AERA/CodeOfEthics(1).pdf

Ali, S., Payne, B.H., Williams, R., Park, H.W. & Breazeal, C. (2019). Constructionism, ethics, and creativity: Developing primary and middle school Artificial Intelligence education. *Proceedings of IJCAI 2019*. http://robotic.media.mit.edu/wp-content/uploads/sites/7/2019/08/Constructionism__Ethics__and_Creativity.pdf.

Alpaydin, E. (2016). *Machine learning: The new AI.* Cambridge, MA: MIT Press.

Ananny, M. & Crawford, K. (2018). Seeing without knowing: Limitations of the transparency ideal and its application to algorithmic accountability. *New Media & Society,* 20 (3), 973–989.

Anderson, C. (2008) The End of theory: The data deluge makes the scientific method obsolete. *WIRED,* 23 June 2008. https://www.wired.com/2008/06/pb-theory/.

Anderson, J.R., Conrad, F.G. & Corbett, A.T. (1989). Skill acquisition and the LISP tutor. *Cognitive Science,* 13 (4), 467–505.

Anderson, J.R., Corbett, A.T., Koedinger, K.R. & Pelletier, R. (1995). Cognitive tutors: Lessons learned. *Journal of the Learning Sciences,* 4 (2), 167–207.

Australian Government (2006). Private sector information sheet 1A: National privacy principles. Sydney: Office of the Privacy Commissioner.

Australian Research Council, National Health and Medical Research Council & Universities Australia (2018). *Australian Code for the Responsible Conduct of Research.* https://www.nhmrc.gov.au/guidelines-publications/r41.

Azevedo, R. & Hadwin, A.F. (2005). Scaffolding self-regulated learning and metacognition: Implications for the design of computer-based scaffolds. *Instructional Science,* 33 (5–6), 367–379.

Baldwin, A. (2016). The hidden dangers of AI for queer and trans people. *Model View Culture,* April 25. https://modelviewculture.com/pieces/the-hidden-dangers-of-ai-for-queer-and-trans-people.

Bakos, Y., Marotta-Wurgler, F. & Trossen, D.R. (2009). Does anyone read the fine print? Testing a law and economics approach to standard form contracts. *New York University Law and Economics Working Papers* 195. https://2ndave.nyu.edu/bitstream/2451/29503/2/Bakos_Marotta-Wurgler_Trossen_09-04.pdf.

Bayne, S. (2015). Teacherbot: Interventions in automated teaching. *Teaching in Higher Education,* 20 (4), 455–467.

Bechmann, A. (2014). Non-informed consent cultures: Privacy policies and app contracts on Facebook. *Journal of Media Business Studies,* 11 (1), 21–38. doi:10.1080/16522354.2014.11073574.

Bechmann, A. & Bowker, G.C. (2019). Unsupervised by any other name: Hidden layers of knowledge production in artificial intelligence on social media. *Big Data & Society,* 6 (January–June), 1–11. doi:10.1177/2053951718819569.

Bechmann, A. & Zevenbergen, B. (2020). AI and machine learning: Internet research ethics guidelines. In franzke, a.s., Bechmann, A., Zimmer, M., Ess, C. & Association of Internet Researchers, *Internet research: Ethical guidelines 3.0* (pp. 33–49). https://aoir.org/reports/ethics3.pdf.

Belpaeme, T., Kennedy, J., Ramachandran, A., Scassellati, B. & Tanaka, F. (2018). Social robots for education: A review. *Science Robotics,* 3 (21), 7–9, p.eaat5954. https://robotics.sciencemag.org/content/robotics/3/21/eaat5954.full.pdf.

Bennett, S., Dawson, P., Bearman, M., Molloy, E. & Boud, D. (2017). How technology shapes assessment design: Findings from a study of university teachers. *British Journal of Educational Technology,* 48 (2), 672–682.

BERA (2018). *Ethical guidelines for educational research* (4th edn). London: British Educational Research Association. https://www.bera.ac.uk/researchers-resources/publications/ethical-guidelines-for-educational-research-2018.

Biswas, G., Leelawong, K., Belynne, K., Viswanath, K., Schwartz, D. & Davis, J. (2004). Developing learning by teaching environments that support self-regulated learning. In *International conference on intelligent tutoring systems* (pp. 730–740). Berlin: Springer.

Bond, M., Zawacki-Richter, O. & Nichols, M. (2019). Revisiting five decades of educational technology research: A content and authorship analysis of the British Journal of Educational Technology. *British Journal of Educational Technology*, 50 (1), 12–63.

boyd, d. & Crawford, K., (2012). Critical questions for big data in information, communication & society: Provocations for a cultural, technological, and scholarly phenomenon. *Communication and Society*, 15 (5), 662–679.

Cheverie, J. (2012). Data protection reform legislation in the European Union. *EDUCAUSE Blog*. https://er.educause.edu/blogs.

Christensen, L.T. & Cheney, G. (2015). Peering into transparency: Challenging ideals, proxies, and organizational practices. *Communication Theory*, 25 (1), 70–90.

Crawford, K. & Calo, R. (2016). There is a blind spot in AI research. *Nature News*, 538 (7625), 311.

Crawford, K., Whittaker, M., Elish, M.C., Barocas, S., Plasek, A. & Ferryman, K. (2016). *The AI Now report: The social and economic implications of artificial intelligence technologies in the near-term*. http://acikistihbarat.com/Dosyalar/AINowSummaryReport-artificial-intelligence-effects-in-near-future.pdf.

Cumming, G. & McDougal, A. (2000). Mainstreaming AIED into education? *International Journal of Artificial Intelligence in Education*, 11, 197–207.

Daley, S.G., Hillaire, G. & Sutherland, L.M. (2016). Beyond performance data: Improving student help seeking by collecting and displaying influential data in an online middle-school science curriculum. *British Journal of Educational Technology*, 47 (1), 121–134.

d'Aquin, M., Troullinou, P., O'Connor, N.E., Cullen, A., Faller, G. & Holden, L. (2018). Towards an ethics by design methodology for AI research projects. In *Proceedings of the 2018 AAAI/ACM Conference on AI, Ethics, and Society* (pp. 54–59). ACM.

Data Protection News (4 June 2019). https://dataprotection.news/edps-flags-data-protection-issues-on-eu-institutions-websites/.

Data Protection News (8 Jan 2020a). https://dataprotection.news/?s=cambridge+analytica.

Data Protection News (6 Feb 2020b). https://dataprotection.news/google-tells-facial-recognition-startup-clearview-ai-to-stop-scraping-photos/.

Data Protection News (6 Feb 2020c). https://dataprotection.news/clearview-ai-slammed-with-new-lawsuit-over-faceprint/.

David, M. (2015). The correspondence theory of truth. In *Stanford Encyclopedia of Philosophy*, 28 May. http://plato.stanford.edu/entries/truth-correspondence/.

Dawson, S. (2006). The impact of institutional surveillance technologies on student behaviour. *Surveillance & Society*, 4 (1–2), 69–84.

Dignum, V. (2018). Ethics in artificial intelligence: introduction to the special issue. *Ethics and Information Technology*, 20, 1–3. doi:10.1007/s10676-018-9450-z.

Eaton, E. (2017). Teaching integrated AI through interdisciplinary project-driven courses. *AI Magazine*, 38 (2), 13–21.

Edwards, R. (2010). The end of lifelong learning: A post-human condition? *Studies in the Education of Adults*, 42 (1), 5–17.

El-Alfy, E.S.M. & Abdel-Aal, R.E. (2008). Construction and analysis of educational tests using abductive machine learning. *Computers & Education*, 51 (1), 1–16.

Ellis, C. (2013). Broadening the scope and increasing the usefulness of learning analytics: The case for assessment analytics. *British Journal of Educational Technology*, 44 (4, SI), 662–664.

ESRC (2015). Research ethics guidance. https://www.ukri.org/councils/esrc/guidance-for-applicants/research-ethics-guidance/framework-for-research-ethics/.

European Commission (EC) (2018). Data protection in the EU. https://ec.europa.eu/info/law/law-topic/data-protection/data-protection-eu_en.

European Union (EU) (2002). e-Privacy directive. https://edps.europa.eu/data-protection/our-work/subjects/eprivacy-directive_en.

Flinders, D.J. (1992). In search of ethical guidance: Constructing a basis for dialogue. *Qualitative Studies in Education*, 5 (2), 101–115.

Fox, A. & Mitchell, R. (2019). Ethical learning from an educational ethnography: The application of an ethical framework in doctoral supervision. In Busher, H. & Fox, A. (eds), *Ethics in educational ethnography: Regulation and practice*. London: Routledge.

franzke, a.s., Bechmann, A., Zimmer, M., Ess, C.M. & Association of Internet Researchers (2020). *Internet research: Ethical guidelines 3.0*. https://aoir.org/reports/ethics3.pdf.

Gilligan, C. (1982). *In a different voice*. Cambridge, MA: Harvard University Press.

González-Marcos, A., Alba-Elías, F. & Ordieres-Meré, J. (2016). An analytical method for measuring competence in project management. *British Journal of Educational Technology*, 47 (6), 1324–1339.

Greene, D., Hoffmann, A.L. & Stark, L. (2019). Better, nicer, clearer, fairer: A critical assessment of the movement for ethical artificial intelligence and machine learning. In *Proceedings of the 52nd Hawaii international conference on system sciences*.

Haigh. C. & Jones, N. (2007). Techno-research and cyber-ethics: Challenges for ethics committees, *Research Ethics Review*, 3 (3), 80–83.

Hansen, H.K. & Flyverbom, M. (2014). The politics of transparency and the calibration of knowledge in the digital age. *Organization*, 22 (6), 872–889.

Hayles, K. (2015). *Future anterior, derivative writing, and the cognitive technosphere*. Keynote at Thinking with Algorithms: Cognition and Computation in the Work of N. Katherine Hayles, February 26–27, Durham, NC.

Hoffmann, A.L. & Jonas, A. (2016). Recasting justice for Internet and online industry research ethics. In Zimmer, M. & Kinder-Kuranda, K. (eds), *Internet research ethics for the social age: New cases and challenges* (pp. 3–18) Bern, Switzerland: Peter Lang.

Hong, J.Y., Suh, E.H. & Kim, S.J. (2009). Context-aware systems: A literature review and classification. *Expert Systems with Applications*, 36 (4), 8509–8522.

Hongladarom, S. (2017). Internet research ethics in a non-Western context. In Zimmer, M. & Kinder-Kuranda, K. (eds), *Internet research ethics for the social age: New cases and challenges* (pp. 151–163). Bern, Switzerland: Peter Lang.

Hudson, J.M. & Bruckman, A. (2004). 'Go away': Participant objections to being studied and the ethics of chatroom research. *The Information Society*, 20, 127–139.

Information Commissioner's Office (2014). *Conducting privacy impact assessments code of practice*. https://iapp.org/media/pdf/resource_center/ICO_pia-code-of-practice.pdf.

Jesus Rodriguez-Triana, M., Martinez-Mones, A., Asensio-Perez, J.I. & Dimitriadis, Y. (2015). Scripting and monitoring meet each other: Aligning learning analytics and learning design to support teachers in orchestrating CSCL situations. *British Journal of Educational Technology*, 46(2, SI), 330–343.

Kay, J. (2012). AI and education: Grand challenges. *IEEE Intelligent Systems*, 27 (5), 66–69.

Kennedy, J., Lemaignan, S. & Belpaeme, T. (2016). *The cautious attitude of teachers towards social robots in schools*, in Proceedings of the Robots 4 Learning Workshop at RO-MAN 2016, New York.

Knapp, S. & VandeCreek, L. (2007). When values of different cultures conflict: Ethical decision making in a multicultural context. *Professional Psychology: Research and Practice*, 38 (6), 660–666.

Knox, D. (2010). A good horse runs at the shadow of the whip: Surveillance and organizational trust in online learning environments. *Canadian Journal of Media Studies*, 7, 7–10. http://cjms.fims.uwo.ca/issues/07-01/dKnoxAGoodHorseFinal.pdf.

Kotsiantis, S.B., Pierrakeas, C.J. & Pintelas, P.E. (2003). Preventing student dropout in distance learning using machine learning techniques. In *International conference on knowledge-based and intelligent information and engineering systems* (pp. 267–274). Berlin: Springer.

Kroll, J.A., Barocas, S., Felten, E.W., Reidenberg, J.R., Robinson, D.G. & Yu, H. (2016). Accountable algorithms. *University of Pennsylvania Law Review*, 165, 633–699.

Latour, B. (2004). Why has critique run out of steam? From matters of fact to matters of concern. *Critical Inquiry*, 30 (2), 225–248.

Leeds University Business School (2010). *ImREAL project.* https://business.leeds.ac.uk/divisions-international-business/dir-record/research-projects/1182/immersive-reflective-experience-based-adaptive-learning-imreal.

Leese, M. (2017). Holding the project accountable: Research governance, ethics, and democracy. *Science and Engineering Ethics*, 23 (6), 1597–1616.

Lewis, K., Kaufman, J. & Christakis, N. (2008). The taste for privacy: An analysis of college student privacy settings in an online social network. *Journal of Computer-Mediated Communication*, 14 (1), 79–100.

Luger, E. & Rodden, T. (2013). An informed view on consent for UbiComp. In *Proceedings of the 2013 ACM international joint conference on pervasive and ubiquitous computing* (pp. 529–538). ACM.

Lupton, D. (2018). How do data come to matter? Living and becoming with personal data. *Big Data & Society* (July–December), 1–11. https://journals.sagepub.com/doi/full/10.1177/2053951718786314.

Markham, A. (2020). An 'impact model' for ethical assessment. In franzke, a.s., Bechmann, A., Zimmer, M., Ess, C. & Association of Internet Researchers, *Internet research: Ethical guidelines 3.0* (pp. 76–77). https://aoir.org/reports/ethics3.pdf.

Markham, A., Tiidenberg, K. & Herman, A. (2018). Ethics as methods: Doing ethics in the era of big data research – introduction. *Social Media + Society*, 4 (3). doi:10.1177%2F2056305118784502.

McAfee, A. & Brynjolfsson, E. (2012). Big data: The management revolution. *Harvard Business Review*, 90 (10), 60–68.

NeurIPS (2019). The machine learning reproducibility checklist (Version 1.2). https://www.cs.mcgill.ca/~jpineau/ReproducibilityChecklist.pdf.

Nissenbaum, H. (2001). Securing trust online: Wisdom or oxymoron? *Boston University Law Review*, 81 (3), 635–664.

Nissenbaum, H. (2009). *Privacy in context: technology: Policy, and the integrity of social life.* Stanford: Stanford University Press.

Nissenbaum, H. (2011). A contextual approach to privacy online. *Daedalus*, 140 (4), 32–48.

Nix, I. & Wyllie, A. (2011). Exploring design features to enhance computer-based assessment: Learners' views on using a confidence-indicator tool and computer-based feedback. *British Journal of Educational Technology*, 42 (1), 101–112.

Papathoma, T. (2019). *MOOC educators: Who they are and how they learn*. PhD thesis, Open University.

Pardo, A. & Siemens, G. (2014). Ethical and privacy principles for learning analytics. *British Journal of Educational Technology*, 45 (3), 438–450.

Payne, R. (2014). Frictionless sharing and digital promiscuity. *Communication and Critical/ Cultural Studies*, 11 (2), 85–102. doi:10.1080/14791420.2013.873942.

Plaut, V. & Bartlett, R. (2007). Blind consent? A social psychological investigation of non-readership of click-through agreements. *Law and Human Behaviour*, 31 (1), 293–311. https://escholarship.org/content/qt3wq2q5dx/qt3wq2q5dx.pdf.

Pickering, A. (2005). Asian eels and global warming: A posthumanist perspective on society and the environment. *Ethics and the Environment* 10 (2), 29–43. doi:10.2979/ ETE.2005.10.2.29.

Prinsloo, P. & Slade, S. (2016). Student vulnerability, agency, and learning analytics: An exploration. *Journal of Learning Analytics*, 3 (1), 159–182.

Robards, B. (2013). Friending participants: Managing the researcher-participant relationship on social network sites. *Young*, 21 (3), 217–235.

Russell, S. & Norvig, P. (2009). *Artificial intelligence: A modern approach* (3rd edn). Upper Saddle River, NJ: Pearson.

Sandvig, C., Hamilton, K., Karahalios, K. & Langbort, C. (2016). When the algorithm itself is a racist: Diagnosing ethical harm in the basic components of software. *International Journal of Communication*, 10, 4972–4990.

Seedhouse, D. (1998). *Ethics: The heart of health care* (2nd edn). Chichester: Wiley.

Self, J. (1999). The defining characteristics of intelligent tutoring systems research: ITSs' care, precisely. *International Journal of Artificial Intelligence in Education*, 10, 350–364.

Slade, S. & Prinsloo, P. (2013). Learning analytics: Ethical issues and dilemmas. *American Behavioral Scientist*, 57 (10), 1510–1529.

Sintov, N., Kar, D., Nguyen, T., Fang, F., Hoffman, K., Lyet, A. & Tambe, M. (2017). Keeping it real: Using real-world problems to teach AI to diverse audiences. *AI Magazine*, 38 (2), 35–47.

Solove, D. (2004). *The digital person: Technology and privacy in the information age*. New York: New York University Press.

Stutchbury, K. & Fox, A. (2009). Ethics in educational research: Introducing a methodological tool for effective ethical analysis. *Cambridge Journal of Education*, 39 (4), 489–504.

Suler, J. (2004). The online disinhibition effect. *Cyberpsychological Behavior*, 7 (3), 321–326. https://pubmed.ncbi.nlm.nih.gov/15257832/.

Suomela, T., Chee, F., Berendt, B. & Rockwell, G. (2019). *Applying an ethics of care to internet research: Gamergate and digital humanities*. *Digital Studies/le Champ Numérique*, 9 (1), 4. doi:10.16995/dscn.302.

Toetenel, L. & Rienties, B. (2016). Analysing 157 learning designs using learning analytic approaches as a means to evaluate the impact of pedagogical decision making. *British Journal of Educational Technology*, 47 (5), 981–992.

Underwood, J. & Luckin, R. (2011a). What is AIED and why does education need it? A report for the UK's TLRP technology enhanced learning–artificial intelligence in education theme. https://www.researchgate.net/profile/Joshua_Underwood/publication/ 241698223_What_is_AIED_and_why_does_Education_need_it/links/56e519d508ae 68afa11068a7/What-is-AIED-and-why-does-Education-need-it.pdf.

Underwood, J. & Luckin, R. (2011b). Themes and trends in AIED research, 2000 to 2010: A report for the UK's TLRP technology enhanced learning–AIED theme.

https://www.researchgate.net/profile/Joshua_Underwood/publication/297995631
_Themes_and_trends_in_AIED_research_2000_to_2010_A_report_for_the_UK's_
TLRP_Technology_Enhanced_Learning_-_AIED_Theme_May_2011_The_Londo
n_Knowledge_Lab/links/5a81b41aa6fdcc6f3ead5f75/Themes-and-trends-in-AIED-
research-2000-to-2010-A-report-for-the-UKs-TLRP-Technology-Enhanced-Learnin
g-AIED-Theme-May-2011-The-London-Knowledge-Lab.pdf.

Veletsianos, G., Collier, A. & Schneider, E. (2015). Digging deeper into learners' experiences in MOOCs: Participation in social networks outside of MOOCs, notetaking and contexts surrounding content consumption. *British Journal of Educational Technology*, 46 (3, SI), 570–587.

Wertheimer, R. (1990). The geometry proof tutor: An 'intelligent' computer-based tutor in the classroom. *Mathematics Teacher*, 83(4), 308–317.

White House (2012). *Consumer data privacy in a networked world*. Washington, DC: US Government.

Whitworth, D.E. & Wright, K. (2015). Online assessment of learning and engagement in university laboratory practicals. *British Journal of Educational Technology*, 46 (6), 1201–1213.

Zevenbergen, B., Brown, I., Wright, J. & Erdos, D. (2013). Ethical privacy guidelines for mobile connectivity measurements (SSRN Scholarly Paper No. ID 2356824). https://papers.ssrn.com/abstract=2356824.

3 AI in education

An opportunity riddled with challenges

Ivana Bartoletti

Introduction

There are very few areas where AI ethics matters more than they do in education, because education – alongside housing, borrowing, and health – is a leveller for improving equal opportunity and social mobility. Regardless of our background, it is through schooling that we can achieve access to knowledge, work, and financial security, with all that those entail. A good education system is one that nurtures ability, cultivates interests, and solicits curiosity, and these are the ingredients behind a desire to learn and aspiration. Therefore, when we bring AI into our education theory, policy, and practice, the first question we should ask ourselves is whether it is there as a springboard for opportunity, to further or hinder the role of education. This is very important as, too often, with the proliferation of new and glamorous AI products, hyped as the latest essential by PR teams across the world, the risk is to use a new technological artefact just because it is there and available, rather than because it is needed.

At the time of writing, the world is living through the COVID-19 pandemic, which will inevitably reshape the way we live and work for decades to come, in ways that are hard to predict. But one thing seems certain: AI should be developed and deployed to serve the needs of society moving forward and help us deal with the challenges ahead. Rather than being shaped by AI and the hype surrounding it, we need AI to support the vision of the world we want, both during and after the pandemic. Education is part of this conversation. Constructing the ethics of AI means recognising unprecedented opportunities alongside the unintended consequences and risks. From early years' education onwards, the focus has to be on what vision we have for education in the age in which we live, and how AI can augment traditional human input to achieve it.

The inherent problem and greatest risk with AI is that it uses existing historical data to answer the problems we have right *now*, rather than contributing to our vision of society and its needs *tomorrow*. In this chapter, I set out why I think this is the greatest risk that we face, and formulate my thinking around three main areas: firstly, a discussion of the meaning of ethics, and why we are talking about it in the context of AI; secondly, how AI in education brings

DOI: 10.4324/9780429329067-5

risks with regard to human agency and the erosion of human skills, alongside the risk of scaling up poor pedagogical ideas; and, thirdly, defining key principles underpinning the development of AI in education, its potential benefits, and the frameworks we need to unlock them. Justifying the use of AI in education involves making the motivation for using the technology explicit, as well as clarifying the key assumptions that underpin the stated motivation. If the motivation is clear, it can be scrutinised, assessed, and challenged. In education, *why* a product is used matters as much as *how* it is used, owing to the role education plays in our society as a catalyst for opportunity, mobility, and equality.

The debate around ethics

As AI proceeds at pace and brings enormous opportunities, alongside unintended consequences and risks, ethical frameworks and guidelines have proliferated – and rightly so. Global organisations, as well as governments and institutions, have set out their approach to ethics to ensure AI works for the common good. All this is happening because over the last few years we have seen enormous leaps in technology, including discoveries and innovative applications that promise to make our lives better: we have seen advances in medicine where machine learning enables better detection of diseases at a much earlier stage (Price, 2020); artificial emotional intelligence, albeit controversial, has brought joy and support to children with autism (Hao, 2020); and much more. At the same time, we have peered into the darker sides of AI. The Cambridge Analytica scandal revealed how our digital ecosystem has spawned a persuasive architecture (Confessore, 2018) whereby manipulation is possible because of what underpins the business model itself: attention grabbing.

The regulators' slow-motion grappling with the challenges of the digital advertising ecosystem is proof that we have allowed the system to grow wild, unfettered and unchecked for too long, and only the heavy machinery of global governance of AI systems and their effects is going to be up to the job.

The introduction of surveillance through facial-recognition techniques (Roussi, 2020) has seen the emergence of the dichotomy between security and privacy, yet again showing how a lack of regulation around something so vital, so pervasive (albeit important to keep us all safe) can lead to a populist and unhelpful approach to the issue (Amnesty International, 2021). When I say that we have seen the worst of technology, I refer to the unchecked use of AI artefacts, be that in behavioural science, surveillance, or automated decisions replacing human ones (in housing or fraud detection, for example). Among those, the proliferation of tools around emotion recognition is perhaps the most worrying example (Wakefield, 2021).

Over the last few years, we have seen these systems dumped on our world unchecked, unchallenged and ungoverned through the frameworks of multistakeholder negotiation that suffice in other areas. For example, a recent Dutch case highlighted how a system used to detect fraud (SyRI) ended up using surveillance primarily to monitor the most vulnerable and impoverished in society, thus making the system prone to bias, discrimination, and representational harm (Privacy International, 2021). The Dutch Court declared that the lack of transparency surrounding the system could potentially lead to unfair decisions, thus harming the basis of trust that is essential in the citizen–state relationship and which underpins a well-managed and functioning state.

Having ungoverned and unfettered AI systems means that algorithms are used increasingly for targeted advertising, determining access to loans and insurance, and calculating interest rates and insurance premiums (MacCarthy, 2019). This murky matchmaking is made more powerful by the addition of neural information, modelled on neuron activity associated with certain attention states. According to MacCarthy, the deployment of AI for decisions that impact so fundamentally on life, including whether to provide benefits to a person in need, is often the outcome of cost-saving exercises operated by cash-strapped local authorities. Short-sighted decisions do not consider the long-term consequences of what is perceived as a quick win. For example, local authorities may deploy tools to identify teenagers at risk of veering into crime (McIntyre & Pegg, 2018). There is little doubt that due to the historical bias in society, reflected in the data pools, the output of the automated system will be to use surveillance, monitoring, and privacy deprivation for some already vulnerable people. Although some may perceive this as a success, are they thinking at all about what the long-term effect of policies driven by algorithms will be?

This is the context of the debate around ethics. In short, we need to prevent misuse to avoid missed opportunities. As I write, there are around 90 guidance documents and principles governing the area of ethical AI (Jobin et al., 2019). These are grounded in a cluster of key principles, often derived from bioethics, as pointed out in the recent study analysing the entire corpus of frameworks. Yet, according to Jobin and colleagues, no single ethical principle seems to be common to the complete body of documents, although there is a convergence around the following principles: transparency, justice and fairness, non-maleficence, responsibility, and privacy.

With regard to transparency, the focus has been on the so-called *explainability* of algorithms; that is, whether and how the outcome of a process is read and interpreted by the person who is then affected by a particular decision. Although this is vital, I find this approach extremely reductive as it places too great an onus on the customer/user, and thus risks perpetuating inequality. It would be more responsible to produce a global system of labelling for higher-risk AI applications, which guarantees that a specific product undergoes a rigorous due-diligence process. Tools such as the British Kitemark, governed at sector level by industry regulators, could prove useful in terms of creating a specification for trustworthy AI systems (Ahamat et al., 2021).

Data-protection authorities at a global level seem to be wading into this debate as, quite rightly, privacy law calls for the transparent collection and processing of personal data. The corpus of access rights of the General Data Protection Regulation (GDPR), for example, provides a solid framework around the transparency of processing as it forces organisations to cater for those rights at both the developmental and deployment stages (Information Commissioner's Office, 2021). Access rights, including the right to explain when decisions are made by machines without human intervention, coupled with accountability, do support a vision of transparency.

Interestingly, a recent ruling issued by the Italian *Courte di Cassazione* (Supreme Court) stated that consent cannot be deemed as valid if the algorithm is not transparent. Without transparency, the Court stated, the data subject could not possibly understand what they were consenting to (Scorza, 2021). But it would be wrong to see AI only through the lens of data protection. AI does not exist in isolation. The opposite is true: AI applications are built into a solid corpus of antidiscrimination, equal opportunities, human rights, competition, and consumer law – all of which can be leveraged and applied to the outcomes of this technology. For example, when it comes to one of the most important (and discussed) features of the ethical debate, fairness of algorithmic decision-making, four dimensions are certainly involved:

- Consumer law – namely the right to non-discrimination;
- Privacy and data protection, especially in relation to a fair distribution of power between the data controller and the individual;
- Competition law, especially in relation to antitrust and removing unfair practices;
- Human rights law, and the protection of human dignity.

It is true that the current legal corpus may need an update to cater for the new challenges posed by technology. For example, it is arguable whether algorithmic discrimination – which is often subtle and much harder to identify, especially as it operates by proxy – can be easily covered by existing non-discrimination law.

However, the main issue is that ethics go far above the law. Over the past few years, we have seen numerous examples of biased outcomes in algorithms. For example, facial-recognition technology still fails to properly recognise black faces, which has had a severe impact on those who have been misidentified (Hardesty, 2018); adverts for low-paying jobs are directed more towards women than men (Gibbs, 2015); and Amazon was about to issue recruitment software which was pulled at the last minute because it was configured to choose only the CVs of male applicants (Dastin, 2018).

Algorithmic bias is not an issue that can be solved by technology alone because the root causes of bias are in the historical data used to train algorithms. Data is not neutral, despite the so-called *futurists* telling us repeatedly that it is thanks to data today that we can predict the future tomorrow. Data is the product of social stratification, patterns of inequalities, and racism. Caroline Criado Perez, in *Invisible Women* (2020), provides a mind-boggling overview of how women have been erased from data collection and analysis – and, therefore, the design of what the reality of our world is today. This ranges from the size of objects we currently use to the training data used in medicine. It is most striking to see how strokes in men are studied and understood, as if women were completely immune from having them. This shouldn't surprise anyone. In what I call 'data violence', the process of ending up in a dataset is never neutral; it is part of the power structure between the (often invisible) hand that places us in it and the one that keeps us out. Women are well accustomed to power structures as they form part of our invisibility (or our struggle for visibility) as we inhabit our world; and that is why I argue that feminist lenses are crucial in the rethinking of how we use data for the common good.

In recent years, we have seen the proliferation of algorithmic fixes to mitigate the risks of bias in AI. The concept underpinning the so-called automation of fairness can be approximately summarised as such: a machine-learning algorithm is only safe and reliable to the extent that it is trained on (1) sufficient volumes of data that (2) are suitably representative of the scenarios in which the algorithm is to be deployed. However, this approach fails to recognise that bias in AI emerges at different stages of the process. Data quality is key, and technical fixes to override the non-neutrality of data can help; but they can only go so far because bias creeps in from the parameters used in the AI system, as well as from the features chosen. So, for example, seemingly neutral things like a postcode can unlock discrimination by proxy as a postcode says much more than simply where someone lives; postcodes indicate class, social background, and even sexual orientation (Prince & Schwarcz, 2020).

That said, algorithms are not based on what we are accustomed to as part of the understanding characteristic of human intelligence. Rather, they are the product of statistical pattern-matching. Therefore, if algorithms and automated decisions are based on data that contains inaccuracies or biases, then these algorithms might well reflect those inaccuracies or biases. The basic truth is that, regardless of a technical solution to *un-bias* the data, this will always be a problem with huge political, ethical, and social implications.

AI, governance, and regulation

With the proliferation of ethical principles and guidelines it is legitimate to ask whether companies are embracing ethics as the ultimate self-regulation strategy. This is clearly a risk of ethics-washing, especially as fairness cannot be reduced to a checklist-ticking exercise (Wagner, 2018). Whether or not an algorithm is fair depends heavily on the context and perceived benefit or detriment of outcomes. What is fair based on one metric, or in one jurisdiction, or in the opinion of one stakeholder, may be considered unfair in another context. Difficult choices must sometimes be made, and companies must decide whether they are satisfied with achieving legal compliance (for example with anti-discrimination obligations) or whether they feel a greater responsibility around fairness related to concepts such as equity and social justice.

The European Union recently published new legislation regulating high-risk AI. This legislation sets out a risk-based approach to AI products, ranging from banned to high and low risk (European Union, 2021). Producers of high-risk systems must comply with both pre-and post-development requirements, including audits, implementation of new risk-management and documentation systems, registration of models on a centralised database, and in-market monitoring. This will involve navigating a balance between the accessibility and legibility of algorithms and commercial secrecy. The new legislation is likely to undergo several changes moving forward. It is a complex piece of law, with a GDPR-like structure, including hefty fines, supervision by new and existing regulatory bodies, and breach-reporting obligations.

The progress made by the EU in this field is certainly welcome. In particular, the idea that concepts such as social scoring and real-time facial recognition are banned (with some exceptions) is an important step. As the EU legislation commences its legislative journey, it is worth remembering that the Council of Europe (CoE) also announced it would soon initiate negotiations around a new AI treaty, although it is not yet known whether it will be binding (Council of Europe, 2021).

The CoE process is important, and for several reasons: first, because the CoE is a vast organisation; and, second, because of the focus on human rights. We do not need to think about the scaremongering visions of *Terminator*: AI as it stands now already creates risks for our human rights and civil liberties, such as an increase in inequality and the reduction of human agency. As Cathy O'Neil puts it, these systems 'tend to punish the poor':

> This is, in part, because they are engineered to evaluate large numbers of people. They specialize in bulk, and they're cheap. That's part of their appeal. The wealthy, by contrast, often benefit from personal input. A white-shoe law firm or an exclusive prep school will lean far more on recommendations and face-to-face interviews than will a fast-food chain or a cash-strapped urban school district. The privileged, we'll see time and again, are processed more by people, the masses by machines.
>
> (O'Neil, 2017, p. 8)

The issue we are facing is that AI systems can often be obscure and unaccountable. The processes, parameters, and features leading to specific decisions, persuasion, or choice-influencing will be obscure to most of us, making it complex to trace potential discrimination, let alone allow a form of redress. This is where standards, due diligence, and certification schemes may be crucial to ensure we can cohabit, and even thrive, with these systems without feeling threatened by them. The degree of human oversight involved is one example of a knotty issue, as increasingly complex and autonomous systems may make it impossible for humans to intervene later to control them, despite being efficient from a purely mathematical perspective. If you believe, as I do, that humans should remain in control at all times, you will see it is not a technological issue but a political one, because it relates to which values underpin innovation, how human-centred it is, and which humans are in charge.

AI in education: An opportunity riddled with challenges

In the previous sections, I showed how data is not neutral and how, by personalising what content we see and are exposed to, algorithms are editors or curators of information that nudge us into making particular choices. We have also looked into the main issues debated in the ethical AI forums and how the deeper incursion of law, standards, and governance could bring some clarity to this discussion.

The deployment of AI in education brings with it all of the above challenges in the context of the world's most powerful catalyst for equality and social mobility – or, too often, the opposite. This is why we need to be cautious yet optimistic about its use. In this section, we will therefore investigate what I consider the main risks related to the unfettered and unchecked deployment of AI in schools and wider education, and offer a framework that may help educators and their representatives.

Risk 1: The scaling-up of poor pedagogical ideas

In recent years, we have been lured by the promise of AI doing amazing things. Some of the time that promise has been met. For example, IBM's Watson Classroom promises cognitive solutions that help educators gain insights into the approaches to learning, preferences, and aptitudes of individual students, taking personalised learning to a whole new level.[1]

However, looking at a number of other offerings across the sector, we must question what these *shiny* products actually give the pupil. Here's how it works: AI-based learning systems would be able to give professors useful information about their students' learning preferences and aptitudes, abilities, and progress, and provide suggestions for how to customise their teaching methods to students' individual needs. The promise is the end of a classroom full of catatonic children as the students receive an education magically tailored to bring out the best from their unique minds and personalities. Is it true, and is this even possible? We have to question whether, alongside these wonderful opportunities, we are at risk of scaling up pedagogical ideas that are not rooted in empirical evidence.

Risk 2: Reading emotions and sentiments

Recently, we have seen a surge in companies producing AI that looks into our emotional make-up by analysing how we look, smile, and react to things (Purdy et al., 2019). In the retail industry, it is often proposed as the panacea to cure all sales slumps, and can reveal with pinpoint accuracy which types of marketing actually work. Emotional AI is supposed to be able to 'read' normally imperceptible movements of our face, lips, and nose to infer whether or not we like a particular product. Advertising images can then be adjusted accordingly, perhaps instantly, at the point of sale.

It can be argued that emotional AI could have benefits. For example, there might be a public interest in recognising fear, or danger. Education might benefit from progressing this space. For example, support systems for children with learning difficulties or behavioural problems could exploit this technology as it progresses. However, as we have seen above, algorithms can discover patterns in data that predict the desired outcome, but which are actually pre-existing patterns of exclusion and inequality. This is why these products bring enormous risks of which we must be aware, and which could be seriously damaging in the area of emotional AI. Could we, for example, end up discriminating against or treating students differently because of their emotional make-up? The problem with all of this is that the answer is hardly technological and computational: a technological fix can help prevent the embedding of society's longstanding stereotypes in AI products; but, ultimately, the real answer to exclusion is political, not computational (McStay, 2020).

It would be particularly ironic if the work done by schools to help societies progress is reversed as tasks are delegated to backward-looking technology – that is, leaving the fox in charge of the chickens.

Risk 3: Automatic nudging

Nudging is a theory which is applied across many sectors (Thaler & Sunstein, 2009). For instance, when local authorities identify pockets of potential fraud (using machine learning applications) they can act in two ways: they can either carry out extra checks on those individuals identified as potential fraudsters; or they can send all service users (including the manifestly honest) a generic message saying that X% of people in their area are committing fraud. The implication of the first action is far-reaching. It could lead to the local authority implementing controls, and thus intervening in what is perhaps an already vulnerable segment of the population. In other words, this would mean focusing surveillance and controls on specific groups, thus leading to further marginalisation through victimisation and shaming.

I appreciate this might be a controversial concept, but we must think about the effect of automating controls and checks with reduced human intervention. Owing to the scalability of automatic systems, we would scale up surveillance on groups of individuals – and we do not know what the effects of this would be. This is why the second approach is much more interesting and convincing as it *nudges* people towards good behaviour without shaming specific individuals by checking on them. Nudging is used to encourage behaviour which society expects us to employ; and it does make sense, as persuasion is certainly worth trying before resorting to enforcement.

Amazon's Alexa device nudges young people into saying 'please' and asking politely for information rather than demanding it rudely. It does so through the positive reinforcement technique of responding more warmly as a reward for good behaviour. As we embed nudging into the education sector, are education professionals convinced that this seemingly humane variation of reward or punishment, or carrot and stick, will work for deeper causes – for example, to instil a lifelong passion for learning?

It is worth asking this question, as AI teaching increasingly supports flesh-and-blood teachers with homework help and other tasks. Once again, the concern is that educational technology could end up being more about the technology than the educational goals. As I write, some of the world's wealthiest people are investing in the crossover between neuroscience and AI (CB Insights, 2019). Glamorous announcements tell us on a daily basis how AI is now able to read the human mind (Arunn Murugesu, 2020). It is estimated that the for-profit sector expends some US$100 million a year on neurotechnology, and this figure is rising rapidly (Sterling, 2018). If neurotechnology is to be deployed in schools and colleges to nudge, understand, and, ultimately, influence students, what framework will these companies apply? How will we define and identify unacceptable manipulation?

Risk 4: The erosion of human agency

I believe that a key aspect of education is to teach the value of human agency. In my opinion, this goes to the heart of learning and is about exercising choice and being responsible for it. Ultimately, this is the meaning of life and how we navigate it.

We must therefore ask ourselves: What happens to human agency as AI enters the education sector, introducing nudging, compelling people to act and replacing tasks? This is a crucial question because, as always, value judgements and ethics underpin the areas of choice, individual and collective responsibility, and action.

So, when an AI learning system is introduced, it is already framed with outcomes before it begins to learn. This means that whoever designed that model chose a point of view, imposed categories and interests, and solidified them into the system to then predict future behaviour. In other words, patterns are codified in one's path. This is rather worrying from political, sociological, and ethical standpoints, especially because it means that our behaviour is predicted by past data. Ultimately, what this translates into is that the patterns used to shape our *future* choices are based on *historical* data. What does this do to human agency, mobility, and creativity? Breaking traditional patterns of behaviour is inherent in human nature. Will AI limit that? In education especially, this is particularly meaningful if we consider education as the primary place for young people to learn how to make true choices and break away from historical patterns of behaviour.

Human agency also impacts the teaching profession as AI systems support educators with homework marking (Hughes, 2019) as well as with understanding and profiling students. This calls for serious considerations about the relationship between professionals and the machines they use and on which they rely. As in the medical profession – where it is legitimate to ask what will happen to medical knowledge as medics increasingly depend on automated systems for the detection, prevention, and assessment of diseases, as well as the personalisation of medicine – so in education we need to understand what the role of educators actually is if the more traditional tasks, such as marking, are performed with the support of machines. One of the alleged merits of AI is to release employees from administrative and repetitive tasks, so there is an argument that marking falls into this category. However, we are already embedded in an educational culture geared more towards exam methodology than learning, so AI's impact on automating this would need a total rethink of the teaching profession – and it could be a good opportunity for doing so.

Risk 5: The public value of privacy

The ubiquity of digitisation brings privacy challenges and questions, irrespective of whether we need to rethink the concept of privacy itself. It is true that privacy is contextual and changes across cultures, generations, and time. However, it would be too simplistic, in my view, to just say that privacy changes because technology is useful and somehow incompatible with the traditional view of personal data.

To an extent, it is. The use of devices and social-media platforms means we are much more accustomed to data-driven systems. This, coupled with deceitful privacy notices (and I do mean deceitful because they are too long and incomprehensible by design), means that our consent-based privacy approach is flawed (Lee & Zong, 2019). Consumers have neither the time nor the knowledge to go through and understand clauses and legalistic notes about the handling of their data. However, surveys do show that people care about privacy and what happens to their personal information (Whitney, 2020), while events such as the Cambridge Analytica scandal have shown the world what can happen when the digital environment is allowed to go unchecked (Confessore, 2018).

The omnipresence of data collection means that we have a lot of data we can use for applications and analysis. Some of this is undoubtedly good – for example, in medicine (Rauch, 2020) – given the limitations discussed earlier regarding the non-neutrality of data and the need to watch out for potential misuse. Let us take an example that has become particularly relevant during the COVID-19 crisis: location data collected via our phones to trace contact between people. "While there is little doubt on the potential of mobile phone data for good, location data contain intimate details of our lives: rich information about our whereabouts, social life, preferences, and potentially even finances" (de Montjoye et al., 2018). Obviously, during an emergency the first and foremost human right becomes the right to life, thus making it reasonable to find a middle ground by stretching privacy laws in a way we wouldn't normally do during non-emergency times.

Movement data can be collected for other useful reasons, such as traffic management, urban development, and logistics around the functioning of smart cities, among others. Many government entities are interested in gaining access to 'anonymous' or 'anonymous and aggregated' location data to observe population-level trends and movements (Gray, 2020). Privacy-by-design methodologies (these are both procedures and technologies aimed to ensure privacy is embedded at the onset and not as an afterthought) can certainly reduce risks; although it has proved very difficult to anonymise personal data, and even aggregated data can eventually be re-identified (Lomas, 2019). This means that there are inherent risks in data collection, and trade-offs need to be navigated based on benefits vs. risk.

In education, privacy is very important, and for a number of reasons. Primarily, the 'datafication' (Williamson, 2020) and algorithmic management of the student population requires a clear assessment of what the trade-offs are. In other words, what are the risks for pupils once they enter databases, once applications are used and their responses monitored? Once a student's personal information has been entered into a specific database, this data can be matched with other data to identify patterns and correlations. So, for example, local authorities could decide to use information about a student's performance and/ or school attendance as part of a data pool to identify patterns of behaviour leading to, for instance, low-level criminality.

The goal is certainly admirable as behaviour can be addressed at a much earlier stage, and prevention is better than cure. However, once again (and as discussed earlier), there are implications around all this. Data reflects social stratifications, and is therefore biased. The outcome of such exercises, if not mitigated, could be to place checks and controls on specific segments of the population. This is not to say that these things should not be done. To an extent, correlations are done by teachers on a daily basis. Every educator will, in their own mind, correlate one student's experience with another's and suggest things that worked in one case in relation to what they perceive as a similar case. The issue with automation is that it could scale up existing inequalities by building on historical data. On the other hand, if there is something that COVID-19 has taught us, it's the value the public attribute to their personal information. During the pandemic, information about a person's whereabouts has been key to safeguarding others. So it is in other areas too: for example, sharing one's cancer diagnosis information is crucial to gathering enough data so that earlier diagnoses can be achieved.

The bottom line is that the insights we can gain about someone from their personal data trail are extraordinary. In 2015, researchers at the Massachusetts Institute of Technology (MIT) discovered that careful analysis of motor behaviour revealed by keyboard strikes on personal devices could help in the early detection of Parkinson's disease (Trafton, 2015). And a 2017 study suggested that mobility model measurements, such as those collected from people carrying smartphones with them throughout the day, could be used to diagnose the initial signs of Alzheimer's (Nieto-Reyes et al., 2017). Therefore, in the education sector we need to ask ourselves what degree of personal information we want to use in order to improve education for all. It's not an easy question, but it is one we must answer.

Risk 6: Teaching AI – the challenges ahead

In the West, we are the heirs of a dualistic culture, one which views scientific and technological activities as separate from humanist disciplines. For example, classical studies are still considered distant from studies involving technology. If we want to succeed with AI development and deployment, we need to move beyond this division. At the present time, it looks as if the only way to succeed in the world is through technological skills. This relegates the humanities to a rather residual space, which is worrying. Along with this, the pressure is on specialisation and forging those profiles that keep up with the demands (both real and perceived, as we do not really know how automation will change our society) of the economy. However, as things in the technological space move so quickly, the risk is that what children are learning now will become obsolete in a short span of time.

The bottom line here is that our education system should, in my view, embrace a multidisciplinary approach – and this should be reflected across all areas of learning. We should find ways to override the dualistic culture that sees science as separate from the humanities as the two, in reality, should merge into one. As I argue in *An Artificial Revolution* (Bartoletti, 2020), every technological artefact is a political one as it reflects cultural, social, and political dynamics. Every single design choice is a decision made by someone with their own cultural background, and their conscious and unconscious bias. The non-neutrality of technological products means that multidisciplinary thinking is essential at a time when the distinction between our digital and non-digital space is becoming non-existent. Right now, we navigate between environments, often unknowingly, and this is reshaping our thinking, daily life, and interactions. I cannot help thinking that the expression 'social distancing' – adopted to signal physical distancing between people – is rather symbolic as it has forced us to redefine the word 'social' at a time when we are moving between environments, countries, spaces, and worlds.

Transforming our world with AI is not just a matter of preparing the younger generation for the professions that will drive the new world. In my opinion, it is really about reframing technology as a multidisciplinary subject that blurs science into the humanities, and vice versa. As product design affects all aspects of our life, design cannot be a technological issue alone. Or, better put, traditional technological thinking will not address the challenges that design must address, such as inclusion, access, and the transformation of the ways we live and work. The other main area that needs addressing urgently is gender disparity in the technological workforce, and this issue is certainly related to the points above in relation to the dualism underpinning Western culture.

At this present time, women make up 24.4% of the computer science workforce and receive median salaries that are only 66% of the salaries of their male counterparts (Synced, 2020). The reasons for this are various and start from the way girls are influenced from a very young age, both in the family and at school. The history of women in technology is a complex one. In the past, computing was very much a female skill and, as with secretarial work, women were in the majority in this field of employment. This explains, for example, why women were very much present at Bletchley Park, where Alan Turing played a key role in defeating Nazi Germany in the Second World War. Later on, however, in around the 1960s, things changed quite dramatically as computing work became more managerial (Bartoletti, 2020). This probably also related to the improvement of computing power alongside the availability of data. As I argue throughout *An Artificial Revolution*, data should be regarded as capital as it reproduces the same patterns as the capitalistic structures of accumulation. Interestingly, companies like IBM turned the computing profession into one of suited and booted managers – all men – which was a drastic change from the earlier *secretarial* vision of coding.

A plethora of organisations such as Women Leading in AI,[2] Black Women in AI,[3] and Women in AI[4] are trying to address the issue of women in the technological workforce, and their efforts are all welcome. However, the road seems rather long, and we cannot wait for early years' education to change this approach as we know that everything starts in a person's early formative years. My view is that reshaping the narrative around technology and the humanities is a crucial step, alongside role models, proactive steps taken by businesses, mentoring, and social-conscience communications initiatives.

An ethics framework: Main elements

Over the last few years, we have seen a proliferation of ethics frameworks across the world. This is necessary in part because the deployment of AI has far-reaching consequences as well as enormous potential. There are a number of limitations to ethical frameworks. The first is that ethics should not become an excuse for self-regulation, however important that may be. Clearly, ethics and regulations are two different domains, and it would be wrong to compare, let alone confuse, them. However, with the proliferation of ethical principles and manifestos, it is legitimate to ask whether companies are only putting great effort into this field in order to avoid legal scrutiny.

I have little doubt that regulation is required; although by regulation I do not mean massive, overarching regulatory structures, but pragmatic, sector-led rules of due diligence with which organisations must demonstrate compliance. Alongside these, I would like to see redress mechanisms for citizens when they have been adversely affected by an automated decision. The problem with this, however, is the difficulty of achieving fairness via an algorithm and, more worryingly, the complexity of spotting and tracing unequal treatment within an AI system, owing to its opacity and intricacy. Quality marks, such as those in the food-labelling industry, could also be valuable tools, in addition to mandatory audits and controls.

Furthermore, ethics frameworks are important as they form part of the spirit of collaboration that should underpin legislation, whereby trust is placed in organisations to take proactive steps. Of course, trusting companies 'to do the right thing' won't suffice, and ethics cannot be the excuse for doing that. However, collaboration is essential, especially in an area where technological development can bring benefits and advantages – if done properly.

This chapter began by stating the importance of ethics in the education sector and by asserting that any deployment of AI in education should reflect the role of education as an engine of equality and development. This is why a correct and meaningful ethics framework should start with *purpose*.

Purpose is about asking whether a specific AI product, whether developed in-house or purchased from outside, furthers rather than hinders the mission of the organisation, and questions how it does so. At a time when the validity of an AI system seems to stem more from PR rather than from its utility in solving pressing problems, purpose is an ethical matter. In education, it is fundamental.

Alongside purpose, the second element of the ethics framework should be *impact*. Impact requires honest consequence-scanning, looking at the short- and long-term impact of the AI system to be introduced. Impact-assessment must be seen as a stakeholder exercise, and this is why a fully functioning ethics board can make the difference. Moreover, I would always recommend consultations with students, parents, teachers, and the wider community. Listening exercises, as well as citizen juries made up of a wider section of the community, can be useful tools. The main problem is that impact depends on the background of those involved in its assessment – diversity is therefore a crucial element.

Once purpose and impact have been assessed, the AI product to be introduced deemed valuable, and all its potential consequences evaluated, then the remaining elements of the ethics framework are, in my view, *justice and fairness*. This is where it is important to look at potential unfair outcomes, as well as at technical solutions to mitigate them. Justice should focus instead on the need to ensure that, regardless of more technical solutions, the outcome desired is in itself just and does not leave anyone behind. In an area such as education this is paramount. In the UK, the GDPR introduces some practical guidance in relation to fairness in the collection and processing of data. Procedural fairness, however, must go hand in hand with fairness of outcomes.

Finally, I think an ethics framework in education should be rooted in *human values*. This means that AI must be driven and controlled by humans. As mentioned above, AI can do a lot of good in education, but can potentially also scale up poor pedagogical ideas. This is why, when developing an AI system, humans need to remain in control; we must be careful not to engage with systems that do not take into account values, outcomes, and principles that we want to instil in our education sector. Human values mean that student autonomy remains pre-eminent, and that we do not introduce tools to limit it by imposing parameters and outcomes based on patterns that rely on historical data. My greatest concern is that we respect the fact that life is perhaps about breaking away from patterns, thus maintaining our individuality as the most valuable contribution to the collective good.

***

Innovating with AI is a challenge that we must embrace.

If we believe that AI can bring positive innovation to education, learning, and teaching, then we must look at the risks and consequences too. Not doing so will be harmful to the social and technological progress our society desperately needs right now.

Notes

1 IBM's data analytic approach towards education is cognitive learning systems. Human beings and machines can communicate with each other by the technologies that use natural language processing (NLP) and machine language together in action.
2 https://womenleadinginai.org/.
3 https://www.blackwomeninai.com/.
4 https://www.womeninai.co/.

References

Ahamat, G., Thomas, C. & Bancroft, J. (2021). Enabling trustworthy innovation by assuring AI systems. *Centre for Data Ethics and Innovation* blog. https://cdei.blog.gov.uk/2021/12/08/enabling-trustworthy-innovation-by-assuring-ai-systems/.

Amnesty International (2021). *Amnesty International Report 2020/21. The State of the World's Human Rights.* https://www.amnesty.org/en/documents/pol10/3202/2021/en.

Arunn Murugesu, J. (2020, March 30). Mind-reading AI turns thoughts into words using a brain implant. *New Scientist.* https://www.newscientist.com/article/2238946-mind-reading-ai-turns-thoughts-into-words-using-a-brain-implant.

Bartoletti, I. (2020). *An Artificial Revolution: On Power, Politics and AI.* Indigo Press.

CB Insights Research. (2019, January 28). 21 neurotech startups: Brain technology, implantables, and neuroprosthetics. *CB Insights Research.* https://www.cbinsights.com/research/neurotech-startups-to-watch/.

Confessore, N. (2018, April 4). Cambridge Analytica and Facebook: The scandal and the fallout so far. *New York Times.* https://www.nytimes.com/2018/04/04/us/politics/cambridge-analytica-scandal-fallout.html.

Council of Europe. (2021). 131st session of the Committee of Ministers (Hamburg (videoconference), 21 May 2021). https://search.coe.int/cm/Pages/result_details.aspx?ObjectID=0900001680a28ddf.

Dastin, J. (2018). Amazon scraps secret AI recruiting tool that showed bias against women. *Reuters.* https://www.reuters.com/article/us-amazon-com-jobs-automation-insight-idUSKCN1MK08G.

de Montjoye, Y.-A., Gambs, S., Blondel, V., Canright, G., de Cordes, N., Deletaille, S., Engø-Monsen, K., Garcia-Herranz, M., Kendall, J., Kerry, C., Krings, G., Letouzé, E., Luengo-Oroz, M., Oliver, N., Rocher, L., Rutherford, A., Smoreda, Z., Steele, J., Wetter, E., … Bengtsson, L. (2018). On the privacy-conscientious use of mobile phone data. *Scientific Data,* 5(1), 180286. doi:10.1038/sdata.2018.286.

European Union. (2021). Proposal for the regulation of the European Parliament and of the Council laying down harmonised rules on artificial intelligence (Artificial Intelligence Act) and amending certain Union legislative acts.

Gibbs, S. (2015, July 8). Women less likely to be shown ads for high-paid jobs on Google, study shows. *The Guardian*. https://www.theguardian.com/technology/2015/jul/08/women-less-likely-ads-high-paid-jobs-google-study.

Gray, S. (2020). A closer look at location data: privacy and pandemics. *Future of Privacy Forum*. https://fpf.org/blog/a-closer-look-at-location-data-privacy-and-pandemics/.

Hao, K. (2020). Robots that teach autistic kids social skills could help them develop. *MIT Technology Review*. https://www.technologyreview.com/s/615288/ai-robots-teach-autistic-kids-social-skills-development/.

Hardesty, L. (2018). Study finds gender and skin-type bias in commercial artificial-intelligence systems. *MIT News*. https://news.mit.edu/2018/study-finds-gender-skin-type-bias-artificial-intelligence-systems-0212.

Hughes, C. (2019). Let the robots mark and the teachers teach. *TES*. https://www.tes.com/news/let-robots-mark-and-teachers-teach.

Information Commissioner's Office. (2021). Right of access. https://ico.org.uk/for-organisations/guide-to-data-protection/guide-to-the-general-data-protection-regulation-gdpr/individual-rights/right-of-access/.

Jobin, A., Ienca, M. & Vayena, E. (2019). Artificial Intelligence: The global landscape of ethics guidelines. *Nature Machine Intelligence*, 1(9), 389–399. doi:10.1038/s42256-019-0088-2.

Lee, C. & Zong, J. (2019, August 30). Consent is not an ethical rubber stamp. *Slate*. https://slate.com/technology/2019/08/consent-facial-recognition-data-privacy-technology.html.

Lomas, N. (2019). Researchers spotlight the lie of 'anonymous' data. *TechCrunch*. https://techcrunch.com/2019/07/24/researchers-spotlight-the-lie-of-anonymous-data.

MacCarthy, M. (2019). Fairness in algorithmic decision-making. Brookings Institution. https://www.brookings.edu/research/fairness-in-algorithmic-decision-making/.

McIntyre, N. & Pegg, D. (2018). Data on thousands of children used to predict risk of gang exploitation. *The Guardian*. https://www.theguardian.com/society/2018/sep/17/data-on-thousands-of-children-used-to-predict-risk-of-gang-exploitation.

McStay, A. (2020). Emotional AI and EdTech: Serving the public good? *Learning, Media and Technology*, 45(3), 270–283.

Nieto-Reyes, A., Duque, R., Montaña, J. L. & Lage, C. (2017). Classification of Alzheimer's patients through ubiquitous computing. *Sensors*, 17(7), 1679.

O'Neil, C. (2017). *Weapons of Math Destruction: How Big Data Increases Inequality and Threatens Democracy*. Penguin.

Perez, C. C. (2020). *Invisible Women: Exposing Data Bias in a World Designed for Men*. Vintage.

Price, S. (2020, October 26). Technological innovations of AI in medical diagnostics. *Health Europa*. https://www.healtheuropa.eu/technological-innovations-of-ai-in-medical-diagnostics/103457/.

Prince, A. E. R. & Schwarcz, D. (2020). Proxy discrimination in the age of artificial intelligence and big data. *Iowa Law Review*. https://ilr.law.uiowa.edu/print/volume-105-issue-3/proxy-discrimination-in-the-age-of-artificial-intelligence-and-big-data/.

Privacy International. (2021). The SyRI case: A landmark ruling for benefits claimants around the world. http://privacyinternational.org/news-analysis/3363/syri-case-landmark-ruling-benefits-claimants-around-world.

Purdy, M., Zealley, J. & Maseli, O. (2019, November 18). The risks of using AI to interpret human emotions. *Harvard Business Review*. https://hbr.org/2019/11/the-risks-of-using-ai-to-interpret-human-emotions.

Rauch, S. (2020, April 10). The growing role of AI and big data in healthcare. https://www.simplilearn.com/role-of-ai-and-big-data-in-healthcare-article.

Roussi, A. (2020). Resisting the rise of facial recognition. *Nature*, 587(7834), 350–353. doi:10.1038/d41586-020-03188-2.

Scorza, G. (2021). 'L'algoritmo deve essere trasparente', la Cassazione rilancia il GDPR. *Agenda Digitale*. https://www.agendadigitale.eu/sicurezza/privacy/lalgoritm o-deve-essere-trasparente-la-cassazione-rilancia-il-gdpr/.

Sterling, B. (2018). Ethical priorities for neurotechnologies. *Wired*. https://www.wired. com/beyond-the-beyond/2018/08/ethical-priorities-neurotechnologies/.

Synced. (2020, March 13). Exploring gender imbalance in AI: Numbers, trends, and discussions. https://syncedreview.com/2020/03/13/exploring-gender-imbalance-in-a i-numbers-trends-and-discussions/.

Thaler, R. H. & Sunstein, C. R. (2009). *Nudge: Improving Decisions about Health, Wealth and Happiness*. Penguin.

Trafton, A. (2015, April 1). Diagnosis by keyboard. *MIT News*. https://news.mit.edu/ 2015/typing-patterns-diagnose-early-onset-parkinsons-0401.

Wagner, B. (2018). Ethics as an Escape from Regulation: From 'Ethics-Washing' to Ethics-Shopping? In E. Bayamlioğlu, I. Baraliuc, L. Janssens & M. Hildebrandt (Eds.), *Being Profiled* (pp. 84–89). Amsterdam University Press. doi:10.2307/j.ctvhrd092.18.

Wakefield, J. (2021). AI emotion-detection software tested on Uyghurs. *BBC News*. https:// www.bbc.com/news/technology-57101248.

Whitney, L. (2020). Most consumers worry about online privacy but many are unsure how to protect it. *TechRepublic*. https://www.techrepublic.com/article/most-consum ers-worry-about-online-privacy-but-many-are-unsure-how-to-protect-it/.

Williamson, B. (2020). Datafication of Education. In H. Beetham & R. Sharpe (Eds.), *Rethinking Pedagogy for a Digital Age* (pp. 212–226). Routledge. doi:10.4324/ 9781351252805-14.

4 Student-centred requirements for the ethics of AI in education

Lionel Brossi, Ana María Castillo and Sandra Cortesi

Introduction

Youth participation via recognizing their diverse identities, perspectives and learning requirements/styles is critical when designing, developing, and implementing AI-based education. This should be taken into account in the planning of education policies, delivery, and management systems. It needs to also inform strategies that empower educators and equip them with the relevant tools to teach and mentor. This ensures enhanced learning and learning assessment to help develop values and skills for life and work, thus promoting equitable and high-quality lifelong learning.

The impact of AI in education is witnessing enormous advances. Global and regional reports, expert consultations, and academic studies indicate that the role of educators and human tutoring is irreplaceable (ITU, 2020; UNESCO, 2018, 2019a, 20219b; UNICEF, 2020a, 2020b; Brossi et al., 2021; Cortesi et al., 2021). However, AI-powered education technology (ed tech) can help enhance educational outcomes and provide engaging and more effective learning experiences (Hasse et al., 2019). AI may also help to significantly improve education management, services, and processes, as well as enhancing lifelong learning opportunities. Likely, the potential impacts of AI will be more significant in some parts of the world as, for now, it reaches only a limited number of youth communities.

Objective number four of the 17 Sustainable Development Goals (SDGs) set by the United Nations Educational, Scientific and Cultural Organization (UNESCO) is dedicated to education, and aims to "ensure inclusive, equitable and quality education and promote lifelong learning opportunities for all" (UN, 2019, p. 10). This framework can serve as a helpful lens through which the identification of opportunities and challenges as well as areas and implications of Artificial Intelligence in the field of education can be discussed. *Artificial Intelligence in Education: Challenges and Opportunities for Sustainable Development* (UNESCO, 2019a) identifies the critical areas. The first area indicates how AI technologies can help improve the equity and quality of education via a) personalization and improvement of the lessons learned; and b) data analysis by government educational institutions. The second area looks at how to prepare students for interaction with

DOI: 10.4324/9780429329067-6

AI systems that are increasingly integrated into everyday life, and how to train teachers to work with and on AI. The third area deals with the challenges that the whole process entails, starting with development of an understandable public policy on AI for sustainable development; ensuring inclusion and equity in AIED; the preparation of teachers for work with AI for education; and the development of inclusive and quality data systems, among others.

This chapter specifically draws upon the recommendations in UNESCO's *Beijing Consensus on Artificial Intelligence and Education* (2019b) to derive insights on why it is imperative to hear and include students' voices when it comes to the design, development, deployment, and regulation of AI in the field of education. It argues that adult-centric perspectives for AI and education may hinder youth from feeling included and empowered to actively engage in matters and decision-making that are important to them and relevant for their future (Gasser, 2019).

The AI ecosystem presents a structure that is concentrated in a few private corporations of developed countries. For these technologies to be aligned with human rights, democracy, and socio-economic justice – as is the case for digital technologies in general – there is a need to decentralize ownership and control of software and hardware (Kwet, 2019).

> There is a push for "data driven development" mediated by private actors. Development donors such as international NGOs and governments rely on data collected by corporations, creating potentially-biased, opaque decision-making systems. We should examine the design of the systems of automation and artificial intelligence that are gradually permeating citizens' lives. We must think about who these systems are designed for, who designs them, how they are designed, and what ends they serve.
>
> (Arun, 2019, pp. 2–3)

Discussions in the intersection of AI and the Global South suggest that consideration of the context can be as important for developing and implementing technologies as it can be for designing housing. For example, a house designed for the cold climate of Northern Europe is not useful for a tropical climate. It is helpful to think of technologies and society from the same architectural perspective to be able to slow the impact of those unilateral and corporate decision-making processes that impact communities in the Global South (Arun, 2019).

Furthermore, this chapter highlights relevant methodological recommendations based on take-aways from recent efforts around student-centred design and academic research in Latin America. It draws special attention to the importance of promoting the use of student-centred methodologies for research and actions that are more responsive to the needs of diverse youth communities.

AI as a Social Concern

AI has the potential to provide many benefits for our society. However, at the same time, it may increase existing inequalities and lead to harmful outcomes that can affect people and communities in different ways. There have been numerous media articles stating, for instance, how AI will replace humans through automation of work in thousands of jobs; or how certain algorithms have generated forms of ethnic, racial, and gender discrimination; or raising concerns regarding the inability of humans to understand how algorithms come to certain decisions, among other threats that may reinforce dynamics of exclusion and discrimination (Deming, 2020; Egan, 2020; Grasso, 2015; Howard, 2021; Hvistendhal, 2019).

The notion of AI can be conceived as a philosophy that allows us to ask questions about human intelligence, as a method that helps test theories about intelligence, and as a tool to resolve problems.

> With AI having now crossed over from a purely scientific domain to practical mainstream applications, AI as a solution has taken the centre stage. However, we believe that this single lens limits our view on the actual strengths and weaknesses of AI in the context of socially embedded practices such as in education, and more broadly as a tool for scientific inquiry into what makes us human. It obscures the need for asking what society we want, instead permitting technological advances (and the few tech specialists behind those) to dictate what society we end up with.
>
> (Porayska-Pomsta & Rajendran, 2019, p. 46)

With the purpose of identifying and confronting potential harms, it is important to take into account the following main actors and elements involved in the processes that go from design to deployment of AI. These actors are developers, data, AI systems, and end-users, as well as people who do not have direct access to these technologies yet may be affected by them.

At his time, Giddens (1991) argued that even the most underprivileged subjects and communities were permeated by institutional components of modernity. With the rapid advancements in the field of Artificial Intelligence, it is granted that all sectors and spheres of society are being and will be affected in some way or another. Thus, thinking about AI and society implies focusing not only on the subjects and communities who design, develop, and use or interact with these technologies but also, and especially, on non-participants in these dynamics.

From the perspective of developers, an approach towards understanding the relation between designers and creators of AI systems and social inclusion is to explore the questions surrounding bias in algorithms. For example, the deployment of AI in education can present bias in certain contexts and the potential to promote dynamics of exclusion. An important question in this sense is how diversity can be at the core of the developer team's mindset for ensuring more accurate, ethical, and inclusive outputs.

If we think about the intersection of AI and data, it is important that fairness, accountability, transparency, and ethics are ensured (Brossi et al., 2019; Holmes et al., 2018; Holstein & Doroudi, 2019; Porayska-Pomsta & Rajendran, 2019). When using data, it is important to consider the view of data in science (Wilkinson et al., 2016). The authors propose that the principles of findability, accessibility, interoperability, and reusability should serve as guides to make any data process transparent and more reliable, which ensures that the process can be reproduced and audited. In many cases, data does not accurately portray the reality it is intended to represent. A model can be trained on data that is skewed in a particular direction, hiding unforeseen data. Thus, datasets must be audited for inherent social biases, starting from the development stage of AI, since machine learning systems may perpetuate or exacerbate those biases, leading to unpredictable harms (UNICEF Innovation et al., 2019).

If we focus on AI systems themselves, we already know they are penetrating different areas of everyday life, ranging from social robots for well-being, self-driving cars, and healthcare robots and home assistants to algorithms used for job recruitment, dissemination of news, justice systems, and education. Following this, there is a need to ask how AI agents can contribute to promoting and improving social participation of traditionally marginalized/excluded groups. Questions such as the following can help identify how to overcome potentially negative and exclusionary consequences of these systems:

How do AI systems communicate their outputs?
What kinds of accents and languages do they recognize?
What are the individuals and groups they serve?
What is their impact on individuals, groups, and society at large?

One of the central aspects to consider in this regard is decision-making by autonomous agents that can face moral dilemmas that directly affect subjects and communities (Conitzer et al., 2017).

Artificial intelligence algorithms make decisions from processes that occur in a "black box" that is unintelligible to humans (Charisi et al., 2017). In that sense, increasing interpretability and explainability of the ways in which autonomous agents make decisions is fundamental for ethical AI (Core et al., 2006).

Approaching the interrelation of end-users with AI systems implies understanding their uses and perceptions of Artificial Intelligence. Including the more vulnerable and/or marginalized subjects and communities as well, we need to explore what they have to say, from their situated contexts and experiences, about the opportunities and challenges that come with the use of AI and related technologies. In other words: how AI is impacting their lives; what their perspectives are; and how they can contribute to the challenge of developing, deploying, and using AI systems for social good.

Developing digital skills for an AI-embedded world can have the potential to motivate and facilitate learning; cultivate knowledge; develop critical thinking; encourage civic and political participation; and foster participation in the consumption, dissemination, and creation of content. However, if we think of children and young people, not all have the same opportunities to develop, learn, and practise AI digital skills. Their opportunities may vary depending on socio-cultural, educational, economic, and demographic factors.

Finally, governments and the private sector are also key actors. As AI is playing a growing role in different aspects of life, efforts to develop it have to be centred on improving the quality of life of individuals and communities before political interests or market priorities.

Historically, human beings have willingly ceded part of their autonomy to technologies, to machines. But nowadays, in the context of the evolution of AI, and particularly machine learning systems, one may ask what can happen when we delegate our decision-making power to an algorithm. Algorithmic outcomes, decisions, or predictions should always be under human scrutiny and close supervision, as an ethical imperative. Thus, humans must be placed at the centre when making decisions in critical situations.

> The dominant discourse around AI in education is about saving time, reducing costs and increasing efficiency, reflecting a continuation of the neoliberal policies driving austerity and cuts to services that have emerged over the past two decades. But there is nothing inevitable about these values and it is reasonable to consider a different set of values against which the fitness function of algorithms could be optimized. For example, instead of developing an algorithm that maximizes cost-effectiveness, profit or attention, there is nothing preventing us from choosing to maximize human well-being instead.
>
> (Rowe, 2019, pp. 156–157)

According to Sadin (2017, pp. 84–85), with the development of Artificial Intelligence we are entering an era of a hybrid condition of humanity through the incorporation of the deductive and predictive power of machines in our actions and decisions, and even in our bodies. They can now work through a double cognitive source, combining human and Artificial Intelligence into a growing number of activities in our daily lives, where the countless positive functions of these advances also need to be isolated from the potential negative effects on individuals and society in general.

The Beijing Consensus on Artificial Intelligence and Education

Artificial Intelligence in the field of education has begun to reconfigure processes of teaching and learning, management, and curriculum design, among others. These technologies are already being used in various countries, reinforcing the often large gap between developed and emerging countries, since AI systems for education require advanced infrastructure and a solid innovation ecosystem for their design and deployment. Reducing this gap between the most advanced and disadvantaged countries goes beyond adopting advanced technologies to facilitate learning. It also implies rethinking curriculum design, methods, and content, among other aspects, so that students can better face the challenges of technological development and take advantage of their opportunities.

The *Beijing Consensus on Artificial Intelligence and Education* is considered the first document to offer guidance and recommendations on how best to harness AI technologies for achieving the Education 2030 Agenda. It was conceived to promote:

> appropriate policy responses aimed at the systematic integration of AI and education to innovate education, teaching and learning, and at leveraging AI to accelerate the delivery of open and flexible education systems that enable equitable, relevant and quality lifelong learning opportunities for all that will contribute to achieving the SDGs and the shared future for mankind.
>
> (UNESCO, 2019b. p. 3)

It also gives a series of recommendations for governments and other stakeholders towards achieving SDG 4 "Ensure inclusive and equitable quality education and promote lifelong learning opportunities for all." Among the recommendations are those aimed towards:

- Planning AI in education policies – taking into account its multidisciplinary nature, the need for investment, and the processing and use of quality data for decision-making;
- Management and delivery – referring to the value of data for evidence-based policy planning, new models for delivering education and training enabled by AI, and making the management and provision of education more equitable, inclusive, open, and personalized;
- AI to empower teaching and teachers – focusing on the importance of human interaction and collaboration between teachers and learners remaining at the core of education, and on training teachers to work in AI-rich educational settings;
- AI for learning and learning assessment – being cognizant of trends regarding the potential of AI to support learning and learning assessments, reviewing and adjusting curricula to promote in-depth integration of AI and transformation of learning methodologies, anticipating risks, and supporting the development of AI tools for interdisciplinary skills and competencies.

The consensus attempts to advocate that all progress in the field of AIED be supported, responsibly, addressing the ethical dilemmas involved. It promotes collective and intersectoral work, enabling, given its global nature, different communities, territories, and cultures to address their particularities and needs.

According to UNESCO's *Global Framework of Reference on Digital Literacy Skills for Indicator 4.4.2* (Law et al., 2018, p. 6),

Digital literacy is the ability to access, manage, understand, integrate, communicate, evaluate, and create information safely and appropriately through digital technologies for employment, decent jobs and entrepreneurship. It includes competences that are variously referred to as computer literacy, ICT literacy, information literacy and media literacy.

In that sense, digital skills are a substantial part of the digital practices of individuals, which "are characterized by showing regularity in the action giving stability and favouring the fluid participation of the subjects in social spheres" (Valdivia et al. 2019, p. 6).[1]

As mentioned, among the existing applications in the use of AI systems in education is the possibility of designing customized learning experiences for each student by predicting the most appropriate and personalized curricular path. AI can also provide predictions of performance, tutorials with machine learning, systems of registration and analysis of automated qualifications, reduce biases in qualifications, and identify AI technologies for collaborative learning, among others (UNESCO, 2019b). Although these technologies can provide enormous benefits in educational processes, and even in the development of educational policies, they also present, as previously mentioned, ethical challenges. In the case of AIED these are mostly related to the handling and use of sensitive data from students – concerns about privacy and security – and the delegation of decisional power to algorithms on topics that are relevant to the lives of the students. Examples of the latter include admission to educational institutions, evaluation and qualification, predictions on teaching–learning processes, behaviour surveillance, and analysis.

Even though the Consensus as such does not have binding power, its adoption is important in that it serves as a guide for the implementation or improvement of policies regarding AIED, and as a guide for any educational institution and stakeholders working in the field.

> The sense of inevitability associated with technological progress is disempowering because it can make us believe that we cannot change its direction or destination. But the reality is that human decisions informed by human values are what drives technological progress and the same must be true of the decisions that inform the implementation of AI in education.
>
> (Rowe, 2019, p. 157)

One aspect of the Consensus that deserves to be highlighted is the fact that humans are placed at the centre of the discussions and as a key factor for beneficial AI. Indeed, in article 7 of its preamble the Consensus affirms that:

> [T]he development of AI should be human-controlled and centred on people; that the deployment of AI should be in the service of people to enhance human capacities; that AI should be designed in an ethical, non-discriminatory, equitable, transparent and auditable manner; and that the

impact of AI on people and society should be monitored and evaluated throughout the value chains.

(UNESCO, 2019b, p. 4)

When we think of the impact of AIED, it will certainly affect people of all ages.

AI-based ed tech may also include the development of "lifelong learning companions" – intelligent systems accessible via mobile devices that accompany youth across all levels of schooling, in and beyond the classroom, offering feedback on tasks, suggested educational resources, and activities that promote 21st century skills, such as leadership and creativity.

(Hasse et al., 2019, p. 9)

AI is being introduced into some mainstream schools as a curriculum in its own right, is being developed to improve online tutoring, and is being researched as a way of enhancing teacher training. In short, the application of AI in educational contexts is growing exponentially, such that by 2024 it is predicted to become a market worth almost $6 billion.

(Holmes et al., 2019, p. 10)

Other aspects of the Beijing Consensus focus on the importance of creating policies that encompass intersectoral and multi-stakeholder views. It refers to the participation of various entities, but does not explain the need for youth participation directly in the teaching–learning processes.

As already mentioned, the Consensus emphasizes the need for a human-centred approach to AI. This opens a window for the inclusion of traditionally marginalized communities and sectors that most commonly do not participate directly in decision-making processes concerning themselves. The aim of supporting the creation of participatory policies where no voices are excluded is clearly drawn from the text; but by not explicitly expressing the importance of the participation of the agents directly involved an adult-centric notion is shown. This vision tries to be inclusive, but allows the policy-making institutions to read the recommendations literally and opt for traditional mechanisms of planning and creating AI, that is, without the participation of youth in processes that concern them.

However, most students in the world are children and young people, which points to a fundamental aspect that is missing from the Consensus: it does not mention or emphasize the importance of student-centred requirements for the ethics of AIED.

Nevertheless, there have been a number of field-shaping publications focusing on AI highlighting youth voices and perspectives, or the need for them (see UNICEF, 2020b). An initial one, *Youth and Artificial Intelligence: Where We Stand* (Hasse et al., 2020), highlights initial learnings and exploratory questions around the ways youth may interact with and be impacted by AI technologies. It aims to inform different stakeholders, including parents and caregivers, to ask the right questions and encourage all of us to further discuss how youth can be empowered to meaningfully engage with AI systems to promote learning, creative expression, and well-being, while also addressing key challenges and concerns. Another recent example is UNICEF's *Policy Guidance on IA for Children* (2020a). This publication was informed by and features consultations with young people from around the globe using participatory methods that allowed active listening and interaction regarding AI in areas such as education, health, and wellbeing. A third example, *The Case for Better Governance of Children's Data: A Manifesto* (Byrne et al., 2021), presents challenges and actions that specifically reflect the relevance and importance of direct youth participation in policies that concern them.

Student-Centred Approaches

The origin of student-centred education is in constructivist developmental theories advanced by figures such as Jean Piaget and John Dewey (Mascolo, 2009). The notion of learner-centred instruction – which is defined as "a system of instruction based on a student's individual choices, interests, needs, abilities, learning styles and educational goals" (Yilmaz, 2009, p. 23) – supports the idea that high student engagement in the learning process produces higher-quality learning in comparison with traditional teaching–learning approaches (Mascolo, 2009).

> The infrastructure of education ensures that control and authority are vested in the teacher who is positioned, both physically and epistemologically, as the only legitimate source of knowledge in the classroom. Students are reminded that their words and personal experiences have no value in their own learning ... and this lack of power dulls their enthusiasm and cultivates an obedience to a system that generates attitudes of conformity.
>
> (Rowe, 2019, p. 152; citations omitted)

This adult-centred authoritarianism is counteracted in the pedagogical field from the constructivist approach. The constructivist paradigm is built on the following principles: learning is a constructive process – it requires an "active examination of learning content and integrating individual experiences and knowledge backgrounds" (Wulf, 2019, p. 48); learning must be self-regulated as well as cooperative; and learning must be considered as a situational process (Wulf, 2019). Adult-centric methodologies not only hinder children and youth agency, but also position them as merely the objects of inquiry.

> A student-centred learning culture is oriented on constructivist findings, considering the activity of learners in the process of knowledge acquisition; emphasizes self-regulated and autonomous learning processes that take place in social interaction; takes into account social, emotional and motivational aspects of the learning process in addition to cognitive

factors; is responsive to varying prior knowledge and experiences; and involves an emancipated relationship between educators and learners in an open and flexible, competence-oriented learning environment.

(Wulf, 2019, p. 49)

A literature review which explored 28 studies of student-centred teaching concluded that, on one hand, students in highly student-centred activities demonstrated improvements in non-academic areas such as behaviour, attitudes, interests, and self-confidence (Din & Wheatley, 2007). On the other hand, these improvements were mainly in non-academic areas.

The notions of "student voice" (Lincoln, 1995; Daniels & Arapostathis, 2005) and "student agency" are closely related to student-centred-approaches. Student voice refers in general to:

student participation and decision making in the structures and practices that shape their educational experiences. … Therefore, student voice requires more than student participation during classroom lessons – instead, it seeks to elevate student ideas and contributions about how learning occurs (or should occur).

(Rennie Center for Education Research & Policy, 2019, p. 3)

However, this conception of learning is not exempt from detractors and debate. Criticism of this concept has ranged from arguing that it promotes active student engagement at the expense of active teaching, to privileging individual experience and building a false dichotomy of student-centred/ teacher-centred in educational theory and practice (Mascolo, 2009, p. 5). Feminist authors also observed that in order to protect and empower female students in class, and possibly to educate males about sexism, feminist teachers should assert their voice, incorporating autobiography in education programmes (Shelton-Colangelo, 1996).

Student-centred pedagogy was embraced by some feminist educational theorists since it was seen as an antidote to more "traditional" or "masculinist" processes of teaching and learning. Additionally, student-centred pedagogy was also seen as positioning the teacher at the margins of classroom life, echoing the stereotypical visions of domestic femininity (Gómez, 2008).

Student-centred approaches in research, as several authors point out, present both methodological and ethical challenges (Bragg, 2010; Bucknall, 2014; Alderson, 2014). Topics such as degrees of participation and involvement, control and power relations between researchers and participants in fieldwork, the consequences of their participation, or the use and ownership of information, among others, are aspects that are repeated in the literature and debates on research involving children and young people. Thus, working from a student-centred approach, both in its design and execution, requires a permanent review of the position in which children and young people remain, as well as fulfilment of the ethical aspects that are involved.

Children and young people have the right to voice their opinion in all matters that affect their lives (Clark et al., 2014). Therefore, social research with children and young people should not be taken uncritically; yet it needs to be problematized in order to develop effective research in an ethical and positive direction.

In participatory methodologies assumptions about children and youth are challenged. When research and interventions contemplate the participation of young minors, special care is required with the generation and use of protocols for fieldwork and for analysis of the results (Alderson, 2014). In addition to the informed consent of managers, teachers, students, and their advocates, authorization for the use and dissemination of audio-visual images must also be given by the students' guardians.

Informed consent for participation will explain in detail who is responsible, the origin and purpose of the study or field of intervention, participation conditions, costs, and benefits; it will ensure that participation is voluntary, as well as assuring anonymity and confidentiality. Any initiative with a student-centred approach must consider the presentation and discussion of results with the young participants, which is one of the ethical criteria that are recommended in research and interventions with young people (Bragg, 2010).

Qualitative research methodologies have long considered the relationship between researchers and research subjects (Corbin & Strauss, 1990; Jenkins, 2006; Castells, 2009; Rainie & Wellman, 2012, Vilches, 2013); but the perspective developed in this chapter tries to go one step further, and suggests a space for young people's participation and creativity. We aim to do this specifically in the topics that concern them as citizens. The case of AI technologies and young people is far more relevant because they and their families provide the data to make the algorithms work (Serwadda et al., 2018), and the design, development, and deployment of those systems that, in the end, will affect them.

Methodologies and Student-Centred Activities: The Case of HabLatam

There is clearly a need to find ways to support students – especially children and youth – to develop the necessary digital literacies to live in a world where AI will permeate most areas of life, and find ways to help them develop critical thinking and evaluative skills. As mentioned before, one of the imperatives for advancing in the field of AIED is to include traditionally marginalized and/or vulnerable subjects and communities. Consider a future where employment in highly paid and high-skill jobs will grow exponentially and non-specialized, lower-paid jobs will tend to disappear (Harari, 2017; West, 2018; Acemoglu & Restrepo, 2018). In this scenario exploring the actual daily digital practices of children and youth – taking into account their situated contexts and their individual perspectives and needs – will provide a stronger base for understanding where AI will impact their life and the educational requirements for thriving in their future.

HabLatam is a regional initiative that involves research in five Latin American countries – Argentina, Brazil, Chile, Colombia, and Uruguay. At the time of writing it included over 300 students from public secondary schools in traditionally marginalized urban areas.[2] The classroom methodologies applied in this project can give some insights on how to incorporate participatory, student-centred activities, including the guidance of tutors or monitors to accompany, motivate, and enrich the discussions and debates avoiding or reducing response bias and adult-centric interventions. The project seeks to investigate, from the young people's perspective and with a special focus on gender, what they understand as digital skills and online content gaps in order to expand, deepen, and improve the quality of knowledge and existing data in the field. It aims to better understand the shifts in young people's engagement with digital technologies, and the opportunities and challenges digital technologies present for them and for their future. The following summarizes the project's aims.

1. Develop and implement methods that capture the perspectives, practices, and attitudes of young people

While existing studies have mapped a variety of perspectives, practices, and skills young people develop and apply in the digital environment (van Deursen et al., 2014, Cabello & Claro 2017, Livingstone et al., 2017; Ministry of Education Chile, 2013), this project seeks to deepen and rate this understanding from the point of view of young people and their practices, interests, and attitudes. With this in mind, the goal is to create, iterate, and implement methodologies that work from the youth perspective while maintaining scientific rigour.

2. Learn from what is happening at the national and regional level

Obtaining a high-quality evidence-base will allow us to not only use that evidence to advance research and policy-making at a national level, but also to learn from other countries in the region and, whenever possible, engage in collaborative and interdisciplinary work to address similar challenges. We hope that this collaborative approach will inspire other stakeholders in the youth and technology space in Latin America and beyond.

3. Focus on digital skills, content gaps, and misinformation

In order for young people to take advantage of the benefits the internet and social media platforms can offer, the need to better navigate online risks and potential harms, to learn a range of skills cultivated across various areas of life that are expanding, cumulative, fluid, and evolving – in part shaped by one's socio-historical context – has become a fundamental prerequisite. These areas of life range from engaging in civic and political efforts, to participating in economic activity to earn different types of capital (e.g. social, cultural, economic), to managing one's privacy and reputation. Across these areas of life are a variety of skills that are highly interconnected, and which can help facilitate participation in contemporary society. These forms of participation include the political, social, cultural, educational, institutional, and informational. In this sense, HabLatam aims to capture the existing skills young people possess and identify which skills they believe are crucial for their future but with which they have not yet been successfully equipped. How young people deal with misinformation is one of the key topics of the project – understanding that they do not evaluate quality according to the established adult-normative criteria emphasizing credibility, accuracy, and authority (Gasser et al., 2012). The qualitative stage of the project involves two phases: exploratory workshops and focus groups.

Phase 1: Exploratory workshops

Four participatory workshops per country were implemented, after institutional review board (IRB) approval, with an average of 20 students per workshop. This initial exploration aimed to pursue the following objectives:

a   Determine and characterize the most significant daily practices in relation to the use of digital technologies according to situated contexts, identifying *what they do, how* and *why do they do it*, and *how they value what they do*.
b   Determine and analyse what digital skills youth have and apply, and what digital skills they don't have but consider important to learn/develop.
c   Identify types of content that are relevant for youth and whether they exist online.
d   Differentiate situated contexts and gender determinants, among others.
e   Explore the relationship between content gap, barriers to access to content, and possibilities to learn and develop digital skills.
f   Identify how students understand the notions of "information quality" and "misinformation" and their practices and perceptions of it.

For this stage, the participatory methodology – co-designed with teachers, students, and experts in the field – includes dynamics where students adopt an active role in the generation of knowledge and are encouraged to discuss and build on their own perspective categories and concepts; in other words, taking the role of co-creators of knowledge. The student-centred approach in this experience by no means implied that facilitators had marginal participation in the dynamics with students. On the contrary; they were actively motivating and guiding students on how to develop critical thinking on the covered issues and to inquire deeply into their own perceptions of their digital practices, encouraging group debate and consensus-building when possible.

Table 4.1 represents a template of a flipchart paper that facilitators delivered to each group of students. It was co-designed with the students to explore their daily digital practices and what they need to know in order to master those practices. Students complete the template by writing their thoughts on sticky notes.

Table 4.1 Template module 1 of HabLatam

Column 1	Column 2
Digital activities we do	Three things we must know/do in order to do the activities in column 1
Example 1: I love Instagram and uploading images to it	(1) Be able to take pictures with my camera (2) Know how to use filters (3) Know which images are coolest (will get me lots of likes)
Example 2: I watch YouTube videos	(1) Be able to figure out how to find cool content on YouTube (2) It helps me to enjoy it more if I subscribe to certain YouTubers (3) Be able to assess the quality of the video, so I check who uploaded it, how many likes it has, and what the comments say about it

The purpose of this activity is to ease the participants into the topic by thinking about and discussing their own digital daily practices. Additionally, it encourages thinking about their present digital skills and the ones they would like or need to acquire without giving them any pre-defined category.

At the end of each module, each group is asked to select one of its members to report back, in which process the facilitator can support the reporter by identifying points of convergence and divergence. The way this report is made will impact how information flows and is shared between all participants. For the case of HabLatam, the report is made in order to be heard and commented on by all groups.

As the student participants were mostly accustomed to traditional, normative, and more conservative didactics in class, they often approached tutors with questions regarding norms and limits for delivering their answers. One of the tutors of a workshop in Chile wrote in her contextual background report: "Many of them [students] asked the facilitators if their answer was fine before writing it or if there was a limit of answers per student".

Generally speaking, the schools where the workshops were implemented use traditional and mostly vertical methodologies in class; and, instead of engaging in activities and contents they are attracted to, students spend much of their time taking notes from what the teacher says, copying from the whiteboard, or using their smartphones to chat or play games.

In the same report, the tutor pointed out that "nevertheless the students observed that in their course on robotics, they had a math professor that did not have any knowledge on the subject nor the resources to buy robots for the class".

The above indicates that, on occasions, what is shown in the official curricular programme does not reflect what really happens in practice, and students may not or do not have any power to change this kind of situation.

to the official explicit curriculum imposed from the hegemonic culture, we can add the implicit (hidden) curriculum, which involves behaviours and attitudes of educational directors and teachers. From these two efficient fronts of symbolic violence, a dual educational discourse is transmitted to students: the explicit curricular discourse, loaded with decontextualized impositions for the students, is confronted by the contradictory example of the practice of directors and teachers, contravening the curricular contents. This is what is called ethical bipolarity in education.

(Martínez & Rondón Herrera, 2018, pp. 24–25)[3]

The fact that the workshop activities are more interactive, allowing conversations and discussions among peers and creating a space of confidence with the facilitators, makes students feel more interested and attracted to the contents, and also eager to learn more about the topics approached.

The tools designed for the workshops allow students to think about and build their own categories to define their digital practices, identify content gaps, and understand and reflect on the determinants of information quality. This encourages creative and critical thinking and, from the research perspective, allows out-of-the-box insights.

The three modules of Phase 1 of the workshop contain similar participatory and co-creation activities for each topic.

Phase 2: Focus groups

The focus groups were held in all participant countries, after IRB approval, with a sample of more than 150 students. This stage of the field study was developed to expand and deepen the insights derived from the co-design workshops.

The methodology of HabLatam can serve as an example of the possibilities to integrate students in the discussion and knowledge production of AIED with a participatory approach while avoiding or considerably reducing adult-centric knowledge and practices.

The first two modules of the project were developed just before the COVID-19 pandemic began. We could learn there was a big gap and disconnection between students' daily digital practices and the incorporation of the digital sphere in the formal school curricula. However, in times of confinement and distance learning, school communities (including leaders, teachers, and families) started to recognize the value and importance of understanding how youth interact with digital technologies in order to implement more efficient educational practices and policy.

Regarding the intersection of AI and digital daily youth practices, we could identify that most students are worried about the collection and use of their personal data, especially what companies are doing with this data. However, they do not tend to take any special action beyond making their profiles private and allowing access only to selected known contacts (friends and family). Participants also acknowledged the fact that the algorithms behind social media platforms and their smartphones personalize contents according to their preferences and interests, without understanding the mechanisms for which this personalization is performed.

Student perspectives, ideas, and knowledge should be included from design to deployment and implementation processes through participatory and student-centred approaches, taking into account all ethical implications and requirements. Youth participation models (i.e. spaces, programmes, and methodologies) come with diverse challenges. Cortesi et al. (2021) propose that for achieving youth participation we need to: promote equity and inclusion as disparities in participation are persistent; make participation more accessible through diverse processes that are more dynamic, rather than gradual or linear; shift the power dynamics in adult–youth relationships; and have an oversight body to ensure that young people's rights and best interests are the guiding principles for all planned methodologies and activities.

As stated by Urs Gasser (2019), conversations on AI are being developed by a limited and small group of technical experts and decision-makers. By not including young people as participants or constituents, advancements in AIED policies will be ineffective.

Student-Centred Approach in the Context of AIED

The emerging AI practices for schools are mostly related to developing critical and technical AI skills. In order to equip students with a basic understanding and prepare them for a world where AI will be more pervasive, the interactions between teachers and students and the processes of student learning must not only be highly regarded; students also need to take an active role in their learning processes, so that students and teachers develop the curriculum together (Chiu, 2021).

The move from 'learning about AI' to 'using AI for teaching and learning processes', AIED becomes especially sensitive. AI systems for education draw from various disciplines to enrich their flexibility, personalization, and effectiveness (Chen et al., 2020). Educational outcomes and students' career paths can be highly enhanced by AI systems; teachers can design pedagogical strategies that are more effective or 'tailored' to the students' needs, interests. and competencies; and school and education management in general can be uplifted and more efficient.

> AI-powered ed tech in the classroom – such as intelligent tutoring systems, AI-based curriculum plans, and intelligent virtual reality – can enhance educational outcomes, and provide engaging learning experiences for young people … Over time, as reduction in costs and increases in Internet connectivity allow more schools and homes to access AI-fuelled technologies, the future of AI in education holds the potential for personalized learning at scale
>
> (Hasse et al., 2019, p. 9)

Despite the beneficial changes and possibilities that have been described and that are already underway, there are still very conservative conceptions that can become barriers to innovation.

The implementation of AIED presents several challenges for policymakers, mainly regarding trust (transparency, explainability, and accountability) and the use of AI systems to serve human-centred values in protecting and securing (personal) data (Vincent-Lancrin & van der Vlies, 2020, p. 13).

One of the major challenges posed by the implementation of these technologies is that AIED systems are extracting and analysing massive amounts of sensitive data from students, very often through questionable or unethical mechanisms or without informed consent from the students, tutors, or parents. As stated by Pedro Hartung (2020, p. 1), "Either due to the lack of choice, the overload of information and consent, or the complexity of data processing, the vast majority of families adhere to the terms of use without full understanding of their meaning." He argues that providers have a great responsibility for children's data protection and rights, and generally, this responsibility often ends up falling on parents and guardians.

Engaging students in designing, assessing, and implementing AIED policies and systems is crucial, addressing challenges for specific types of problems and context-specific situations (Raji et al., 2021).

The integration of Artificial Intelligence technologies into the classroom also means a challenge to the authoritarian adult-centric culture. Teachers, in this context, are usually disconnected from the students' perspective and from new technological innovations, so dealing with both tends to be hard. Working with or without AI in the classroom challenges the identity of the adults, who perceive themselves as "professional creator[s] of learning spaces, with which the message and its format become very important" (Contreras, 2014, p. 67). This requires a paradigm shift that is suggested from the training of teachers and researchers. This does not mean that authority has been re-centred – from teachers to AI technologies or to AI developers – or that we may be facing the de-professionalization of teachers. On the contrary; thanks to adequate implementation of AIED, "teachers can begin to understand much more about the process of learning itself, which might then be applied to mainstream classroom practices" (Holmes et al., 2019, p. 83), and, together, students and teachers can make better decisions to design, prepare, and evaluate content and lessons.

Conclusions and Recommendations for Action

The development and implementation of AIED is already expanding the gap between those who can design, develop, and access these technologies and those who cannot. Within the history of the evolution of digital technologies it is an old story with new elements. Even though AI technologies are not yet extensively applied in the field of education around the globe, the Global South has already advanced far into enjoying its benefits (Montoya & Rivas, 2019; Okolo, 2020). Thus, there is a risk of the gap continuing to grow if the design, deployment, regulation, ethics, and governance of Artificial Intelligence are monopolized by only a few private corporations and governments from developed countries. Furthermore, inequalities can be reinforced if AIED technologies are mainly adopted in developed countries and primarily by private sector education systems. But, according to the Innovation Centre for Brazilian Education (CIEB), AIED can also be a structural pillar for innovative education policies if equity measures are implemented to: (i) democratize access to these technologies in different regions, especially in emerging countries; (ii) support training in public education networks; and (iii) promote the universalization of AIED for the most diverse contexts, profiles, and educational community needs (in Dino & Senne, 2019).

It is often expressed by representatives of AI companies and a number of governments that too much regulation may hinder innovation in the field of AI. However, this is an unsustainable premise. There are models in which regulation, ethical concerns, social justice, and innovation can advance from the design stages while preventing potential harm to subjects and society. These include the layered model of governance proposed by Urs Gasser and Virgilio Almeida (2017), among others. On occasions, AIED policies and actions are market oriented, with a considerable lack of ethical requirements for involving children and youth. This should be considered in order to achieve ethical design and deployment of AIED.

The incorporation of AIED policies must be accompanied by the adoption of a paradigm focused on the right to education, where respect for individual identity, diversity, and socio-cultural conditions are at the centre of the new developments. Involving children and youth in all AIED stages and processes is fundamental to their own future and to a more democratic and fair development of AI in the field. Ethical concerns and reflexive engagement must accompany all processes and interventions in order to ensure that the rights, dignity, and wellbeing of children and young people are protected. Apart from the informed consent of tutors, parents, and the students themselves, other aspects that should be addressed include: whether the research or intervention is necessary and should be undertaken; students' readiness and capacity to be part of the student-centred processes; assumptions about childhood and youth involved; and the impact on children's experiences, disparities in power, and status (Graham et al., 2013, p. 5).

Children and youth will actually experience how social roles may drastically change in an AI-embedded future. Therefore, it is now imperative to establish new requirements for designing and implementing these technologies. Furthermore, advancements in transparency, explainability, predictability, safety, and privacy (among other important AIED matters) should not be performed without the insights from the subjects affected: students and educational communities at large. With a solid ethical framework, adequate regulation, and future-minded as well as inclusive thinking, improvements in AIED can provide enormous opportunities for today's children and young people to thrive in the future and for generations to come.[4]

Notes

1 Translation by the authors.
2 To find out more about the HabLatam project visit http://www.hablatam.org. Pro ject financed by Fondo Sectorial de Educación, modalidad Inclusión Digital. ANII-Fundación Ceibal.
3 Translation by the authors.
4 Special thanks to Dr Gabriella Kakonyi, Research Associate in the Department of Civil and Structural Engineering at the University of Sheffield, for her review of an earlier draft of this chapter.

References

Acemoglu, D. & Restrepo, P. (2018). Artificial intelligence, automation and work. National Bureau of Economic Research Working Paper.

Alderson, P. (2014). Ethics. In Clark, A., Fletwitt, R., Hammersley, M. & Robb, M. (eds.), *Understanding research with children and young people*. London: Sage. pp. 85–102.

Arun, C. (2019). AI and the global south: Designing for other worlds. In Dubber, M. D., Pasquale, F. & Das, S. (eds.), *The Oxford Handbook of Ethics of AI*. Oxford University Press.

Bragg, S. (2010). *Consulting young people: A literature review* (2nd ed.). Newcastle upon Tyne: Creativity, Culture and Education. Retrieved from: https://www.researchgate.net/p ublication/42797884_Consulting_Young_People_A_Review_of_the_Literature.

Brossi, L., Dodds, R. & Passerón, E. (eds.) (2019). *Inteligencia Artificial y Bienestar de las Juventudes en América Latina*. Santiago: LOM Ediciones.

Brossi, L., Olivera, M., Valdivia, A., Passeron, E., Lombana-Bermudez, A., Cortesi, S., Morales, M. J., Castillo, A.M., Palenzuela, Y. & Ibáñez, M. J. (2021). *Informe de Resultados Entrevistas a Escolares y Docentes*. Proyecto de Investigación "Jóvenes, Habilidades Digitales, Brechas de Contenido y Calidad de la información en América Latina (Hablatam)".

Bucknall, S. (2014). Doing qualitative research with children and young people. In Clark, A., Fletwitt, R., Hammersley, M. & Robb, M. (eds.), *Understanding research with children and young people*. London: Sage. pp. 69–84.

Byrne, J., Day, E. & Raftree, L. 2021. *The case for better governance of children's data: A manifesto*. New York: UNICEF. https://www.unicef.org/globalinsight/media/1741/ file/UNICEF%20Global%20Insight%20Data%20Governance%20Manifesto.pdf.

Cabello, P. & Claro, M. (2017). *General results: Kids online survey Chile*. Santiago: Kids Online Chile.

Castells, M. (2009). *Comunicación y Poder*. Madrid: Alianza Editorial.

Charisi, V., Dennis, L., Lieck, M. F. R., Matthias, A., Sombetzki, M. S. J., Winfield, A. F. & Yampolskiy, R. (2017). Towards moral autonomous systems. arXiv:1703.04741.

Chen, X., Xie, H. & Hwang, G.-J. (2020). A multi-perspective study on artificial intelligence in education: Grants, conferences, journals, software tools, institutions, and researchers. *Computers and Education: Artificial Intelligence*, 1. doi:10.1016/j.caeai.2020.100005.

Chiu, T. K. (2021). A holistic approach to the design of artificial intelligence (AI) education for K-12 schools. *TechTrends*, 65(5), 796–807.

Clark, A., Flewitt, R., Hammersley, M. & Robb, M. (eds.). (2014). *Understanding research with children and young people*. Los Angeles: Sage.

Conitzer, V., Sinnott-Armstrong, W., Borg, J. S., Deng, Y. & Kramer, M. (2017). Moral decision-making frameworks for artificial intelligence. Retrieved from: https://users.cs. duke.edu/~conitzer/moralAAAI17.pdf.

Contreras, C. (2014). El desarrollo docente del formador de profesores: una propuesta orientada hacia el análisis de incidentes críticos auténticos. *Estudios Pedagógicos*, 40, 49–69. Retrieved from: https://www.redalyc.org/articulo.oa?id=1735/173533385004.

Corbin, J. & Strauss, A. (1990). Grounded theory research: Procedures, canons, and evaluative criteria. *Qualitative Sociology*, 13(1), 3–21.

Core, M. G., Lane, H. C., Van Lent, M., Gomboc, D., Solomon, S. & Rosenberg, M. (2006). Building explainable artificial intelligence systems. *Proceedings of the Association for the AAAI Conference* (pp. 1766–1773).

Cortesi, S., Hasse, A. & Gasser, U. (2021). *Youth participation in a digital world: Designing and implementing spaces, programs, and methodologies*. Berkman Klein Center for Internet & Society. https://cyber.harvard.edu/publication/2021/youth-participation-in-a-digital-world.

Daniels, E. & Arapostathis, M. (2005). What do they really want? Student voices and motivation research. *Urban Education*, 40(1), 34–59.

Deming, D. (2020). The robots are coming. Prepare for trouble. *New York Times*. January 30. Retrieved from https://www.nytimes.com/2020/01/30/business/artificial-intelligence-robots-retail.html.

Din, F. S. & Wheatley, F. W. (2007). A literature review of the student-centred teaching approach: National implications. *National Forum of Teacher Education Journal*, 17(3), 1–17.

Dino, L. A. & Senne, P. (2019). Plataformas digitales y aprendizaje: indicadores sobre el acceso, actividades y habilidades digitales de niños y adolescentes en Brasil. In Brossi, L. *et al.* (eds.), *Inteligencia Artificial y Bienestar de las Juventudes en América Latina*. Santiago: Lom Ediciones (pp. 149–163).

Egan, M. (2020). Workers fear humans implanted with microchips will steal their jobs. *CNN Business*. September 18. Retrieved from: https://edition.cnn.com/2020/09/18/business/jobs-robots-microchips-cyborg/index.html.

Gasser, U. (2019). AI innovators should be listening to kids. *Wired*. November 26. Retrieved from: https://www.wired.com/story/ai-innovators-should-be-listening-to-kids/.

Gasser, U. & Almeida, V. A. (2017). A layered model for AI governance. *IEEE Internet Computing*, 21(6), 58–62.

Gasser, U., Cortesi, S., Malik, M. M. & Lee, A. (2012). Youth and digital media: From credibility to information quality. Berkman Klein Center for Internet & Society, 2012–1.

Giddens, A. (1991). *Modernity and self-identity: Self and society in the late modern age*. Stanford University Press.

Gómez, D. S. (2008). Women's proper place and student-centred pedagogy. *Studies in Philosophy and Education*, 27(5), 313–333.

Graham, A., Powell, M., Taylor, N., Anderson, D. & Fitzgerald, R. (2013). *Ethical research involving children*. Florence: UNICEF Office of Research–Innocenti.

Grasso, A. (2015). *Will machines replace us or work with us? Wired*. January. Retrieved from: https://www.wired.com/insights/2015/01/will-machines-replace-us-or-work-with-us/.

Harari, Y. N. (2017). Reboot for the AI revolution. *Nature News*, 550(7676), 324.

Hartung, P. (2020). The children's rights-by-design standard for data use by tech companies. UNICEF Office of Global Insight and Policy Issue Brief no. 5, November.

Hasse, A., Cortesi, S., Lombana-Bermudez, A. & Gasser, U. (2019). Youth and artificial intelligence: Where we stand. Berkman Klein Center for Internet & Society. Retrieved from: https://dash.harvard.edu/handle/1/40268058.

Holmes, W. *et al.* (2018). Co-designing a real-time classroom orchestration tool to support teacher–AI complementarity. *Journal of Learning Analytics*, 6(2), 27–52.

Holmes, W., Bialik, M. & Fadel, C. (2019). *Artificial intelligence in education: Promises and implications for teaching and learning.* Boston: Center for Curriculum Redesign.

Holstein, K. & Doroudi, S. (2019). Fairness and equity in learning analytics systems (FairLAK). In *Companion Proceedings of the Ninth International Learning Analytics & Knowledge Conference (LAK'19).* ACM.

Howard, A. (2021). Real Talk: Intersectionality and AI. *MIT Sloan Management Review.* August. Retrieved from: https://sloanreview.mit.edu/article/real-talk-intersectionality-and-ai/.

Hvistendahl, M. (2019). Can we stop AI outsmarting humanity? *The Guardian.* March 28. Retrieved from: https://www.theguardian.com/technology/2019/mar/28/can-we-stop-robots-outsmarting-humanity-artificial-intelligence-singularity.

ITU (2019). *Guidelines for parents and educators on child online protection.* Geneva: International Telecommunication Union.

Jenkins, H. (2006). *Convergence culture.* New York, NY: New York University Press.

Kwet, M. (2019). Digital colonialism: US empire and the new imperialism in the global south. *Race & Class*, 60(4), 3–26.

Law, N., Woo, D., de la Torre, J. & Wong, G. (2018). *A global framework of reference on digital literacy skills for Indicator 4.4.2.* Montreal: UNESCO Institute for Statistics.

Lincoln, Y. S. (1995). In search of students' voices. *Theory into Practice*, 34(2), 88–93.

Livingstone, S., Ólafsson, K., Helsper, E., Lupiáñez-Villanueva, F., Veltri, G. & Folkvord, F. (2017). Maximizing opportunities and minimizing risks for children online: The role of digital skills in emerging strategies of parental mediation. *Journal of Communication*, 67(1), 82–105.

Martínez, R. M. & Rondón Herrera, G. (eds.) (2018). *Formación docente y pensamiento crítico en Paulo Freire.* Buenos Aires: CLACSO.

Mascolo, M. F. (2009). Beyond student-centered and teacher-centered pedagogy: Teaching and learning as guided participation. *Pedagogy and the Human Sciences*, 1(1), 3–27.

Ministry of Education Chile. (2013). Matriz de Habilidades para el aprendizaje. Retrieved from: http://www.enlaces.cl/sobre-enlaces/habilidades-tic-en-estudiantes/.

Montoya, L. & Rivas, P. (2019). *Government AI readiness meta-analysis for Latin America and the Caribbean.* IEEE International Symposium on Technology and Society (ISTAS), 1–8. doi:10.1109/ISTAS48451.2019.8937869.

Okolo, C. T. (2020). AI in the "real world": Examining the impact of AI deployment in low-resource contexts. arXiv:2012.01165.

Porayska-Pomsta, K. & Rajendran, G. (2019). Accountability in human and artificial decision-making as the basis for diversity and educational inclusion. In Knox, J., Wang, Y. & Gallagher, M. (eds.), *Artificial intelligence and inclusive education: Speculative futures and emerging practices.* Singapore: Springer. pp. 39–59.

Rainie, L. & Wellman, B. (2012). *Networked: The new social operating system.* Cambridge, MA: MIT Press.

Raji, I. D., Scheuerman, M. K. & Amironesei, R. (2021, March). You can't sit with us: Exclusionary pedagogy in AI ethics education. In *Proceedings of the 2021 ACM Conference on Fairness, Accountability, and Transparency* (pp. 515–525).

Rennie Center for Education Research & Policy (2019). *Student voice: How young people can shape the future of education.* Boston, MA: Rennie Center for Education Research & Policy. https://files.eric.ed.gov/fulltext/ED594106.pdf.

Rowe, M. (2019). Shaping our algorithms before they shape us. In Knox, J., Wang, Y. & Gallagher, M. (eds.), *Artificial intelligence and inclusive education: Speculative futures and emerging practices.* Singapore: Springer. pp. 151–164.

Sadin, E. (2017). *La humanidad aumentada.* Buenos Aires: La Caja Negra.

Serwadda, D.*et al.* (2018). Open data sharing and the global south: Who benefits? *Science,* 359(6376), 642–643.

Shelton-Colangelo, S. (1996). Tara's story: The feminist teacher's voice in the "student-centered" classroom. *WILLA,* 5, 24–29.

UNESCO (2018). *Global education monitoring report 2019: Migration, displacement and education – building bridges, not walls.* doi:10.18356/22b0ce76-en.

UNESCO (2019a). *Artificial intelligence in education: Challenges and opportunities for sustainable development.*

UNESCO (2019b). *Beijing Consensus on Artificial Intelligence and Education.*

UNICEF (2020a). *Policy guidance on IA for children.* Retrieved from: https://www.unicef.org/globalinsight/media/1171/file/UNICEF-Global-Insight-policy-guidance-AI-children-draft-1.0-2020.pdf.

UNICEF (2020b). *Resources to complement the UNICEF policy guidance on AI for children: Resources per requirement for child-centred AI.* Retrieved from: https://docs.google.com/spreadsheets/u/0/d/1zKmFPZgnaOeuQafmcWRRp6l8BeyxSts2pC7wPndcYaM/htmlview?urp=gmail_link.

UNICEF Innovation, Human Rights Center & UC Berkeley (2019). *Memorandum on artificial intelligence and child rights.* Retrieved from: https://www.unicef.org/innovation/reports/memoAIchildrights.

United Nations (2019). Special edition: Progress towards the Sustainable Development Goals. Report of the Secretary-General.

Valdivia, A., Brossi, L., Cabalin, C. & Pinto, D. (2019). Alfabetizaciones y prácticas digitales desde agencias juveniles. Desafíos para la educación en Chile. *Pensamiento Educativo, Revista de Investigación Latinoamericana,* 56(2), 1–16. doi:10.7764/PEL.56.2.2019.1.

van Deursen, A. J. A. M., Helsper, E. & Eynon, R. (2014). *Measuring digital skills: From digital skills to tangible outcomes project report.* Enschede: University of Twente.

Vilches, L. (2013). *Convergencia y transmedialidad. La ficción después de la TDT en Europa e Iberoamérica.* Barcelona: Gedisa.

Vincent-Lancrin, S. & van der Vlies, R. (2020). Trustworthy artificial intelligence (AI) in education: Promises and challenges. OECD Education Working Papers, No. 218. doi:10.1787/a6c90fa9-en.

West, D. M. (2018). *The future of work: Robots, AI, and automation.* Washington, DC: Brookings Institution Press.

Wilkinson, M. D. *et al.* (2016). The FAIR guiding principles for scientific data management and stewardship. *Scientific Data,* 3, 160018. doi:10.1038/sdata.2016.18.

Wulf C. (2019). "From teaching to learning": Characteristics and challenges of a student-centred learning culture. In Mieg, H. A. (ed.), *Inquiry-based learning – undergraduate research: The German multidisciplinary experience.* Cham: Springer. pp. 47–55.

Yilmaz, K. (2009). Democracy through learner-centred education: A Turkish perspective. *International Review of Education,* 55(1), 21–37.

5 Pitfalls and pathways for Trustworthy Artificial Intelligence in education

Nathalie A. Smuha

Introduction

Artificial Intelligence (AI) may well be one of the most hyped technologies of our time; yet its increasing ubiquity in all areas of our lives attests it to being more than hype. AI is an umbrella term for an array of technologies demonstrating aspects of intelligent behaviour, from natural language processing (enabling text analysis and translation) to voice and image recognition (enabling interaction with virtual assistants, or the identification of objects and faces). The most recent successes booked by AI build on increased computing power at lower cost, research advances (particularly in the AI subfield called *machine learning*), and the growing availability of big data (on which machine learning heavily relies). Being a general-purpose technology that can be used to execute tasks more efficiently in a wide range of sectors and domains, AI-applications have the ability to generate substantial economic and societal benefits (European Commission 2018; McKinsey 2018). It is thus no surprise that governments across the globe eagerly adopted AI strategies to secure sufficient capital, talent, and infrastructure to become AI powerhouses – from China's 'Next Generation AI Development Plan' (2017), to the UK's 'AI Sector Deal' (2018), the European Union's 'Communication on Artificial Intelligence for Europe' (2018) or the United States' 'Executive Order on Maintaining Leadership in AI' (White House 2019).

The adoption of AI is also growing in the realm of education, where it can build on the accomplishments of *educational technology* (EdTech) more generally. As part of their national strategies, some countries also explicitly state their support for the use of AI in education. Thus China's plan includes a section on 'intelligent education', in which it aims to use AI to 'reform' teaching methods, 'establish new-type education systems, including intelligent learning and interactive learning', and 'launch the construction of intelligent campuses' as well as 'develop intelligent educational assistants' (Webster et al. 2017). The US Executive Order speaks of prioritizing, among other things, 'curricula that encourage the integration of AI technologies into courses in order to facilitate personalized and adaptive learning experiences for formal and informal education and training' (White House 2019).

DOI: 10.4324/9780429329067-7

The use of AI-based applications extends to various educational environments – from traditional schools to specialized language centres – aiming to support students, teachers, and schools to achieve their objectives more effectively (Southgate et al. 2018; Francesc et al. 2019). This development was further spurred by the COVID-19 pandemic, which led many educational institutions to become dependent on (AI-enabled) digital learning tools to continue their activities amidst restrictive measures.

The development and use of AI, however, also presents certain risks. These risks are not new, yet are becoming the subject of broader public scrutiny. Thanks mainly to engaged researchers and practitioners, vocal civil society organizations, and committed journalists, the technology's adverse impacts are increasingly being brought to light (Mittelstadt et al. 2016; O'Neil 2017; Leenes et al. 2017; Yeung 2019; Benjamin 2019). Consider in this regard, for instance, the work of Joy Buolamwini and Timnit Gebru (2018) on bias in automated facial analysis, or the advocacy undertaken by the American Civil Liberties Union (ACLU) and the research institute AI Now (Crawford et al. 2019). Over the past years, certain AI-applications have led to public outrage when the harm caused thereby – to individuals or society – became more widely known (Isaak and Hanna 2018; Coughlan 2020; Bedingfield 2020). This triggered a broader discussion on the ethical challenges raised by AI, and on how they should be addressed. Consequently, along with strategies to boost AI uptake, reflections on how to minimize, prevent, and overcome AI's risks also emerged, both at the national and international level.

Moreover, beyond the assessment of AI's risks from a horizontal perspective, calls are also increasingly made to analyse and address the technology's ethical challenges from a vertical or sectorial perspective. Evidently, an erroneous prediction made by an AI-system about a movie one may be interested in watching does not have the same impact as an erroneous prediction about a medical treatment or the downgrading of students' exam results (Afifi-Sabet 2020). Since many of AI's risks are context-dependent, a number of initiatives have also started to map these risks in more 'sensitive' domains. This sensitivity can stem, for instance, from the involvement of vulnerable individuals or groups, from a manifestation of asymmetries of information or power, or, more generally, from the fact that human rights or democratic values can be adversely impacted. Surprisingly, however, despite the unquestionable sensitivity of the educational realm, thus far only little attention has been paid to the specific risks arising in the context of Artificial Intelligence in education (AIED). As will be discussed further below, this is slowly changing; yet a lot of work still lies ahead to map and address AI's ethical conundrums in this field.

This chapter aims to contribute to that work, by assessing the ethical challenges posed by the use of AIED. The normative framework of this assessment consists of the seven requirements for Trustworthy AI, as set out in the Ethics Guidelines of the European Commission's High-Level Expert Group on AI. After an overview of the broader context in which the seven requirements took shape, the chapter examines each requirement in the educational realm, as well as the pitfalls that must be addressed to enable their realization. Particular attention is given to the special role of education to shape people's minds, and the manner in which this role can be used both to empower and exploit individuals. The examination highlights how AIED's main strengths – offering education on a wider scale through more flexible and individualized learning methods, and through the closer monitoring of students' reception of the materials – also constitute its main liabilities when left unchecked. Finally, the chapter discusses various pathways that policymakers should consider to foster Trustworthy AIED beyond the adoption of guidelines, before offering some concluding remarks.

The Landscape of AI Ethics

The Ethics Guidelines for Trustworthy AI in context

Although the term 'Artificial Intelligence' was coined by computer scientist John McCarthy only in 1956, the philosophy of AI already kick-started a few years earlier in 1950, when Alan Turing published a seminal paper raising the question: Can machines think? (Turing 1950). Over the following decades, Turing's imagined 'universal computer' became a reality, and information technologies (IT) more generally became incorporated into our everyday lives. Besides questions of theoretical philosophy, the increased use of IT in more practical contexts – and the increased possibilities they created for harm or misuse – also started giving rise to questions of practical philosophy or ethics. Within the domain of ethics, it is the field of *applied ethics* that deals with the question of what a person ought to do in a specific situation or domain of action. *AI ethics* is hence a sub-field of applied ethics, and focuses on the ethical conundrums raised by the development and use of AI-systems.

The field of AI ethics includes various ethical theories, all putting forward specific ethical guidance to follow in the context of AI (Lin et al. 2014). While some believe that traditional ethical theories (for instance based on virtue ethics, deontology, or utilitarianism) provide a sufficient ethical framework for AI's development and use, others consider these theories inadequate to tackle the specific issues raised by AI, and instead put forward new ethical theories (often heavily drawing on – or containing a mix of – more traditional ones). This difference of opinions immediately clarifies that there is not just 'one' ethics or 'one' ethics of AI, but that multiple ethical theories around AI coexist, which, depending on the context or timing, can prescribe different actions or outcomes to pursue. The increased use of AI in society has also triggered an increase of attention to AI ethics, resulting in a proliferation of guidelines in this sphere (Jobin et al. 2019). The principles contained in these guidelines are typically addressed to developers and deployers of AI-systems, who are considered to have an ethical duty – in addition to legal obligations they can have – to secure compliance therewith.

At the European level, the most influential guideline document stems from the European Commission's High-Level Expert Group on AI (HLEG on AI). This independent group gathered 52 experts from academia, industry, and civil society with different backgrounds, and was tasked inter alia with the drafting of the *Ethics Guidelines for Trustworthy AI* (the Guidelines). Rather than using the notion of *ethical AI*, the HLEG on AI framed its foundational ambition as *Trustworthy AI*, which it defined as AI that is not only ethical but also legal and robust.[1] To be deemed trustworthy, the Guidelines state, AI first and foremost needs to comply with all legal rules that already apply thereto – such as privacy or safety legislation (*legal AI*). Second, it must respect ethical principles, which may or may not be embedded in legislation (*ethical AI*). Third, it needs to be technically robust, ensuring that no unintentional harm occurs – for instance due to inadequate security measures leading to hacks or data leaks (*robust AI*). These three conditions should be guaranteed throughout the system's lifecycle. The Guidelines hence take a *values-by-design* approach, in which the need for compliance should already be reflected in the system's design rather than being a mere afterthought.

The Guidelines do not set out the legal obligations that need to be respected in the context of AI, but instead provide guidance on how the ethical and robust character of AI-systems can be secured, doing so in three steps – from the most abstract to the most concrete (Smuha 2019). The first step sets out four overarching ethical principles that should be upheld in the context of AI, drawn from human rights law, namely: respect for *human autonomy, prevention of harm, fairness,* and *explicability*. From these four principles, in a second step, seven requirements for Trustworthy AI are derived, namely, respect for: (1) *human agency and oversight*; (2) *technical robustness and safety*; (3) *privacy and data governance*; (4) *transparency*; (5) *diversity, non-discrimination, and fairness*; (6) *societal and environmental wellbeing*; and (7) *accountability*. Finally, the third step provides an assessment list to operationalize each of the seven requirements by raising concrete questions for reflection and implementation.[2] The seven requirements were supported by a subsequent EC document that encouraged all organizations to implement them (European Commission 2019).

Beyond guidelines

While many of these requirements are already partially reflected in existing legislation, no legislation currently covers them in a comprehensive manner. In February 2020, the European Commission therefore published a White Paper that identified some legal gaps it intended to tackle (European Commission 2020). It focused particularly on AI-applications with a high risk to individuals' safety and fundamental rights, and examined a number of legislative options for a new AI-specific regulation to complement ethical guidance. Building on that White Paper, in April 2021 the Commission published a formal proposal for a new European AI regulation, taking a risk-based approach to AI. The proposed regulation would impose new requirements for certain 'high-risk' AI-systems.

Simultaneously, the Council of Europe – counting 46 Member States – also started to explore the feasibility of implementing new binding regulation in this field (Council of Europe 2019). Building on its Feasibility Study, which was published in December 2020, the Council of Europe's Ad Hoc Committee on AI (CAHAI) adopted possible elements of a binding legal framework for AI – for instance, in the form of a new treaty – to ensure that the design, development, and use of AI respects human rights, democracy, and the rule of law (Council of Europe 2020).

The ongoing regulatory initiatives of the European Commission and the Council of Europe are primarily focusing on a horizontal approach, intended to apply to AI-systems that pose a heightened level of risk, rather than only focusing on one particular sector. However, within these risk-assessment frameworks, the specificity of the sector can play a role, as the risk level of an application is at least partially defined by the sensitivity of the sector in which the application is used. As noted above, many of the ethical risks raised by the development and use of AI are context-specific. Therefore, any horizontal approach to ethical guidance or regulation should ideally be complemented by a vertical one, recognizing the particular risks arising from the domain in which a system is used. While the seven requirements for Trustworthy AI can provide an overarching framework to assess AI's trustworthiness, the concrete implementation thereof should be tailored to the particular concerns raised in a given context.

As regards the educational sector, several reports describe the benefits and risks arising from the use of AI in this field (Francesc et al. 2019; Vincent-Lancrin 2020). The *Beijing Consensus on Artificial Intelligence and Education*, adopted by UNESCO Member States in May 2019, also contains a section on the need to ensure the 'ethical, transparent and auditable use of education data and algorithms', thus acknowledging the risks AIED might generate (UNESCO 2019). Furthermore, the European Commission's proposed AI Act (2021) also covers a few AIED applications as 'high risk' AI-systems on which new requirements are imposed. Recital 35 of the proposal states that:

> AI systems used in education or vocational training, notably for determining access or assigning persons to educational and vocational training institutions or to evaluate persons on tests as part of or as a precondition for their education should be considered high-risk, since they may determine the educational and professional course of a person's life and therefore affect their ability to secure their livelihood. When improperly designed and used, such systems may violate the right to education and training as well as the right not to be discriminated against and perpetuate historical patterns of discrimination.

Nevertheless, tailored ethical guidance for the development and use of AIED remains sparse (note, however, Aiken and Epstein 2000). AIED does not operate in a legal vacuum, and numerous legal rules already apply thereto.

Yet AIED developers, educational institutions, and impacted stakeholders have little guidance at their disposal to understand and assess the specific ethical pitfalls that should be considered when developing or using AIED. A positive development is that, in 2021, the European Commission launched a new expert group to develop ethics guidelines on AI and data in education and training, which will build further on the *Ethics Guidelines for Trustworthy AI*. Simultaneously, the Council of Europe established the Working Group on Artificial Intelligence in Education (WG-AIEd) to explore opportunities for policy and legal instruments in that area. These developments demonstrate increased awareness of the importance of ensuring Trustworthy AI in education.

AI ethics and education

Within the domain of education, AI techniques can be used for many different applications and aims (Kulkarni 2019). Examples include: AI-applications that teach content, such as language-training apps, AI-systems that suggest personalized learning trajectories based on student profiles; systems that correct exams through natural language processing or that evaluate oral presentations through video analysis; chatbots that answer students' questions; facial recognition applications used for exam proctoring or to monitor students' class attendance; facial analysis applications to assess students' understanding of the materials or their attention span; and AI-based evaluation systems that predict and assess students' grades and progress more generally. Besides student-oriented applications, AIED applications can also be tailored to teachers, or even be used to evaluate teachers' performance, for instance through value-added-models (Amrein-Beardsley 2014).

While all these applications belong to the sphere of education, their purposes and ways of functioning are very different. These applications do not all have the same level of (proven) effectiveness; they do not all collect the same amount or type of data; and they do not all have the same level of intrusiveness into a student's or teacher's life. AIED cannot be reduced to one type of application, and not all AIED applications raise particular ethical concerns. The ethical assessment of educational AI-applications thus requires an approach that is tailored to the specific use or case.

At the same time, within the broader sphere of education, some common ethical concerns with regard to the use of AI can be identified. Arguably, the most important concern to consider in AIED context is whether the application entails the direct involvement of vulnerable individuals. These are typically children but, in some situations, can also comprise adults who, for instance, are at risk of exclusion (Prinsloo and Slade 2016). In addition, educational settings are typically characterized by asymmetries of power and of information. These asymmetries tend to manifest themselves at three different levels.

First, asymmetries of power and information are inherent in virtually all student–teacher relationships, regardless of the student's age. By definition, teachers have more knowledge on certain topics than their students, whom they are also meant to evaluate. This asymmetry is exacerbated when another aspect of vulnerability is at stake, such as a young age, minority background, or (learning) disability. Second, these asymmetries also exist between teachers and schools, as teachers typically depend upon schools for their employment and, by extension, for their livelihood. As a consequence, they may find themselves in a difficult position when facing concerns about certain AI-applications in their classrooms – whether these concerns arise from the application's ethical risks or lack of effectiveness – especially where their employer has heavily invested in the technology and strongly supports its use. Finally, asymmetry of information is often also a factor in the relationship between educational institutions and AI developers that commercialize AIED products. Schools – and by extension teachers and students – typically lack the expertise to accurately understand how educational AI-systems work, what data they collect and process, how they arrive at their decisions or recommendations, and what the consequences of the use of these systems might be, including potential adverse effects.

As a consequence, when assessing AIED's ethical challenges, it is essential to look beyond the student–teacher relationship. All stakeholders should be considered to identify where vulnerabilities or asymmetries – in whichever form – might exist and could potentially lead to an exacerbation of AI's risks (Aiken and Epstein 2000). To identify and counter these risks, the seven requirements listed in the above-mentioned Guidelines for Trustworthy AI might be a helpful starting point. While not claiming to provide an exhaustive overview of potential concerns, these Guidelines can stimulate a reflection not only on what the ethical challenges of a specific AIED application may be, but also how these challenges could be mitigated. Such reflection should occur *ex ante*, prior to the system's use – and ideally also prior to its development.

While all AIED stakeholders have their own part to play in securing the requirements for Trustworthy AI (see also Chapter 6 in this book by Holstein and Doroudi), the Guidelines particularly highlight the role of three sets of stakeholders, which can be translated into the educational domain as follows:

1 Developers of AIED applications (often but not always commercial companies, as well as researchers in the field) – they should implement and apply the requirements in their design and development processes;
2 Deployers of AIED applications (typically schools, whether primary, secondary, tertiary, or non-traditional educational institutions – and in some instances, this can also include public entities): they should ensure that the systems they use, and the products and services they offer, meet the requirements;
3 End-users (typically students or teachers) and all other parties affected by AIED (including parents, but also society at large): they should be informed about these requirements and be able to request and enforce accountability.

Arguably, to the extent the educational sector is also a regulated one – or at least one in which the government typically plays a considerable role – a fourth stakeholder and responsibility should be included:

4   Regulators (whether at local, national, or international level): they should ensure that developers and deployers of AIED implement the requirements, and that those affected by AIED – either directly or indirectly – are safeguarded from any adverse impact thereof.

Attention to AIED-related risks has so far mainly focused on privacy concerns, particularly in light of AI-enabled processing of students' personal data, for instance with the aim of fostering personalized or adaptive learning applications. These concerns also played an important role in the fall of US-based EdTech company inBloom even before it was properly launched, which in turn triggered a backlash against AI-applications in schools more globally (Bulger et al. 2017). Breach of privacy was also at stake in August 2019 in Europe, when a Swedish school that introduced AI-based facial recognition to monitor student attendance received a substantial fine for breaching EU data protection law (Hanselaer 2019). While privacy risks are certainly important to consider, AIED can raise other risks too, as was for instance demonstrated by the UK's system downgrading A-level results (Coughlan 2020; Afifi-Sabet 2020). It is therefore essential that the ethical assessment of AIED is sufficiently comprehensive and covers all seven requirements for Trustworthy AI, of which privacy is only one. To this end, in what follows each of these requirements is discussed in the context of education.

Trustworthy AI in Education: Requirements and Risks

Human agency and oversight

By automating certain tasks and decisions that are normally undertaken by human beings, AI by definition has an impact on human agency – yet this is not necessarily problematic. After all, the objective of AI-systems is to ease people's lives by taking over some of their work. AI-systems can, for instance, execute tasks that are deemed too dull or repetitive to be of human interest (such as replying to 200 student emails asking the same basic questions). They can help carry out tasks on a much larger scale (such as correcting 2000 identical student exams). And in some instances, they can carry out tasks with more precision and effectiveness than humans could (such as providing personalized curricula for 2000 students based on individual preferences and abilities in a short time span). As long as human beings can meaningfully decide when and under what conditions decisions are delegated to an AI-system, human agency is not only preserved, but can even be empowered. At the same time, the delegation of certain tasks to AI-systems also carries some risks, especially when the delegated decisions can have a direct – and potentially negative – impact on individuals. Importantly, the choice to delegate decisions to AI-systems is a human choice, and thus falls under human responsibility.

   Safeguarding human agency hence means that all those who are involved in the decision to deploy or use an educational AI-system – be it schools, teachers, students, and/or their parents – are enabled to make an informed and autonomous decision. For this purpose, they first need the knowledge to understand how a particular AI-application works, and should have the possibility to challenge the decisions it makes where needed. While it can – and should – be expected from the schools that choose to deploy AI to inform and educate themselves about the capacities and limitations of the system prior to its use, for (end-)users (such as students and teachers) this information should be proactively provided. This will then enable individuals to exercise their human agency and to assess the appropriateness of the task delegation and the potential risks to be considered.

Human agency can also be hampered in more subtle ways. AI can, for instance, be used to influence student behaviour in a manner that is more difficult to detect – through covert manipulation or deception, or by providing targeted (dis)information. Of course, all educational activities aim to shape human minds in a certain sense, whether by providing new skills and knowledge or by providing additional or new perspectives. In fact, education is often explicitly put forward as a crucial tool to foster socially and individually beneficial behaviour. Yet this powerful ability of education to shape minds – especially when it concerns young minds that are typically more malleable – can also be used to foster behaviour that might benefit those developing and deploying the technology while not necessarily being in the learners' interest. More far-reaching, it can also be used to teach certain beliefs that run counter to the values of human rights, democracy, and the rule of law, and that foster instead more oppressive or totalitarian goals. Unfortunately, examples of the instrumentalization of education towards such aims are not only historical (Kunzer 1938; Gallo 2015), but are also found today (Zenz 2019; Raza 2019). And while the use of education for (political) indoctrination does not necessitate AI, the availability of an AI-powered educational infrastructure offers significant advantages to achieve such aims.

Technologies, including those enabled by AI, are inevitably moulded by the knowledge, norms, culture, and power relationships as well as (unconscious) biases and prejudices of their creators, and hence value-laden, even if unintentional and barely perceivable (van de Poel and Kroes 2014). In a bleak scenario, this feature can hence be used to purposefully mould AIED so as to influence, nudge, and even manipulate students in a more effective manner, whether openly or covertly. Moreover, potential resistance to the curriculum's changes by human teachers could be more easily circumvented or overridden, as the role of human intermediaries might become smaller. In other words, one of the main strengths of AI-based education – its ability to offer education on a much wider scale, at a faster pace, through more flexible methods, and in a way that allows for the closer monitoring of students' understanding and reception of the materials – is in this sense also one of its biggest liabilities. Evidently, the extent of this risk is directly correlated with the role that AIED plays in the classroom. Most democratic societies already have some regulatory safeguards in place in this regard, for instance by regulating the mandatory content that each student should be taught. Moreover, this risk is less present when AIED is used outside of traditional educational institutions rather than in primary and secondary schools. Yet the potential for (covert) nudging to influence students in more subtle ways – akin to the use of such techniques on social media – remains relevant. While this concern is present with EdTech applications more generally, the use of AI-enabled nudging techniques can amplify it.

One of the most important ways to counter the use of AI that may (un)intentionally hamper human agency or cause other adverse impacts is the establishment of strong human oversight mechanisms. The Guidelines mention three particular types of oversight that can help achieve this, which – depending on the use case – should be used complementarily. The first is a human-in-command (HIC) approach, whereby the overall activity of the educational AI-system is overseen, as well as the broader implications it has from an ethical, societal, legal or economic perspective. This also encompasses responsibility for a decision on whether or not to use an AI-system in a given situation in the first place, and – if so – how the system should be used. It is, for instance, one thing for a school to decide, together with its teachers, that an AI-based value-added model will be used to help provide insights into teachers' performance. It is another thing for a school to decide that, based solely on the evaluations of such a model, teachers may get fired (O'Neil 2017).

The second oversight approach mentioned in the Guidelines is a human-on-the-loop (HOTL) approach. This approach not only enables human intervention during the design phase of the AI-system, but also ensures that – once the system is in operation – its use is closely monitored. The third is a human-in-the-loop (HITL) approach, whereby human intervention is made possible in every decision cycle of the AI-system. While the latter approach would be too demanding for an AI-system that only presents low or no tangible risks, more continuous human intervention may nevertheless be a necessary safeguard for AI-applications that can significantly impact students' or teachers' lives. As already stressed, context matters. The same intensity of oversight is unlikely to be warranted for an AI-chatbot that answers frequently asked questions and for an AI-system that is supposed to generate students' final exam results, and thereby co-determines their future.

It is the responsibility of those involved – including the organizations that develop the system and the entities that decide to use it, each within their own role – to assess on a case-by-case basis which oversight mechanism is needed to ensure that the system meets the requirements throughout its lifecycle. This assessment also necessitates prior reflection on the various rights and interests at stake when implementing the system. In this regard, the UN Convention on the Rights of the Child, which lists some important rights to be considered whenever children are involved, can be recalled in particular. In addition, ongoing initiatives that aim to map the impact of AI specifically on children can also provide a helpful framework.[3]

Technical robustness and safety

Like all software systems, AI is only as good as its technical infrastructure. A lack of attention to the system's robustness can still lead to numerous types of harm, which developers and deployers of AI should strive to avoid. Especially where AI relies on (personal) data of students, adequate security measures must be taken to ensure that no data leaks can occur. AI-systems should be protected against technical vulnerabilities by making them resilient to attacks on their software (comprising their data and model) or on their hardware. Moreover, whenever AI-systems are embedded in – or linked to – hardware, such as robotics, additional caution is also needed for physical damage that can potentially ensue, whether through the exposure of the system to use situations that were not initially foreseen or through the system's intentional corruption by malicious actors. These risks must be assessed and addressed before AI-applications are introduced in educational settings, to secure the physical and mental integrity of all those who might be impacted.

Technical robustness also implies that the system can make correct or accurate judgements. Depending on the use case, inaccurate decisions, predictions, or recommendations can have negative consequences for those involved. Examples in the educational context range from an AI-system that recommends the wrong content based on an inaccurate assessment of the student's ability, to one that wrongly evaluates students or teachers, or that provides them with inaccurate feedback. Accuracy problems are especially relevant for AI-systems that claim to have the ability to read cognitive or emotional states, besides posing significant risks to privacy (Lieberman 2018). This type of technology is increasingly used in other sectors, for instance to analyse video-interviews of prospective job candidates (Harwell 2019), and has started to be deployed in classrooms too. Importantly, however, numerous researchers have pointed to the inherent flaws of such technologies and the unscientific grounding thereof (Bjørnsten and Zacher Sørensen 2017; Barrett et al. 2019). In addition to being generally inaccurate, those systems are disproportionately inaccurate when it concerns students with different profiles, such as those having a disability or coming from a different cultural background than the profiles on which the system was trained (Crawford et al. 2019). While human beings are not immune to inaccurate judgements either, their mechanisms to learn, adapt, correct, and re-plan are not comparable to those of AI-systems, which can also manifest this problem on a much wider scale.

Finally, the Guidelines also list reliability and reproducibility as necessary attributes under the umbrella of AI's technical robustness. Reliability denotes the need for AI-systems to work properly within a range of inputs and situations, and to effectively carry out the tasks they claim to execute. This means the system must be able to perform these tasks not only within the conditions of the (digital) lab in which it was developed and tested, but also in real school settings. Reproducibility demands that AI-systems yield the same outcome when used under the same conditions, and are hence able to reproduce their behaviour. While the responsibility to verify and secure the technical robustness of AIED rests primarily with the companies developing it, schools and other deployers of AIED must ensure that the systems they use meet these criteria, and – in case of harm – should not deflect their responsibility on to the developers.

Privacy and data governance

The importance of the right to privacy and the protection of personal data – two distinct fundamental rights under EU law – is not new in EdTech debates. Yet the emergence of AIED – and in particular applications based on learning-techniques – only raised the privacy stakes to a higher level, in view of the large amount of data they require. The role of data is not only essential during the system's training phase, but also once it is used. Moreover, data generated in the course of the system's operation can also be reused as new input. Developers and deployers of AIED applications often operate under the premise that the collection and analysis of as much relevant data as possible about students and their (historical and actual) performance can help assess their abilities and provide tailored tools for enhancement (Rouhiainen, 2019). While the analysis of student data can be used for many beneficial applications, it also comes with an important responsibility as it can be used in ways that are not in the students' interests or even run counter thereto.

In order to build a personalized learning trajectory based on individual student profiles, for instance, data is typically collected on their grades, acquired knowledge, and learning capacities; but it is potentially collected also on their character traits, preferences, health status, family situation, and various other aspects that might be of relevance to map their abilities and set out their learning path. Even if not all these data points are explicitly collected, inferences of a personal nature can still be made – including from information as limited as the movements of a computer mouse (Hibbeln et al. 2017). Companies developing AIED typically monetize such data primarily through their products. Yet questions around the ownership of both the collected data and the outcomes of the analyses based on that data are often undefined, which opens up further risks (Herold 2018). The collected or inferred data could for instance be sold to third parties (including online marketers, insurers, or employers) who develop their own AI products and who might use the acquired information for their own purposes.

As raised above, students are not only in a vulnerable position because of their young age, but also because of their dependency on the school and teachers. They are hence not always in a position to challenge the collection of their data. Furthermore, due to the inherent power imbalance in educational contexts, it can even be questioned whether consent can ever be used as a valid legal basis to process student data. To be valid, consent needs to be *freely* given. However, recital 43 of the EU General Data Protection Regulation (GDPR) specifies that 'consent should not provide a valid legal ground for the processing of personal data in a specific case where there is a clear imbalance between the data subject and the controller.' In this regard, the crucial role of parents or guardians who, depending on the student's age, can be required to give consent on their behalf should also be considered – not least because, in some situations, tensions may arise between the interests of the child and the interest of the parents.

The question can also be raised whether a genuine opportunity to opt out of the technology's use still exists once it is adopted by the school. Opting out might become de facto impossible, either because of the pressure exerted upon students and parents to conform to the will of the majority who might believe the application's benefits outweigh the risks or because the physical infrastructure is put in place and does not technically allow for deviations in the system's use. As noted above, data can also be collected on teachers (for instance, to evaluate their teaching abilities (as in O'Neil 2017)) – which, in light of the specific employer–employee relationship, can raise the same question of power imbalance and validity of consent.

Assuming that a valid legal basis for the collection of personal data exists, developers and deployers of AIED must protect such data throughout the lifecycle of the system. Moreover, this protection should also extend to all the inferred data, or the output generated by the system based on the initially collected data. It can be noted that not all AI-systems necessarily rely on personal data to operate. However, systems that do not process personal data can potentially have a (negative) impact on individuals and groups – an example thereof being an application that helps correct anonymized exams but fails to do so accurately, and thus erroneously fails a student. Accordingly, even with AIED applications where no or only little personal data is processed, their impact on the private lives of those involved must be assessed.

The protection of privacy and personal data is not only an ethical but also a legal requirement which is now well established in the educational realm. However, ensuring the ethical handling of data covers more than merely meeting legal standards. Trustworthy AIED also requires that mechanisms for good data governance are established. The quality of the datasets used must be assessed and held to high standards (Hasselbalch 2019). Any AI-system will, after all, only be as good as the data it is fed. Therefore, prior to training an AIED application, developers must take measures to eliminate, as far as possible, inaccuracies as well as unjust biases from the datasets they use. Securing data integrity throughout the system's lifecycle is essential as the inclusion of erroneous data in the system can change its behaviour in a damaging way. Sound data governance also requires protocols to govern data access, outlining who can access information and under what conditions. While AIED developers have the primary task of testing and documenting the steps taken to secure privacy and good data governance, as already stressed above, organizations deploying AIED have an equally important responsibility to ensure that the applications they purchase meet these requirements.

Transparency

To secure Trustworthy AIED, the various elements constituting the AI-application need to be made transparent, including the type of data, the system's model, and the business model for which it is used. Transparency hence functions not just as an ethical value in itself, but rather as a meta-value that sheds light on whether and how all other requirements for Trustworthy AI are respected. In its Guidelines, the HLEG on AI lists three sub-requirements that need to be fulfilled in order to enable this meta-value: traceability, explainability, and communication.

Traceability pertains to rendering visible the traces of how a particular decision taken by an AI-system was reached. This requires the availability of documentation that logs what data was gathered and under what conditions (during the training, testing, and use phase of the application); the choices made for data labelling and categorization; selection of the algorithm; and the criteria or variables selected for the algorithm's optimization. The decisions made by the AI-system (and how these decisions might change under different conditions – for instance in case of slightly different datasets or models) should also be documented, as this not only increases transparency but also allows us to determine why a specific decision was erroneous and how such errors can be prevented in the future. While documenting these elements might sound resource-intensive, various (technological) tools can be used to facilitate this task. Moreover, documenting these elements not only forces developers of AIED to be explicit about the design choices they make, and hence to rationally reflect thereupon, but it also enables the auditability of the system by third parties (for instance independent auditors or government agencies). Of course, private companies that develop AI-systems are entitled to intellectual property rights and to protect potential trade secrets associated with their systems. However, traceability requirements need not hinder those rights and can coexist therewith.

Especially when the system is used by public entities and has the ability to affect the interests of a large number of students or teachers, documentation that enables the auditability of a system should be provided not only *ex post* (after the system has been implemented) but also *ex ante* (prior to the system's use). The example of the algorithm used by the UK's Office of Qualifications and Examinations Regulation (Ofqual) during the COVID-19 pandemic to predict students' A-level grades in the absence of traditional exams illustrates this (Afifi-Sabet 2020; Bedingfield 2020). If Ofqual had made information about the algorithm and its intended purpose publicly available prior to its implementation, stakeholders and independent experts would have been able to assess the algorithm's robustness and its intended scope of application. On that basis, they would have been able to suggest adaptations to the model or to the manner in which Ofqual envisaged deploying it. In turn, this would have enabled both sounder and more legitimized policymaking. While this reasoning especially holds true when the system is applied to a country's entire student population, it also holds true for AI-systems that are used at a smaller scale and are able to significantly affect the interests of only a few (Han 2020).

Enabling an AI-system's traceability also helps to fulfil the requirement of explainability. Explainability demands not the documentation but the explanation of the (technical) processes of an AI-system. This also includes explanation of the human decisions relating to the system, such as in which modality the system is used within the organization, the rationale for the design choices made, and in which area of application it is used. For AI-systems used in learning platforms, an explanation should for instance be given as to why one specific learning trajectory was recommended rather than another; or, in the context of AI-enabled grading, it should be explained based on which criteria a specific grade was attributed to a student. Whenever the use of an AI-system can have a significant impact on a person's life, such explanation should always be given proactively, allowing the person to understand how the impacting decision came about. This explanation needs to be provided in language adapted to the knowledge of the person concerned. In other words, this explanation will not be the same when given to a child, an adult student or parent, or an expert. Without such explanation, the individual concerned will not be able to challenge the decision, and will also not be able to seek correction or redress if it is erroneous or biased.

Lastly, the requirement of transparency necessitates appropriate communication by developers and deployers of AI-systems. This means that, first of all, those interacting with – or subject to – the AI-system need to be aware that they are not interacting with a human being. Such misunderstanding can particularly occur in the context of chatbots that can be used to communicate with students. The option not to interact with an AI-system but instead to rely on a human interlocutor should also be considered, hence enabling a right to opt out. In addition, the capabilities and limitations of the AIED applications should be communicated both to the deployers of the AI-system (e.g. the school that acquires the application) and to the users of the system (e.g. the teachers and students interacting therewith). Such communication should occur in a manner that is adapted to the intended audience. For this purpose, a mapping exercise should be undertaken of the various stakeholders involved with the AIED application in question – covering schools, teachers, students, parents, and others – and their various needs for information about the system's functioning within its overall environment. Adequate communication is particularly important to avoid over-expectations about the system's capabilities.

Diversity, non-discrimination and fairness

Bias – the inclination of prejudice towards or against a person, group, object, or position – is an inherent part of society and of how human beings operate (Steinbock 1978; Banaji et al. 1993; Begby 2013). As subjective individuals, we are unable to grasp anything we encounter in a purely objective manner, but always do so through the filter of our personal knowledge and experience – which in turn constitutes a reflection of our upbringing, education, cultural exposure, personality, and numerous other traits. In this broad sense, bias is not necessarily bad. Yet, under certain conditions, bias can be unfair or lead to discrimination. AI-systems are developed by human beings, and fed data collected and shaped by human beings. It is hence no surprise that their decisions also reflect the individual and societal biases of their creators and users – for better or worse (Silberg and Manyika 2019; Ntoutsi et al. 2020). It is thus crucial to address this risk, even if unjust bias in machines is not always easily perceptible – in particular if it slips in through proxies rather than through legally protected criteria such as gender, age or, ethnicity (Benjamin 2019; Crawford et al. 2019).

Unfair bias can manifest itself in numerous ways in AIED. Often, biased predictions or decisions are the result of a biased dataset on which the algorithm is trained. Consider in this context the use of AI-based speech recognition systems to evaluate a student's (language) skills or knowledge. If these systems are trained on a dataset that contains primarily male and accent-less voice recordings, they will not be suitable to analyse the voices of a wide range of users, and will be negatively biased against women, migrants with accents, or people with speech disabilities (Johar 2016; Guo et al. 2019; Koenecke et al. 2020). Similarly, facial recognition technology is often predominantly trained on images of white males, and is therefore less accurate as regards faces of women or people of colour (Crawford et al. 2019). Hence, if an educational institution for instance resorts to exam proctoring based on a biased facial recognition system, certain students will be unfairly disadvantaged. This is precisely what happened when such a proctoring application was used during the pandemic and students of colour saw themselves forced to project a white light on to their faces during an exam so as to ensure the application would continue to recognize them (Johnson 2020; ACLU 2020).

Bias can also emanate from a biased algorithmic model, or it can arise because a system is trained in a given context but thereafter used in a context that was not initially foreseen. It can also emerge at a later stage, during the system's use phase for instance, if the system learns from and adapts itself to biased interactions with users. Finally, the AI-system can also be deployed in a discriminating fashion. This can be illustrated by revisiting the previously raised example of Ofqual's A-level algorithm. Ofqual's choice to only use the algorithm for schools with larger classes posed an unfair disadvantage for students in larger – often public (state) rather than private (independent) – schools (Bedingfield 2020).

Problematically, the unfair biases set out above are often difficult to detect due to their unintentionality, and due to the non-transparency of the algorithmic decision-making process and of the human decisions relating to the algorithm's use. Moreover, these biased systems tend to exacerbate existing inequalities by disproportionately affecting those who are already disadvantaged. To counteract these risks, oversight processes should be put in place from the system's design phase onwards. Efforts are already starting to be made towards this within the AIED community – as for instance described in Chapter 6 (Holstein and Doroudi), Chapter 7 (Kizilcec and Lee), and Chapter 10 (Howley, Mir and Peck) of this book. A clear analysis of the system's purpose, operational sphere, constraints and requirements should be made, as well as an assessment of the instances in which unfair bias can emerge – for instance data collection or selection, codification of rules, development of the algorithmic model or the deployment by (end)users. Diversity in the teams that design and train AI-systems – not only in terms of culture and gender but also in terms of disciplines and areas of expertise – can help limit these risks as it fosters a range of perspectives that can be embedded in the system.

In addition, AIED developers must ensure sufficient attention to user-centricity, allowing users from diverse backgrounds and with diverse traits and abilities to have access to the AI-application without being disadvantaged thereby. The standards for *universal design* as set out by the United Nations Convention on the Rights of Persons with Disabilities can be a guiding framework in this regard, so that the widest possible range of users can benefit from the technology – hence truly democratizing education (United Nations 2006). Finally, the Guidelines also suggest the organization of stakeholder consultations, so that those directly or indirectly affected by the AI-system can contribute to (the decisions on) its design and use. The solicitation of feedback from those involved – whether schools, teachers, students, or parents – is beneficial not only to detect potential errors or bias in the system but also to further improve the utility as well as the user-friendliness of the application. While both are important contributors to the system's quality, utility is determined by the system's usefulness in light of its purpose, whereas user-friendliness focuses on how easy it is to understand the system and learn how to use it to interact with the system's interface, how practical the system is, and whether it can ensure a certain level of user satisfaction.

Societal and environmental wellbeing

Besides assessing the immediate impact of AI-applications in the area of education, an assessment should ideally also be made of the wider effects that the development and use of such applications can have.

An indirect but critical effect of the use of AI in an educational context concerns the social impact on students, for instance in light of their interaction with machines rather than human beings. Depending on the specific purpose of the system and the role it plays in the classroom, AIED might change students' conception of social agency, alter the social relationship between student and teacher (which typically goes far beyond a mere pedagogical role), as well as impacting students' sense of engagement. Only little research has been conducted on the long-term effects of increased or ubiquitous machine interaction in learning environments and the impact on students' social skills and mental wellbeing. In addition, the use of AI-enabled cameras or monitoring systems might also lead to a chilling effect as students (but also teachers) might feel observed, potentially leading to changes in their behaviour and hampering their ability to act authentically. The severity of this risk is directly related to the invasiveness of the AI-application in the student's curriculum, and hence strongly case-dependent. However, as already mentioned above, both in explicit and implicit ways, AI-applications can change not only how we behave but also how we think, and the social consequences thereof need better mapping.

In addition, while some are cautioning about the potential emergence of intellectual laziness (for instance due to constant interaction with machines that are 'superior' in knowledge), others have raised concerns about how the limitations of these systems shape our learning environments and needs, rather than the other way around (Yujie 2019). The data that can be collected on students' reports, grades and progress to feed AI-systems are most useful to track and assess abilities and skills that can be measured by numbers and performance metrics. The more standardized these metrics are – and the tests and surveys that aim to assess them – the easier for the system to compare and analyse. There is thus a risk that – as the usefulness of AI-systems is strongest when measuring capabilities in a standardized way – schools will reinforce the use of standardized tests to further enhance the systems' usefulness. However, skills that are easily measurable are also precisely the skills that will be increasingly automated (Bulger 2016). While this does not automatically render these skills less valuable, it does provide an additional reason to ensure they are not the sole focus of student curricula. It is hence crucial that sufficient attention is also given to the development of other capacities that are less easily tracked and measured, including soft skills such as teamwork abilities, communication proficiency, empathy, and emotional intelligence, as well as critical and creative thinking – even if AIED may not be the best tool to foster this.

A comprehensive impact assessment of the use of AI-systems in education also entails an examination of the resources they use throughout their lifecycle and their impact on the environment. Many AI-applications require the processing and storing of huge amounts of data, which turns them into notorious energy consumers and undermines their sustainability (Schwartz et al. 2019; Strubell et al. 2019; Hao 2019). While AI can be used to help foster the UN's Sustainable Development Goals (Vinuesa et al. 2020) – including quality education – in order to be truly sustainable, its impact on the planet and on future generations must be borne in mind. Therefore, regardless of whether an AI-system is used in the education sector or in another domain, its environmental footprint – and that of its entire value chain – should be minimized.

Finally, AI's impact on society and democracy can also be considered more broadly. Scandals like Cambridge Analytica have already demonstrated how AI can be used to influence the democratic decision-making process by influencing what type of content people see, thereby shaping their thoughts and emotions in very subtle and almost imperceptible ways (Stark 2018; Isaak and Hanna 2018; Brkan 2019). It is, however, underexplored what a similar use of AI could mean in education, where the task is essentially to shape the democratic citizens and voters of tomorrow. As noted above, while the use of education as a weapon to shield totalitarian and repressive regimes from criticism is not new, AI-enabled educational infrastructure facilitates this risk, not only in terms of scale and timing but also in terms of subtleness, thus limiting awareness of the problematic manipulation. It was already stressed that bias is an inherent aspect of human society. Therefore, every educational intervention – whether it concerns an account of history, geography, literature, language, art, economy, or biology – will reflect a certain bias by the teacher, whether human or machine. In liberal democracies this bias will in principle be coloured by values such as political, religious, and scientific freedom, human dignity and equality, respect for human rights, and, more generally, the stimulation of critical thinking. In authoritarian regimes this bias may reflect values that better sustain the regime's power continuity. It is, therefore, important that developers and deployers of AIED acknowledge this responsibility and strive to ensure that educational applications – not only in terms of their content but also in terms of their teaching method – reflect a bias towards the values of democracy, human rights, and the rule of law.

Accountability

The final requirement for Trustworthy AI – accountability – can be seen as a reiteration of all the requirements above, coupled with a demand for guarantees that these are not only proclaimed but also implemented. It entails the need for human beings to take responsibility for the outcomes and consequences of the AI-systems they develop and deploy, during the systems' entire lifecycle, and that they can be held accountable when adverse impacts ensue. An important aspect to enable accountability is the AIED system's auditability. A system is auditable when its design process, algorithms, and data can be assessed and evaluated, not only by internal auditors but also by external auditors or other third parties. Given the importance of the role of education in society, independent oversight of the auditing process – for instance through public entities or approved third-party auditors – is not an unnecessary luxury.

The outcomes of these audits could subsequently be made public to enhance the trustworthiness both of the system and of the processes surrounding it, including the human decisions regarding its use. These evaluation reports can also indicate the (effectiveness of) measures taken to minimize unfair bias, to safeguard the system's technical robustness and safety, to render the decision-making processes more transparent, and to ensure adequate human oversight. Closely linked to this requirement is the assessment and reporting of potential negative impacts of the AIED application, and the measures taken to address these. Such assessment needs to be tailored to the educational context in which the AI-system is used, to the type of users (students, teachers, others), and must stand in proportion to the risks posed. Moreover, if the AIED system is actually deployed, the assessment needs to be carried out periodically so as to allow continual evaluation. Indeed, accountability should be seen as a process rather than a set state (Porayska-Pomsta and Rajendran 2019).

An element that often lacks sufficient attention when ensuring accountability for AIED concerns the importance of a protective framework for those who report on adverse impacts thereof – be it an unfair bias, a safety issue, an unfounded claim of effectiveness, or another deficiency – in situations where such reporting could go against the interests of the school or of other stakeholders, or more generally raise difficulties. Whistle-blowers have already played a crucial role in shedding light on some of the problematic uses of AI in other contexts, and thereby contributed to rendering the developers and deployers of AI more accountable (Crawford et al. 2019). In the context of education, it is important that students, teachers, parents, employees of AIED-developing companies, and other actors feel comfortable to report their concerns on an application's potential negative impacts without fear of potential repercussions, in whatever form.

Ensuring accountability for AIED also entails acknowledgement that tensions may arise between the above-mentioned requirements. These requirements can be implemented in multiple ways, and will in some situations necessitate balancing acts and trade-offs. It is important that these trade-offs are not only acknowledged and documented but also assessed in a rational and methodological manner, examining the various interests involved as well as the consequences of the design and implementation choices for those interests. In this manner, the accountability of the entity making the trade-off can be ensured. When no ethically acceptable trade-off exists, the AIED application should not be developed or used in that form; it either necessitates an overhaul of its design and purpose or consideration of alternative tools to reach the aspired goals. Finally, it is crucial that, whenever the development or use of AIED leads to an unjust harm – whether to students, teachers, or any other stakeholder – redress can easily be sought. Those responsible, for instance the educational institution deploying AIED, should clearly communicate about the availability of redress mechanisms.

Additional considerations for a Trustworthy AIED assessment

In addition to the seven requirements set out above, some further considerations are listed below for developers and deployers of AIED applications to keep in mind in the context of a contextual Trustworthy AIED assessment.

First, while the *Ethics Guidelines for Trustworthy AI* do not explicitly contain a 'requirement zero', it has been argued that such a requirement should nevertheless be considered when contemplating the use of AI-systems in sensitive contexts (Muller 2020). Prior to implementing an educational AI-application, and especially when this application can have an impact on students' or teachers' lives, it is worth asking whether the problem that needs to be solved, or the task that requires a more effective execution, actually necessitates an AI-based solution. In some instances, it may be more beneficial to instead keep relying on human intervention only, or to rely on other (technological) tools that provide adequate results.

This consideration can, firstly, be made from an ethical *risk-benefit* perspective. Even when the AI-application as such can be used legally, ethically and robustly, it should still be considered whether any potential negative impact the application might have is proportionate to the increase in benefits. Second, this consideration can also be made from an economic *cost-benefit* approach. In certain situations, developing an AI-system that accurately performs a task might be very costly due to the difficulty of gathering the necessary data or due to the significance of the amount of data that needs to be gathered and curated – which may not weigh up against the benefits the system could provide as compared to other tools. Although drawn from a different sector, the example of Correctional Offender Management Profiling for Alternative Sanctions (COMPAS) – a predictive AI-system assessing the likelihood of recidivism based on the analysis of 137 information points about an individual – can serve as an illustration. Besides struggling with issues of bias, studies showed that a similar predictive accuracy could be achieved by using only seven information points instead of 137, and by relying either on a simple linear predictor or even on (non-expert) human beings (Dressel and Farid 2018).

This example is also relevant when designing an AIED application that, for instance, is meant to evaluate certain features of students or teachers. If the job can be done just as well with a much simpler algorithm or with far less (personal) data – and less risk – an alternative should be considered. In other words, just because an AIED application can be built does not mean it also should be built. Furthermore, there are tasks for which no AI model is easily developed, for instance due to a lack of appropriate metrics base on which a model can be created. AI is not a solution to every problem. For differing reasons, other tools can sometimes be more suited to fulfil a given task. This also raises the need to appraise the effectiveness and added value of a given AIED application more generally, which – just like for other EdTech solutions – is not always easy to do (Livingstone 2012; Selwyn 2013). Importantly, when prospective deployers of AIED applications assess costs, benefits, and alternative options, they should rely not only on the expertise of the company developing or selling the AIED but on other expert opinions too.

Second, AIED applications can be based on different AI-techniques. There is no such thing as 'one' AI, and applications based on deep learning will present different risks from applications based on rule-based AI. In the same vein, not all uses of AI within the educational sector raise the same types of issue. More vigilance will be needed for AIED applications that directly interact with or have an impact on students or teachers, as opposed to applications that merely help reduce administrative backlogs or optimize logistical aspects in a school's organization. It also matters whether AI is used in public education – where no easy opt-out may be available – or in voluntary educational programmes. In sum, the various situations in which AIED is used should be differentiated from each other so that a case-by-case assessment can be made of the measures needed to safeguard the requirements for Trustworthy AI.

Third, no uniform definition of AI exists, which may further complicate matters for those involved (Buiten 2019). The current hype around AI – and the investments focused thereon – has even led some companies to falsely claim the use of AI, in the hope that this would attract new funds (Kelnar 2019). Another definitional complication is that the boundaries of applications considered as 'intelligent' are continually changing in view of the so-called AI effect (McCorduck 2004). This definitional question should however not stand in the way of securing a proper assessment of the ethical issues that an AIED application might raise. All the requirements for Trustworthy AI can be equally applicable to automated decision-making systems that may not uniformly be considered as 'AI'. Rather than fixating on AI definitions, thorough mapping should be made of the potential risks posed by the specific application and of how these risks can be mitigated – regardless of whether it concerns a simple, advanced, or professed AI-system.

Finally, such a risk assessment should be contextual and – for each risk identified – take into account factors such as the extent, likelihood, ubiquity, and reversibility thereof. A contextual risk assessment also requires attention to the level of maturity of the individuals involved. Indeed, children have different levels of comprehension, which is a relevant factor when assessing the manner in which requirements such as transparency, explainability, or human agency should be implemented in AIED applications. In this regard, inspiration can also be drawn from the ample literature that already exists on the impact of technology and the internet more generally on children. Important research on this has, for instance, been carried out from a sociological and educational perspective (for example, Livingstone 2011; Kardefelt-Winther 2017; Livingstone et al. 2012), which can be a basis for further reflection in the context of AIED-specific assessments.

Pathways to secure Trustworthy AIED

Despite the slow start, the debate on ethical AI is finally reaching the educational domain. This was (at least in part) spurred by the COVID-19 pandemic, which led to a fast-paced adoption of digital and AI-based educational solutions across the world – albeit not always in a manner that aligned with ethical values. Indeed, the deployment of certain AIED applications sparked public outrage precisely because adequate assessment and mitigation of ethical risks was lacking. The increased attention on ethical AIED is a welcome development. It not only enriches the public debate, but also enhances the awareness of those directly involved that AIED can come with certain risks for which responsibility needs to be taken. It also sends a signal to regulators that some of these risks may require regulatory responses that go beyond non-binding guidance.

In the sections above, an overview was provided of the seven requirements for Trustworthy AI and the specific challenges faced by the educational sector to ensure their implementation. While the Guidelines – and, in particular, the assessment list that helps operationalize the seven requirements – can provide a useful tool for AIED developers and deployers, the question however remains: are horizontal guidelines sufficient? Even if they are duly implemented in a manner that is tailored to the educational realm, does a voluntary approach to comply with these requirements suffice? If not, what is the way forward to ensure that the ethical risks raised by AIED are adequately tackled, and that those involved can be held accountable when this does not occur? An appropriate balance should be found between, on the one hand, taking courage from the fact that organizations are increasingly aware of AI's ethical issues and are starting to take measures to mitigate them and, on the other hand, being naive in thinking that commercial interests are fully aligned with the interests of those who can be negatively impacted. Besides disseminating and encouraging adherence to non-binding guidance, a number of alternative and complementary pathways are open to policymakers who – given the extent of some of the risks posed by AIED – have a responsibility to ensure their careful consideration.

Awareness and education

To start with, they should acknowledge that the increasing ubiquity of AI necessitates broader awareness and understanding of this technology by society at large. Education can not only be an application domain for AI-systems; it can – and should – also be used as an enabler to foster knowledge on this technology and ensure that the benefits, challenges, and limitations thereof are duly explained. It is especially important to stimulate awareness of ethical risks (and responsibility for these risks) in computer science courses and other curricular areas through which future AI developers are trained, as stressed in Chapter 10 of this volume. However, such awareness-raising should also go beyond this setting.

Digital literacy classes can serve this aim more broadly, and should thus not be restricted to the development of ICT skills. Rather, they should also encompass education on digital rights (such as privacy and data protection, as well as freedom of speech and thought), digital communication, digital safety and security, digital identity, and other capabilities that are needed for a holistic picture of AI-systems. For this purpose, work is also needed to educate the educators, and ensure that teachers are able to address these topics with their students in a critical manner. At the very least, the use of AIED in classes should be coupled with lessons on how AI works and in which ways it is limited. While an updated curriculum is not the panacea to counter the ethical risks raised by AIED, it is both useful and essential.

Thorough reflection on the role of commercial actors

Second, policymakers should carefully reflect upon the role of commercial actors in the educational sphere. This debate is not new, as many EdTech solutions – including those using AI techniques – are developed by private companies, and are hence at least partially guided by commercial interests. Those companies – and the beneficial AIED innovations they may generate – can make important contributions to the quality and availability of education. At the same time, national governments and educational institutions alike depend on these private actors when seeking to procure or deploy AIED.

Given the ethical challenges set out above, and the impact that some of these applications can have both on the educational process and on people's lives and minds, it should be ensured that the commercial nature of AIED applications does not interfere with the rights and interests of those involved, but rather empowers them. To this end, policymakers adopting strategies on technology and education should foster a broader reflection on how this can be ensured (Selwyn 2016). As noted above, such reflection should go beyond considerations of cybersecurity and data protection – to which the UK's strategy, for instance, currently seems limited (UK Department for Education 2019).

Appropriate regulatory oversight, mindful of power and information asymmetries

Third, for certain AIED applications, more far-reaching measures may be needed. For instance, the invasiveness of applications that entail the physical or mental tracking of students through biometric recognition techniques renders them an important candidate for mandatory regulatory oversight. AI-applications that run on such data – including emotional tracking, behavioural identification, affect recognition, voice and tone recognition, facial recognition, and the analysis of micro-expressions – constitute significant intrusions of individuals' privacy (McStay 2020). Not only are many of the applications that gather such data unable to deliver their promised benefits, but they are also prone to erroneous judgements and bias, which can negatively impact those who are subjected thereto. Also for other AIED applications that can have an impact on the rights of students or teachers – such as the right to non-discrimination – enhanced oversight may be warranted.

As noted above, a number of regulators are currently considering the adoption of new regulation for AI-applications. Given the prominence of power asymmetries in the educational realm, and given the prevalent involvement of vulnerable individuals, it is important that regulators acknowledge the educational sector as meriting heightened scrutiny. While many AIED applications can undoubtedly benefit the stakeholders involved, and not all such applications raise the same level of risks, for all the reasons set out above, new legal requirements that may apply to 'high-risk' AI-systems under upcoming legislative proposals should also apply to high-risk AI-systems in the education sector. The European Commission's proposed AI Act forms a good basis to do so, but still leaves much scope for improvement (Smuha et al. 2021).

Across the globe, including in Europe, many schools are still facing difficulties securing basic educational IT infrastructure such as an internet connection and properly functioning soft- and hardware. Among and within countries, strong inequalities exist between the level of education that students enjoy and the digital literacy they are taught. While AIED promises to make education more broadly accessible, and hence can help reduce these inequalities (see Chapter 7), it can just as well exacerbate them and widen the digital literacy gap. At the same time, data is increasingly used as a currency, traded off against services claiming to be free. There is hence a danger that schools unable to afford AIED applications will instead be encouraged to use the currency of (their students') data as a commodity in exchange for the technology's promised benefits – without any mapping of the potential adverse impacts, without ethical safeguards, and without any sound evidence that the claimed benefits are worth the risks. In this context, consent must be treated with extreme care when used as a legal basis for processing (sensitive) data, and additional safeguards will be needed to ensure respect not only for privacy but also for all the other requirements of Trustworthy AI.

Such safeguards can, for instance, consist of mandatory documentation obligations for certain AIED applications. Besides enhancing the traceability – and hence auditability – of these applications, such documentation could also describe the methodology that was used to secure a system's technical robustness, explain the design choices made, and describe the implemented testing and verification procedures to tackle unfair bias and other risks. Public authorities – and relevant independent third parties such as non-governmental organizations (NGOs) – should be able to audit these systems to assess whether they match their documentation and whether they abide by applicable laws. In addition, when AIED applications are acquired through tender procedures or public procurement processes, governments should demand a comprehensive assessment of the system's ethical impact. Finally, it is essential that attention is given not only to the individual and collective harms that may arise from the use of AIED, but also to the societal harms (Smuha 2021), especially in light of education's role in society.

Specific guidance and compliance mechanisms for the educational domain

Complementary to the above pathways, the development of tailored guidelines for the use of AI in education would not be a luxury given the specific ethical issues raised by AIED. Furthermore, besides more tailored guidelines and legal safeguards, the development of certification procedures specifically for AIED can also be of help as it provides AIED developers with a tool to not only claim but also to demonstrate compliance. It should, however, be stressed that any regulation, domain-specific guidelines, and certification mechanisms should be developed in a multi-stakeholder and multidisciplinary setting (see Chapter 6), bringing together AIED developers and data scientists, pedagogists, teachers, ethicists, psychologists, and other experts, but ideally also students or student representatives.

Given that research on the impact of AI's mid- and longer-term consequences is lacking, a risk-based approach is warranted that duly takes into consideration the essential role of education in our society, as well as in the lives of the 2 billion children around the world. If, for every euro of research into the development and analysis of the potential benefits of AIED a euro could also be spent on research into its ethical risks and the measures that can help address these, the goal of attaining Trustworthy AIED will come a little closer.

Conclusions

Artificial Intelligence is altering all domains of our lives, from the way we communicate and work to the way we behave and think. Like virtually all technologies, it can be used for beneficial purposes, it can be used for harmful purposes, and it can be used in ways that cause harm in entirely unintentional ways. The extent of this harm is strongly dependent on the application in question and the context in which it is used, as well as on those directly or indirectly involved. The question should hence be: who does the claimed beneficial purpose of AI-systems serve, and who might be impacted in potentially harmful ways? While AI-applications and EdTech more broadly have the potential to foster higher-quality education across the globe, they can also exacerbate existing inequalities and discrimination, widen the digital literacy gap, infringe on individuals' privacy, inadvertently influence or manipulate their users, and pose other significant risks in a democratic society. The particular role of education in our societies also raises a number of domain-specific sensitivities for the development and use of AI in the educational context. This particular role, and the opportunities and risks it entails, is exemplified in quotes by two notorious historical figures – one of them is considered as one of the most morally reprehensible individuals of the last century, and the other as one of the most morally valued:

Whoever has the youth has the future – Adolf Hitler

Education is the most powerful weapon which you can use to change the world – Nelson Mandela

Both recognized the importance of education as a tool to shape society, and both strove to embed their ideals in the educational systems of their respective jurisdictions. It is a collective responsibility to safeguard the ideals of a liberal and democratic society and to make sure that AI used in the domain of education reflects these ideals, both as regards the educational content it provides and the manner in which it operates. Notwithstanding sensational media reporting about the subject, AI is not something that suddenly overcomes us. While undoubtedly being a powerful technology, it remains up to human beings to decide how and for what purposes it is developed, when and where it can be deployed, and under which conditions and safeguards it should be used. This responsibility is particularly important when those involved do not (yet) have a strong voice of their own, either because of their young age or because of their more vulnerable position in society (Porayska-Pomsta and Rajendran 2019).

While it is necessary to distinguish between the different applications of AIED – which certainly do not all present the same type and extent of risk – a public debate needs to be held, in an informed manner and with the involvement of all relevant stakeholders, to collectively decide how we wish to deal with these risks. Forgoing such a debate risks leading us to one of two undesired paths: a lack of trust in the technology, leading to a technological backlash and missing out on the benefits that Trustworthy AIED can bring; or the proliferation of untrustworthy AIED applications that fail to take into account the risks they pose and can lead to irreparable harm.

Adherence to ethical guidelines such as those drafted by the European Commission High-Level Expert Group on AI is a necessary step to secure the goal of Trustworthy AIED, but a first step only. These guidelines can help stimulate reflection on the choices made throughout AIED's lifecycle, and stress the non-negligible fact that these choices have ethical consequences. However, they are voluntary, the overview of ethical issues they provide is non-exhaustive, and they still need to be tailored to the educational context and to the specific AI-application that is envisaged. Moreover, the invasiveness of certain AIED applications renders even the development of education-specific ethics guidelines an insufficient safeguard. Instead, high-risk AIED-applications should be able to demonstrate their legal, ethical, and robust nature. For these applications, policies should therefore be established to secure mandatory safeguards, be that through documentation obligations, auditability requirements, or the creation of sectorial certification mechanisms – or a combination of all.

Ultimately, however noteworthy the benefits of AIED might be, they will not be able to fulfil the purpose of enhancing learners' capabilities without taking into account not only their educational but also their moral, mental, and physical wellbeing. The various effects of the use of AI in the educational context – in particular when minors are involved – are still not fully mapped. Accordingly, further research on this subject should be fostered, as well as the mapping of appropriate technical and non-technical tools to help address any negative effects. At the same time, the increased attention on ethical AI in the educational sector allows for cautious optimism. Out of the increasingly loud calls for ethical AI, a path towards building Trustworthy AIED is slowly emerging. To truly reap the benefits thereof – not only in the short but also in the longer term – all stakeholders have a responsibility to ensure it stays on track.

Acknowledgements

The author is grateful for the helpful feedback she received from Gry Hasselbalch on an early draft of this chapter. The author's research is funded by the FWO (Research Foundation - Flanders).

Notes

1 It can be pointed out that striving for 'trust' in the context of AI has been deemed controversial, given that trust is an inter-human emotion that cannot be granted to machines (Tschopp 2020; Bryson 2020), and given that the concept of trust entails a delegation of control without any supervision – which is undue in the context of AI. It has also been argued that trust cannot be based on purely voluntary requirements. These interpretations, however, do not correspond to the meaning of Trustworthy AI as put forward by the Guidelines. Rather, it concerns an overarching concept denoting a number of requirements that should be fulfilled by human beings when designing, developing, and using AI. The term is hence less important than the requirements it embodies. Moreover, AI systems do not exist independently, but are part of a broader socio-technical environment. Ensuring their trustworthiness hence requires a systemic approach, focusing on the trustworthiness of all actors and processes involved (High-Level Expert Group on AI 2019; Ala-Pietilä and Smuha 2021).
2 The assessment list of the High-Level Expert Group was revised after a feedback gathering process. Its revised version was published in July 2020, and is accessible at: https://ec.europa.eu/digital-single-market/en/news/assessment-list-trustworthy-artificial-intelligence-altai-self-assessment.
3 https://www.unicef.org/globalinsight/media/1171/file/UNICEF-Global-Insight-policy-guidance-AI-children-draft-1.0-2020.pdf.

References

ACLU. 2020. 'ACLU Civil Rights Concerns with Potential Use of Facial Recognition in Proctoring the California Bar Examination', 16 July. www.aclunc.org/sites/default/files/ACLU_Advocacy_Letter_re_Online_Bar_Exam.pdf.

Afifi-Sabet, Keumars. 2020. 'UK Gov's "Unfair" A-Level Algorithm Faces Several Legal Challenges'. *IT Pro*, August 2020.

Aiken, Robert M., and Richard G.Epstein. 2000. 'Ethical Guidelines for AI in Education: Starting a Conversation'. *International Journal of Artificial Intelligence in Education* 11 (January): 163–176.

Ala-Pietilä, Pekka, and Nathalie A. Smuha. 2021. 'A Framework for Global Cooperation on Artificial Intelligence and Its Governance'. In *Reflections of AI for Humanity*, edited by B. Braunschweig and M. Ghallab. Cham: Springer.

Amrein-Beardsley, Audrey. 2014. *Rethinking Value-Added Models in Education: Critical Perspectives on Tests and Assessment-Based Accountability*. New York: Routledge.

Banaji, Mahzarin R, Curtis Hardin, and Alexander JRothman. 1993. 'Implicit Stereotyping in Person Judgment'. *Journal of Personality and Social Psychology* 65 (2): 10.

Barrett, Lisa Feldman, Ralph Adolphs, Stacy Marsella, Aleix M. Martinez, and Seth D. Pollak. 2019. 'Emotional Expressions Reconsidered: Challenges to Inferring Emotion from Human Facial Movements'. *Psychological Science in the Public Interest* 20 (1): 1–68. doi:10.1177/1529100619832930.

Bedingfield, Will. 2020. 'Everything that Went Wrong with the Botched A-Levels Algorithm'. *Wired UK*, 19 August. https://www.wired.co.uk/article/alevel-exam-algorithm.

Begby, Endre. 2013. 'The Epistemology of Prejudice'. *Thought: A Journal of Philosophy* 2 (2): 90–99. doi:10.1002/tht3.71.

Benjamin, Ruha. 2019. *Race after Technology: Abolitionist Tools for the New Jim Code*. Medford, MA: Polity.

Bjørnsten, Thomas Bøgevald, and Mette-Marie Zacher Sørensen. 2017. 'Uncertainties of Facial Emotion Recognition Technologies and the Automation of Emotional Labour'. *Digital Creativity* 28 (4): 297–307. doi:10.1080/14626268.2017.1383271.

Brkan, M. 2019. 'Artificial Intelligence and Democracy'. *Delphi: Interdisciplinary Review of Emerging Technologies* 2 (2): 66–71. doi:10.21552/delphi/2019/2/4.

Bryson, Joanna. 2020. 'It's (Still) Not about Trust: No One Should Buy AI If Governments Won't Prosecute Liability', 23 September. https://joanna-bryson.blogspot.com/2020/09/its-still-not-about-trust-no-one-should.html.

Buiten, Miriam C. 2019. 'Towards Intelligent Regulation of Artificial Intelligence'. *European Journal of Risk Regulation* 10 (1): 41–59. doi:10.1017/err.2019.8.

Bulger, Monica. 2016. 'Personalized Learning: The Conversations We're Not Having'. *Data & Society*, 29 July.

Bulger, Monica, Patrick McCormick, and Mikaela Pitcan. 2017. 'The Legacy of inBloom', *Data & Society*, 2 February.

Buolamwini, Joy, and Timnit Gebru. 2018. 'Gender Shades: Intersectional Accuracy Disparities in Commercial Gender Classification'. *Proceedings of Machine Learning Research*, 81: 1–15. http://proceedings.mlr.press/v81/buolamwini18a/buolamwini18a.pdf.

Coughlan, Sean. 2020. 'Why Did the A-Level Algorithm Say No?' *BBC News*, 14 August. https://www.bbc.com/news/education-53787203.

Council of Europe. 2019. 'Terms of Reference for the Ad Hoc Committee on Artificial Intelligence (CAHAI)'. https://search.coe.int/cm/Pages/result_details.aspx?ObjectId=0900001680972f20.

Council of Europe. 2020. 'Ad Hoc Committee on Artificial Intelligence (CAHAI): Feasibility Study'. https://rm.coe.int/cahai-2020-23-final-eng-feasibility-study-/1680a0c6da.

Crawford, Kate, Roel Dobbe, Theodora Dryer, Genevieve Fried, Ben Green, Elizabeth Kaziunas, Amba Kak *et al.* 2019. *AI Now 2019 Report*. New York: AI Now Institute. https://ainowinstitute.org/AI_Now_2019_Report.pdf.

Dressel, Julia, and Hany Farid. 2018. 'The Accuracy, Fairness, and Limits of Predicting Recidivism'. *Science Advances* 4 (1): eaao5580. https://doi.org/10.1126/sciadv.aao5580.

European Commission. 2018. 'Artificial Intelligence for Europe'. COM (2018) 237 final. https://ec.europa.eu/newsroom/dae/document.cfm?doc_id=51625.

European Commission. 2019. 'Building Trust in Human-Centric Artificial Intelligence'. COM (2019) 168 final. https://ec.europa.eu/newsroom/dae/document.cfm?doc_id=58496.

European Commission. 2020. 'White Paper on Artificial Intelligence: A European Approach to Excellence and Trust'. COM (2020) 65 final.

European Commission. 2021. 'Proposal for a Regulation of the European Parliament and the Council laying down harmonised rules on Artificial Intelligence (Artificial Intelligence Act) and amending certain Union legislative acts'. 2024 COM (2021) 206 final.

Francesc, Pedró, Miguel Subosa, Axel Rivas, and Paula Valverde. 2019. 'Artificial Intelligence in Education: Challenges and Opportunities for Sustainable Development'. UNESCO. https://unesdoc.unesco.org/ark:/48223/pf0000366994.

Gallo, David. 2015. 'La politique de formation idéologique de la SS (1933–1945). Une étude sur la transmission de la normativité nazie'. *Revue historique* 676 (4): 875. doi:10.3917/rhis.154.0875.

Guo, Anhong, Ece Kamar, Jennifer Wortman Vaughan, Hanna Wallach, and Meredith Ringel Morris. 2019. '*Toward Fairness in AI for People with Disabilities: A Research Roadmap*'. ACM ASSETS, 2019 Workshop on AI Fairness for People with Disabilities, 9.

Han, Hye Jung. 2020. 'An Algorithm Shouldn't Decide a Student's Future'. *Politico*, 13 August 2020. https://www.politico.eu/article/an-algorithm-shouldnt-decide-stu dents-future-coronavirus-international-baccalaureate/.

Hanselaer, Sarah. 2019. 'Facial Recognition in School Renders Sweden's First GDPR Fine'. European Data Protection Board. 22 August 2019. https://edpb.europa.eu/ news/national-news/2019/facial-recognition-school-renders-swedens-first-gdpr-fine_en.

Hao, Karen. 2019. 'Training a Single AI Model Can Emit as Much Carbon as Five Cars in their Lifetimes'. *MIT Technology Review* (blog). 6 June 2019. https://www. technologyreview.com/2019/06/06/239031/training-a-single-ai-model-can-emit-a s-much-carbon-as-five-cars-in-their-lifetimes/.

Harwell, Drew. 2019. 'A Face-Scanning Algorithm Increasingly Decides Whether You Deserve the Job'. *Washington Post*, 6 November 2019. https://www.washingtonpost. com/technology/2019/10/22/ai-hiring-face-scanning-algorithm-increasingly-deci des-whether-you-deserve-job/.

Hasselbalch, Gry. 2019. 'Making Sense of Data Ethics: The Powers behind the Data Ethics Debate in European Policymaking'. *Internet Policy Review* 8 (2). doi:10.14763/ 2019.2.1401.

Herold, Benjamin. 2018. 'Ed-Tech Companies Tracking Students' Emotions, Mind-sets: A Push to Use New Technology to Understand the "Whole Child" Is Sparking Privacy Fears'. *Education Week; Bethesda* 37 (36). http://search.proquest.com/doc view/2058514954?rfr_id=info%3Axri%2Fsid%3Aprimo.

Hibbeln, Martin, Jeffrey Jenkins, Christoph Schneider, Joseph Valacich, and Markus Weinmann. 2017. 'How Is Your User Feeling? Inferring Emotion through Human-Computer Interaction Devices'. *MIS Quarterly* 41 (1): 1–21. doi:10.25300/MISQ/ 2017/41.1.01.

High-Level Expert Group on AI. 2019. *Ethics Guidelines for Trustworthy AI*. Brussels: European Commission.

Isaak, Jim, and Mina J. Hanna. 2018. 'User Data Privacy: Facebook, Cambridge Analy-tica, and Privacy Protection'. *Computer* 51 (8): 56–59. doi:10.1109/MC.2018.3191268.

Jobin, Anna, Marcello Ienca, and Effy Vayena. 2019. 'The Global Landscape of AI Ethics Guidelines'. *Nature Machine Intelligence* 1: 389–399.

Johar, Swati. 2016. *Emotion, Affect and Personality in Speech*. Springer Briefs in Electrical and Computer Engineering. Cham: Springer. doi:10.1007/978-3-319-28047-9.

Johnson, Khari. 2020. 'ExamSoft's Remote Bar Exam Sparks Privacy and Facial Recognition Concerns'. *VentureBeat* (blog). 29 September 2020. https://venturebea t.com/2020/09/29/examsofts-remote-bar-exam-sparks-privacy-and-facial-recogni tion-concerns/.

Kardefelt-Winther, Daniel. 2017. 'How Does the Time Children Spend Using Digital Technology Impact their Mental Well-Being, Social Relationships and Physical Activity? An Evidence-Focused Literature Review'. *Innocenti Discussion Papers* 2017/ 02. https://doi.org/10.18356/cfa6bcb1-en.

Kelnar, David. 2019. 'The State of AI 2019: Divergence'. MMC Ventures. https:// www.mmcventures.com/wp-content/uploads/2019/02/The-State-of-AI-2019-Diver gence.pdf.

Koenecke, Allison, Andrew Nam, Emily Lake, Joe Nudell, Minnie Quartey, Zion Mengesha, Connor Toups, John R. Rickford, Dan Jurafsky, and Sharad Goel. 2020. 'Racial Disparities in Automated Speech Recognition'. *Proceedings of the National Academy of Sciences* 117 (14): 7684–7689. doi:10.1073/pnas.1915768117.

Kulkarni, Andrea. 2019. 'AI in Education: Where Is It Now and What Is the Future?' *Lexalytics*. 6 September 2019. https://www.lexalytics.com/lexablog/ai-in-education-present-future-ethics.

Kunzer, Edward J. 1938. 'The Youth of Nazi Germany'. *Journal of Educational Sociology* 11 (6): 342. doi:10.2307/2262246.

Leenes, Ronald, Erica Palmerini, Bert-Jaap Koops, Andrea Bertolini, Pericle Salvini, and Federica Lucivero. 2017. 'Regulatory Challenges of Robotics: Some Guidelines for Addressing Legal and Ethical Issues'. *Law, Innovation and Technology* 9 (1): 1–44. doi:10.1080/17579961.2017.1304921.

Lieberman, Mark. 2018. 'Sentiment Analysis Allows Instructors to Shape Course Content around Students' Emotions'. *Inside Higher Ed*. 20 February 2018. https://www.insidehighered.com/digital-learning/article/2018/02/20/sentiment-analysis-allows-instructors-shape-course-content.

Lin, Patrick, Keith Abney, and George A. Bekey, eds. 2014. *Robot Ethics: The Ethical and Social Implications of Robotics*. Cambridge, MA: MIT Press. https://mitpress.mit.edu/books/robot-ethics.

Livingstone, Sonia. 2011. 'Internet, Children, and Youth'. In *The Handbook of Internet Studies*, edited by Mia Consalvo and Charles Ess, 348–368. Oxford: Wiley-Blackwell. doi:10.1002/9781444314861.ch16.

Livingstone, Sonia. 2012. 'Critical Reflections on the Benefits of ICT in Education'. *Oxford Review of Education* 38 (1): 9–24. doi:10.1080/03054985.2011.577938.

Livingstone, Sonia M., Leslie Haddon, and Anke Görzig, eds. 2012. *Children, Risk and Safety on the Internet: Research and Policy Challenges in Comparative Perspective*. Bristol: Policy Press.

McCorduck, Pamela. 2004. *Machines Who Think*. 2nd ed. Natick, MA: A. K. Peters.

McKinsey. 2018. 'Notes from the AI Frontier: Modeling the Impact of AI on the World Economy'. Discussion Paper. https://www.mckinsey.com/featured-insights/artificial-intelligence/notes-from-the-ai-frontier-modeling-the-impact-of-ai-on-the-world-economy.

McStay, Andrew. 2020. 'Emotional AI and EdTech: Serving the Public Good?' *Learning, Media and Technology* 45 (3): 270–283. doi:10.1080/17439884.2020.1686016.

Mittelstadt, BrentDaniel, PatrickAllo, MariarosariaTaddeo, SandraWachter, and Luciano Floridi. 2016. 'The Ethics of Algorithms: Mapping the Debate'. *Big Data & Society* 3 (2): 205395171667967. doi:10.1177/2053951716679679.

Muller, Catelijne. 2020. 'The Impact of Artificial Intelligence on Human Rights, Democracy and the Rule of Law'. CAHAI (2020)06-fin. Report Prepared in the Context of the Council of Europe's Ad Hoc Committee on AI (CAHAI). Strasbourg: Council of Europe. https://www.coe.int/en/web/artificial-intelligence/cahai.

Ntoutsi, Eirini, Pavlos Fafalios, Ujwal Gadiraju, Vasileios Iosifidis, Wolfgang Nejdl, Maria-Esther Vidal, Salvatore Ruggieri, *et al.* 2020. 'Bias in Data-Driven Artificial Intelligence Systems: An Introductory Survey'. *WIREs Data Mining and Knowledge Discovery* 10 (3): e1356. doi:10.1002/widm.1356.

O'Neil, Cathy. 2017. *Weapons of Math Destruction*. Penguin.

Porayska-Pomsta, Kaśka, and Gnanathusharan Rajendran. 2019. 'Accountability in Human and Artificial Intelligence Decision-Making as the Basis for Diversity and Educational Inclusion'. In *Artificial Intelligence and Inclusive Education: Speculative Futures and Emerging Practices*, edited by Jeremy Knox, Yuchen Wang, and Michael Gallagher, 39–59. Perspectives on Rethinking and Reforming Education. Singapore: Springer. doi:10.1007/978-981-13-8161-4_3.

Prinsloo, Paul, and Sharon Slade. 2016. 'Student Vulnerability, Agency and Learning Analytics: An Exploration'. *Journal of Learning Analytics* 3 (1): 159–182. doi:10.18608/jla.2016.31.10.

Raza, Zainab. 2019. 'China's "Political Re-Education" Camps of Xinjiang's Uyghur Muslims'. *Asian Affairs* 50 (4): 488–501. doi:10.1080/03068374.2019.1672433.

Rouhiainen, Lasse. 2019. 'How AI and Data Could Personalize Higher Education'. *Harvard Business Review*, 14 October 2019. https://hbr.org/2019/10/how-ai-and-data-could-personalize-higher-education.

Schwartz, Roy, Jesse Dodge, Noah A. Smith, and Oren Etzioni. 2019. 'Green AI'. *ArXiv:1907.10597 (Cs, Stat)*, August. http://arxiv.org/abs/1907.10597.

Selwyn, Neil. 2013. *Distrusting Educational Technology: Critical Questions for Changing Times.* New York: Routledge. doi:10.4324/9781315886350.

Selwyn, Neil. 2016. *Is Technology Good for Education?* Cambridge: Polity Press. http://limo.libis.be/primo-explore/fulldisplay/32LIBIS_ALMA_DS71200759640001471/KULeuven.

Silberg, Jake, and James Manyika. 2019. 'Notes from the AI Frontier: Tackling Bias in AI (and in Humans)'. McKinsey Global Institute. https://www.mckinsey.com/~/media/McKinsey/Featured%20Insights/Artificial%20Intelligence/Tackling%20bias%20in%20artificial%20intelligence%20and%20in%20humans/MGI-Tackling-bias-in-AI-June-2019.pdf.

Smuha, Nathalie A. 2019. 'The EU Approach to Ethics Guidelines for Trustworthy Artificial Intelligence'. *Computer Law Review International* 20 (4): 97–106.

Smuha, Nathalie A. 2021. 'Beyond the Individual: Governing AI's Societal Harms'. *Internet Policy Review* 10 (3). doi:10.14763/2021.3.1574.

Smuha, Nathalie A., Emma Ahmed-Rengers, Adam Harkens, Wenlong Li, James MacLaren, Riccardo Piselli, and Karen Yeung. 2021. 'How the EU Can Achieve Legally Trustworthy AI: A Response to the European Commission's Proposal for an Artificial Intelligence Act'. doi:10.2139/ssrn.3899991.

Southgate, Erica, Karen Blackmore, Stephanie Pieschl, Susan Grimes, Jessey McGuire, and Kate Smithers. 2018. *Artificial Intelligence and Emerging Technologies in Schools.* Newcastle, NSW: University of Newcastle, Australia.

Stark, Luke. 2018. 'Algorithmic Psychometrics and the Scalable Subject'. *Social Studies of Science* 48 (2): 204–231. doi:10.1177/0306312718772094.

Steinbock, Bonnie. 1978. 'Speciesism and the Idea of Equality'. *Philosophy* 53 (204): 247–256.

Strubell, Emma, Ananya Ganesh, and Andrew McCallum. 2019. 'Energy and Policy Considerations for Deep Learning in NLP'. *ArXiv:1906.02243 (Cs)*, June. http://arxiv.org/abs/1906.02243.

Tschopp, Marisa. 2020. 'Digital Transformation: Three Wrong Questions about Trust and AI'. *Swiss Post.* 23 September 2020. https://digital-commerce.post.ch/en/pages/blog/2020/trust-in-artificial-intelligence.

Turing, Alan. 1950. 'Computing Machinery and Intelligence'. *Mind* 59 (236): 433–460.

UK Department for Education. 2019. *Realising the Potential of Technology in Education: A Strategy for Education Providers and the Technology Industry.* https://assets.publishing.service.gov.uk/government/uploads/system/uploads/attachment_data/file/791931/DfE-Education_Technology_Strategy.pdf.

UNESCO. 2019. *Beijing Consensus on Artificial Intelligence and Education.* Outcome document of the International Conference on Artificial Intelligence and Education "Planning Education in the AI Era: Lead the Leap"'. Beijing: UNESCO. https://unesdoc.unesco.org/ark:/48223/pf0000368303.

UNICEF. 2020. 'Policy Guidance on AI for Children (Draft)'. https://www.unicef.org/globalinsight/media/1171/file/UNICEF-Global-Insight-policy-guidance-AI-children-draft-1.0-2020.pdf.

United Nations. 2006. *United Nations Convention on the Rights of Persons with Disabilities*. https://treaties.un.org/Pages/ViewDetails.aspx?src=TREATY&mtdsg_no=IV-15&chapter=4&clang=_en.

van de Poel, Ibo, and Peter Kroes. 2014. 'Can Technology Embody Values?' In *The Moral Status of Technical Artefacts*, edited by Peter Kroes and Peter-Paul Verbeek, 103–124. Dordrecht: Springer. doi:10.1007/978-94-007-7914-3_7.

Vincent-Lancrin, Stéphan. 2020. 'Trustworthy Artificial Intelligence (AI) in Education: Promises and Challenges'. OECD Education Working Paper No. 218. doi:10.1787/a6c90fa9-en.

Vinuesa, Ricardo, Hossein Azizpour, Iolanda Leite, Madeline Balaam, Virginia Dignum, SamiDomisch, AnnaFelländer, Simone DanielaLanghans, MaxTegmark, and Francesco Fuso Nerini. 2020. 'The Role of Artificial Intelligence in Achieving the Sustainable Development Goals'. *Nature Communications* 11 (1): 233. doi:10.1038/s41467-019-14108-y.

Webster, Graham, Rogier Creemers, Paul Triolo, and Elsa Kania. 2017. 'Full Translation: China's "New Generation Artificial Intelligence Development Plan (2017)"'. *New America*. http://newamerica.org/cybersecurity-initiative/digichina/blog/full-translation-chinas-new-generation-artificial-intelligence-development-plan-2017/.

White House. 2019. 'Executive Order on Maintaining American Leadership in Artificial Intelligence'. https://www.whitehouse.gov/presidential-actions/executive-order-maintaining-american-leadership-artificial-intelligence/.

Yeung, Karen. 2019. 'Why Worry about Decision-Making by Machine?' In *Algorithmic Regulation*, edited by Karen Yeung and Martin Lodge, 21–48. Oxford University Press. doi:10.1093/oso/9780198838494.003.0002.

Yujie, Xue. 2019. 'Camera above the Classroom'. *Sixth Tone*. 26 March 2019. https://www.sixthtone.com/news/1003759/camera-above-the-classroom.

Zenz, Adrian. 2019. '"Thoroughly Reforming Them towards a Healthy Heart Attitude": China's Political Re-Education Campaign in Xinjiang'. *Central Asian Survey*38 (1): 102–128. doi:10.1080/02634937.2018.1507997.

Part II

Introduction to Part II

Kaśka Porayska-Pomsta and Wayne Holmes

The questions regarding the ethical implications of AI in Education have only recently begun to emerge *within* the AIED community. This is despite AIED having a relatively long history among the AI disciplines, and despite being centrally concerned with interacting with and impacting human thinking and behaviour. In 2000, Aiken and Epstein published their ethical guidelines for AI in Education in a bid to start a conversation about how AI might affect learners and educators, and how it might be situated in the broader context of a future educational system, i.e. by highlighting the need for the community to interrogate the role that AIED may play in fundamentally revolutionising education (Aiken & Epstein, 2000). More than two decades later, although some predictions may require a qualified re-evaluation in light of technological innovations, progress within the AIED field, and our habituated usage of technologies, most of their concerns are strikingly on target (e.g. the guideline: Respect differences in cultural values; avoid "cultural imperialism").

The relevance of Aiken and Epstein's conversation starter is especially apparent given what we now know about AI's role in amplifying and proliferating social inequalities, injustice, and discrimination. However, despite the paper having raised some fundamental questions about AIED's ethical implications, the conversation that Aiken and Epstein had intended to start does not seem to have taken place. The community, it appears, was not ready to appreciate the importance or the urgency of the ethics of AIED until sometime after concerns started to surface in the context of the more recent debates about AI more broadly. As a consequence of this, the work conducted within the AIED community in relation to the ethical challenges and implications, and how these might be addressed within AIED, is only now emerging as a recognised and a critical area within the field (Holmes et al., 2021). As well as defining the identity of the field in the broader ethical AI research landscape, AIED researchers have now begun also to map out the key concerns and challenges for the field by recognising the overlaps with broader ethical AI principles (e.g. Floridi & Cowles, 2019), the aspects that are unique to education as a domain of AI application, and practical approaches to addressing those challenges at the AIED systems' design, engineering, evaluation, and deployment stages.

DOI: 10.4324/9780429329067-8

As AIED is fundamentally a design discipline, identifying the unique role and traits of AI applications in education also involves defining the design requirements for such applications and the technical challenges that relate to building and deploying ethical AIED systems. Through this emergent work, it has become apparent that examining the ethics of AI within the educational domain can shine a sharp light on how the general ethical principles advocated for by researchers and activists operating outside the AIED: (i) may be contextualised and actioned; (ii) what further challenges arise that are specific to how AI may impact human psychology and behaviour; (iii) whether current AIED systems serve all learners equally, and how AIED may need to be conceptualised, designed, evaluated, and deployed to deliver on its promise of inclusivity; (iv) how the AIED pedagogies may need to be reconsidered and audited; and (v) how we might nurture new generations of AI engineers for whom the ethics of AIED ought to be as necessary a component of their practices as the programming languages they use to write the software.

The chapters in Part II provide detailed examinations of the questions set out above by researchers and thinkers from within the AIED community. They represent carefully considered contributions that are based on the authors' in-depth understanding of the field of *AI in Education as a transdisciplinary domain* that integrates theoretical research and practices from education, cognitive and psychological sciences, sociology, AI engineering, technology design, and philosophy. As such AIED is often an uncomfortable scientific space, always residing at the edge of knowledge. As the chapters in Part II reveal, this space cannot be filled simply with descriptive accounts of what is or might go wrong in the context of AI ethics. Instead, akin to civil engineering domains, AIED demands actionable approaches to addressing the existing and potential implications of AI being used in and for education, while being transparent about the inevitable compromises involved.

Part II begins with Chapter 6, where Ken Holstein and Shayan Doroudi provide a detailed examination of the socio-technical landscape within which AIED research and technologies sit and operate. Through adopting the different lenses available within this landscape, they demonstrate the need to consider the questions of how and why AIED systems may carry the risk of amplifying the pre-existing social inequities through the multiple stakeholder perspectives, in order to then develop clear pathways towards more informed and equitable AIED of the future that responds to the needs of front-line, real-world contextual demands. By linking AIED systems and use to human psychology of decision-making, the chapter at once demonstrates the critical importance of considering AI designs from the human-centred perspective, and the need for transdisciplinary methods and thinking in order to nurture AIED that is ethical by design.

In Chapter 7, René Kizilcec and Hansol Lee drill down into concepts of algorithmic fairness – an important subset of the pathways that could lead to inequity in AIED systems considered by Holstein and Doroudi. They provide detailed definitions of fairness, walk-through examples of how fairness may become manifest in concrete AI implementations, and a demonstration of the essential incompatibility of the different vantage points (individual vs group fairness, process vs outcome fairness) on the questions of what is and is not fair in a specific educational context of university admissions. They carefully tease apart the different definitions of fairness to highlight both the inevitable compromises embedded in the AIED designs and applications, and demonstrate why standardised, community-wide auditing practices are essential to safeguarding against AI amplified harms, and how this may be achieved.

Michael Madaio, Su Lin Blodgett, Elijah Mayfield, and Ezekiel Dixon-Román dedicate Chapter 8 to the exploration that extends beyond algorithmic fairness into a detailed discussion of the structural inequities that are encoded in AI in Education research and systems by virtue of the field being bound up and grounded in the historical structural injustice and lack of equity in society at large. By doing so, they put into sharp relief some fundamental questions that the AIED community should be asking in relation to its research and practices, and expose the field's blind spots that compromise AIED's overarching ambitions to support the best education for all. These questions relate to who is served by the AIED systems and research and who tends to be systematically underserved. As part of this, the authors interrogate how the pedagogies chosen might perpetuate injustice and persistent exclusion of certain groups, either because those groups are not represented in AIED research or because the systems that are built can only adapt to learners who are capable of conforming to mainstream modes and dominant cultures of learning. The chapter offers powerful arguments for how the AIED community can and ought to extend its thinking about what is important to learn and how learners should learn, to seize the opportunity to genuinely innovate education and promote inclusion and fairness of outcomes.

In Chapter 9, Ben du Boulay interrogates the ethics of AIED from the perspectives of both professional teacher practices and broader aims and ambitions of the AIED field. The chapter confronts the recent criticisms of the AIED community that relate to the AIED systems potentially violating two central principles underlying the ethics of teaching practices – i.e. the principle of *doing one's best* and the principle of not abusing teachers' position of responsibility and power. Du Boulay provides a detailed examination of what doing one's best means from the perspective of pedagogic best practices, and points to the dilemmas that are inherent to teaching. These dilemmas include practices which in other domains might be considered unethical (e.g. the need to challenge, discomfort, confuse the learners, etc.), but which respond to the long-term aims of nurturing learning. As AIED is largely based on human teaching practices that are pervaded with dilemmas of the short-term discomforts vs the long-terms gains for the learners, du Boulay provides some take-home recommendations for how the related ethical concerns may be mitigated through developing processes for auditing of the AIED pedagogies, teacher training with respect to best practices in the human-AIED blended contexts, and the need for co-design of AIED systems that respond to the needs of their users.

Part II concludes with Chapter 10, which focuses on the need to develop the next generation of AI practitioners and engineers who consider the ethics of AI systems as a necessary and inherent property of the technologies that they develop. While this need has been long advocated by social scientists and philosophers of technology, Iris Howley, Darakhshan Mir, and Evan Peck raise more specific questions of how computer science course curricula can be infiltrated with ethics as a necessary part of the design and engineering practices taught. They also consider what sort of ethics-related skills are expected from AI engineers. The chapter is centred on use-cases from the perspective of educational practitioners who attempt to integrate AI ethics into computer science curricula, from early introduction of the topics to upper-level courses. The use-cases offer a concrete basis for considering both the practices and the challenges of engaging students in a reflection on ethics of AI, and in exploring what it means to build ethical AI that responds to and is mindful of the potential implications for individual users and society.

References

Aiken, R. M. & Epstein, R. G. (2000). Ethical Guidelines for AI in Education: Starting a Conversation, *International Journal of Artificial Intelligence in Education*, 11, pp. 163–176.

Floridi, L. & Cowles, J. (2019). A Unified Framework of Five Principles for AI in Society, *Harvard Data Science Review*, 1(1). doi:10.1162/99608f92.8cd550d1.

Holmes, W., Porayska-Pomsta, K., Holstein, K., Sutherland, E., Baker, T., Shum, S. B., Santos, O. C., Rodrigo, M. T., Cukurova, M., Bittencourt, I. I., & Koedinger, K. R. (2021). Ethics of AI in Education: Towards a Community-Wide Framework. *International Journal of Artificial Intelligence in Education*. doi:10.1007/s40593-021-00239-1.

6 Equity and Artificial Intelligence in education

Kenneth Holstein and Shayan Doroudi

Introduction

With increasing awareness of the societal risks of algorithmic bias and encroaching automation, issues of fairness, accountability, and transparency in data-driven AI systems have received growing academic attention in multiple high-stakes contexts, including healthcare, loan-granting, and hiring (e.g. Barocas & Selbst, 2016; Holstein, Wortman Vaughan, et al., 2019; Veale et al., 2018). While questions of how to design more transparent and accountable systems have received some attention within the academic field of AI in education (e.g. Bull & Kay, 2010; 2016; Conati et al., 2018; Holstein, Wortman Vaughan, et al., 2019; Buckingham Shum, 2018), issues of fairness and equity in educational AI (AIED) systems have received comparatively little attention (Blikstein, 2018; Ferguson, 2019; Holmes, Bialik et al., 2019; Holstein & Doroudi, 2019; Buckingham Shum & Luckin, 2019).

The development of AIED systems has often been motivated by their potential to promote educational equity and reduce achievement gaps across different groups of learners – for example, by scaling up the benefits of one-on-one human tutoring to a broader audience (e.g. Kizilcec et al., 2017; O'Shea, 1979; Reich & Ito, 2017; VanLehn, 2011; 2016) or by filling gaps in existing educational services (e.g. Madaio et al., 2020; Saxena et al., 2018; Uchidiuno et al., 2018). Given these noble intentions, why might AIED systems have inequitable impacts?

In this chapter, we ask whether AIED systems will ultimately serve to *Amplify* Inequities in **Ed**ucation or, alternatively, whether they will help *Alleviate* existing inequities. We discuss four lenses that can be used to examine how and why AIED systems risk amplifying existing inequities: (1) factors inherent to the overall *socio-technical system design*; (2) the use of *datasets* that reflect historical inequities; (3) factors inherent to the underlying *algorithms* used to drive machine learning and automated decision-making, and (4) factors that emerge through a complex *interplay* between automated and human decision-making. Building from these lenses, we then outline possible paths towards *more equitable futures* for AIED, and highlight debates surrounding each proposal. In doing so, we hope to provoke new conversations around the design of equitable AIED and push ongoing conversations in the field forward.

DOI: 10.4324/9780429329067-9

Pathways toward Inequity in AIED

We begin by presenting four lenses to understand how AIED systems might amplify existing inequities or even create new ones (cf. Buckingham Shum, 2018). While each lens provides a different way of examining pathways towards inequity in AIED, all are pointed at the same underlying socio-technical system. Figure 6.1 provides a coarse-grained overview of the broader social-technical systems in which AIED systems are embedded, and some of the components we will refer to in the four lenses. The accumulated, collective decisions of designers, researchers, policy-makers, and other stakeholders shape these systems' designs. In addition to *using* or being *affected by* AIED systems, on-the-ground stakeholders such as students, teachers, or school administrators may also play a role in shaping their designs – whether *directly*, through participatory design processes, or *indirectly* through the passive generation of training data while interacting with an AIED interface. In turn, decisions regarding what data is used to shape an AIED system's design (e.g. as training data for use with machine learning methods) can shape an AIED system's algorithmic behaviour (e.g. instructional policies learned from data). This relationship is often bidirectional: the AIED system's algorithmic behaviour also determines and constrains the kinds of data that are subsequently generated via user interactions.

Designing more equitable AIED technologies requires reasoning at multiple levels of abstraction, rather than only thinking about one level in isolation. However, looking at these challenges through different lenses at times can reveal different kinds of potential solutions. Thus, these four lenses differ

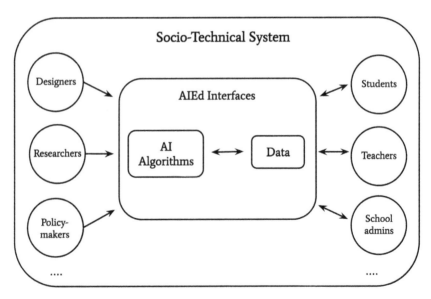

Figure 6.1 High-level overview of AIED systems and the broader socio-technical systems in which they are embedded

primarily in *where they place their focus*, with each dedicating higher resolution to particular components of the overall socio-technical system. Indeed, different research communities have tended to tackle issues of fairness and equity in AI systems, both within and outside the area of education, through different sets of lenses. While AI and machine learning communities have historically studied these issues primarily through the second (Data) and third (Algorithmic) lenses, fields such as human–computer interaction (HCI) and the learning sciences have largely approached these issues through the first (System) and fourth (Human–Algorithm) lenses. As we discuss below, designing more equitable AIED systems will likely require meaningful integration across all four lenses.

Kizilcec and Lee (Chapter 7, this volume) discuss the particular concern of algorithmic fairness in educational systems in greater depth, including an exposition of technical definitions of fairness, which we do not discuss in this chapter. Baker and Hawn (2021) also provide an overview of the sources of algorithmic bias throughout the machine learning pipeline, providing examples of pathways that go beyond the ones discussed here. We see issues of algorithmic fairness as constituting an important subset of the pathways that could lead to inequity in AIED systems that we discuss in this chapter. Kizilcec and Lee characterize three steps in the design and use of an algorithmic system that can result in unfairness: measurement, model learning, and action. These roughly correspond to our data, algorithmic, and human–algorithm lenses respectively. However, since we take a broader view of inequity in AIED systems, each of these three lenses also includes ways in which inequity can emerge even in the absence of using data-driven techniques. Overall, these recent overviews of algorithmic fairness in education are complementary to the broader discussion of equity in AIED presented in this chapter.

Lens 1 (System): Factors Inherent to the Overall Socio-Technical System Design

We first discuss factors related to the design of AIED technologies *other than* their use of AI algorithms that may contribute to inequities in education. These factors are highlighted in Figure 6.2. They include the components of a technology that does not explicitly involve the use of AI, such as the user interface, the learning theories and pedagogical principles underpinning the system, and the way domain knowledge is represented in the system. This lens also considers all the relevant factors of the broader socio-technical system in which the technology lives, which includes various human stakeholders, values, beliefs, business models, the context in which the system is used, and so on.

Under this lens, one major source of inequity of AIED technologies lies in *disparities of access*, where a technology is more accessible to certain groups of learners than others. For example, costlier technologies may be more likely to be adopted by wealthier schools or families. Although the cost of computers (including mobile devices such as phones) has greatly declined, computer access remains a source of disparity. A 2015 survey found that 5% of families

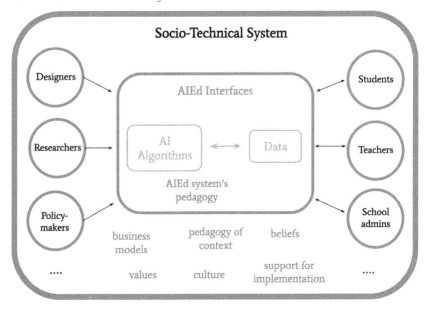

Figure 6.2 Lens 1 (System): Focus on overall socio-technical system design rather than actual AI or data-driven aspects of an AIED system

Note: In this and subsequent figures, the highlighted components show the focus of the current lens.

in the US with children under the age of 18 do not have *any computer* in their household (desktop, laptop, or handheld device) and 15% have no Internet subscription (Ryan & Lewis, 2017). Moreover, these numbers are lower for underrepresented minorities than for white and Asian families. Rideout and Katz (2016) found that even though the percentage of families without any kind of Internet access is relatively small, many low- and moderate-income families with nominal Internet access were still found to be under-connected in one or more ways (e.g. slow Internet access, computer sharing, mobile-only access, and limited data plans). Under-connectivity can in turn affect the degree to which children use digital technologies for educational purposes; for example, Rideout and Katz found that only 35% of children with mobile-only access would often use the Internet for interest-driven learning, as compared to 52% of those who had desktop or laptop access.

Yet even if all students have physical access to a given technology, disparities of access may remain. For example, an AIED system that provides guidance (e.g. on-demand hints or scaffolding questions) only in English will limit access to non-English speakers, and may serve to disadvantage non-native versus native English speakers. Where AIED systems assume use of a mainstream dialect, students from minoritized groups who use other dialects at home may be disadvantaged. For example, Finkelstein et al. (2013) showed that African American students displayed more scientific reasoning when taught by a virtual avatar that spoke entirely in African American Vernacular English (AAVE) compared with an avatar that spoke Mainstream American English (MAE). Such disparities can also arise when educational *content* is implicitly tailored toward particular cultural contexts. Chipman et al. (1991) found that the familiarity of situations described in math word problems affected performance on those problems, even when the underlying mathematical structure was held constant. Moreover, unless AIED technologies are explicitly designed with accessibility in mind, these technologies risk accelerating learning for some groups of learners while decelerating learning for others. This can happen, for example, if a school implements the technology to replace a previously accessible activity with one that is less accessible (Guo et al., 2019; Rose, 2000; Wen et al., 2019).

Inequities due to the overall socio-technical system design extend well beyond disparities of access. Reich and Ito (2017) synthesize a body of research showing that even when schools and individual learners have *equal access*, "new technologies tend to be used and accessed in unequal ways, and they may even exacerbate inequality" (p. 3). Different schools and teachers will use the same technologies in different ways, for example due to differences in values and beliefs surrounding education and technology. For instance, Rafalow (2020) found that teachers in schools with different demographic compositions adopted different attitudes toward students' digital literacy skills and expressions based on (racial) stereotypes about the student body. Notably, schools that are better resourced and that serve students from more privileged backgrounds tend to use technologies in more innovative ways. While this is not solely a technical challenge, designers of AIED technologies should be aware of systematic differences in the ways these technologies are implemented or adopted, and consider ways of measuring, responding to, and designing for such differences. Even when students in the same school have similar levels of access *and* comparable levels of digital literacy, Sims (2014) observed that different social groups might form "differentiating practices" around the use of technology, which could exacerbate social divisions. Further, Reich and Ito identified that providing open access to educational resources (e.g. massive open online courses), *does not* mean everyone will benefit from those technologies equally. MOOCs are disproportionately used by students with high socio-economic status, many of whom already have advanced degrees. This could be due to socio-cultural barriers that prevent individuals from using certain technologies, even when they are free. However, Kizilcec et al. (2017) showed that simple social belonging and value-affirmation interventions could increase the persistence and completion rate of MOOCs for students from less developed countries, potentially eliminating the gap in MOOC completion between students in less versus more developed countries. Similarly, designers of AIED technologies should consider interventions to reduce gaps in who *chooses to use* their technology. Simply improving access is not enough.

A key factor that may contribute to inequities in AI-supported education is the "social distance between developers and those they seek to serve" (Reich &

Ito, 2017). Even in cases where teams explicitly design technologies to help underserved populations, if the design process is not guided by representative voices from those populations, the resulting technologies may fail to serve the needs of those populations, or may even amplify existing equity gaps (as discussed further in the next section).

So far, we have largely discussed factors that apply to educational technologies in general, not only AIED systems. However, common design features of AIED systems have been identified which may contribute to inequities in use. For instance, many AIED systems, such as intelligent tutoring systems, are designed for *one-on-one interaction* with a student. One-on-one interaction is assumed not only in these systems' interface designs but also in the choices of the AI algorithms that these systems rely upon to adapt and personalize instruction, such as Bayesian Knowledge Tracing (Corbett & Anderson, 1995). If the system is used in a different way in practice, it may make decisions that are suboptimal or even harmful to students (see our third lens below, as well as Olsen et al., 2015). Yet research has shown that, in certain cultural contexts, students tend to work with these technologies *collaboratively* rather than individually (Ogan, Walker et al., 2015; Ogan, Yarzebinski, et al., 2015).

Another factor is the lack of flexibility or adaptability of AIED systems. Since AIED technologies are often complex systems with many interlocking components, these systems tend to permit limited end-user customization. In particular, AIED systems rarely support flexible customization options, to help teachers adapt these systems to the needs of their local contexts (Nye, 2014). On the other hand, simpler educational technologies that do not rely (extensively) on AI may lend themselves to such customization more easily, by default. For example, in lieu of advanced forms of adaptivity, the ASSISTments system is designed to support teacher-driven adaptability, allowing teachers to create or customize their own assignments so they can better meet the needs of their students (Heffernan & Heffernan, 2014). This support for teacher-driven adaptability means that teachers are not required to rely on pre-set assignments with which they may be unfamiliar, or which may poorly fit their contexts (e.g. by presenting word problems with which their students cannot connect).

Lens 2 (Data): Use of Data that Reflect Historical Inequities

AIED systems have great potential to address inequities in education, for example by filling gaps in the educational services otherwise available to learners (Madaio et al., 2020; Saxena et al., 2018; Uchidiuno et al., 2018). However, insofar as these technologies are shaped or driven by historical data, they risk perpetuating or even amplifying any social inequities reflected in these data (Mayfield et al., 2019; Selbst et al., 2019; Veale et al., 2018). This second lens considers the ways in which biases and inequities in the ways in which data was collected or generated can propagate in AIED systems. The focus of this lens is depicted in Figure 6.3.

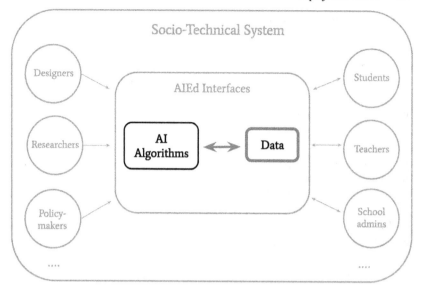

Figure 6.3 Lens 2 (Data): Decisions regarding the data that an AIED system relies upon (including the ways in which this data is used or generated)
Note: Designing datasets or data-generating mechanisms that support more equitable outcomes is a central goal.

The risks of "scaling up" inequities via data-driven approaches have inspired new research communities focusing on fairness in machine learning (e.g. the ACM Conference on Fairness, Accountability, and Transparency), which have begun to influence research on educational data mining and learning analytics. Through this second lens, inequities may arise via a number of possible pathways.

The first pathway highlights the fact that biases in data need not arise only when machine learning or data-driven techniques are explicitly used. Here, we consider the impact of social distance discussed under the first lens through this data-centric lens, centring the roles of *sampling processes and biases* in the design of a system. Even if a given AIED system's behaviour is not shaped through machine learning, its design process may still be guided by the use of data. This data may often consist of observations from a limited set of contexts and feedback from a limited set of stakeholders. Meaney and Fikes (2019) discuss "Early-adopter Iteration Bias" in the design of learning analytics systems and other educational technologies – the notion that the educational practitioners and students most likely to participate at the earliest stages of the design process tend to represent a relatively privileged subpopulation. In the presence of such recruitment biases, the designs of novel educational technologies may be skewed towards the needs of these early adopters, while failing to reflect the needs of marginalized, underserved, and otherwise risk-averse populations (who may participate more heavily in later design cycles).

As a second major pathway, when an AIED system's behaviour is developed in a data-driven manner, inequities may arise due to *misalignments* between system developers' educational goals, the datasets used to train and evaluate models, and the dynamics of the contexts in which these systems will eventually be used. If particular learner subpopulations or educational contexts are overrepresented in datasets used to train and evaluate models offline, the resulting models may encode associations that fail to generalize to other learners and contexts, and which may even cause harm if deployed in these contexts (Ocumpaugh et al., 2014). For example, the use of proctoring software during the COVID-19 pandemic has raised several equity concerns, including difficulties in identifying the faces of students of colour, presumably due to the biases in the datasets that the facial recognition technologies were trained on (García-Bullé, 2021; Teninbaum, 2021).

Moreover, in cases where AIED systems' assessment or pedagogical models are learned from the ratings or observed behaviours of human decision-makers (e.g. school administrators, teachers, parents, or students), the resulting models may serve to scale up not only beneficial practices but also *undesirable biases* exhibited by these educational stakeholders (as discussed further under our fourth lens below). For example, it is known that K-12 teachers (of children aged 5–18) often exhibit biases in assessing the written work of students from marginalized populations (representing mismatches between teachers' educational goals and their actual assessment practices). Furthermore, prior work has demonstrated that when human teachers' scores are uncritically used as the "ground truth" for student performance, such assessment biases can easily be encoded into automated essay scoring systems used at scale (e.g. Madnani et al., 2017; Mayfield et al., 2019). As discussed in the next lens, the extent to which a given AIED system serves to propagate or even amplify historical inequities may depend in part on the choices of *models and algorithms* used to develop these systems.

A third major pathway is discussed below under our fourth lens (Human–Algorithm). When machine learning-based AIED systems are deployed in real-world educational contexts, historical biases may not only replicate but also *compound* via feedback loops.

Lens 3 (Algorithmic): Factors Inherent to the Underlying Algorithms

AIED algorithms are often implicitly designed to reduce equity gaps, for example, by attempting to personalize instruction for each learner. Giving students the right amount and types of instruction at the right time can mitigate concerns around one-size-fits-all instruction that tends to amplify existing achievement gaps. Nonetheless, due to various factors, the use of AI algorithms may fall short of this vision by engendering inequitable outcomes for learners through a number of possible pathways. This lens focuses on the use of AI algorithms – including the ways in which these algorithms utilize or are shaped by data – as depicted in Figure 6.4.

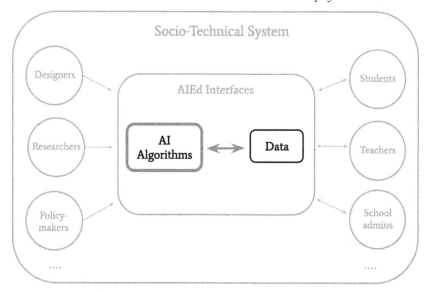

Figure 6.4 Lens 3 (Algorithmic): Design decisions regarding an AIED system's under-lying AI algorithms (including the ways in which these algorithms use or are shaped by data)
Note: Designing algorithms that support more equitable outcomes is a central goal.

First, as discussed above, machine learning algorithms will tend towards further propagating, or even exacerbating, existing biases present in historical datasets unless explicitly designed to counteract these biases. For example, when fitting a model to an automated essay scoring dataset where teachers' essay grades systematically encode certain biases, the model will naturally make predictions that are biased in similar ways. Note that such scenarios can play out *even if no demographic variables are used* in a machine learning model, because other variables can (and often will) correlate with demographic variables in non-obvious ways (Barocas & Selbst, 2016; Datta et al., 2017, Dwork et al., 2012; Kilbertus et al., 2017). For example, Gardner and colleagues (2019) found that across a variety of MOOC datasets and different machine learning models used to predict dropout rates, the models exhibited disparities in accuracy across males and females, even though none of the models used gender or other demographic variables as explicit features. Although the source of such disparities may be understood under our second lens to lie in the choices of data used to train these models, particular choices of models and learning algorithms may be more prone to amplify such biases than others (Elzayn et al., 2019).

Even if theoretically *there were no undesirable historical biases* in a dataset, machine learning algorithms could still be unfair when the amount of data we have for different demographic groups vary. In particular, most machine learning algorithms will be *inherently biased* against minority groups in our data (Hardt, 2014). This is because the algorithm will try to optimize overall accuracy of a model; and if it can achieve that accuracy by tailoring its predictions to that of a majority group (at the expense of minority groups), it will do so. For example, a learning analytics algorithm that detects "at-risk" students trained on data from a majority-white college can be very accurate overall by learning how to make nuanced predictions for the white students and possibly making less nuanced predictions for Black students or Native American students for whom it may have much less data. To reiterate, this can result simply from the fact that minority groups will naturally be less represented in a dataset where they are in a minority, rather than systematic historical biases (although, in practice, certain groups may be undersampled in available datasets due to historical biases). In some cases, this concern might be resolved by intentionally collecting more data from minority groups, even if that is not representative of the population.

Machine learning algorithms can also contribute to inequitable decision-making due to *model misspecification*. This is especially relevant when fitting statistical models of student learning, since learning is a complex, unobservable phenomenon, and any simple model is bound to be an imperfect representation of the true underlying processes. For example, Doroudi and Brunskill (2019) examined contexts where a student model is used for mastery learning (i.e. to decide how much practice a student should receive on each of a set of targeted skills or knowledge components). The authors demonstrated two major kinds of model misspecification that can cause inequitable outcomes. First, if learners learn at different rates (i.e. there are faster and slower learners), but the student model is not individualized (i.e. a single model is fit to aggregate data from faster and slower learners), then slower learners may be more likely to receive less practice than they need as compared to fast learners. Second, if the functional form of the model is fundamentally misspecified, then slower learners could again face disadvantages (receiving suboptimal practice). In particular, the authors showed that if, in reality, students learn according to the Additive Factor Model, but a Bayesian Knowledge Tracing model is used for mastery learning (as is typically the case in intelligent tutoring systems), then *even if* separate models are fit for slower versus faster learners, inequitable outcomes across these groups persist as a result of the underlying model misspecification.[1] Therefore, in order to ensure equitable outcomes, AIED system developers should not only strive to develop student models that more faithfully capture student learning processes, but also aim to develop algorithmic interventions that are robust to potential model misspecification.

Finally, AIED algorithms can also be inequitable *even when they are not data-driven*. For example, using a heuristic for mastery learning, such as assuming students have learned a skill when they display N consecutive correct responses for that skill (Kelly et al., 2015; Hu, 2011), could also contribute to inequitable outcomes (Doroudi & Brunskill, 2019). Implicitly, such a heuristic is making assumptions about student learning that may not actually hold in practice in all contexts (Doroudi, 2020). In general, algorithms that make different decisions for students based on their performance, while key to providing adaptive instruction, can be susceptible to such risks. For example, a proposed game-theoretic mechanism for incentivizing students to accurately self-assess their work (Labutov & Studer, 2016) can *inherently* lead to artificial deflation of lower-performing students' grades. That is, lower-performing students could receive much lower grades than they would otherwise receive if they were not asked to self-assess their work. Outside of the research setting, similar scoring rules have been used to grade students in several university courses on decision analysis (Bickel, 2010). Yet researchers have not discussed the consequences of these incentive mechanisms with respect to equity in educational outcomes.

Lens 4 (Human–Algorithm): Interplay between Automated and Human Decision-making

When AIED systems are used in real-world educational contexts, they do not act upon students in a vacuum. Rather, their impacts result from a complex interplay between the AI systems themselves, the human teams who design and develop them, and the human decision makers who use these systems – e. g. teachers, school administrators, and students (Holstein et al., 2018b; Holstein, Wortman Vaughan et al., 2019; Mayfield et al., 2019; Madaio, Stark et al., 2020). As such, achieving more equitable futures for AI in Education requires carefully designing for this interplay (cf. De-Arteaga et al., 2020; Holstein et al., 2019) – moving beyond a focus on AIED interfaces, datasets, or algorithms in isolation – as depicted in Figure 6.5.

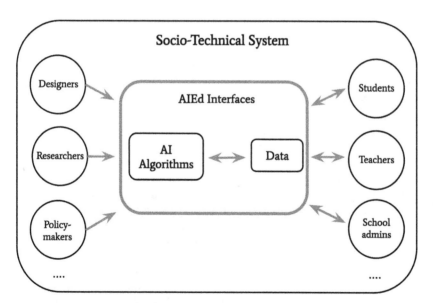

Figure 6.5 Lens 4 (Human-Algorithm): The complex interactions between AIED systems and human decision-makers
Note: Under this lens, designing to shape these (often bidirectional) interactions in ways that support more equitable outcomes is a central goal.

In cases where an educational AI or learning analytics system does not necessarily encode harmful *algorithmic* biases (e.g. where the system does not present disparities in predictive accuracy across subgroups of students), it is still possible that real-world *use* of the system may systematically contribute to inequitable outcomes. For instance, consider two alternative designs of a decision-support tool for classroom teachers that both rely upon the same underlying student modelling algorithms, yet present the outputs of these algorithms to teachers in different ways. Despite the use of common algorithms, different methods of presentation may interact with teachers' existing decision-making biases in very different directions (see Holstein et al., 2018a, 2018b; Martinez-Maldonado, 2013; van Leeuwen 2015; van Leeuwen & Rummel, 2020). If a tool design leads teachers to *challenge* their existing beliefs about individual students' abilities and potential for growth, then this design has the potential to nudge teachers towards more equitable practices (Holstein et al., 2018b). By contrast, if a tool design has the primary effect of making teachers feel *validated* in their existing beliefs, even when these beliefs are incorrect, then this design risks maintaining or even amplifying inequitable patterns of teacher behaviour (Holstein et al., 2018a; 2019; van Leeuwen, 2015).

Such interactions between human and machine biases may have compounding effects – for better or worse – in the presence of human–AI *feedback loops* in learning or decision-making (cf. Lum & Isaac, 2016; Elzayn et al., 2019; Veale et al., 2018). For example, in the context of predictive policing, Lum and Isaac showed that PredPol, a popular predictive policing software, reinforced existing biases in the dataset and targeted Black people at disproportionately high rates (twice as high as white people, even though drug use was roughly equal between the two groups); this is a typical inequitable outcome as per the second lens. However, they further showed via simulation that if police are more likely to find crime in areas where they are actively policing (as a result of PredPol's predictions), which in turn affects the crime rates in the data used by the algorithm, then the algorithm will become further biased in a feedback loop that amplifies existing biases.

In cases where deployed AI systems both *shape* the behaviours of learners and educators (e.g. by presenting particular predictions, recommendations, or behavioural nudges) and *are shaped by* these evolving behaviours (continuously learning and adjusting based on incoming educational data), the dynamics of the resulting educational system can be challenging to anticipate. Given a longstanding focus on the development of data-driven, self-improving systems for education (Doroudi et al., 2019; O'Shea, 1979), measuring, modelling, and designing for such cyclical interactions should be a central focus of future work. If intentionally designed as such, these cycles may have the potential to serve as positive, regulative loops (cf. VanLehn, 2016) – helping humans to mitigate undesirable impacts of algorithmic decision-making and helping machines to mitigate undesirable impacts of human decision-making.

Towards More Equitable Futures for AI-supported Education

In the following, we present brief examples of some possible paths towards more equitable futures for AI in Education. We first discuss promising paths towards *avoiding amplification* of existing inequities through AIED, addressing some of the risks discussed in the last section. After seeing how we might mitigate such negative outcomes, we then return to the promise of AIED as a means of combating inequity, presenting some possible paths for AIED to *alleviate* existing inequities in education.

For each path presented, we also present one or more critiques of the proposed path, followed by potential resolutions. In presenting each path in the style of a dialectic (inspired by repeated conversations we have had with AIED researchers and practitioners), we intend to highlight the challenges that we may face ahead, while also acknowledging their complexity. Our goal is to both provoke new conversations and to push ongoing conversations forward. However, note that the following is *far from an exhaustive set* of promising paths forward or an exhaustive discussion of associated challenges and critiques.

Pathways to Avoid Amplifying Inequities

Path 1: Invest in developing tools and processes to support AIED practitioners in developing and deploying more equitable technologies

We could further invest, as a field, in research and practical methods for assessing and addressing inequitable impacts of AIED technologies. For example, we could develop specialized toolkits and organizational processes to support equity-focused design, testing, and deployment in the area of AI-supported education (Cramer et al., 2019; Holstein, Wortman Vaughan, et al., 2019; Madaio, Stark, et al., 2020). AIED development teams could then *continuously* monitor for unwanted disparate impacts of their technologies across different educational contexts and groups, and iteratively refine these technologies to address such disparities.

Critique 1: How will AIED companies be held accountable?

Will companies simply be able to announce that they are auditing for inequitable impacts of their technologies, to improve public relations, but without actually reporting all issues they uncover or addressing these issues (cf. Bietti, 2020)?

Possible resolution: We can and should design mechanisms to promote increased accountability and transparency. For instance, support for company-internal auditing should exist alongside (and ideally in close coordination with) mechanisms for auditing and regulating AIED systems from the outside (cf. Cramer et al., 2019; Madaio, Stark, et al., 2020; Raji & Buolamwini, 2019).

Critique 2: In addressing one form of inequity, AIED developers may inadvertently create others.

By trying to satisfy a particular notion of fairness (e.g. according to a particular quantitative definition proposed in prior literature), one might actually cause harm in another dimension without realizing it (Holstein, Wortman Vaughan, et al., 2019; Kleinberg et al., 2016; Zhu et al., 2018).

Possible resolution: Nonetheless, we need to try our best. Ultimately, the notions of fairness we choose for a particular application depend on what we, and those we include in the design process, find most salient and important. Where fundamental design trade-offs exist, we *need to take a stance* and make these trade-offs. This means accepting responsibility, which is better than the alternative of denying responsibility. Moreover, by continuously auditing for fairness, we avoid making a small one-off fix that leads to unanticipated long-term side effects.

Path 2: Design AIED systems that can clearly communicate their own capabilities and limitations, and hand off control to humans as needed

Future AIED systems can be designed to communicate their uncertainties and potential biases to the humans-in-the-loop (e.g. when reporting analytics), allowing relevant human decision-makers (e.g. teachers and students) to override their recommendations when needed (Amershi et al., 2019; De-Arteaga et al., 2020; Fancsali et al., 2018; Holstein et al., 2018b; 2019).

Critique: "Lifting the curtain" on AIED systems will reduce trust.

By increasing transparency and making people more aware of the boundaries of AIED systems' capabilities, we risk promoting *under-trust* in these systems. Ultimately, these kinds of efforts will make people less likely to use systems that would otherwise be beneficial to students.

Possible resolution: If such systems are designed carefully, with an awareness and understanding of the ways human and algorithmic decision-making interact (e.g. algorithmic aversion or over-reliance), we can support teachers and students in achieving *the right levels of trust* in particular instances. Ideally, AIED systems should support teachers and students in trusting their predictions and recommendations only when they are *trustworthy*, and should otherwise support teachers and students in second-guessing or overriding such information (cf. Bull & Kay, 2016; Conati et al., 2018; Holstein et al., 2019). Prior research suggests that increased transparency in AI systems can have the overall effect of improving trust rather than diminishing it, at least when paired with corresponding, meaningful options for *user control* (Lee & Baykal, 2017).

Path 3: Incorporate equity-related outcomes, not just individual student learning outcomes, into the objective functions of AIED systems

"Rich get richer" effects are often observed in classrooms using AIED systems, where systems behave in ways that systematically benefit students coming in with higher prior domain knowledge *more* than they benefit students coming in with lower prior knowledge (e.g. Doroudi & Brunskill, 2019; Hansen & Reich, 2015; Holstein et al., 2018b; Rau, 2015). As a result, although AIED systems may show favourable results at the individual student level, at the population level they risk *further widening achievement gaps*. To address this, we should work towards designing algorithms for AIED systems that optimize not only for individual student learning outcomes, but should also take into account outcomes at higher levels (e.g. at the class, school, district, or region level). See Kizilcec and Lee (Chapter 7 this volume) for a related discussion of this issue.

Critique: We should not suppress advanced students' progress simply to avoid widening achievement gaps across students.

A positive framing of the "rich get richer" argument is the notion that AIED systems can help advanced students reach their full potential faster than they would otherwise. It may not be ethical or desirable to suppress these students' progress in the name of equity. Education is complex, and narrowing achievement gaps is *not our only goal*.

Possible resolution: Ultimately, it may be that we may need to make trade-offs. However, we should make sure that we do so consciously and deliberately, rather than making these kinds of trade-offs "by default." As a field, we should critically reflect on our goals for learning, both at the individual and population levels, as well as the trade-offs we are willing to make among these goals. It might also be the case that we can overcome certain trade-offs through thoughtful design. For example, many AIED systems that involve adaptive problem selection will allow advanced students to progress to later material in a curriculum as quickly as they can reach this material (such that, in the same class, one student might be working on "Chapter 3" while another is already working on "Chapter 25"). However, an alternative design for such technologies, which might have some desirable properties with respect to equity, might instead keep different students relatively synchronized in the curriculum, while providing challenging enrichment opportunities for those students who move through the material more quickly (e.g. allowing advanced students to *deepen* their knowledge of a particular area, but without necessarily supporting them in moving far ahead of others in the curriculum, possibly by having them help tutor their struggling peers).

Pathways to Alleviate Existing Educational Inequities

Path 1: Broaden (meaningful) participation in AIED system design to serve diverse populations more equitably

The design of AIED systems should take into account voices from diverse perspectives that are representative of the students and teachers these systems aim to serve (e.g. in socio-economic background, culture, and language). This could include involving diverse educational stakeholders (e.g. students, teachers, and parents from a range of backgrounds) in a co-design process, or hiring a more diverse team to lead the design of the technology. However, this should not mean teams should hire "token" members of particular demographic groups simply to cross off a checklist (Arnstein, 1969). A constant effort needs to be made to seek out relevant voices that are not being represented, and to ensure that these voices can actually have a *meaningful* impact on AIED system designs (Holstein et al., 2019; Madaio, Stark, et al., 2020; Young et al., 2019).

Critique 1: Students and teachers are not scientific experts.

By enabling broad participation, we allow students and teachers with poor knowledge of good educational practices to potentially lower the quality of these systems. For example, what if a teacher wants to design a system that adapts to student "learning styles" – an intervention that scientific research suggests may be ineffective or even *harmful* to students (Pashler et al., 2008)?

Possible resolution: By enabling broader participation in the design of these systems, *we do not lose our own agency* as learning scientists, designers, researchers, and developers. Rather, a participatory, collaborative approach acknowledges that there may be much that we do not know, but which stakeholders know quite well (e.g. regarding their day-to-day lived experiences), and that we similarly hold considerable knowledge that other stakeholders may lack. Our challenge is then to figure out how best to balance between various stakeholders' desires and perceived needs and existing scientific or design knowledge. From this perspective, we are empowered by knowledge of different stakeholder groups' desires, boundaries, and challenges, not limited by this knowledge. Understanding students' and teachers' perspectives and experiences can also help in anticipating whether and how an AIED technology might be implemented across different educational contexts. For example, if teachers believe firmly in learning styles, they may adopt a certain technology in a way that attempts to tailor instruction to learning styles. It is advantageous for AIED developers to know about both positive and negative adoption patterns, and incorporate that knowledge in the design of such systems.

Critique 2: Can broadening participation yield discriminatory outcomes?

In some cases, truly taking into account the needs of different groups of students, teachers, and educational contexts may require designing different technologies for different groups of users. Even if the technologies are optimized to serve the needs of these different groups, such *disparate treatment* might ultimately serve to stigmatize members of these groups.

Possible resolution: Disparate treatment is already ubiquitous in education, and is often necessary in avoiding *disparate outcomes* across groups. For example, mastery learning and in fact, *all adaptive systems* enact forms of disparate treatment. If a student is struggling, we often wish to give them more opportunity to succeed than a student who quickly masters the same material. Ultimately, we need to design interventions with members of these communities to ensure that these targeted interventions are viewed as helpful, but not stigmatizing or discriminatory.

Path 2: Fill existing gaps in educational services with AIED technologies

AIED systems can fill gaps, providing educational services where few or none previously existed; for example, by offering instruction in the midst of a multi-week teachers' strike, as in the case study by Madaio, Yarzebinski, et al. (2020).

Critique: AIED will function as such an attractive "sticking plaster" that we will neglect to heal the underlying wounds.

The presence of such gap-filling AIED systems may be used as an "excuse" by policy-makers not to invest in higher-quality, longer-term fixes for social problems surrounding education (e.g. the presence of these technologies might ultimately lead to funding cuts for teachers and public schools or to increasing class sizes). Similarly, already under-resourced schools might be more likely to adopt this option to cut costs, potentially exacerbating existing inequities (Watters, 2014).

Possible resolution: This is a serious critique that should not be taken lightly. AIED systems can do enormous good by filling gaps; but ultimately AIED researchers, practitioners, and policy-makers share a responsibility to ensure they do not have a net negative impact on society. Our community should continue to discuss, with heightened urgency, what we can do to ensure our work is not used as sticking plasters or excuses not to address deeper problems in our education systems (Blikstein, 2018).

Path 3: AIED as a force to overcome harmful human biases

As discussed above, AIED systems have many biases; but many of the paths toward inequity are actually rooted in human biases, including biases that teachers might have – e.g. teachers' beliefs influencing how they use educational technology (in lenses 1 and 4) and teachers' biases encoded in data used by AIED technologies such as automated essay graders (in lens 2). AIED systems can actually serve as a tool to push against human educators, as needed, to help them notice and overcome their own biases.

Critique: If AI systems can encode harmful biases, how can they be used to help humans overcome harmful biases?

By using AIED systems to nudge teachers towards more equitable decision-making, we may inadvertently do the opposite. For example, AIED systems may incorrectly push against teacher biases that actually represent helpful heuristics (e.g. based on rich contextual knowledge to which the teacher has access but the AI does not), or may even push their own harmful biases onto teachers.

Possible resolution: AIED systems might be designed with an awareness of their own fallibility, and avoid offering confident prescriptions for teacher action, as described in Path 1 under "Pathways to Avoid Amplifying Existing Inequities." Even though an AIED system may encode some harmful biases of its own, these biases may differ from those held by a human educator. By calling teachers' attention to *discrepancies* between their own judgements and those of an AIED system, the system may promote productive teacher reflection and learning (cf. An et al., 2019; 2020; De-Arteaga et al., 2020; Holstein et al., 2019). AIED systems (or system developers) can in turn take feedback from teachers to help pinpoint and mitigate biases that the AIED system may have.

Conclusions

The use of Artificial Intelligence in education represents one possible means towards improving educational systems and reducing existing inequities. However, as with any attempt to address the wicked problems of education, AIED systems can easily have unintended impacts, amplifying existing inequities rather than alleviating them. We have described multiple lenses through which to understand how this can occur, each of which focuses on a different aspect of the complex socio-technical system within which AIED technologies operate. Ultimately, only by examining the many ways in which AIED systems can amplify inequities can we realize the true potential of AIED to *alleviate* inequities in education. Looking ahead, we must foster honest, critical discussions around the many challenges that lie in our path. It is our hope that this chapter serves to further ongoing conversations and spark new ones within the area of AI-supported education.

Note

1   Misspecifying the functional form of a student model may not always result in worse results for low-performing students, so this should be studied on a case-by-case basis.

References

Amershi, S., Weld, D., Vorvoreanu, M., Fourney, A., Nushi, B., Collisson, P., Suh, J., Iqbal, S., Bennett, P. N., Inkpen, K. & Teevan, J. (2019). Guidelines for human–AI interaction. In *Proceedings of the 2019 CHI Conference on Human Factors in Computing Systems (CHI'19)* (pp. 1–13). ACM.

An, P., Bakker, S., Ordanovski, S., Taconis, R., Paffen, C. L. & Eggen, B. (2019). Unobtrusively enhancing reflection-in-action of teachers through spatially distributed ambient information. In *Proceedings of the 2019 CHI Conference on Human Factors in Computing Systems* (pp. 1–14). ACM.

An, P., Holstein, K., d'Anjou, B., Eggen, B. & Bakker, S. (2020). The TA framework: Designing real-time teaching augmentation for K-12 classrooms. In *Proceedings of the ACM CHI Conference on Human Factors in Computing Systems (CHI'20)* (pp. 1–17). ACM.

Arnstein, S. R. (1969). A ladder of citizen participation. *Journal of the American Institute of Planners*, 35 (4), 216–224.

Baker, R. S. & Hawn, A. (2021). Algorithmic bias in education. doi:10.35542/osf.io/pbmvz.

Barocas, S. & Selbst, A. D. (2016). Big data's disparate impact. *California Law Review*, 104, 671–732.

Bickel, J. E. (2010). Scoring rules and decision analysis education. *Decision Analysis,* 7 (4), 346–357.

Bietti, E. (2020). From ethics washing to ethics bashing: A view on tech ethics from within moral philosophy. In *Proceedings of the 2020 Conference on Fairness, Accountability, and Transparency (FAT*20)* (pp. 210–219).

Blikstein, P. (2018). *Time to make hard choices for AI in education.* Keynote talk at the 2018 International Conference on Artificial Intelligence in Education.

Buckingham Shum, S. J. (2018). *Transitioning education's knowledge infrastructure.* Keynote talk at the 2018 International Conference of the Learning Sciences.

Buckingham Shum, S. J. & Luckin, R. (2019). Learning analytics and AI: Politics, pedagogy and practices. *British Journal of Educational Technology,* 50 (6), 2785–2793.

Bull, S. & Kay, J. (2010). Open learner models. In R. Nkambou, R. Mizoguchi & J. Bourdeau (eds), *Advances in Intelligent Tutoring Systems* (pp. 301–322). Springer.

Bull, S. & Kay, J. (2016). SMILI☺: A framework for interfaces to learning data in open learner models, learning analytics and related fields. *International Journal of Artificial Intelligence in Education,* 26 (1), 293–331.

Conati, C., Porayska-Pomsta, K. & Mavrikis, M. (2018). AI in education needs interpretable machine learning: Lessons from Open Learner Modelling. arXiv:1807.00154.

Corbett, A. T. & Anderson, J. R. (1995). Knowledge tracing: Modeling the acquisition of procedural knowledge. *User Modeling and User-adapted Interaction,* 4 (4), 253–278.

Chipman, S. F., Marshall, S. P. & Scott, P. A. (1991). Content effects on word problem performance: A possible source of test bias? *American Educational Research Journal,* 28 (4), 897–915.

Cramer, H., Holstein, K., Wortman Vaughan, J., DauméIII, H., Dudík, M., Wallach, H., Reddy, S. & Garcia-Gathright, J. (2019). *Challenges of incorporating algorithmic fairness into industry practice.* Tutorial at the ACM Conference on Fairness, Accountability, and Transparency (FAT* '19).

Datta, A., Fredrikson, M., Ko, G., Mardziel, P. & Sen, S. (2017). Proxy non-discrimination in data-driven systems. arXiv:1707.08120.

De-Arteaga, M., Fogliato, R. & Chouldechova, A. (2020). A case for humans-in-the-loop: Decisions in the presence of erroneous algorithmic scores. In *Proceedings of the ACM CHI Conference on Human Factors in Computing Systems (CHI'20)* (pp. 1–12). ACM.

Doroudi, S. (2020). Mastery learning heuristics and their hidden models. In *International Conference on Artificial Intelligence in Education* (pp. 86–91). Berlin: Springer.

Doroudi, S. & Brunskill, E. (2019). Fairer but not fair enough on the equitability of knowledge tracing. In *Proceedings of the 9th International Conference on Learning Analytics and Knowledge* (pp. 335–339).

Doroudi, S., Aleven, V. & Brunskill, E. (2019). Where's the reward? A review of reinforcement learning for instructional sequencing. *International Journal of Artificial Intelligence in Education,* 29 (4), 568–620.

Dwork, C., Hardt, M., Pitassi, T., Reingold, O. & Zemel, R. (2012). Fairness through awareness. In *Proceedings of the 3rd Innovations in Theoretical Computer Science Conference* (pp. 214–226).

Elzayn, H., Jabbari, S., Jung, C., Kearns, M., Neel, S., Roth, A. & Schutzman, Z. (2019). Fair algorithms for learning in allocation problems. In *Proceedings of the Conference on Fairness, Accountability, and Transparency* (pp. 170–179).

Fancsali, S. E., Yudelson, M. V., Berman, S. R. & Ritter, S. (2018). *Intelligent Instructional Hand Offs.* International Educational Data Mining Society.

Ferguson, R. (2019). Ethical challenges for learning analytics. *Journal of Learning Analytics*, 6 (3), 25–30.

Finkelstein, S., Yarzebinski, E., Vaughn, C., Ogan, A. & Cassell, J. (2013). The effects of culturally congruent educational technologies on student achievement. In *International Conference on Artificial Intelligence in Education* (pp. 493–502). Berlin: Springer.

García-Bullé, Sofia. (2021). The dark side of online exam proctoring. *Observatory of Educational Innovation*. https://observatory.tec.mx/edu-news/dark-side-proctored-exams.

Gardner, J., Brooks, C. & Baker, R. (2019). Evaluating the fairness of predictive student models through slicing analysis. In *Proceedings of the 9th International Conference on Learning Analytics and Knowledge* (pp. 225–234).

Guo, A., Kamar, E., Wortman Vaughan, J., Wallach, H. & Morris, M. R. (2019). Toward fairness in AI for people with disabilities: A research roadmap. arXiv:1907.02227.

Hansen, J. D. & Reich, J. (2015). Democratizing education? Examining access and usage patterns in massive open online courses. *Science*, 350 (6265), 1245–1248.

Hardt, M. (2014). How big data is unfair. *Medium*. https://medium.com/@mrtz/how-big-data-is-unfair-9aa544d739de.

Heffernan, N. T. & Heffernan, C. L. (2014). The ASSISTments ecosystem: Building a platform that brings scientists and teachers together for minimally invasive research on human learning and teaching. *International Journal of Artificial Intelligence in Education*, 24 (4), 470–497.

Holmes, W., Bialik, M. & Fadel, C. (2019). *Artificial intelligence in education: Promises and implications for teaching and learning*. Boston, MA: Center for Curriculum Redesign.

Holstein, K. & Doroudi, S. (2019). Fairness and equity in learning analytics systems (FairLAK). In *Companion Proceedings of the Ninth International Learning Analytics & Knowledge Conference (LAK 2019)*.

Holstein, K., McLaren, B. M. & Aleven, V. (2018a). Informing the design of teacher awareness tools through Causal Alignment Analysis. In *Proceedings of the 13th International Conference of the Learning Sciences (ICLS 2018)* (pp. 104–111).

Holstein, K., McLaren, B. M. & Aleven, V. (2018b). Student learning benefits of a mixed-reality teacher awareness tool in AI-enhanced classrooms. In *Proceedings of the 19th International Conference on Artificial Intelligence in Education* (pp. 154–168). Cham: Springer.

Holstein, K., McLaren, B. M. & Aleven, V. (2019). Co-designing a real-time classroom orchestration tool to support teacher–AI complementarity. *Journal of Learning Analytics*, 6 (2), 27–52.

Holstein, K., Wortman Vaughan, J., Daumé III, H., Dudik, M. & Wallach, H. (2019). Improving fairness in machine learning systems: What do industry practitioners need? In *Proceedings of the 2019 CHI Conference on Human Factors in Computing Systems* (pp. 1–16). ACM.

Hu, D. (2011). How Khan Academy is using machine learning to assess student mastery. http://david-hu.com/2011/11/02/how-khan-academy-is-using-machine-learning-to-assess-student-mastery.html.

Kelly, K., Wang, Y., Thompson, T. & Heffernan, N. (2015). Defining mastery: Knowledge tracing versus. In *Proceedings of the 8th International Conference on Educational Data Mining*. ACM.

Kilbertus, N., Carulla, M. R., Parascandolo, G., Hardt, M., Janzing, D. & Schölkopf, B. (2017). Avoiding discrimination through causal reasoning. In *Advances in Neural Information Processing Systems* (pp. 656–666).

Kizilcec, R. F., Saltarelli, A. J., Reich, J. & Cohen, G. L. (2017). Closing global achievement gaps in MOOCs. *Science*, 355 (6322), 251–252.

Kleinberg, J., Mullainathan, S. & Raghavan, M. (2016). Inherent trade-offs in the fair determination of risk scores. arXiv:1609.05807.

Labutov, I. & Studer, C. (2016). *Calibrated Self-Assessment.* International Educational Data Mining Society.

Lee, M. K. & Baykal, S. (2017). Algorithmic mediation in group decisions: Fairness perceptions of algorithmically mediated vs. discussion-based social division. In *Proceedings of the 2017 ACM Conference on Computer Supported Cooperative Work and Social Computing.* (pp. 1035–1048). ACM.

Lum, K. & Isaac, W. (2016). To predict and serve? *Significance*, 13 (5), 14–19.

Madaio, M., Yarzebinski, E., Zinszer, B., Kamath, V., Akpe, H., Seri, A.B., Tanoh, F., Hannon-Cropp, J., Cassell, J., Jasinska, K., Ogan, A. (2020). Motivations and barriers for family engagement with a home literacy technology in rural communities. In *Proceedings of the 2020 CHI Conference on Human Factors in Computing Systems.* ACM.

Madaio, M. A., Stark, L., Vaughan, J. W. & Wallach, H. (2020). Co-designing checklists to understand organizational challenges and opportunities around fairness in AI. In *Proceedings of the 2020 CHI Conference on Human Factors in Computing Systems* (pp. 1–14). ACM.

Madnani, N., Loukina, A., Von Davier, A., Burstein, J. & Cahill, A. (2017). *Building better open-source tools to support fairness in automated scoring.* In *Proceedings of the First ACL Workshop on Ethics in Natural Language Processing* (pp. 41–52).

Martinez-Maldonado, R., Dimitriadis, Y. & Kay, J., Yacef, K. & Edbauer, M. (2013). MTClassroom and MTDashboard: Supporting analysis of teacher attention in an orchestrated multi-tabletop classroom. *CSCL 2013 Proceedings*, 1, 119–128.

Mayfield, E., Madaio, M., Prabhumoye, S., Gerritsen, D., McLaughlin, B., Dixon-Roman, E., Black, E. (2019). Equity beyond bias in language technologies for education. In *Proceedings of the 14th Workshop on Innovative Use of NLP for Building Educational Applications (pp. 444–460).*

Meaney, M.J. and Fikes, T. (2019). Early-adopter iteration bias and research-praxis bias in virtual learning environments. In *Companion Proceedings of the 2019 International Conference on Learning Analytics and Knowledge (LAK'19).*

Nye, B. D. (2014). Barriers to ITS adoption: A systematic mapping study. In *Proceedings of the 12th International Conference on Intelligent Tutoring Systems* (pp. 583–590). Cham: Springer.

Ocumpaugh, J., Baker, R., Gowda, S., Heffernan, N. & Heffernan, C. (2014). Population validity for educational data mining models: A case study in affect detection. *British Journal of Educational Technology*, 45 (3), 487–501.

Ogan, A., Walker, E., Baker, R., Rodrigo, M. M. T., Soriano, J. C. & Castro, M. J. (2015). Towards understanding how to assess help-seeking behavior across cultures. *International Journal of Artificial Intelligence in Education*, 25 (2), 229–248.

Ogan, A., Yarzebinski, E., Fernández, P. & Casas, I. (2015). Cognitive tutor use in Chile: Understanding classroom and lab culture. In *International Conference on Artificial Intelligence in Education* (pp. 318–327). Cham: Springer.

Olsen, J. K., Aleven, V. & Rummel, N. (2015). Predicting student performance in a collaborative learning environment. In *Proceedings of the 8th International Conference on Educational Data Mining* (pp. 211–217). International Educational Data Mining Society.

O'Shea, T. (1979). A self-improving quadratic tutor. *International Journal of Man-Machine Studies*, 11 (1), 97–124.

Pashler, H., McDaniel, M., Rohrer, D. & Bjork, R. (2008). Learning styles: Concepts and evidence. *Psychological Science in the Public Interest*, 9 (3), 105–119.

Raji, I. D. & Buolamwini, J. (2019). Actionable auditing: Investigating the impact of publicly naming biased performance results of commercial AI products. In *Proceedings of the 2019 AAAI/ACM Conference on AI, Ethics, and Society* (pp. 429–435).

Rafalow, M. H. (2020). *Digital Divisions*. University of Chicago Press.

Rau, M. A. (2015). Why do the rich get richer? A structural equation model to test how spatial skills affect learning with representations. In *Proceedings of the 8th International Conference on Educational Data Mining* (pp. 350–357).

Reich, J. & Ito, M. (2017). *From good intentions to real outcomes: Equity by design in learning technologies*. Irvine, CA: Digital Media and Learning Research Hub.

Rideout, V. J. & Katz, V.S. (2016). *Opportunity for all? Technology and learning in lower-income families: A report of the Families and Media Project*. New York: Joan Ganz Cooney Center at Sesame Workshop.

Rose, D. (2000). Universal design for learning. *Journal of Special Education Technology*, 15 (3), 45–49.

Ryan, C. L. & Lewis, J. M. (2017). *Computer and internet use in the United States: 2015*. Washington, DC: US Department of Commerce, Economics and Statistics Administration, US Census Bureau.

Saxena, M., Pillai, R. K. & Mostow, J. (2018). Relating children's automatically detected facial expressions to their behavior in RoboTutor. In *Thirty-Second AAAI Conference on Artificial Intelligence*.

Selbst, A. D., Boyd, D., Friedler, S. A., Venkatasubramanian, S. & Vertesi, J. (2019). Fairness and abstraction in sociotechnical systems. In *Proceedings of the Conference on Fairness, Accountability, and Transparency (FAT* '19)* (pp. 59–68). New York: ACM. doi:10.1145/3287560.3287598.

Sims, C. (2014). From differentiated use to differentiating practices: Negotiating legitimate participation and the production of privileged identities. *Information, Communication & Society*, 17 (6), 670–682.

Teninbaum, G. H. (2021). Report on ExamSoft's ExamID feature (and a method to bypass it). *Journal of Robotics, Artificial Intelligence, and Law*. doi:10.2139/ssrn.3759931.

Uchidiuno, J., Yarzebinski, E., Madaio, M., Maheshwari, N., Koedinger, K. & Ogan, A. (2018). Designing appropriate learning technologies for school vs home settings in Tanzanian rural villages. In *Proceedings of the 1st ACM SIGCAS Conference on Computing and Sustainable Societies* (pp. 1–11).

van Leeuwen, A. (2015). Learning analytics to support teachers during synchronous CSCL: Balancing between overview and overload. *Journal of Learning Analytics*, 2 (2), 138–162.

van Leeuwen, A. & Rummel, N. (2020). Comparing teachers' use of mirroring and advising dashboards. In *Proceedings of the 2020 Conference on Learning Analytics and Knowledge (LAK'20)* (pp. 26–34). SoLAR.

VanLehn, K. (2011). The relative effectiveness of human tutoring, intelligent tutoring systems, and other tutoring systems. *Educational Psychologist*, 46 (4), 197–221.

VanLehn, K. (2016). Regulative loops, step loops and task loops. *International Journal of Artificial Intelligence in Education*, 26 (1), 107–112.

Veale, M., Van Kleek, M. & Binns, R. (2018). Fairness and accountability design needs for algorithmic support in high-stakes public sector decision-making. In *Proceedings of the 2018 CHI Conference on Human Factors in Computing Systems* (pp. 1–14).

Watters, A. (2014). *The monsters of education technology*. CreateSpace.

Wen, Z. A., Amog, A. L. S., Azenkot, S. & Garnett, K. (2019). Teacher perspectives on math e-learning tools for students with specific learning disabilities. In *21st International ACM SIGACCESS Conference on Computers and Accessibility* (pp. 516–518).

Young, M., Magassa, L. & Friedman, B. (2019). Toward inclusive tech policy design: A method for underrepresented voices to strengthen tech policy documents. *Ethics and Information Technology*, 21 (2), 89–103.

Zhu, H., Yu, B., Halfaker, A. & Terveen, L. (2018). Value-sensitive algorithm design: Method, case study, and lessons. In *Proceedings of the ACM on Human-Computer Interaction, 2(CSCW)*, 1–23.

7 Algorithmic fairness in education

René F. Kizilcec and Hansol Lee

Introduction

Educational technologies increasingly use data and predictive models to provide support and analytic insights to students, instructors, and administrators (Baker & Inventado, 2014; Luckin & Cukurova, 2019). Adaptive systems like cognitive tutors help students achieve content mastery by providing them with different study materials based on predictions about what content they have already mastered (Pane et al., 2010). Automated scoring systems provide immediate feedback on open-ended assessments based on predictions of what scores and comments a human grader would give (Yan et al., 2020). Student support systems identify struggling students to automatically offer them assistance or flag them to instructors or administrators based on predictions about which students are likely to disengage from the learning platform, get a low score on an upcoming assessment, or experience affective states of confusion, boredom, and frustration (Hutt, Grafsgaard, et al., 2019; Prenkaj et al., 2020). Some educational technologies use data-driven predictions to directly change the learning experience, such as skipping over a module that a student is predicted to have mastered already. This can occur with or without explicit notification to the student, rendering the "intelligence" of a system either overt or hidden. Other educational technologies present model predictions to students, instructors, or administrators to support their process of interpretation and decision making. The presentation format of such predictions varies substantially with the learning context, target audience, and desired response; it can be in the form of a dedicated dashboard for instructors to track students or for students to monitor their own progress, indicators embedded in learning activities for immediate feedback, or subtle changes in the digital learning environment that affect student attention and behavior. The influence of Artificial Intelligence in education is growing in K-12, higher, and continuing education with the increasing adoption of algorithmic systems that employ predictive models developed using big data in education.

The increasing use of algorithmic systems in education raises questions about its impact on students, instructors, institutions, and society as a whole.

DOI: 10.4324/9780429329067-10

How much and under what circumstances do such technologies benefit these stakeholders? What characteristics of algorithmic systems in education are associated with greater benefits? And what counts as a beneficial impact on these stakeholders? These questions encourage a critical analysis of AI in education that also attends to its perhaps unintended and unforeseen negative consequences. Those have been a subject of significant public and academic discourse in other domains including credit decisions, employment screening, insurance eligibility, marketing, delivery of government services, criminal justice sentencing and probation decisions (MacCarthy, 2019; O'Neil, 2016). The use of data-driven decision systems in these domains has raised concerns about fairness, bias, and discrimination against members of protected classes in the United States (women, seniors, racial, ethnic, religious, and national minorities, people with disabilities, genetic vulnerabilities, and pre-existing medical conditions). It is time to widen the scope of this research effort to examine potential issues of fairness arising from the use of algorithmic systems in educational contexts. This chapter is an introduction to algorithmic fairness in education with a focus on how discrimination emerges in algorithmics systems and how it can be mitigated by considering three major steps in the process: measurement (data input), model learning (algorithm), and action (presentation or use of output). Building on extensive research on algorithmic fairness in other domains, we examine common measures of algorithmic fairness, most of which focus on the model learning, and how a better understanding of threats to algorithmic fairness can advance the responsible use of Artificial Intelligence in education. In another chapter in this book, Holstein and Doroudi (2021) holistically examine the socio-technical system surrounding Artificial Intelligence in education to explore how it risks amplifying inequalities in education.

Fairness in Education

Considerations of fairness are deeply rooted in the field of education and focused on concerns of bias and discrimination. Long before the adoption of digital learning environments in schools and homes, education scholars have studied inequalities and inequities in educational opportunities and outcomes, such as school segregation and achievement gaps. In fact, this work foreshadowed more recent formal definitions of algorithmic fairness in machine learning (Hutchinson & Mitchell, 2018). In 1954, the U.S. Supreme Court stated in *Brown v. Board of Education*, "it is doubtful that any child may reasonably be expected to succeed in life if he is denied the opportunity of an education." The legal recognition of the value that an education provides and the state's role in its provision put an end to state-sanctioned school segregation in the U.S. After all, if state-supplied education is of such critical value, according to *Brown v. Board of Education*, it "must be available to all on equal terms." This ruling shaped decades of research and public discourse on equal opportunities to educational access (Reardon & Owens, 2014), and it can be understood as a requirement for fairness in educational access. At least since the Coleman report of 1966, academic achievement gaps have become a focus of educational reform efforts (Coleman, 2019). Colman and many others have argued that a combination of home, community, and in-school factors give rise to systematic differences in educational performance between groups of students based on their socioeconomic status, race-ethnicity, and gender (Kao & Thompson, 2003). The presence of achievement gaps can be understood as a shortcoming of fairness in educational outcomes, especially if it is the result of discriminatory behavior: it is unfair if students from low-income families score lower test scores for lack of access to study resources available to high-income families, but it is especially unfair if they score lower because their teacher, or an algorithmic scoring system, is biased against them. Given the long tradition of scholarship on inequities in education, the term algorithmic fairness in the academic community almost exclusively refers to bias and discrimination involving algorithmic systems.

Any notion of fairness is inherently based in social comparison. The impact of an educational policy or technology can be assessed for groups of individuals, and how the impact compares in magnitude between them has fairness implications. Figure 7.1 shows three stylized representations of how an innovation, such as the use of an intelligent tutoring system for mathematics, might affect educational outcomes for groups and individuals under the assumption that the innovation is beneficial in general and that there are pre-existing gaps in outcomes. Each panel shows how an innovation can affect members of an advantaged and a disadvantaged group on average. Although the average outcome improves in both groups, the relative level of improvement in the advantaged group here determines whether the innovation reduces the pre-existing gap (closing gap), expands it (widening gap), or leaves it unchanged (constant gap). Most studies of the impact of educational technology on student outcomes find evidence consistent with the widening gap scenario (Attewell & Battle, 1999; Boser, 2013; Warschauer et al., 2004; Wenglinsky, 1998), though there are some exceptions that offer evidence of constant or even closing gaps (Kizilcec et al., 2021; Roschelle et al., 2016; Theobald et al., 2020). Most observers would agree that a widening gap is less fair than a constant gap, and some may find a constant gap to be less fair than a closing gap even though the overall improvement in outcomes is lower. All three scenarios are certainly fairer than one where the disadvantaged group does not benefit at all or even sees decrements in average outcomes. Fairness should therefore be measured on a continuous and not binary scale, and there are multiple ways to measure fairness, as we will discuss in more detail. Note that the points presented in Figure 7.1 represent group averages, which can mask important distributional group differences (e.g. spread and skew of outcomes within groups) that can raise additional fairness concerns and warrant closer inspection in practice.

Equality and equity are two common notions of fairness in education that are also represented in Figure 7.1. An innovation achieves equality in its impact if the groups benefit the same amount no matter what their

Figure 7.1 Stylized representations of how a generally beneficial innovation can influence outcomes for members of an advantaged group and a disadvantaged group

pre-existing outcomes are (constant gap); but to achieve equity, its impact has to be more beneficial to the group with lower outcomes to close pre-existing gaps (closing gap). Most observers would ascribe different levels of fairness to these two outcomes. In one case, groups of students who are different in terms of their outcomes (and perhaps in other ways) receive the same benefit and remain different; in the other case, different groups of students receive different benefits to render them more alike. But what about students who are similar to begin with? Dwork and colleagues (2012) propose a definition of individual fairness whereby similar individuals are to be treated similarly. Albeit a simple and intuitive approach to measure fairness, it raises a different challenge in adequately measuring the similarity of individuals: which individual characteristics are considered of those that are available and how they are combined can interfere with the assessment of individual fairness. Most definitions of fairness used in practice are therefore at the group level and compare the average individual across different groups; examples in education include the assessment of enrolment and graduation rates and achievement gaps

Scholars have grappled with issues of algorithmic fairness in high-stakes settings like healthcare and criminal justice, where machine learning models have become widely adopted in practice (Corbett-Davies & Goel, 2018; Lum & Isaac, 2016; Wiens et al., 2019). Although considerations of fairness in education are not novel, the consideration of *algorithmic* fairness is more recent and motivated by the growing number of students who are affected by algorithmic systems in educational technologies today (Hutchinson & Mitchell, 2018). This chapter provides an introduction to algorithmic fairness in education by examining the components of an algorithmic system and where considerations of fairness enter in the process of developing and deploying these systems. Our focus is on algorithmic fairness defined by the absence of bias and discrimination in a system, rather than the presence of due process. An algorithmic system such as college admission by random number generator is unfair for using an arbitrary and unaccountable process, but it is still unbiased and non-discriminatory. We review different ways of defining and assessing fairness, and initial evidence on algorithmic fairness in education. We conclude by offering recommendations for policymakers and developers of educational technology to promote fairness in educational technology.

Algorithmic Fairness and Antidiscrimination

A fair algorithm does not discriminate against individuals based on their membership in protected groups. Then what does it mean for an algorithm to discriminate and what are protected groups? The latter question can have a legal answer, which in countries like the US or UK includes groups defined based on age, sex, colour, race, religion, nationality, citizenship, veteran status, genetic information, and physical or mental ability (Government Equalities Office, 2013). Yet the list of protected groups can be extended or modified to fit the specific application of an algorithmic system. Ocumpaugh and colleagues (2014) tested the accuracy of a student affect detector on students in urban, suburban, and rural schools. Their interest in algorithmic fairness focused on protected groups defined based on urbanicity of students' location, because their affect detector was developed with data from predominantly urban students and would eventually get adopted in more rural schools. Doroudi and Brunskill (2019) tested how an intelligent tutoring system affects learning outcomes for fast and slow learners. Their interest in algorithmic fairness focused on protected groups defined based on students' learning speed to evaluate if the self-paced system discriminates against students from either group. Although definitions of protected groups vary across applications and contexts, it is necessary to specify a priori which protected groups' algorithmic fairness is to be determined.

To explain what it means for a system to discriminate against individuals, we consider traditional forms of discrimination involving human agents, which may be intentional or unintentional in nature. American antidiscrimination laws distinguish between disparate treatment and disparate impact to draw a distinction based on an actor's intent. For example, in the context of college admissions, direct consideration of applicants' race in admissions decisions (outside of holistic review) is a form of disparate treatment, because the rule that is being applied is not neutral with respect to a protected attribute. If applicants' race is omitted from consideration in the process and yet disproportionately fewer applicants from some racial groups are admitted, it is a form of disparate impact but not treatment, which does not require proof that it was intentional. Now, consider a college admissions algorithm that ranks applicants according to their predicted academic performance based on historical data from applicants and their subsequent college achievement. If this algorithmic system ranks applicants from one racial group disproportionately lower than others, it may be said that it discriminates against individuals in that protected group. Barocas and Selbst (2016) argue that this is almost always due to pre-existing patterns of bias in historical data or unintentional emergent properties of the system's use, rather than conscious choices by its programmers. In the absence of demonstrable intent, the system's discrimination is a case of disparate impact, not treatment. Including protected attributes as inputs into the algorithm does not typically change its discriminatory effects, and without a case for intentional discrimination, it does not amount to disparate treatment. Most unfair algorithmic systems thus discriminate against individuals in unintentional ways that create disparate impact. We acknowledge the importance of addressing systemic patterns of injustice that contribute to unfair algorithms and the hazards of treating the status quo as fixed. At the same time, computational research on algorithmic fairness in education can play a valuable role in affecting social change (Abebe et al., 2020).

How Discrimination Emerges in Algorithmic Systems

In the absence of discriminatory intent, how do algorithmic systems produce disparate impact among protected groups? To answer this question, we deconstruct how a generic algorithmic system is developed and used, and identify how issues of fairness can arise in the process even without deliberate intent to discriminate. A typical data-driven algorithmic system makes predictions about future or previously unseen cases based on what it "learns" from historical data. The development and use of the system can be deconstructed into a sequence of three steps visualized in Figure 7.2: measurement, model learning, and action. Measurement is the process of collecting data about an environment. Model learning is the process of using the collected data (i.e. training data) to develop a representation of the environment as a set of correlations. Action is the process of using predictions of the learned model for new cases for judgement and decision making. It can be a system-based action or a human action by a number of different stakeholders, including students, instructors, teaching staff, and administrators.

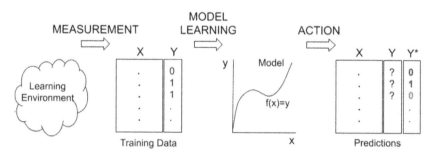

Figure 7.2 Development and use of a generic algorithmic system
Note: Data is collected from a learning environment of interest, with each datapoint represented by some fixed set of attributes X with an outcome of interest Y (Measurement); the collected data is used to learn a model f that represents the relationship between X and Y (Model Learning); the learned model is used to predict outcomes Y^* for new data with unknown true outcome Y to inform system or stakeholder actions (Action).

We return to the example of an algorithmic system designed to support the college admissions process by predicting students' college success from their application data (Friedler et al., 2016; Kleinberg et al., 2018). In the measurement step, a training dataset is assembled by quantifying college success (e.g. cumulative GPA, degree completion) as the target variable y for each student with a set of individual features $\{x_1 ..., x_n\}$ X from the application information. Student features may include high school grades, standardized test scores, the number of extracurricular activities and leadership positions, and linguistic features extracted from the essay. Once the training dataset is assembled, the model learning step can begin. There is a wide variety of prediction algorithms to choose from. For instance, a (penalized) linear regression algorithm might be used to learn a model for a continuous outcome like cumulative GPA, while a random forest algorithm might be used to learn a model for a binary outcome like on-time graduation. The learned model is then used to generate predictions for new applicants whose eventual college success is yet unknown. These predictions can be used in the action step to inform judgement and decision-making about applicants in a number of ways. Admissions officers may still review all applicants manually, but take the model predictions into account as an additional input into their decisions. Alternatively, the algorithmic system may provide admissions officers the option to further review only applicants whose predicted college success rate is above a certain threshold. In theory, following careful evaluation of its feasibility and impact, the entire admissions process could be automated based on the model predictions. Using this example of a college success prediction system, we examine how unintended discrimination can arise in each of the three steps visualized in Figure 7.2.

Measurement

Measurement may appear like the simplest step in the process, but it presents some of the greatest challenges for developing fair algorithmic systems. The first task is to define the prediction problem and measure the target variable. The number of recent articles emphasizing the importance of defining appropriate outcomes in educational settings and the dangers of optimizing for inappropriate ones is evidence that this task calls for careful consideration of potential options and their consequences (DeBoer et al., 2014; Duckworth & Yeager, 2015; Gašević et al., 2015; Schwartz & Arena, 2013). In the context of college admissions, selecting a target measure of college success is not only a task that requires subjective judgements of what constitutes success (academics, extracurriculars, community service, etc.), it also depends on the characteristics and objectives of the admitting college (its graduation rates, goals for student diversity, etc.). Consider college GPA as a target measure of college success, which has been used in prior research (e.g. Kleinberg et al., 2018). This measure arguably captures a limited notion of college success, as students can be successful in other ways than achieving high grades in their classes. Most target measures, including college

GPA, inherit prejudices of prior decision-makers and encode widespread biases that exist in society. For instance, persistent demographic gaps in the GPA of college graduates may not reflect true differences in college success (de Brey et al., 2019): structural barriers like access to learning resources, psychological factors like stereotype threat, and (implicit) bias among graders can all reduce GPA for historically disadvantaged students. A learning algorithm will discover the correlation between student demographics and college GPA in the training data, even though it is a reflection of historic patterns of prejudice, discrimination, or data integrity issues. The subjectivity of the choice of the target variable and the possibility that it encodes bias can adversely affect the fairness of an algorithmic system. The target variable is particularly influential in this regard because it alone encodes what the algorithm optimizes for, but the choice and measurement of features presents its own set of challenges (Nabi & Shpitser, 2018).

The selection of features to measure alongside the target measure involves a reduction of a rich state of the world into a fixed and relatively narrow set of values. Due to this distillation, the collected data won't capture the full complexity of individual differences and contextual factors. This raises concerns for algorithmic fairness if historically disadvantaged and vulnerable members of society are differentially affected in the process. For instance, the inclusion of Advanced Placement (AP) grades as a feature in the training data for an algorithmic admissions system can result in bias against students who do not have access to AP classes in their high school, which disproportionately affects students in low-income school districts. Moreover, historical patterns of bias can be embedded in measured features in the same way as the target variable. Standardized test scores such as ACT or SAT scores are commonly used in the admissions process as an indicator of academic potential, even though they are highly correlated with students' socioeconomic status and could therefore disadvantage minority and low-income students (Sackett et al., 2009). The predictive power of features can also vary across groups. For example, features extracted from the college admissions essay may vary in how well they forecast college success depending on students' native language and home country, as evidenced by research demonstrating cultural variation in the predictive power of motivational factors on student achievement (Li et al., 2021).

Beyond the problem definition, the process of measurement almost always requires sampling data from a population. Whether sampling is done intentionally or unintentionally, it warrants careful consideration because it raises questions of representativeness and generalizability. These terms are often vaguely defined and used inconsistently across fields such as politics, statistics, and machine learning (Chasalow & Levy, 2021). In general, the closer the training data is to the test data for which the algorithm is going to make predictions, the more accurate its predictions are going to be; however, this is not always the case (Yudelson et al., 2014). Ocumpaugh and colleagues (2014) demonstrated this in the case of a student affect detector that exhibited higher prediction accuracy for students from rural, suburban, and urban regions if it was trained on a sample drawn from the same locale. Likewise, Gardner and colleagues (2019) showed in the context of student dropout prediction that training datasets that skew male provide lower prediction accuracy for females. The underrepresentation of some groups in the training data due to the sampling strategy can thus present a threat to algorithmic fairness by disadvantaging members of historically underrepresented groups (Chawla et al., 2002).

Model Learning

The model learning step typically begins with pre-processing the collected training data. Pre-processing can take many different forms and commonly includes the removal of duplicate data, correction of inconsistencies, removal of outliers, and handling of missing data. According to a recent review paper on predictive student modelling, very few studies provide a detailed account of the pre-processing procedures that were applied (Cui et al., 2019). Friedler and colleagues (2019) show that different choices made during pre-processing can lead to notable differences in the performance of algorithmic systems and should therefore be well-documented and held constant when comparing model learning strategies.

Model learning is the process of approximating the relationship between the features and the target measure based on the pre-processed training data. The resulting model is therefore subject to potential biases embedded in the data. Some biases can be mitigated in the measurement step itself, but others will enter into the model learning process and without an intervention, the resulting model is likely to reflect these biases. To illustrate this point, consider that without intervention, a natural language model trained on textual data collected from a large real-world corpus like Google News will learn gender stereotypes such as "male" is to "computer programmer" as "female" is to "homemaker" (Bolukbasi et al., 2016). This shows that even if the training dataset is remarkably large and the embedded biases are relatively subtle, the learned model is still likely to mirror the bias in its predictions if left unchecked. Studies in education that found reduced prediction accuracy for students who are underrepresented in the training data could for instance use case weights to raise the relative influence of underrepresented students in the model learning process (Gardner et al., 2019; Ocumpaugh et al., 2014).

Two major choices in the model learning step are the type of model and evaluation strategy. In practice, most software packages render it quick and easy to try different types of models and compare their performance against each other: for example, *scikit-learn* in Python (Pedregosa et al., 2011) and *caret* in R (Kuhn & Others, 2008). Early research on how the choice of a type of model affects algorithmic fairness does not suggest that some model types are generally fairer than others; instead, the level of algorithmic fairness varies across datasets, and even within datasets for different random splits into training and testing data (Friedler et al., 2019; Gardner et al., 2019). This finding emphasizes the role of the model evaluation strategy and metrics in assessing algorithmic fairness. A common evaluation strategy is to compute model performance as the overall prediction accuracy on a held-out testing dataset. However, the high overall accuracy can hide the fact that the model has much lower accuracy for individuals who are underrepresented in the data. Gardner and colleagues (2019) advocate for a "slicing analysis" to consider model accuracy for sub-groups explicitly and quantify the gap in accuracy. Others have proposed modifications to learning algorithms to additionally optimize a fairness constraint (Calders & Verwer, 2010; Kamishima et al., 2012; Zafar et al., 2017; Zemel et al., 2013). How analytic choices in model learning raise issues of algorithmic fairness is a relatively novel and active area of research, and much remains to be learned (for a recent survey, see d'Alessandro et al., 2017).

Action

The final step in the process is taking action using the learned model to make predictions for new cases and guide human decision-makers (students, instructors, administrators, etc.) or have the algorithmic system act upon the predictions directly. In the case of an algorithmic system for college admissions, predictions for college success will be made for new applicants who were not in the training dataset and for whom the true outcome such as college GPA is unknown. The resulting predictions could be used in various ways, from merely complementing the standard application materials that admissions offers review, to entirely automating admissions decisions. The predictions are however only as valid as the underlying training data and learned model. If biases in the underlying data result in biased predictions, for instance underpredicting college success for minority and low-income students, it can affect admissions decisions and contribute to disparate impact. It is therefore recommended to monitor the accuracy of model predictions over time and set expectations that the model will likely require tuning when fairness issues are discovered. Failing to test an algorithmic system for potential fairness issues, known as auditing the algorithmic system, can result in disparate impact (Saleiro et al., 2018). Yet the growing complexity of algorithmic systems is making it more difficult to test them.

As algorithmic systems have grown in complexity, it has become more difficult for human decision-makers who use these systems to understand why and how a model is making certain predictions. The rise of "black box" systems has raised concerns about the trustworthiness of model predictions, the extent to which predictive models should also be explanatory in nature, and what happens when predictions drive automated decisions that may have discriminatory effects (Hosanagar, 2020). These concerns have motivated research on *interpretable machine learning* which aims to design models that are transparent and understandable (Conati et al., 2018; Doshi-Velez & Kim, 2017). If predictive models provided explanations for their predictions, such as why a given student applicant is predicted to have low college success, then decision-makers could use these explanations to qualitatively assess various criteria including fairness. Concerns about model transparency and explainability have come up in the knowledge tracing literature, which has been dominated by simple and interpretable Bayesian models (Corbett & Anderson, 1995) when a new deep learning model was proposed with substantially more parameters and lower interpretability (Piech et al., 2015). How to communicate the prediction outcomes to the decision-maker or user of the system is a human-computer interaction question. Deciding just how much transparency to provide about an algorithmic system is a critical consideration that can determine how much users will trust the system and its predictions (Kizilcec, 2016). An erosion of trust in an algorithmic system can lead decision-makers to disregard its predictions, which can result in discriminatory action that reinforces prevailing stereotypes when decisions are also subject to confirmation bias (Nickerson, 1998). For example, an admissions officer who does not have trust in the algorithmic system may question its predictions when they violate her expectations (stereotypes) but not otherwise.

Another potential issue that can arise even if the model is thoroughly tested and highly accurate, is the misinterpretation of a fundamentally correlational prediction as a causal one. Most algorithmic systems are developed based on historical data for which they learn to represent empirical relationships between features and the target measure. Model predictions therefore indicate correlational but not causal quantities in most cases; and yet, causal interpretations of predictive models are abundant. SAT scores are predictive of college success in terms of GPA, but it does not mean that if SAT scores were raised for some students by signing them up for a test preparation course, that it would cause them to earn a college GPA according to the prediction. Instead, numerous individual and contextual factors about a student correlate with both SAT score and college GPA to strengthen the correlation between these two measures. Using said predictions to support the college admissions process may therefore result in disparate impact, by more frequently denying admission to low-income students who tend to have both lower SAT scores and college GPA (Sackett et al., 2009). This provides another potential source of unfairness in algorithmic systems, especially if it establishes a negative feedback loop by biasing future training data used to update the model of the algorithmic system (O'Neil, 2016).

For some prediction problems, it may not be possible to achieve a high level of prediction accuracy even with access to a rich dataset and state-of-the-art machine learning algorithms. Salganik and colleagues (2020) demonstrated this in a competition involving hundreds of researchers to predict major life outcomes including educational achievement based on years of detailed longitudinal survey data. The best performing model was only slightly better than a simple baseline and explained only 20% of the variation in high school GPA. Predicting who should receive what kind of educational intervention can be even harder because it requires causal inference. Kizilcec and colleagues (2020) used data from a massive field experiment in online higher education and state-of-the-art machine learning to target behavioural science interventions to individual students, but even the best models produced no better student outcomes than simply assigning everyone the same intervention or a random one. These studies highlight practical limits of data-driven models for prediction and potential risks of stakeholders placing too much confidence in algorithmic systems.

Measures of Algorithmic Fairness

The previous section showed how issues of fairness can arise in every step of the process of developing and deploying an algorithmic system. This can result in discriminatory action and disparate impact in the absence of any malicious intent. In this section, we take a closer look at what unfairness means by reviewing a number of formal definitions of fairness that have been proposed in the literature to date and how they can be applied in the context of education. Specifically, we review statistical, similarity-based, and causal notions of fairness in relation to an example of an algorithmic system that predicts student dropout. Research on fairness in machine learning is rapidly evolving and this review is based on the most recent work in the field (for further reading, we recommend Barocas and colleagues' online book on fair machine learning and Verma and Rubin's detailed review of definitions; Barocas et al., 2019; Verma & Rubin, 2018). Measures of algorithmic fairness have focused on the predictions resulting from the model learning step in the process of developing an algorithmic system. This step lends itself to quantifying fairness because of the standardized approaches to evaluating models, such as a confusion matrix of correct and incorrect predictions. In contrast, to quantify bias and discrimination in the measurement and action steps, significantly more contextual knowledge is required to quantify dataset bias (e.g. what population it should be representative of), discriminatory problem definitions (e.g. predicting affective states that are subject to cultural variation), stigmatizing responses to model predictions (e.g. flagging at-risk students in ways that discourages performance), and biased representations of predicted outcomes (e.g. visualizations that make small predicted differences seem large).

To compare different definitions of fairness in the context of AI in education, we consider the case of student dropout prediction which has received substantial research attention in various learning environments. Let random variables X represent a set of observed features for each student, Y their true dropout outcomes, D the algorithmic decisions (predictions of y), and G a protected attribute of each student. For standard dropout prediction, this is a binary classification problem where $Y=\{0,1\}$, though it can be generalized to multivariate or regression problems. The algorithmic system uses a prediction model $f(X)$ that returns a probability distribution over the possible values of for each individual (i.e. $Pr(D|X)$). D is determined using a deterministic threshold, where if $D=1$ if $f(X) > t$, and 0 otherwise. We examine whether an algorithmic system that predicts the likelihood of students' dropout from a course is fair for male and female students (i.e. G in this case).

Statistical Notions of Fairness

We begin by reviewing three statistical notions of fairness: independence, separation, and sufficiency. They are a foundation for understanding many statistical fairness criteria in the literature, which can be expressed as a derivation of one of these three definitions. **Independence** requires that an algorithm's decision be independent of group membership. Formally, in the case of binary classification, it requires that

$$Pr(D = 1|G = g_i) = Pr(D = 1|G = g_j)$$

for all protected groups g_i, g_j in G. Independence is satisfied if the same percentage of male and female students are classified as at-risk for dropping out ($D = 1$). Figure 7.3 visualizes outcomes of a dropout prediction algorithm that satisfies independence. Independence represents the desirable long-term goal of equity for different groups of students (i.e. male and female students persist at equal rates) and using it as a measure of fairness may advance efforts to reduce historical inequalities (Räz, 2021). However, a limitation of independence as a notion of fairness in settings like dropout prediction is that it ignores students' true tendency to drop out. If female students were more likely to drop out in the first week of class than male students, for instance because they initially enrol in more courses to find the best fit, then it would seem reasonable to account for the actual gender difference in dropout in the predictions. To address this limitation of independence, which results from only considering the protected group G and algorithmic decision D, the definition of fairness as separation additionally considers the true outcome Y.

Separation requires that an algorithm's decision be independent of group membership conditional on true outcomes. Formally, in the case of a binary classification, separation requires that both

$$Pr(D = 1|Y = 1, G = g_i) = Pr(D = 1|Y = 1, G = g_j)$$
$$Pr(D = 1|Y = 0, G = g_i) = Pr(D = 1|Y = 0, G = g_j)$$

for all protected groups g_i, g_j in G. Separation encodes the belief that a fair algorithm makes correct and incorrect predictions at similar rates for different groups.

This is visualized in Figure 7.4 (left panel) which shows the same true positive rate (60%) and false positive rate (20%) for male and female students. If the dropout prediction algorithm has a higher false positive rate for female students than for male students, it falsely flags well-performing female students as at-risk more often than well-performing male students. Instructors may lower their expectations about students flagged as at-risk and act towards them in ways that reduce their academic performance – a phenomenon known as the Pygmalion effect (Brookover et al., 1969). This describes one way that an algorithmic system with a higher false positive rate for female students can be unfair towards female students. Likewise, if the dropout system has a lower true positive rate for female students than male students, it will fail to identify struggling female students more often than similarly struggling male students. A targeted intervention to help students predicted to be at-risk may inadvertently help male students more than it helps female students. To achieve separation, an algorithmic system typically needs to set different decision thresholds t for each protected group. However, this violates another notion of fairness such as individual fairness, according to which individuals should not be treated differently on the basis of protected attributes.

Where as separation requires that algorithmic decisions are independent of protected attributes conditional on true outcomes, **sufficiency** requires that true outcomes are independent of protected attributes conditional on algorithmic decisions. Formally, in the case of a binary classification, Sufficiency can be expresses as

$$Pr(Y = 1|D = 1, G = g_i) = Pr(Y = 1|D = 1, G = g_j)$$

for all protected groups g_i, g_j in G. Sufficiency encodes the belief that algorithmic decisions should carry the same level of significance for all groups, such that for all student predicted to drop out, the same percentage of students predicted to drop out, the same percentage of students in each group actually drop out. This is visualized in Figure 7.4 (top panel) which shows that 30 male and 35 female students are predicted to drop out, and 60% in each group actually drop out. The predictions therefore carry the same significance for male and female students. However, satisfying sufficiency may offer only a weak guarantee for fairness. To see this, suppose that the true dropout rate is 25% for males and 50% for females. An algorithmic system could naively

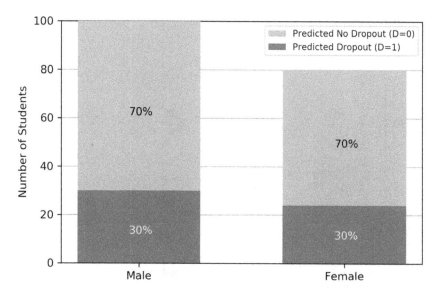

Figure 7.3 Illustration of dropout predictions that satisfy fairness as independence
Note: Given a total of 100 male and 80 female students, independence is satisfied with $Pr(D = 1 | G = \text{male}) = Pr(D = 1 | G = \text{female}) = 30\%$ predicted to be at risk of dropping out.

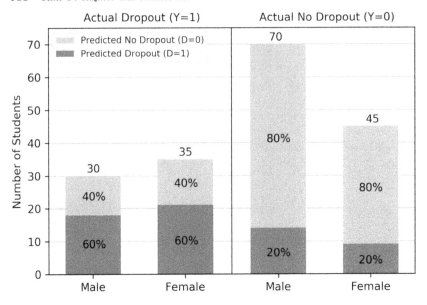

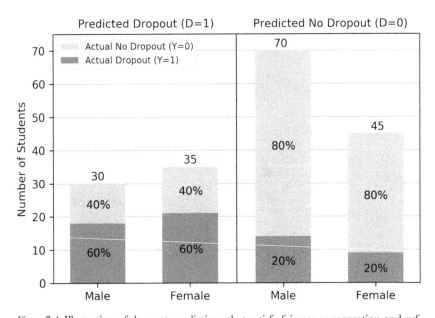

Figure 7.4 Illustration of dropout predictions that satisfy fairness as separation and sufficiency for a total of 100 male and 80 female students

Note: Separation is satisfied with $Pr(D = 1 | Y = 1, G = \text{male}) = Pr(D = 1 | Y = 1, G = \text{female}) = 60\%$ and $Pr(D = 1 | Y = 0, G = \text{male}) = Pr(D = 1 | Y = 0, G = \text{female}) = 20\%$.

Sufficiency is satisfied with $Pr(Y = 1 | D = 1, G = \text{male}) = Pr(Y = 1 | D = 1, G = \text{female}) = 60\%$.

predict all male students to be at-risk to achieve a precision of 25% and predict only a few female students to be at-risk to also achieve a precision of 25%. This algorithmic system satisfies sufficiency, but it is clearly not fair. If additional resources were allocated to students predicted to be at-risk, then this system would have all of the male students receive this academic intervention, while withholding it from truly at-risk female students.

Similarity-Based Notions of Fairness

Statistical notions of fairness consider algorithmic decisions D, true outcomes Y, and group membership G, but they ignore all individual features of cases X. They are also known as group fairness measures because they ignore individual differences. Whereas statistical notions of fairness require some kind of group-level parity, similarity-based notions of fairness require parity for pairs of similar individuals based on their observed features. We review two approaches to achieving similarity-based fairness: fairness through unawareness and individual fairness. Both approaches encode the belief that algorithmic decisions should not be influenced by any protected attributes that are irrelevant to the prediction task at hand.

Fairness through unawareness is an approach to achieve similarity-based fairness by omitting protected attributes from the feature set (Kusner et al., 2017). It avoids the appearance of disparate treatment because the algorithmic system does not take the protected attribute into account during model learning and action. However, this approach falls short of being blind to protected attributes, because a learned model can inadvertently reconstruct protected attributes from a number of seemingly unrelated features. For example, even if gender is removed from the feature set, a dropout prediction algorithm can still predict as if it had students' gender as a feature, because it has access to multiple features that are slightly correlated with gender. The consequences of fairness through unawareness can therefore be unexpected. Kleinberg and colleagues (2018) found that including race as a feature improves both overall accuracy and demographic parity of an algorithmic admissions system that predicts college success. By explicitly considering the applicant's race, the system's predictions of college success become more accurate and the fraction of black applicants who are predicted to succeed increases. Yu and colleagues (2020) found that predictions are more accurate if the feature set includes student demographic information in an algorithmic system that predicts student performance in college courses on the basis of learning management system data. In contrast, Yu and colleagues (2021) found that the inclusion of student demographics does not affect the overall performance and algorithmic fairness of a college dropout prediction model trained on university registrar data for online and in-person college students. In light of these findings, it is unclear whether the inclusion of protected attributes adds predictive value to algorithmic systems, and the merits of fairness through unawareness may be mostly symbolic. Critics of the fairness-through-unawareness approach have noted its similarities to racist ideologies such as colour-blindness (Bonilla-Silva, 2006; Burke, 2018).

Individual fairness goes one step further to address the issue of algorithms inadvertently reconstructing protected attributes from the feature set by quantifying the similarity between individuals directly (Dwork et al., 2012). This approach has domain experts construct a distance metric to capture the similarity between individuals for a given prediction task. Individual fairness requires that algorithmic decisions be similar for any pair of individuals that is close according to the task-specific distance metric. The similarity of algorithmic decisions is defined by the distance between the probability distributions over outcomes generated by a prediction model f. In the case of student dropout prediction, suppose that domain experts determine that academic preparedness for a course is the single best predictor of dropout and there exists an accurate measure of this student attribute. Students with similar levels of academic preparedness should then be classified similarly by the algorithmic system to satisfy individual fairness. In contrast, an unfair system, as depicted in Figure 7.5, predicts substantially different dropout probabilities for two similar students in terms of their academic preparedness, such that the discrepancy in predictions is not accounted for. A significant challenge with individual fairness is that it depends heavily on the choice of the distance metric, which itself can be subject to fairness issues. Moreover, treating similar individuals similarly may not produce outcomes that satisfy group-level fairness; it can for instance result in a rising tide scenario as shown in Figure 7.1. Specifically, if male and female students have the same tendency to drop out, then imposing individual fairness is a specific version of the group fairness notion of independence; but if the two groups differ in their likelihood of dropping out, then imposing individual fairness will violate independence.

Causal Notions of Fairness

Statistical and similarity-based notions of fairness are based purely on observations of random variables, but algorithmic fairness can also be approached from a causal perspective. **Counterfactual fairness** is grounded in a causal approach to fairness. It encodes the belief that an algorithmic decision is fair if the prediction remains unchanged under the counterfactual scenario where

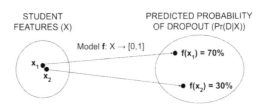

Figure 7.5 Illustration of dropout predictions that violate individual fairness
Note: A prediction model f maps two similar students x_1 and x_2 to different predicted probabilities of dropout, such that x_1 is predicted to be much more likely to drop out (70%) than x_2 (30%).

the individual belongs to a different protected group (Kusner et al., 2017). Compared to individual fairness, which demands that pairs of similar individuals receive similar predictions, counterfactual fairness demands that any individual receives similar predictions regardless of their group membership. Evaluating how the individual's predictions would change for different group memberships requires causal inference. For example, a dropout prediction system that satisfies counterfactual fairness would predict the same dropout probability for a given student with their actual sex and with the opposite sex, keeping all other features constant. The challenge with this approach is making these causal inferences in the absence of a credible identification strategy, and especially if it requires extrapolating outside of the training set (i.e. no student in the training set with similar individual features is of the opposite sex) (Russell et al., 2017). Just as individual fairness hinges on the definition of a valid distance metric to measure similarity, counterfactual fairness hinges on the validity of a causal model for deriving causal quantities mostly from observational data (Wu et al., 2019).

This review of fairness definitions is not exhaustive, but it covers fundamental notions of fairness that many of the definitions that have been proposed in the literature can be related to. An overview of many proposed definitions of algorithmic fairness categorized by the fundamental notion they are related to is provided in Table 7.1. The various fairness definitions are either equivalent to or a relaxation of the statistical, similarity-based, and causal notions of fairness notions reviewed here.

Table 7.1 Definitions of algorithmic fairness categorized by general notions of fairness

Fairness notion	Related definitions of algorithmic fairness
Statistical fairness: Independence	Statistical parity/group fairness (Dwork et al., 2012); demographic parity (Feldman et al., 2015); conditional statistical parity (Corbett-Davies et al., 2017); Darlington criterion (4) (Darlington, 1971)
Statistical fairness: Separation	Equal opportunity/equalized odds (Hardt et al., 2016); ABROCA (Gardner et al., 2019); conditional procedure accuracy (Berk et al., 2018); avoiding disparate mistreatment (Zafar et al., 2017); balance for the positive/negative class (Kleinberg et al., 2016); predictive equality (Chouldechova, 2017); equalized correlations (Woodworth et al., 2017); Darlington criterion (3) (Darlington, 1971)
Statistical fairness: Sufficiency	Conditional use accuracy (Berk et al., 2018); predictive parity (Chouldechova, 2017); calibration within groups (Chouldechova, 2017); Darlington criteria (1), (2) (Darlington, 1971)
Similarity-based fairness	Fairness through unawareness (Kusner et al., 2017); individual fairness (Dwork et al., 2012)
Causal fairness	Counterfactual fairness (Kusner et al., 2017); no unresolved discrimination/no proxy discrimination (Kilbertus et al., 2017); fair inference (Nabi & Shpitser, 2018)

Choosing a Measure of Algorithmic Fairness

The number and variety of available measures of algorithmic fairness raises an important question for researchers and practitioners alike: how does one decide on which measure to evaluate and monitor the fairness of a given algorithmic system? Answering this question requires careful consideration of how the algorithmic system is to be used (i.e. the action step): evaluating the fairness of a given system can require different measures depending on the use case, such as using dropout predictions for placing students on academic probation versus assigning them a personal tutor. To narrow down the options, one can choose to either ensure fairness at the group level using statistical notions or at the individual level using similarity-based and causal notions. Measures of individual-level fairness, such as similarity-based and causal fairness, provide more fine-grained information than group-level definitions, but they are generally harder to compute and implement. The extent to which they are feasible depends on the application context. For example, counterfactual fairness can be appropriate and feasible for an algorithmic system that delivers interventions to at-risk students with some degree of randomness to examine intervention efficacy, because the randomness offers an identification strategy for credible causal inference. Similarity-based fairness can also be feasible in applications where domain experts agree on a valid distance metric to quantify individual similarity. It is worth considering the possibility of applying individual-level fairness measures in education, where educational technologies facilitate randomization of course materials and where the availability of student data and frequent assessments facilitates the definition of robust distance metrics.

Group-level fairness is consistent with the ideal of allocating scarce educational resources to various groups of students in an equitable fashion. An advantage of group-level statistical notions of fairness is that they are easy to measure by computing conditional probabilities of different random variables. However, various statistical notions of fairness are inherently in conflict with each other, as formalized in the impossibility of fairness results (Chouldechova, 2017; Kleinberg et al., 2016), which have since been demonstrated in the contexts of automated English proficiency test scoring (Loukina et al., 2019) and university student at-risk prediction (Lee & Kizilcec, 2020). Since any two notions of statistical fairness cannot be satisfied simultaneously (except in unrealistic scenarios), one has to prioritize one notion of fairness over others. Which notion of statistical fairness should be prioritized in educational contexts? Independence advances the goal of allocating resources equally to all students regardless of their background or qualification. As we have seen, independence is more appropriate if there is an even playing field to begin with or if the action taken with the algorithmic system has negative consequences for individuals, but less appropriate otherwise. Separation and sufficiency, both considered merit-based fairness measures, advance the goal of allocating resources equally across *qualified* individuals independent of their group membership. Merit-based fairness measures are most appropriate in applications like student dropout prediction for allocating additional study resources, where the goal is to estimate students' true tendency to drop out as accurately as possible. Some algorithmic systems in education seek a middle ground between these two ideals of resource allocation and therefore need to satisfy a (weighted) combination of fairness criteria; for instance, an algorithmic admissions system is expected to rank the most qualified applicants highest while also maintaining socio-demographic diversity.

The choice of a fairness measure can also be informed by one's understanding of the relationship between students' true and observed attributes. Friedler and colleagues (2016) define two different worldviews that highlight the tension between group- and individual-level fairness: WYSIWYG (what you see is what you get) and WAE (we're all equal). The WYSIWYG worldview represents the belief that observed attributes (e.g. a student's GPA or standardized test score) are an accurate reflection of unobserved attributes (e.g. a student's merit or potential). In contrast, the WAE world view represents the belief that there are no innate differences between groups of individuals in the unobserved attributes. In the example of college admissions, the WYSIWYG worldview assumes that observed attributes, such as GPA or standardized test scores, correlate well with unobserved attributes, such as merit or potential. This worldview encourages comparing the true aptitude of individual applicants using the observed student attributes, once any noise or structural bias in the observed attributes are appropriately accounted for. On the other hand, the WAE worldview assumes that different groups of applicants are all equal in their intrinsic abilities in the unobserved space, so any differences in the observed features are due to factors irrelevant to student ability (e.g. availability of resources for college preparation, or quality of neighbourhood schools). Considering these two opposing worldviews makes the choice of fairness notions explicit, as only individual fairness notions are desirable under the WYSIWYG worldview, and only group fairness notions are desirable under the WAE worldview.

As different fairness notions all highlight different angles of fairness, it may not be sufficient to satisfy only one fairness definition in order to certify that an algorithmic system is non-discriminatory. Corbett-Davies and Goel (2018) point out a limitation of separation as a fairness criterion by showing that differential error rates across groups may just be a consequence of different underlying risk distributions, rather than a discriminatory algorithm. It can therefore be misleading to assess the fairness of a dropout prediction system solely based on separation without careful examination of the underlying distributions for each group, since a violation of separation may just be a natural consequence of male and female students having different probabilities of dropout. In some contexts, for example in automated essay scoring where an algorithmic system attempts to replicate a complex task performed by experts, it is possible to compare model predictions to reference values, such as the scores a human assigns to the same work. While human scores should not simply be treated as a gold standard because of biases that can enter in the scoring process, the comparison between human and algorithmic scores for various subgroups can offer an intuitive method to measure fairness in contexts such as TOEFL and GRE essay scoring (Bridgeman et al., 2009, 2012).

No single definition of fairness will be appropriate across all algorithmic systems in education. It is the responsibility of the researcher and practitioner to evaluate their specific situation and decide what criteria are most important to them (Makhlouf et al., 2020). It is also relatively easy to compute several group-level fairness measures to assess how an algorithmic system performs across various criteria. The effects of imposing different fairness criteria can be evaluated based on the long-term effects on affected populations (Liu et al., 2018), their trade-offs between social utilities (Corbett-Davies et al., 2017), their society-wide distributional effects (Hu & Chen, 2018), and changes in strategic behavior of affected individuals (Milli et al., 2019). This demonstrable need to carefully evaluate fairness criteria for each application scenario encourages active discussion about fairness priorities among a wide range of stakeholders.

Advancing Algorithmic Fairness in Education

Advances in algorithmic fairness in education rely on stakeholders raising questions about the presence and nature of disparate impacts of algorithmic systems in academic contexts. These questions apply to algorithmic systems that are currently in use, under consideration for procurement from external vendors, and new systems that analysts and researchers are planning to develop. Despite the recent enthusiasm about Artificial Intelligence, algorithmic systems are not silver bullets for solving problems in education (Reich, 2020). They are tools that in some cases impact many people, operate in opaque ways, and inadvertently cause harm in education as well as other domains (O'Neil, 2016). This is why it is critical for stakeholders to scrutinize the way that algorithmic systems are working in relation to how they expect them to work. We have seen how bias and discrimination can enter in every step of developing and deploying an algorithmic system, from measurement to model learning to action. We have also reviewed various notions of algorithmic fairness to measure how the system is actually working from different angles. We now offer recommendations for techniques that can be adopted at each step to improve algorithmic fairness in education. Fairness-enhancing techniques are an active area of research that has gained momentum over recent years (see Friedler et al., 2019 for an in-depth survey). The current best practice is to implement discrimination-aware unit tests at each step – measurement, model learning, and action – so that fairness issues can be identified and addressed in a timely and targeted manner (d'Alessandro et al., 2017). In the future, education technology providers may be expected to provide a fairness report to communicate benchmarked properties of their algorithmic systems to academic stakeholders (Mitchell et al., 2018).

To improve fairness in the measurement step, it is important to scrutinize the concrete prediction problem that the algorithmic system is set up to solve and remember that the underlying data is not neutral. Data reflect any existing biases and discriminatory behavior that exist in the real world. We reviewed several kinds of bias that can be present in the target measure as well as the feature set. Considering what is not included in the measured data can be just as important as what is included with respect to both missing information and sampling. Students in underrepresented groups may need to be oversampled to ensure that sufficient data is available in the model learning step to produce an accurate prediction for their group. Likewise, missing data may be more common among non-traditional students (e.g. standardized test scores, records from other learning technologies), which may inadvertently introduce bias in the model learning step. The collected data should therefore be carefully reviewed and corrected for potential bias before it is used to train prediction models. A number of techniques for de-biasing training data have been proposed (Calmon et al., 2017; Feldman et al., 2015; Kamiran & Calders, 2012). For example, Feldman and colleagues (2015) propose modifying individual features to standardize them across protected attributes to remove potentially discriminatory information encoded in the features. We encourage academic policymakers to interrogate the measurement step with questions about the definition of the prediction problem (e.g. "what is the system's definition of student success/failure?"), the data collection process (e.g. "what student data sources are used in the system?"), checks for bias in the training data (e.g. "how were students in the training dataset selected?"), and what de-biasing techniques were applied.

To improve fairness in the model learning step, developers of algorithmic systems in education can be explicit about which data pre-processing steps are necessary (Friedler et al., 2019), use model evaluation metrics that are sensitive to biases in prediction performance (Gardner et al., 2019), and add fairness constraints or regularizers to learning algorithms (Calders & Verwer, 2010; Kamishima et al., 2012; Zafar et al., 2017; Zemel et al., 2013). Friedler and colleagues (2019) find that different modifications to learning procedures result in a trade-off between model accuracy and fairness, and that the efficacy of a particular modification varies across different datasets. It is therefore important for developers of educational technology to carefully report and evaluate the choices made in model learning procedures, including pre-processing of student data as well as consideration of feature sets and learning algorithms. Model evaluation metrics like ABROCA (Gardner et al., 2019; Hutt, Gardner, et al., 2019) that account for group-specific model performance can reveal sources of discrimination for models that are trained to maximize overall accuracy. For example, differences in ABROCA values across student demographic groups can reveal a source of bias in a student predictive model that may otherwise be hidden if the model was only evaluated on standard metrics that consider the student sample as a whole. The model learning procedure can be modified by adding fairness constraints or regularizers to remove relationships with protected attributes that exist in the training data. For example, Dwork and colleagues (2012) suggest adding a fairness constraint to the optimization problem that maximizes accuracy and encodes the notion of individual fairness that similar individuals should receive similar predictions. We encourage academic policymakers to inquire about the use and consideration of fairness requirements in the model learning process and how its effects on students, instructors, and administrators are evaluated.

To improve fairness in the action step, it is important to remain vigilant for how the trained model is working for different stakeholders in education. If the model predictions do not achieve a desirable outcome for different groups, it is possible to improve the model in a post-learning step by modifying its predictions in a principled way (Hardt et al., 2016; Kamiran & Calders, 2012; Woodworth et al., 2017). For example, Hardt and colleagues (2016) suggest adjusting the resulting predictions of a trained model such that separation can be achieved post-hoc. Open-source toolkits such as Aequitas (Saleiro et al., 2018) and AI Fairness 360 (Bellamy et al., 2018) can be used in the action step to monitor a trained model for potential disparate impact by developers of algorithmic systems in education for internal audits and by education policymakers for external and periodic audits. Aequitas provides an interface for developers and policymakers to evaluate a prediction model based on several fairness metrics, along with a "fairness tree" to help them select a relevant metric for a given use case. AI Fairness 360 provides a more extensive toolkit that includes an interface for both detecting and mitigating unfairness of an algorithmic system. The design of these toolkits highlights the benefits of evaluating a variety of fairness measures in combination with a variety of bias-mitigation strategies. Last but not least, to improve fairness in the action step, algorithmic interfaces designed for students, instructors, and administrators can provide more information on the purpose and intended use of the algorithmic system and how it is working to promote trust in the system and avoid unintended types of usage that have adverse consequences (Conati et al., 2018; Doshi-Velez & Kim, 2017; Kizilcec, 2016; Marcinkowski et al., 2020). Individual perceptions of algorithmic fairness, for example with respect to procedural and distributive justice, can diverge from objective measures of fairness based on how a system is presented to students in the context of peer assessment (Kizilcec, 2016) or college admissions (Marcinkowski et al., 2020).

A vibrant new area of work on bias and discrimination in algorithms, which has become known as algorithmic fairness, is intersecting with new uses of algorithms and longstanding concerns about bias and discrimination in educational settings. The use of algorithmic systems in education is raising questions about its impact on students, instructors, institutions, and society as a whole. There is promising evidence that these technologies can benefit various stakeholders in different educational environments, but more work is required to fully understand the ways in which algorithmic systems that are in common use in education impact different groups or individuals differently. More critical analysis of AI in education that attends to its unintended and unforeseen negative consequences is necessary in light of the many recent examples of big data algorithms that reinforce pre-existing inequality (O'Neil, 2016). We anticipate many new investigations into algorithmic fairness in education in the coming years as the ideas and techniques reviewed in this chapter are gaining traction in our community.

References

Abebe, R., Barocas, S., Kleinberg, J., Levy, K., Raghavan, M. & Robinson, D. G. (2020). Roles for computing in social change. *Proceedings of the 2020 Conference on Fairness, Accountability, and Transparency*, 252–260.

Attewell, P. & Battle, J. (1999). Home Computers and School Performance. *The Information Society*, *15*(1), 1–10.

Baker, R. S. & Inventado, P. S. (2014). Educational data mining and learning analytics. In *Learning Analytics* (pp. 61–75). Springer New York.

Barocas, S., Hardt, M. & Narayanan, A. (2019). *Fairness and machine learning*. fairmlbook.org.

Barocas, S. & Selbst, A. D. (2016). Big Data's Disparate Impact. *California Law Review*, *104*, 671.

Bellamy, R. K. E., Dey, K., Hind, M., Hoffman, S. C., Houde, S., Kannan, K., Lohia, P., Martino, J., Mehta, S., Mojsilovic, A., Nagar, S., Ramamurthy, K. N., Richards, J., Saha, D., Sattigeri, P., Singh, M., Varshney, K. R. & Zhang, Y. (2018). AI Fairness 360: An Extensible Toolkit for Detecting, Understanding, and Mitigating Unwanted Algorithmic Bias. In *arXiv (cs.AI)*. arXiv. http://arxiv.org/abs/1810.01943

Berk, R., Heidari, H., Jabbari, S., Kearns, M. & Roth, A. (2018). Fairness in Criminal Justice Risk Assessments: The State of the Art. *Sociological Methods & Research*. https://doi.org/10.1177/0049124118782533

Bolukbasi, T., Chang, K.-W., Zou, J. Y., Saligrama, V. & Kalai, A. T. (2016). Man is to Computer Programmer as Woman is to Homemaker? Debiasing Word Embeddings. In D. D. Lee, M. Sugiyama, U. V. Luxburg, I. Guyon & R. Garnett (Eds.), *Advances in Neural Information Processing Systems 29* (pp. 4349–4357). Curran Associates, Inc.

Bonilla-Silva, E. (2006). *Racism without Racists: Color-Blind Racism and the Persistence of Racial Inequality in the United States*. Rowman & Littlefield Publishers.

Boser, U. (2013). Are Schools Getting a Big Enough Bang for Their Education Technology Buck? *Center for American Progress*. https://eric.ed.gov/?id=ED565372

Bridgeman, B., Trapani, C. & Attali, Y. (2009). Considering fairness and validity in evaluating automated scoring. *Annual Meeting of the National Council on Measurement in Education, San Diego, CA*. https://www.academia.edu/download/52116920/AER-A_NCME_2009_Bridgeman.pdf

Bridgeman, B., Trapani, C. & Attali, Y. (2012). Comparison of Human and Machine Scoring of Essays: Differences by Gender, Ethnicity, and Country. *Applied Measurement in Education*, *25*(1), 27–40.

Brookover, W. B., Rosenthal, R. & Jacobson, L. (1969). Pygmalion in the Classroom: Teacher Expectation and Pupils' Intellectual Development. In *American Sociological Review* (Vol. 34, Issue 2, p. 283). https://doi.org/10.2307/2092211

Burke, M. (2018). *Colorblind Racism*. John Wiley & Sons.

Calders, T. & Verwer, S. (2010). Three naive Bayes approaches for discrimination-free classification. In *Data Mining and Knowledge Discovery* (Vol. 21, Issue 2, pp. 277–292). https://doi.org/10.1007/s10618-010-0190-x

Calmon, F., Wei, D., Vinzamuri, B., Natesan Ramamurthy, K. & Varshney, K. R. (2017). Optimized Pre-Processing for Discrimination Prevention. In I. Guyon, U. V. Luxburg, S. Bengio, H. Wallach, R. Fergus, S. Vishwanathan & R. Garnett (Eds.), *Advances in Neural Information Processing Systems 30* (pp. 3992–4001). Curran Associates, Inc.

Chasalow, K. & Levy, K. (2021). Representativeness in Statistics, Politics, and Machine Learning. In *Proceedings of the 2021 ACM Conference on Fairness, Accountability, and Transparency* (pp. 77–89). Association for Computing Machinery.

Chawla, N. V., Bowyer, K. W., Hall, L. O. & Kegelmeyer, W. P. (2002). SMOTE: Synthetic Minority Over-sampling Technique. *The Journal of Artificial Intelligence Research, 16*, 321–357.

Chouldechova, A. (2017). Fair Prediction with Disparate Impact: A Study of Bias in Recidivism Prediction Instruments. *Big Data, 5*(2), 153–163.

Coleman, J. S. (2019). *Equality And Achievement In Education*. Routledge.

Conati, C., Porayska-Pomsta, K. & Mavrikis, M. (2018). AI in Education needs interpretable machine learning: Lessons from Open Learner Modelling. In *arXiv preprint*. arXiv:1807.00154

Corbett, A. T. & Anderson, J. R. (1995). Knowledge tracing: Modeling the acquisition of procedural knowledge. In *User Modelling and User-Adapted Interaction* (Vol. 4, Issue 4, pp. 253–278). https://doi.org/10.1007/bf01099821

Corbett-Davies, S. & Goel, S. (2018). The Measure and Mismeasure of Fairness: A Critical Review of Fair Machine Learning. In *arXiv (cs.CY)*. arXiv. http://arxiv.org/abs/1808.00023

Corbett-Davies, S., Pierson, E., Feller, A., Goel, S. & Huq, A. (2017). Algorithmic Decision Making and the Cost of Fairness. In *Proceedings of the 23rd ACM SIGKDD International Conference on Knowledge Discovery and Data Mining–KDD '17*. https://doi.org/10.1145/3097983.3098095

Cui, Y., Chen, F., Shiri, A. & Fan, Y. (2019). Predictive analytic models of student success in higher education. In *Information and Learning Sciences* (Vol. 120, Issue 3/4, pp. 208–227). https://doi.org/10.1108/ils-10–2018-0104

d'Alessandro, B., O'Neil, C. & LaGatta, T. (2017). Conscientious Classification: A Data Scientist's Guide to Discrimination-Aware Classification. In *Big Data* (Vol. 5, Issue 2, pp. 120–134). https://doi.org/10.1089/big.2016.0048

Darlington, R. B. (1971). ANOTHER LOOK AT "CULTURAL FAIRNESS"1. In *Journal of Educational Measurement* (Vol. 8, Issue 2, pp. 71–82). https://doi.org/10.1111/j.1745–3984.1971.tb00908.x

DeBoer, J., Ho, A. D., Stump, G. S. & Breslow, L. (2014). Changing "Course": Reconceptualizing Educational Variables for Massive Open Online Courses. *Educational Researcher, 43*(2), 74–84.

de Brey, C., Musu, L., McFarland, J., Wilkinson-Flicker, S., Diliberti, M., Zhang, A., Branstetter, C. & Wang, X. (2019). *Status and Trends in the Education of Racial and Ethnic Groups 2018*. National Center for Education Statistics.

Doroudi, S. & Brunskill, E. (2019). Fairer but Not Fair Enough On the Equitability of Knowledge Tracing. In *Proceedings of the 9th International Conference on Learning Analytics & Knowledge – LAK19*. https://doi.org/10.1145/3303772.3303838

Doshi-Velez, F. & Kim, B. (2017). *Towards A Rigorous Science of Interpretable Machine Learning*. http://arxiv.org/abs/1702.08608

Duckworth, A. L. & Yeager, D. S. (2015). Measurement Matters: Assessing Personal Qualities Other Than Cognitive Ability for Educational Purposes. *Educational Researcher, 44*(4), 237–251.

Dwork, C., Hardt, M., Pitassi, T., Reingold, O. & Zemel, R. (2012). Fairness through awareness. In *Proceedings of the 3rd Innovations in Theoretical Computer Science Conference on – ITCS '12*. https://doi.org/10.1145/2090236.2090255

Feldman, M., Friedler, S. A., Moeller, J., Scheidegger, C. & Venkatasubramanian, S. (2015). Certifying and Removing Disparate Impact. In *Proceedings of the 21st ACM SIGKDD International Conference on Knowledge Discovery and Data Mining – KDD '15*. https://doi.org/10.1145/2783258.2783311

Friedler, S. A., Scheidegger, C. & Venkatasubramanian, S. (2016). *On the (im)possibility of fairness*. http://arxiv.org/abs/1609.07236

Friedler, S. A., Scheidegger, C., Venkatasubramanian, S., Choudhary, S., Hamilton, E. P. & Roth, D. (2019). A comparative study of fairness-enhancing interventions in machine learning. In *Proceedings of the Conference on Fairness, Accountability, and Transparency – FAT* '19*. https://doi.org/10.1145/3287560.3287589

Gardner, J., Brooks, C. & Baker, R. (2019). Evaluating the Fairness of Predictive Student Models Through Slicing Analysis. In *Proceedings of the 9th International Conference on Learning Analytics & Knowledge*. https://doi.org/10.1145/3303772.3303791

Gašević, D., Dawson, S. & Siemens, G. (2015). Let's not forget: Learning analytics are about learning. *TechTrends, 59*(1), 64–71.

Government Equalities Office. (2013, February 27). *Equality Act 2010: guidance*. GOV.UK; GOV.UK. https://www.gov.uk/guidance/equality-act-2010-guidance

Hardt, M., Price, E. & Srebro, N. (2016). *Equality of Opportunity in Supervised Learning*. http://arxiv.org/abs/1610.02413

Holstein, K. & Doroudi, S. (2021). Equity and Artificial Intelligence in Education: Will "AIED" Amplify or Alleviate Inequities in Education? In K. Porayska-Pomsta & W. Holmes (Eds.), *Ethics in AIED: Who Cares? Data, algorithms, equity and biases in educational contexts*. Routledge Press.

Hosanagar, K. (2020). *A Human's Guide to Machine Intelligence: How Algorithms Are Shaping Our Lives and How We Can Stay in Control*. Penguin Books.

Hu, L. & Chen, Y. (2018). *Welfare and Distributional Impacts of Fair Classification*. http://arxiv.org/abs/1807.01134

Hutchinson, B. & Mitchell, M. (2018). *50 Years of Test (Un)fairness: Lessons for Machine Learning*. https://doi.org/10.1145/3287560.3287600

Hutt, S., Gardner, M., Duckworth, A. L. & D'Mello, S. K. (2019). Evaluating Fairness and Generalizability in Models Predicting On-Time Graduation from College Applications. *International Educational Data Mining Society*. http://files.eric.ed.gov/fulltext/ED599210.pdf

Hutt, S., Grafsgaard, J. F. & D'Mello, S. K. (2019). Time to Scale: Generalizable Affect Detection for Tens of Thousands of Students across An Entire School Year. *Proceedings of the 2019 CHI Conference on Human Factors in Computing Systems*, 1–14.

Kamiran, F. & Calders, T. (2012). Data preprocessing techniques for classification without discrimination. In *Knowledge and Information Systems* (Vol. 33, Issue 1, pp. 1–33). https://doi.org/10.1007/s10115-011–0463-8

Kamishima, T., Akaho, S., Asoh, H. & Sakuma, J. (2012). Fairness-Aware Classifier with Prejudice Remover Regularizer. In *Machine Learning and Knowledge Discovery in Databases* (pp. 35–50). https://doi.org/10.1007/978–3-642–33486-3_3

Kao, G. & Thompson, J. S. (2003). Racial and Ethnic Stratification in Educational Achievement and Attainment. In *Annual Review of Sociology* (Vol. 29, Issue 1, pp. 417–442). https://doi.org/10.1146/annurev.soc.29.010202.100019

Kilbertus, N., Rojas Carulla, M., Parascandolo, G., Hardt, M., Janzing, D. & Schölkopf, B. (2017). Avoiding Discrimination through Causal Reasoning. In I. Guyon, U. V. Luxburg, S. Bengio, H. Wallach, R. Fergus, S. Vishwanathan & R. Garnett (Eds.), *Advances in Neural Information Processing Systems 30* (pp. 656–666). Curran Associates, Inc.

Kizilcec, R. F. (2016). How much information? Effects of transparency on trust in an algorithmic interface. *Proceedings of the 2016 CHI Conference on Human Factors in Computing Systems*, 2390–2395.

Kizilcec, R. F., Makridis, C. A. & Sadowski, K. C. (2021). Pandemic response policies' democratizing effects on online learning. *Proceedings of the National Academy of Sciences of the United States of America*, *118*(11). https://doi.org/10.1073/pnas.2026725118

Kizilcec, R. F., Reich, J., Yeomans, M., Dann, C., Brunskill, E., Lopez, G., Turkay, S., Williams, J. J. & Tingley, D. (2020). Scaling up behavioral science interventions in online education. *Proceedings of the National Academy of Sciences of the United States of America*. https://doi.org/10.1073/pnas.1921417117

Kleinberg, J., Ludwig, J., Mullainathan, S. & Rambachan, A. (2018). Algorithmic Fairness. *AEA Papers and Proceedings*, *108*, 22–27.

Kleinberg, J., Mullainathan, S. & Raghavan, M. (2016). *Inherent Trade-Offs in the Fair Determination of Risk Scores*. http://arxiv.org/abs/1609.05807

Kuhn, M. & Others. (2008). Building predictive models in R using the caret package. *Journal of Statistical Software*, *28*(5), 1–26.

Kusner, M. J., Loftus, J. R., Russell, C. & Silva, R. (2017). Counterfactual Fairness. In I. Guyon, U. V. Luxburg, S. Bengio, H. Wallach, R. Fergus, S. Vishwanathan & R. Garnett (Eds.), *Advances in Neural Information Processing Systems 30* (pp. 4066–4076). Curran Associates, Inc.

Lee, H. & Kizilcec, R. F. (2020). Evaluation of Fairness Trade-offs in Predicting Student Success. *Fairness, Accountability, and Transparency in Educational Data Cyberspace Workshop*. Educational Data Mining (EDM).

Liu, L. T., Dean, S., Rolf, E., Simchowitz, M. & Hardt, M. (2018). Delayed Impact of Fair Machine Learning. In J. Dy & A. Krause (Eds.), *Proceedings of the 35th International Conference on Machine Learning* (Vol. 80, pp. 3150–3158). PMLR.

Li, X., Han, M., Cohen, G. L. & Markus, H. R. (2021). Passion matters but not equally everywhere: Predicting achievement from interest, enjoyment, and efficacy in 59 societies. *Proceedings of the National Academy of Sciences of the United States of America*, *118*(11). https://doi.org/10.1073/pnas.2016964118

Loukina, A., Madnani, N. & Zechner, K. (2019). The many dimensions of algorithmic fairness in educational applications. *Proceedings of the Fourteenth Workshop on Innovative Use of NLP for Building Educational Applications*, 1–10.

Luckin, R. & Cukurova, M. (2019). Designing educational technologies in the age of AI: A learning sciences-driven approach. *British Journal of Educational Technology: Journal of the Council for Educational Technology*, *50*(6), 2824–2838.

Lum, K. & Isaac, W. (2016). To predict and serve? *Significance. Statistics Making Sense*, *13*(5), 14–19.

MacCarthy, M. (2019, December 6). *Fairness in algorithmic decision-making*. Brookings; Brookings. https://www.brookings.edu/research/fairness-in-algorithmic-decision-making/

Makhlouf, K., Zhioua, S. & Palamidessi, C. (2020). On the Applicability of ML Fairness Notions. In *arXiv (cs.LG)*. arXiv. http://arxiv.org/abs/2006.16745

Marcinkowski, F., Kieslich, K., Starke, C. & Lünich, M. (2020). Implications of AI (un-) fairness in higher education admissions: the effects of perceived AI (un-)fairness on exit, voice and organizational reputation. *Proceedings of the 2020 Conference on Fairness, Accountability, and Transparency*, 122–130.

Milli, S., Miller, J., Dragan, A. D. & Hardt, M. (2019). The Social Cost of Strategic Classification. *Proceedings of the Conference on Fairness, Accountability, and Transparency– FAT* *'19*, 230–239.

Mitchell, M., Wu, S., Zaldivar, A., Barnes, P., Vasserman, L., Hutchinson, B., Spitzer, E., Raji, I. D. & Gebru, T. (2018). Model Cards for Model Reporting. In *arXiv (cs. LG)*. arXiv. http://arxiv.org/abs/1810.03993

Nabi, R. & Shpitser, I. (2018). Fair Inference On Outcomes. *Proc. Conf. AAAI Artif. Intell.*, 1931–1940.

Nickerson, R. S. (1998). Confirmation Bias: A Ubiquitous Phenomenon in Many Guises. In *Review of General Psychology* (Vol. 2, Issue 2, pp. 175–220). https://doi.org/ 10.1037/1089-2680.2.2.175

Ocumpaugh, J., Baker, R., Gowda, S., Heffernan, N. & Heffernan, C. (2014). Population validity for educational data mining models: A case study in affect detection. In *British Journal of Educational Technology* (Vol. 45, Issue 3, pp. 487–501). https://doi. org/10.1111/bjet.12156

O'Neil, C. (2016). *Weapons of Math Destruction: How Big Data Increases Inequality and Threatens Democracy*. Crown Books.

Pane, J. F., McCaffrey, D. F., Slaughter, M. E., Steele, J. L. & Ikemoto, G. S. (2010). An experiment to evaluate the efficacy of cognitive tutor geometry. *Journal of Research on Educational Effectiveness*, *3*(3), 254–281.

Pedregosa, F., Varoquaux, G., Gramfort, A., Michel, V., Thirion, B., Grisel, O., Blondel, M., Prettenhofer, P., Weiss, R., Dubourg, V. & Others. (2011). Scikit-learn: Machine learning in Python. *The Journal of Machine Learning Research*, *12*, 2825–2830.

Piech, C., Bassen, J., Huang, J., Ganguli, S., Sahami, M., Guibas, L. J. & Sohl-Dickstein, J. (2015). Deep Knowledge Tracing. In C. Cortes, N. D. Lawrence, D. D. Lee, M. Sugiyama & R. Garnett (Eds.), *Advances in Neural Information Processing Systems 28* (pp. 505–513). Curran Associates, Inc.

Prenkaj, B., Velardi, P., Stilo, G., Distante, D. & Faralli, S. (2020). A survey of machine learning approaches for student dropout prediction in online courses. *ACM Computing Surveys*, *53*(3), 1–34.

Räz, T. (2021). Group Fairness: Independence Revisited. In *Proceedings of the 2021 ACM Conference on Fairness, Accountability, and Transparency* (pp. 129–137). Association for Computing Machinery.

Reardon, S. F. & Owens, A. (2014). 60 Years AfterBrown: Trends and Consequences of School Segregation. In *Annual Review of Sociology* (Vol. 40, Issue 1, pp. 199–218). https://doi.org/10.1146/annurev-soc-071913-043152

Reich, J. (2020). *Failure to Disrupt: Why Technology Alone Can't Transform Education*.

Roschelle, J., Feng, M., Murphy, R. F. & Mason, C. A. (2016). Online Mathematics Homework Increases Student Achievement. *AERA Open*, *2*(4), 2332858416673968.

Russell, C., Kusner, M. J., Loftus, J. & Silva, R. (2017). When Worlds Collide: Integrating Different Counterfactual Assumptions in Fairness. In I. Guyon, U. V. Luxburg, S. Bengio, H. Wallach, R. Fergus, S. Vishwanathan & R. Garnett (Eds.), *Advances in Neural Information Processing Systems 30* (pp. 6414–6423). Curran Associates, Inc.

Sackett, P. R., Kuncel, N. R., Arneson, J. J., Cooper, S. R. & Waters, S. D. (2009). Socioeconomic Status and the Relationship between the SAT® and Freshman GPA: An Analysis of Data from 41 Colleges and Universities. Research Report No. 2009-1. *College Board*. https://eric.ed.gov/?id=ED562860

Saleiro, P., Kuester, B., Hinkson, L., London, J., Stevens, A., Anisfeld, A., Rodolfa, K. T. & Ghani, R. (2018). *Aequitas: A Bias and Fairness Audit Toolkit.* http://arxiv.org/abs/1811.05577

Salganik, M. J., Lundberg, I., Kindel, A. T., Ahearn, C. E., Al-Ghoneim, K., Almaatouq, A., Altschul, D. M., Brand, J. E., Carnegie, N. B., Compton, R. J., Datta, D., Davidson, T., Filippova, A., Gilroy, C., Goode, B. J., Jahani, E., Kashyap, R., Kirchner, A., McKay, S., … McLanahan, S. (2020). Measuring the predictability of life outcomes with a scientific mass collaboration. *Proceedings of the National Academy of Sciences of the United States of America, 117*(15), 8398–8403.

Schwartz, D. L. & Arena, D. (2013). *Measuring What Matters Most: Choice-Based Assessments for the Digital Age.* MIT Press.

Theobald, E. J., Hill, M. J., Tran, E., Agrawal, S., Arroyo, E. N., Behling, S., Chambwe, N., Cintrón, D. L., Cooper, J. D., Dunster, G., Grummer, J. A., Hennessey, K., Hsiao, J., Iranon, N., Jones, L., 2nd, Jordt, H., Keller, M., Lacey, M. E., Littlefield, C. E., … Freeman, S. (2020). Active learning narrows achievement gaps for underrepresented students in undergraduate science, technology, engineering, and math. *Proceedings of the National Academy of Sciences of the United States of America, 117*(12), 6476–6483.

Verma, S. & Rubin, J. (2018). Fairness definitions explained. *Proceedings of the International Workshop on Software Fairness–FairWare '18,* 1–7.

Warschauer, M., Knobel, M. & Stone, L. (2004). Technology and Equity in Schooling: Deconstructing the Digital Divide. *Educational Policy, 18*(4), 562–588.

Wenglinsky, H. (1998). *Does it compute?: The relationship between educational technology and student achievement in mathematics.* Educational Testing Service. https://www.ets.org/Media/Research/pdf/PICTECHNOLOG.pdf

Wiens, J., Saria, S., Sendak, M., Ghassemi, M., Liu, V. X., Doshi-Velez, F., Jung, K., Heller, K., Kale, D., Saeed, M., Ossorio, P. N., Thadaney-Israni, S. & Goldenberg, A. (2019). Do no harm: a roadmap for responsible machine learning for health care. *Nature Medicine, 25*(9), 1337–1340.

Woodworth, B., Gunasekar, S., Ohannessian, M. I. & Srebro, N. (2017). Learning Non-Discriminatory Predictors. In S. Kale & O. Shamir (Eds.), *Proceedings of the 2017 Conference on Learning Theory* (Vol. 65, pp. 1920–1953). PMLR.

Wu, Y., Zhang, L. & Wu, X. (2019). Counterfactual Fairness: Unidentification, Bound and Algorithm. In *Proceedings of the Twenty-Eighth International Joint Conference on Artificial Intelligence.* https://doi.org/10.24963/ijcai.2019/199

Yan, D., Rupp, A. A. & Foltz, P. W. (2020). *Handbook of Automated Scoring: Theory into Practice.* CRC Press.

Yudelson, M., Fancsali, S., Ritter, S., Berman, S., Nixon, T. & Joshi, A. (2014). Better data beats big data. *7th International Conference on Educational Data Mining (EDM 2014),* 205–208.

Yu, R., Lee, H. & Kizilcec, R. F. (2021). Should College Dropout Prediction Models Include Protected Attributes? *Proceedings of the ACM Conference on Learning at Scale (L@S'21).*

Yu, R., Li, Q., Fischer, C., Doroudi, S. & Xu, D. (2020). Towards Accurate and Fair Prediction of College Success: Evaluating Different Sources of Student Data. *Proceedings of the 13th International Conference on Educational Data Mining (EDM '20).*

Zafar, M. B., Valera, I., Rodriguez, M. G. & Gummadi, K. P. (2017). Fairness Beyond Disparate Treatment & Disparate Impact. In *Proceedings of the 26th International Conference on World Wide Web.* https://doi.org/10.1145/3038912.3052660

Zemel, R., Wu, Y., Swersky, K., Pitassi, T. & Dwork, C. (2013). Learning Fair Representations. *International Conference on Machine Learning,* 325–333.

8 Beyond "fairness"

Structural (in)justice lenses on AI for education

Michael Madaio, Su Lin Blodgett, Elijah Mayfield and Ezekiel Dixon-Román

Introduction

During the COVID-19 pandemic, countries around the world closed their schools in successive waves, impacting nearly 1.25 billion students across all levels of education.[1] As institutions shifted to distance learning, or a hybrid of in-person and remote instruction (Reich et al., 2020), educational leaders increasingly turned to technological solutions to provide continuity of learning for students (Teräs et al., 2020). Administrators and teachers moved students into remote learning environments that may have never been chosen if the world had stayed as it was in 2019. Students and the global education system will be impacted in enduring ways as the pandemic continues to exacerbate existing systemic inequities in education (Aguliera and Nightengale-Lee, 2020, Dorn et al., 2020).

As educational technologies are proposed as a solution for crisis-induced remote learning (Teräs et al., 2020, Kizilcec et al., 2021), discussion of equity often centres on the assumption that increasing access to learning technologies will reduce inequity in educational opportunities (Hall et al., 2020, Holmes et al., 2021). While some educational technologies may be beneficial for some learners (Kulik and Fletcher, 2016), the logic of distributive justice that equates access to technology as a form of equity (e.g. Holmes et al., 2021, Greene, 2021, Pei and Crooks, 2020) has motivated widespread adoption of learning technologies, as well as widespread data collection on computational traces of students' learning—data that is then used as part of educational algorithmic systems. Substantial research on data-driven algorithmic systems (often referred to as Artificial Intelligence, or AI[2]) in other domains has demonstrated the potential for such systems to reproduce and amplify societal biases in a variety of ways (see Barocas and Selbst (2016) for an overview), or introduce novel sources of unfairness through disparities in their performance (e.g. Buolamwini and Gebru, 2018), in domains as widespread as criminal justice (Richardson et al., 2019), healthcare (Obermeyer et al., 2019), and hiring (Raghavan et al., 2020). In spite of these known issues for AI systems, enthusiasm for AI in education has never been higher, with millions of dollars in funding for institutes in the field[3] and a recent US National Science Foundation report on educational AI (Roschelle et al., 2020) that optimistically

DOI: 10.4324/9780429329067-11

treats such systems as inherently beneficial, arguing that such systems may be solutions to educational inequity (cf. du Boulay, Chapter 9 this volume).

In education research, quantitatively oriented researchers may be motivated to use their training to evaluate biases in educational AI as a neatly quantifiable construct, with error bars and standard deviations, reporting differences in system performance or students' learning outcomes by demographic groups (e.g. race, gender, etc.), as in Kizilcec and Lee (Chapter 7 this volume). Indeed, this has been the dominant paradigm in the nascent field of algorithmic fairness (see (Hanna et al., 2020) for a critique). But social scientists and critical theorists of education have argued (e.g. Dixon-Román (2017), Williamson (2017)) that such an approach to quantifying biases misses the bigger picture—that socio-historical processes both within and outside of the classroom shape the design, use, and evaluation of educational AI.

In an educational crisis, it may be the case that concerns about equity are sublimated in the interest of using any means necessary to continue business as usual within systems of schooling. Naomi Klein (2007), writing about the response to Hurricane Katrina's impact on education in New Orleans, described how "disaster capitalists" such as Milton Friedman saw in that crisis an opportunity to "radically reform the educational system" of New Orleans through immense cuts to public education in favour of subsidies to for-profit private charter schools. Friedman's response to the Katrina crisis was to redirect resources for public education towards for-profit schools.

Yet, there are other responses to a crisis. Social philosopher Pierre Bourdieu (1977) describes how moments of crisis present opportunities to challenge and shift dominant schemes of thought by "rupturing" existing social structures. The coronavirus pandemic is a global crisis in nearly every sector. Rather than further enabling techno-capitalist interests in selling products that weave technology inextricably into the fabric of civic life,[4] the pandemic could instead be used as an inflection point for education decision-makers, researchers, and technologists to radically rethink the way that education is done and how our technologies are designed Moore et al. (2021).[5] Given the known risks for (un)fairness and (in)-equity in AI more generally, and recent enthusiasm about data-driven *educational* algorithms specifically (or, educational AI), it is thus imperative that concerns about structural injustice are taken seriously so that our educational AI systems do not simply reproduce legacies of inequity through their design.

This chapter draws on lenses from critical theory to interrogate and rethink what equity means for educational AI. We begin by summarizing the current state of research on algorithmic fairness, including approaches to measuring fairness of algorithms and their limitations at capturing more fundamental issues of structural injustice, informed by Black feminist theory. We then discuss the historical legacies of (un)fairness and (in)equity in systems of schooling more broadly,[6] and critically examine the operating logics of several widely researched classes of educational AI systems. We use these categories of educational AI not to suggest that they are exhaustive, but instead to suggest that they may be fertile sites to examine how educational AI may fundamentally perpetuate structural injustice, regardless of the quantitative "fairness" of the underlying algorithms' performance. Finally, we call for new methods and visions for justice-oriented approaches to research and design of learning science and educational technology, drawing on related calls for design justice, counter hegemony, and technology refusal in adjacent fields. We argue for the need for radical visions for the design (or dismantling) of educational AI in order to bring about a more equitable and justice-oriented educational future.

Methods and Challenges to Measuring Fairness in AI

The rhetorical promise from designers of data-driven educational algorithms (i.e. educational AI) is that they are able to increase learning overall while reducing inequities by helping all students learn in more personalized ways. One need only look at the theme of the 2019 AI in Education conference, "Education for All in the XXI Century," which solicited papers to explore how AI systems might contribute to reducing educational inequity. This line of thinking follows a broader tradition in technical fields that critics call *technosolutionism* (Morozov, 2013). Fundamentally, work in this vein assumes that technology can solve deep-seated, complex social issues or that technology is inherently less biased than humans. However, there is reason to be deeply suspicious of this theory of change. Before we explore those critiques further, though, we will first review prior work on measuring fairness in education, and then discuss the current state of research on defining and measuring (un) fairness in data-driven algorithmic systems, including machine learning and AI and for such systems used in education. In other words, what *does* it mean for a machine learning or AI system to be fair?

Measuring fairness in educational assessments

Statistical evaluations of equality for test questions across race and gender has a long history in the psychometrics of high-stakes exams like the Scholastic Assessment Test (SAT), going back at least six decades (Anastasi, 1961, Donlon, 1981, Sehmitt and Dorans, 1990). In 1968, Cleary studied the problem of fair test use across Black and white students for admissions to universities that had only just been racially integrated (1968). Later, with Educational Testing Services (ETS), Linn (1973) undertook an extensive quantitative review of test subgroup fairness in the SAT, leaning on definitions from Thorndike (1971). From those early days to more modern research, the primary questions have long been the same: Are the psychometric properties of a test variant or invariant across groups? Is there differential performance for different groups, and, if so, does the test produce valid estimates for each group? Are the items on the test equally difficult for all students, holding their estimated abilities constant; and, if so, are there systematic reasons for such differential item functioning? In more recent decades, Samuel Messick's and Lee Cronbach's concerns for the social consequences of test score use and interpretation have been given more attention. Older versions of these standardized tests famously included culturally discriminatory world knowledge like polo, regattas, ballet, and horseback riding (Weiss, 1987). The approach to solving this has been nearly uniform within the psychometric field: measure marginal distributions of outcomes by demographic group, and make use of items and tests that meet a set of defined criteria for group-level fairness (Hutchinson and Mitchell, 2019).

These research traditions have been focused on achieving reliable measurement and valid predictions of student ability across student populations. However, more fundamental questions have been side-lined from the mainstream discourse in the field—questions such as any interrogation of how "ability" was defined, or whether the basic prediction goal was desirable (or desired by the students), or who such an assessment might disproportionately harm, even if it was functioning "correctly" (Dixon-Román, 2017, Karabel, 2006, Lemann, 2000). These are thorny questions, and they are fundamental to interrogating the meaning of equity in educational technologies.

Measuring fairness in AI and machine learning

Critiques of the social implications of technology are of course not limited to educational technologies. For decades, scholars such as Langdon Winner (1980) and others (Winograd et al., 1986) have argued that technology instantiates social and political relationships. Early work in this area examined several types of bias arising from computational systems (Friedman and Nissenbaum, 1996), with other work critiquing the "mythology" of Big Data—"the widespread belief that large datasets offer a higher form of intelligence and knowledge that can generate insights that were previously impossible, with the aura of truth, objectivity, and accuracy" (boyd and Crawford, 2012)—while other work questioned the ability of existing American anti-discrimination law to address algorithmic discrimination (Barocas and Selbst, 2016). In spite of this rich variety of interdisciplinary critical scholarship, the field of AI and machine learning has recently converged on a narrower framing of how to understand the harms that AI systems might engender.

In recent years, academic approaches arising from the nascent field of fairness, accountability, transparency, and ethics in AI and machine learning (FAccT) have primarily centred on evaluating the *fairness* of algorithmic decision-making systems.[7] Algorithmic decision systems are used in a variety of high-stakes domains to support, or in some cases replace, decisions about access to resources and opportunities for applications as varied as healthcare services (Obermeyer et al., 2019), parole sentencing (Angwin et al., 2016, Dixon-Román et al., 2019), and student–school matching (Robertson and Salehi, 2020). Current approaches to assessing biases in such algorithms have developed mathematical formulations of *group fairness* (Kleinberg et al., 2016, Corbett-Davies and Goel, 2018) and *individual fairness* (Dwork et al., 2012), largely for algorithms that perform classification tasks (i.e. predicting one (or more) of a set of categorical labels, as in Kotsiantis et al., 2007).

Group fairness metrics for classifiers typically measure the equality of predictive performance across groups defined by protected attributes.[8] By contrast, individual fairness approaches look at similar *individuals*, defining similarity in a task-specific way that typically does not rely on demographic labels, and ask whether similar users of a given technological system can expect similarly allocated decisions, error rates, or system quality and effectiveness (Gillen et al., 2018, Kim et al., 2018). Proposed solutions for mitigating unfairness have typically involved developing more "diverse" datasets (i.e. more data from "under-represented" social groups) and algorithmic mitigation approaches (Agarwal et al., 2018), although there are reasons for wariness about both proposed solutions.

Challenges to measuring algorithmic fairness

Challenges to measuring algorithmic fairness abound. For instance, Chouldechova (2017) showed that a number of common fairness metrics cannot be simultaneously satisfied (while population base rates are different), requiring an ultimately socio-political choice by practitioners of which fairness metric to use. These choices have serious consequences for any fairness evaluation, and belie the rhetoric that developing more fair systems is a straightforward task and that models can simply be "de-biased" (Bolukbasi et al., 2016). In addition, investigations into how multiply marginalized individuals are affected by decision-making systems are critical, but scarce. Buolamwini and Gebru (2018)'s path-breaking examination of facial recognition systems' performance at the intersections of race and gender—finding that such systems perform particularly poorly on images of Black women—represents a notable exception.

Moreover, measuring (and attempting to mitigate) algorithmic (un)fairness also typically requires gathering demographic data in the first place, which may threaten the privacy of marginalized groups, who have historically been most vulnerable to data collection and surveillance (Eubanks, 2018). Studying if a lending system is racially biased, for instance, often involves collecting customers' racial information, which can be a fraught process that requires categorization of identities into a small number of fixed labels and the collection of potentially sensitive demographic data. Data collection and privacy concerns are not new for education researchers. There is significant regulation in some countries designed to protect students' privacy, such as the Family and Educational Rights and Privacy Act (FERPA) in the US (Daggett, 2008), although there is contention about its ability to account for modern data infrastructures (Zeide, 2015). There has also been substantive critical writing about student data privacy issues in learning analytics, including concerns about the storage, sharing, and afterlives of student data (Slade and Prinsloo, 2013).

Finally, approaches to evaluating algorithmic fairness have mostly been developed for domains where decision-making systems allocate opportunities or resources—e.g. lending decisions, criminal sentencing, or university admissions decisions (Kleinberg et al., 2016); errors by such systems give rise to what has been called *allocational* harms (Crawford, 2017). However, AI systems, including many systems used in education, often do more than simply allocate opportunities or resources. Recent scholarship is also identifying the ways in which group-based and individual fairness approaches may be inadequate for the social or dignitary harms that may also arise, which Crawford (2017) has termed harms of *representation*—for instance, the reproduction of racist characterizations arising from Google Photos' labelling Black faces as gorillas (Simonite, 2018, Noble, 2018) or the reproduction of gendered expectations by digital assistants who respond coyly to sexual harassment (Fessler, 2017). These represent fundamentally different kinds of harms than those described above, and may not be well-captured by existing group or individual fairness approaches.

Measuring fairness in educational algorithms

Researchers working on educational algorithms, recognizing that their systems are not exempt from the same threats to fairness as in AI systems more broadly, have begun to apply methods for evaluating the disparate impact of educational algorithms, predominantly applying group-based approaches to conceptualizing fairness. In their review of the state of algorithmic fairness in education, Kizilcec and Lee (Chapter 7, this volume) discuss existing approaches to assessing fairness in educational algorithms, including research evaluating how the accuracy of a system designed to detect student affect (e.g. confusion, frustration, boredom) differed for groups of students in urban and rural schools (Ocumpaugh et al., 2014); research evaluating how the accuracy of a model designed to predict the likelihood of student dropout differed by the gender of the student (Gardner et al., 2019), and more (Doroudi and Brunskill, 2019, Lee and Kizilcec, 2020). In spite of extant work that takes a more critical lens to understanding such phenomena—such as work exploring the ethical implications of resource allocation based on automated prediction (Prinsloo and Slade, 2014) or the implications of making decisions to de-prioritize individual support on the basis of group outcome measures (Scholes, 2016)—such critical work has been side-lined in favour of group-based fairness approaches popular in the AI and machine learning community more broadly. The implicit assumption of much work on algorithmic fairness, made explicit in Kizilcec and Lee (Chapter 7, this volume), is that "the innovation is beneficial in general" and the work to be done is to ensure that the benefits are fairly distributed (a stance echoed in recent work by other educational AI researchers as well, as reported in Holmes et al., 2021). Such an approach, however, fails to address other types of harms, such as the representational harms previously described, as well as the second-order consequences of data collection. More fundamentally, there is good reason to be sceptical that this optimistic assumption is in fact true (see Chapter 6 for more discussion of other frames (cf. Selbst et al., 2019) with which to understand ethics in educational AI).

Structural critiques of group-based fairness approaches

As research on algorithmic fairness has developed, scholars (particularly from sociology and science and technology studies (STS)) have brought more fundamental challenges to the algorithmic fairness approaches described previously, critiquing the orientation of such approaches towards technical issues of models and datasets rather than towards the larger social and historical context (e.g. institutions and social structures) of injustice that manifests in socio-technical systems. More specifically, sociological (and Black feminist) scholarship has long recognized that social forces of racism, sexism, cis heteronormativity, ableism, settler colonialism, and so forth have shaped the foundations of our institutions and social structures.[9] Central to these analyses is the understanding that these oppressions are *systems*, encompassing unjust distributions of political power and economic resources as well as the ideologies and discourses that justify these distributions (Feagin and Ducey, 2000, Delgado and Stefancic, 2017). These systems are also ordinary, reproduced by the "routines, practices, and institutions that we rely on to do the world's work" (Delgado and Stefancic, 2017). Finally, they are interlocking; the systems of sexism, racism, and so forth do not operate independently, but are intersecting structuring forces.

This last property is captured by two conceptual models developed by Black feminist scholars: *intersectionality* and the *matrix of domination*. Intersectionality is a term coined by Kimberlé Crenshaw as part of her ground-breaking analysis showing that anti-discrimination law—which addressed gender- and race-based discrimination separately—was inadequate to address the overlapping discrimination experienced by Black women (Crenshaw, 1989, 1990). By highlighting how Black women were marginalized both by the feminist movement and by the civil rights movement, Crenshaw's analyses illustrated the need to move beyond single-axis analyses of injustice. Patricia Hill Collins' "matrix of domination," meanwhile, is a model that "helps us think about how power, oppression, resistance, privilege, penalties, benefits, and harms are systematically distributed" (Collins, 1990) (see Costanza-Chock, 2018 for a discussion of the matrix of domination in technology). This scholarship suggests that technologies developed in a world whose institutions are thus structured will reflect the values and legacies of this social and historical context, as they are steeped in the ideologies and discourses that maintain these institutions and their interlocking systems of oppression. It is thus critical to analyse these technologies through the lens of these oppressive institutions, ideologies, and discourses. Indeed, emerging scholarship is beginning to identify the consequences of existing fairness approaches' failure to account for this broader social and historical context. We outline a few of them here.

First, in attempting to treat different demographic groups the same, *group fairness*-based approaches ignore the reality that institutions and ideologies work to maintain profoundly unequal social orderings, with the result being that different groups are not treated the same in society. Hanna et al. describe this situation in their examination of race in algorithmic fairness:

By abstracting racial categories into a mathematically comparable form, group-based fairness criteria deny the hierarchical nature and the social, economic, and political complexity of the social groups under consideration … In short, group fairness approaches try to achieve sameness across groups without regard for the difference between the groups … This treats everyone the same from an algorithmic perspective without acknowledging that people are not treated the same.

(Hanna et al., 2020, p.508)

Second, in ignoring the sociological complexity of race, gender, and other frequently used attributes, fairness measurements may be inappropriate or inconsistent; for example, Hanna et al. delineate the many ways in which race has been operationalized in measurements of algorithmic fairness, from interviewer-observed, appearance-based classifications to self-declared racial classifications. Fairness approaches also often measure with respect to a single attribute, ignoring the complexities of interlocking oppressions, thereby making it impossible to understand how people who are multiply marginalized experience technologies differently (Costanza-Chock, 2020).

To illustrate this disconnect, consider data-driven algorithms designed to detect toxic language in online social media. These systems are well-documented as treating African American Language (AAL) social media messages as more toxic than Mainstream US English (MUSE) ones (Davidson et al., 2019); and for this performance difference the systems have been rightly critiqued from a group fairness perspective (Sap et al., 2019). But, using the lens of structural injustice, researchers must also recognize the ideologies of language driving this outcome, which construct MUSE as acceptable and normal and AAL as ungrammatical or inappropriate, and acknowledge the impact of these systems—namely the reproduction of harmful patterns of linguistic stigmatization, discrimination, and disenfranchisement that maintain hierarchies of language and race and naturalize unjust political and economic arrangements (Rosa and Flores, 2017). These findings have clear implications for educational technologies (e.g. Mayfield et al., 2019, Loukina et al., 2019), which we describe in more depth in the following section.

More broadly, analyses that do not engage with technologies' social and historical context fail to recognize how that context drives decisions at many points in AI systems' development and deployment pipeline, from the choice of problem definition itself (e.g. "what is the problem to be solved?") to the choices of data (e.g. "whose data is prioritized?" or, more likely, "whose data can be easily acquired?") and choice of evaluation metrics (Passi and Barocas, 2019). Without examining this context, fairness approaches often treat biases as emerging incidentally rather than as reflections of the institutions and ideologies structuring society (Benjamin, 2019b), or, even when such structuring forces are acknowledged, as in Kizilcec and Lee (2020, p.4), they are sidelined in favour of group-based fairness evaluations. Such approaches address only individual undesirable features, models, and datasets rather than the larger ideologies, institutions, and practices that produce them (Hoffmann, 2019). These approaches also fail to recognize how technologies (re)produce social meanings (cf. Winner, 1980), thereby maintaining these institutions and ideologies. In this way, algorithmic biases are treated as disconnected from both their origins outside of technology and their impact on society.

Finally, in proposing solutions that are technical in nature—involving data collection, more sophisticated model development, etc.—algorithmic fairness approaches assume that continued technological development is the solution to unfairness in AI systems, rather than asking whether some systems should be fundamentally re-designed, or perhaps not built at all (Cifor et al., 2019, Green, 2018, Keyes, 2019a, Bennett and Keyes, 2019, Hoffmann, 2019, Baumer and Silberman, 2011, Barocas et al., 2020). Thus, algorithmic fairness approaches maintain traditional power relations between technologists and communities by privileging technologists in the decision-making processes about how technologies should be designed and deployed (Hoffmann, 2021, Kalluri, 2020). In sum, the current state of the art in understanding differential harms of AI largely centres on evaluating group-based and individual fairness metrics. Given the historical legacy of group-based approaches to evaluating educational assessments, it is understandable why the educational AI field has similarly adopted such approaches. However, as we have outlined, conceptual models from critical theory and Black feminist scholarship suggest that a lens of structural injustice can help shed light on the fundamental equity issues posed by data-driven educational technologies (i.e., educational AI).

Injustice in Educational AI

One approach to engaging with equity in AI systems in education—what appears to be the dominant view—might be to see them as inherently beneficial for education and to seek to make those systems accessible and accurate for as many learners as possible (e.g. Holmes et al., 2021, Kizilcec and Lee, 2020, Hansen and Reich, 2015). Indeed, if one adopted the group-based fairness approaches from AI research wholesale, one might simply seek to improve the relative performance of an educational AI system for different populations of learners (Madnani et al., 2017, Loukina et al., 2019, Lee and Kizilcec, 2020, Kizilcec and Lee, 2020). However, given the interlocking systems of oppression in a settler colonialist, patriarchal, cis heteronormative, ableist society such as the United States, we argue that educational AI technologies that simply reproduce the status quo under such a "matrix of domination" will be fundamentally unjust.

Thus, following other critical interventions in reviews of education research (e.g. Kumashiro, 2000, North, 2006), in this section we examine several widely studied paradigmatic categories of educational technologies using lenses drawn from critical theory to identify how their operational logics may reproduce structural injustice in education, regardless of the parity of their algorithmic performance. We highlight these categories of educational AI systems not as an exhaustive list but as a demonstration of how lenses from critical theory may help shift the focus of the dominant paradigm of educational algorithmic fairness discourse towards a focus on structural injustice.

Legacies of educational systems of oppression

The policies, practices, and discourses that have shaped (and are shaped by) interlocking systems of oppression have influenced every part of the current educational landscape, from the nature of the curriculum to the pedagogical methods used to teach it, to the systems of assessing what students know, to the technologies designed to teach and assess that curriculum in specific ways. At the time of this writing, Black children in America are more than twice as likely as white children to attend high-poverty schools,[10] and such intertwined oppressions have led to worse educational outcomes for Black students in high-poverty schools (García, 2020).

Educational policies and funding mechanisms, ostensibly motivated by wanting to support greater equity, have instead reproduced the status quo of historical legacies of structural injustice in education. For decades, government funding for education has been largely tied to schools' performance on standardized testing, tracing back to the 1983 publication of *A Nation at Risk* by the US National Commission on Excellence in Education and through the measurement-focused era of No Child Left Behind. The logic here is that schools must first assess students to understand gaps in performance between students from different backgrounds in order to allocate resources to close those gaps—a similar logic to the group-based approach to algorithmic fairness described earlier, with similar shortcomings. Indeed, performance on standardized tests has been shown to be highly correlated with parental wealth and families' ability to pay for expensive test-prep for their children—opportunities not often available to many marginalized learners (Dixon-Román, 2017).

This assessment-focused paradigm has driven investment in and adoption of educational technologies to support these assessments, ostensibly to first measure and then mitigate gaps in students' performance. In the 2010s, American government funding for education was disbursed through the Race to the Top program, driving a surge in spending to move from summative to ongoing formative assessments, motivating increased adoption of educational technology in the classroom to deliver such ongoing assessments. But these investments in the early 2010s met numerous logistic hurdles, such as readily available broadband and Wi-Fi access, and the ongoing challenges of maintaining sufficiently updated computing devices (Boser, 2012, Fox et al., 2012). These gaps in access to educational technology infrastructures again fell disproportionately on already disadvantaged learners, further widening inequities in access to educational materials along socio-economic lines, which in the US often means racialized communities (Warschauer and Matuchniak, 2010).

It is important to step back and critically question the assumption underpinning those investments—that the issue at hand is simply providing access to the right technology that will reverse legacies of structural injustice impacting marginalized communities. This is a self-perpetuating logic, where group-level performance differences on assessments lead to investment and adoption of educational technologies in order to provide so-called personalized learning opportunities to reduce those performance differences for different groups of learners. In this "distributive justice" paradigm (Pei and Crooks, 2020), the goal is thus to ensure all students have equivalent access to those technologies (i.e. reducing group-level differences in access).

With the transition to primarily online instruction during the COVID-19 pandemic, this paradigm became the dominant one. As schools around the world transitioned to remote learning during the crisis, school administrators, teachers, and parents looked to technology to support "continuity of learning" (Reich et al., 2020, Teräs et al., 2020, Williamson, 2020). Much of the conversation has centred on how to provide equitable access to learning technologies, be that devices on which to learn or access to digital learning platforms. Although providing continued access to educational opportunities in a crisis is certainly important, and ensuring equitable access to those learning opportunities is an important first step, it is critical to consider whether that enthusiastic adoption of technology has opened the door for data-driven educational AI algorithms that, once provided, will reproduce or amplify the structural injustices of the education system more broadly.

To provide one brief example, consider classroom discussion practices. In her book *Teaching to Transgress*, bell hooks (1994, p.30) argues that "our ways of knowing are forged in history and relations of power."[11] Her classic example of this is the white male faculty member in a university English department who primarily teaches books by "great white men" and whose pedagogical practices perpetuate a white supremacist ideology. In many such classrooms, white male students may feel more comfortable volunteering in discussions more often, and may thus be called on more often by instructors (hooks, 1994). When those discussions are mediated by technology—or moved entirely to a digital format, as in the now-ubiquitous remote learning exacerbated by the COVID-19 pandemic—those inequitable pedagogical practices are reproduced and amplified. One can imagine this playing out in a number of ways, from a technology that tracks students' participation in class or awards them points for such participation (perhaps inspired by work such as Ahuja et al., 2019), to educational language technologies that summarize group meetings or class discussions (cf. Li et al., 2019, Zhao et al., 2019).

We thus extend hooks' argument to make the case that *educational AI technologies* are forged in historical relations of power. Classroom pedagogical practices shape the design paradigms and goals of learning technologies; shape the data available for training educational AI systems; shape the ways in which those technologies are deployed in the classroom; and, more broadly, shape the values that are enacted by these systems (cf. Winner, 1980). Thus, the problem to solve is not simply providing *more* students with access to such systems, or improving the accuracy of the systems' predictive models for different subgroups of learners (cf. Kizilcec and Lee, 2020). Researchers and educational technologists must grapple with the legacies of historical disenfranchisement of marginalized learners and the impact those legacies have on the design paradigms of educational technology.

In the following sections, we will discuss a few such design paradigms of educational AI systems that reproduce historical legacies of educational inequity. We will discuss how a lens of structural injustice makes visible—and may allow us to challenge—the interlocking systems of oppression structuring the development and deployment of educational AI that a more narrowly scoped algorithmic fairness approach cannot. Through serious attention to these criticisms, we hope to generate provocative questions and directions toward alternative futures of educational AI technologies in the final section of the chapter.

Biopolitical educational technologies

Here, we trace examples of categories of educational AI systems that may reproduce structural injustices—regardless of the models' accuracy or fairness. We start first with biopolitical AI systems, or approaches that model students' socio-emotional states, in order to induce students to act in desired ways. Such socio-emotional systems are based on and perpetuate racialized ideologies about behaviours and emotions deemed appropriate or beneficial for learning (Williamson, 2017).[12] In the Artificial Intelligence in Education community (AIED) and adjacent communities such as Educational Data Mining (EDM) and others, many papers have been published on the design and evaluation of systems that purport to model learners' "affective state" (e.g. Henderson et al., 2019, Mandalapu and Gong, 2018, D'Mello and Graesser, 2010) and systems that use those estimates of learners' affective state to recommend specific types of content to learners (e.g. Tsatsou et al., 2018, Athanasiadis et al., 2017). These systems use audio, video, and other data sources to label student "affect," or emotional state, as one of a set of predetermined labels, as defined by the researchers, following from the broader field of affective computing (Picard, 2000). Research in educational affect detection has largely converged around a set of purportedly beneficial affective states (cf. Zembylas, 2021), including boredom, confusion, and frustration (D'Mello and Graesser, 2010), with some researchers also including "engagement" or "flow" (Csikszentmihalyi, 1997), delight, and other states (Okur et al., 2017, Chang et al., 2018).

The fundamental assumptions underlying these systems are that learners' affective states are legible to technology and that some affective states are more productive for learning than others (e.g. Craig et al., 2004, Csikszentmihalyi, 1997). One implication of this is that if AI models can identify such states, they can also "nudge" students into affective states that the systems' designers may believe to be more conducive for learning. Even if you believe that these affective states are associated with learning for all learners (cf. Zembylas, 2021)—and setting aside unresolved questions of causality—the belief that one should thus nudge students *into* these states represents an ideology akin to what Foucault and others have called *biopolitics* or biopower: that is, a belief in the role of technology and policy to control people's biophysical states through detection, persuasion, coercion, or, when control is not possible, discipline (Williamson, 2017, Foucault, 1979). Biopolitical educational AI systems contribute to broader systems of algorithmic control through codifying the complex emotional states of learners in narrowly defined ways that are legible to the technologies, and which serve to reinforce particular, often racialized, ideologies about which emotions and behaviours are valued in the classroom and which are punished (Gregory and Fergus, 2017).

Behavioural management and discipline in schools—particularly in America—is shaped by ideologies that reproduce structural injustices. School policies such as zero tolerance have led to racial disparities in student suspension and expulsion rates (Keleher, 2000, Bottiani et al., 2017, Hoffman, 2014), with doubly marginalized students receiving greater disciplinary infractions (García, 2020). These racist disciplinary practices have contributed to the "school-to-prison pipeline" whereby racialized students are disciplined at higher rates, suspended, expelled, and funnelled into the prison system (Heitzeg, 2009, Kim et al., 2010). Structural injustice in schools' disciplinary practices is multifaceted, involving multiple, interlocking systems of oppression. In the US education company GLSEN's 2017 National School Climate Survey, a majority of LGBTQ+ students (62%) reported that their school had discriminatory policies or practices, such as disciplining public displays of affection disproportionately for LGBTQ+ students, with many reporting policies specifically targeting transgender students (Kosciw et al., 2018). Moreover, LGBTQ+ students with disabilities were more likely to be disciplined in school and to drop out of school than LGBTQ+ students without disabilities (Palmer et al., 2016). Without considering structural injustice, the historical legacies of these policies and practices of schooling become baked into technological infrastructures underlying educational AI.

Let us take one educational technology company, ClassDojo, as an example. Despite plucky rhetoric around "building classroom communities,"[13] ClassDojo was designed to allow teachers to track and reward students (via points) to incentivize what teachers feel is appropriate behaviour in the classroom (and occasionally beyond) (Williamson, 2017). While ClassDojo is not currently a data-driven system in the same way as educational AI such as affect detection systems (which use data to train algorithms to identify affective states), the underlying logic of systems like ClassDojo arises from the same biopolitical ideology as affect detection AI, and directly contributes to the creation of behavioural data that may be used to train biopolitical educational AI. A longer critique of biopolitical educational technologies such as ClassDojo is beyond the scope of this chapter (see (Williamson, 2017 or Brynjarsdottir et al., 2012 for a critique of "persuasive" technologies more generally). However ClassDojo is a clear example of how educational technologies may reinforce dominant ideologies of behavioural appropriateness—which construct racialized, LGBTQ+, disabled,[14] neurodivergent, and other marginalized students' behaviour as inappropriate or criminal—instantiated into biopolitical technologies of behavioural discipline and control. Thus, the racialized disciplinary and behavioural practices and policies of schooling are reproduced and amplified by educational AI technologies that detect, track, and influence students' emotional states and behaviours in the classroom.

During the ed tech boom driven by COVID-19 (Teräs et al., 2020), educational institutions have increasingly turned to technology to extend their behavioural control into students' homes, with one egregious example being automated proctoring systems.[15] Such systems encode particular ideologies of what is considered to be normal and abnormal (and thus suspicious) behaviour during a remote test, ideologies that reflect and reproduce structural injustices in the education system more broadly. The algorithms that power such systems, including computer vision for facial detection and behaviour detection algorithms, have been shown in other contexts to perform worse for women and people of colour (Buolamwini and Gebru, 2018). However, even if these models were to be tweaked in order to achieve parity of predictive performance across groups, the assumptions undergirding these systems is that there is a set of normal— and thus desirable—behaviours, and that behaviours other than these are suspected of being indicative of academic dishonesty. For neurodivergent learners, disabled learners, or learners with children or other caregiving responsibilities that might require them to behave in ways outside the narrow boundaries of what is considered to be normal behaviour, the design of such systems reinforces larger systems of oppression that marginalize and punish any who fall outside of those encoded definitions of normality (Davis, 1995, Swauger, 2020, Cahn et al., 2020). This ideology algorithmically encodes and perpetuates the carceral logics (i.e. "cop shit"[16]) of an education system that punishes marginalized learners in innumerable ways via the disciplinary practices of schooling.

Educational surveillance technologies

Underlying and enabling these educational algorithms of biopolitical control— and for educational AI more generally—lies an ed tech surveillance infrastructure that collects data on students under the guise of care.[17] Educational technologies—such as the aforementioned affect detection systems—often rely on or deploy a pervasive surveillance apparatus to collect multimodal (i.e. audio and video) data on learners' behaviour, including in some cases from cameras deployed in classrooms to monitor students' posture, gestures, and movements (Ahuja et al., 2019, Martinez-Maldonado et al., 2020, D'Mello et al., 2015). Although not all educational surveillance approaches use AI, many draw on data-driven algorithmic methods to detect the presence of people and their body movements (e.g. Ahuja et al., 2019) or on language technologies for surveillance of students' communication (e.g. Beckett, 2019). In addition, educational surveillance assemblages provide the crucial infrastructure that ratifies and enables AI systems (as discussed in Krafft et al., 2021). In a recent report from the University of Michigan's School of Public Policy, Galligan et al. argue that "cameras in the classroom" (or educational surveillance tools more broadly) reinforce systemic racism and discrimination, normalize surveillance for children, and further marginalize vulnerable groups.[18]

Although some have argued that classroom surveillance systems can be used as a tool to help students or support teachers' professional development (Ogan, 2019), the reality of how these systems are marketed and used in schools around the world may belie this optimistic view, as classroom surveillance technologies are deployed often without students' awareness or consent and, once deployed, may be used for purposes other than they were intended for.[19] In fact, although some tools for classroom monitoring appear to have been co-designed with input from teachers and students (Holstein et al., 2019), the vast majority do not appear to incorporate student or teacher input. Even in such cases where students or teachers were involved in their design, such approaches may merely be engaging in what has been referred to as "participation-washing," where stakeholders' involvement in the design is used to ratify decisions already made by the system designers (Sloane et al., 2020, Cooke and Kothari, 2001), a point to which we return in the final section. Moreover, the normalization of cameras in the classroom, under the guise of care for students, has now, during COVID-19, led to the pervasive extension of surveillance into learners' homes via Zoom (or other video conference platforms used for learning) and the aforementioned automated proctoring systems.

In addition to cameras in classrooms and homes, as part of a pervasive state of surveillance, some school districts have deployed AI-driven language-based surveillance systems to monitor and extract text data from students' email and messaging platforms (e.g. Beckett, 2019). These systems use natural language processing (NLP) models to flag messages or words that are hypothesized to be indicators that students will commit violent acts. The rhetoric of these platforms posits that schools that use them will be better able to protect their students' safety, following a similar logic of paternalistic care as in other educational surveillance initiatives. However, educational technologies often act as "racializing forces" that encode and perpetuate racialized ideologies about language (Dixon-Román et al., 2020), reinforcing the stigmatization and marginalization of minoritized language varieties and speakers (Rosa and Flores, 2017, Blodgett et al., 2020). Consider the earlier discussion of how language technologies have been shown to identify speakers of African American Language on social media as more toxic than speakers of Mainstream US English (Davidson et al., 2019).

Similarly, NLP systems have been shown to have higher false positive rates on text containing LGBTQ-related terms when attempting to detect hate speech (Dixon et al., 2018). On social media platforms, when these algorithms erroneously flag such language as hate speech, users may experience social or dignitary harms where language about LGBTQ+ topics is stigmatized as inappropriate or offensive, and where (if such language is removed) their ability to participate in public discourse about these topics is diminished (Blodgett et al., 2020). This is bad enough. But in a school context, when a student has a message flagged as harmful or potentially violent, schools may dispatch social workers or disciplinary officers to intervene, thus (at a minimum) creating a disciplinary record for that student (Beckett, 2019), or leading to serious harm for those students' lives and safety from the encounter with the carceral state. By creating disciplinary records and forcing interactions with institutions they might not otherwise have come into contact with, these surveillance systems directly construct "misbehaviour" or "criminality" out of minoritized students' language use, and may lead to their inclusion in databases of state apparatuses (cf. Eubanks, 2018).

This approach to widespread educational surveillance in the name of security—like the ubiquitous surveillance of the post-9/11 world—operates under what Brian Massumi (2015) has called the operative logic of pre-emption. These operative logics of mutual deterrence and pre-emptive strikes are not limited to war and statecraft, but infuse themselves into other aspects of our lives. Classroom surveillance technologies are one such platform, where a military logic of pre-emption informs the design and adoption of ubiquitous sensing infrastructure. Schools that purchase surveillance platforms such as the "appearance recognition" system Avigilon[20] or email and chat surveillance platforms Gaggle and Securly (Beckett, 2019) are able to argue that they have taken steps to make their schools safer from the supposedly ever-present threat of future school shootings, while having little evidence of their actual efficacy in pre-empting this future state. In the meantime, as surveillance infrastructure is adopted ever more widely, marginalized learners are the ones who are most harmed (Weinstein, 2020). During the COVID-19 pandemic, similar logics of care and pre-emption have motivated school districts to contract with surveillance tech companies looking to capitalize on the crisis, leading to (among other surveillance efforts) proposals for students to wear badges to track their movements around schools.[21] The persistent legacy of racist school disciplinary practices suggests that these surveillance technologies will continue to reproduce structural injustice for marginalized learners.

At-risk prediction technologies

The broad class of dropout prediction systems is another category of educational AI systems that reproduces structural injustice, regardless of the accuracy of such systems. Such systems focus on predicting learners' risk of failing to complete a class or a degree program, using behavioural data from interactions with a given course (e.g. Tang et al., 2018, Nur et al., 2019, Lykourentzou et al., 2009, Liang et al., 2016, Márquez-Vera et al., 2016). The underlying interventionist logic of this line of research is that if researchers can identify which students are "at-risk" of dropping out of a course or a program, someone can intervene and prevent the student from dropping out.[22] Decades of educational reformers have painted the "dropout" as a scary Other, designed to motivate learners through their fear of becoming part of this maligned class (Meyerhoff, 2019).[23] This Other has a racialized history. Educational researchers in the 1960s described minority learners as "culturally deprived" and argued that these students should be considered "potential dropouts"—with a too-brief caveat on the negative effect of such labels (Hunt, 1966). Although the terms have changed, the underlying ideology of stigmatizing the "dropout" persists today, manifested in dropout risk prediction algorithms.

Much like other research efforts for biopolitical educational technologies and surveillance systems that have found enthusiastic adoption in school systems, some universities are deploying what they describe as "early warning systems" that use predictive models to trigger an administrative action when a potential risk of dropout is detected, ostensibly in support of those students (Nam and Samson, 2019). This line of research on so-called "Student Early Warning Systems"[24] evokes analogous risk modelling efforts in other domains, such as early warning systems for missile launches, disaster modelling, and financial risk models (Ahmad et al., 2013, Lando, 2009, Basch et al., 2000). But there are consequences to viewing students as missiles or natural disasters.[25] Classifying or labelling learners as "at-risk" has historically had inequitable consequences for marginalized learners (Hunt, 1966) in ways that become self-fulfilling prophecies, particularly when educators begin viewing students as at-risk. The language implicit in dropout "risk" prediction evokes the alarmism of the educational reform report *A Nation At Risk*, which spurred panic about minoritized learners and led to decades of testing and policies ostensibly designed to help learners "at risk." Further, the underlying data used to train these models is often a set of profoundly inequitable educational outcomes, the result of decades of racist educational practices (hooks, 1994, Giroux, 2001, Keleher, 2000, Kim et al., 2010). When such systems are used to predict college enrolment from student behaviours in middle school (Pedro et al., 2013), these systems risk further entrenching legacies of historical injustice in future learning opportunities.

Beyond all of this, even if the models do successfully identify whether students may be likely to fail a course or drop out of a program, it is not clear how they may be used to *prevent* students from leaving the course. One approach to this has been to use the output of the risk models to provide targeted advising to students, as in Purdue University's Course Signals program. Other universities have used such models to support what has been unsettlingly called "intrusive advising" or providing proactive advising to students they think need it (Glennen and Baxley, 1985, Varney, 2012). As in other AI systems in education, some researchers have begun to investigate the differential performance of these dropout prediction systems for different populations (Hutt et al., 2019). Left unanswered (or largely unasked) by these algorithmic fairness approaches is the question of whether these models should exist at all, or the consequences for marginalized learners of being thus labelled.

During the COVID-19 pandemic, as schools moved online and many high-stakes assessments were cancelled, several school systems decided to use algorithmic predictions of end-of-semester grades in lieu of assessments or teacher-assigned grades. Several high-profile examples of this highlight the risks of predictive modelling approaches to grades.[26] In the UK, algorithmic predictions of students' A-level exams were found to be biased against students from schools in lower-income areas.[27] Historical patterns of disinvestment in education and broader societal inequities were instantiated in the algorithm, reproducing these historical legacies of oppression. However, after many students saw their final predicted course grades deviated from what they expected, massive protests erupted, with rallying cries of "F*ck the algorithm."[28] The UK Department for Education later cancelled the algorithm; but it provides a cautionary tale for educational technologists who intend to develop predictive algorithms to model students' performance or risk (in part because the models may be repurposed for other goals, such as grade assignment). Even if this algorithm had been assessed for group-based fairness (Kizilcec and Lee, 2020), its underlying premise was to assign grades on high-stakes assessments on the basis of historical performance in those assessments, reproducing systemic biases (cf. Papageorge et al., 2020).

Without a critical lens to question the historical legacy and socio-political context of scoring on assessments, these algorithms may perpetuate structural injustice. At-risk prediction algorithms thus continue to harm marginalized students (whether via the racialized othering of students "at risk" or via socioeconomic inequities as in the UK A-level algorithm) in ways often left unquestioned in more optimistic views on educational technology. In this section, we have discussed three classes of educational AI systems—biopolitical algorithms; the surveillance infrastructure that draws on and enables educational AI; and risk prediction. These categories of educational AI offer instructive sites with which to understand how educational AI may reproduce structural injustice in education, despite the best intentions of the researchers and designers, and in ways not accounted for by traditional group-based approaches to algorithmic fairness.

Where Might We Go from Here?

The question at this point is not *whether* inequity exists in educational AI. The unequal treatment of students in today's educational settings is well-established, and we have argued that data-driven educational algorithms that fail to grapple with those socio-historical structures may reproduce and amplify existing inequities. Identifying group-based performance differences for various educational AI systems may be a good start, but it remains insufficient if those systems are built on—and further reproduce—existing systems of oppression such as, for instance, racist language ideologies. However, individual researchers may feel unable to make significant changes to their research agenda—as suggested by related findings on industry AI research (Holstein et al., 2018, Madaio et al., 2020, Rakova et al., 2020), much of which has been built up over years and is hard to pivot. In the face of this, how might we as a research community re-imagine a better future, and confront the structural injustice of educational AI?

The limits of representation and participation

One common response to these concerns is to acknowledge the risk of biases from technologies, and then shift to argue for their resolution through more diverse voices involved in the design and decision-making process. This push for representation as a solution is an important step towards addressing issues of access and opportunity to the knowledge, practices, and spaces that are shaping educational AI. As one example, there is a push to train more data scientists from underrepresented backgrounds; in addition to the inherent value of this, the argument is that if more diverse voices were part of the AI design process, their perspectives would be able to shape the design of algorithms.[29]

While these efforts are laudable, as postmodern feminist and political philosopher Iris Marion Young argued (1990), a focus on identity and inclusion is not enough to address the non-material processes of power and oppression. Parisi and Dixon-Román (2020) argue that this approach is based on a politics of inclusion, which makes assumptions that diverse or representative participation will shift the epistemology and logic of socio-technical systems. However, they argue that this approach fails to address the normative disciplinary practices that produce knowledge and shape educational systems (cf. Hoffmann, 2021). Adding diversity to who is included at the table of decision-making is an important initiative; but, as Benjamin (2019b, p.62) argues "so much of what is routine, reasonable, intuitive, and codified reproduces unjust social arrangements, without ever burning a cross to shine light on the problem." Parisi and Dixon-Román further argue that politics of inclusion fundamentally do not transform the norms and logic that make up the epistemology of the system, but may in fact maintain and reify the colonialist logic of hierarchies of difference that was formed in the post-Enlightenment and inherited by science and technology. In other words, the issue at hand is not just about representation in design; it is fundamentally about the epistemological *hegemony* of educational AI—that is, questions about what it means to produce knowledge, which kinds of knowledge are valued, and who determines what knowledge is valued in the design of technology. Thus, the idea of just adding (for instance) more diverse team members may not fundamentally shift or change the underlying ways of thinking and knowing, and the structures of power that animate those ideologies. The recent example of Google firing the co-leads of their Ethical AI research group, Drs Timnit Gebru and Margaret Mitchell, for raising concerns about the authenticity of the company's diversity and inclusion efforts, as well as their critical stance towards large-scale AI systems, throws into stark relief the limits of representation and inclusion of diverse voices in the research and design of AI systems, given existing power structures within technology companies.[30]

An alternative theory of change looks to research programs that include more participatory design and community-based co-design research(ers).[31] This would ideally mean that research teams involve members of marginalized stakeholder groups as meaningful, co-equal members of the research team, or as advisors to the research projects, whose voices are given equal weight in framing the goals from the start, and who should be able to say that the research should not continue if there is no way to make it equitable. This is in contrast to simply offering tokenized feedback to an already finished project or a project that can only be altered at the margins (cf. Arnstein, 1969, Sloane et al., 2020). One can see such participatory approaches used in public policy (Corbett and Le Dantec, 2018) and community-engaged health research (Balls-Berry and Acosta-Perez, 2017), as well as in the tradition of participatory design and co-design in human–computer interaction (HCI) (Harrington et al., 2019, Muller, 2007), which also is emerging in the learning analytics field (Holstein et al., 2019).[32]

While this is a positive step, much like calls for more diverse voices on AI development teams, there is reason to be sceptical of this type of "reformist" approach to change. Simply "adding users and stirring" (Muller, 2007) will do little to change the underlying power structures shaping educational AI systems (see Holstein and Doroudi, Chapter 6 this volume, for additional discussion of this point). Addressing structural injustice through participatory design will require reconsideration of what it means for stakeholders to participate in AI research. Researchers must ensure that their work does not further reproduce existing power dynamics and hierarchies in the broader society, both within the research teams and with their relationships to stakeholders (Sloane et al., 2020, Cooke and Kothari, 2001). Such work will also need to avoid overburdening marginalized communities, by compensating them adequately for the full scope of their newly expanded participation and avoiding what some have referred to as the "epistemic burden" of extractive forms of participatory design (Pierre et al., 2021). Truly empowered participation by marginalized groups in these research agendas requires the ability to change ways of knowing and what evidence looks like. It will require a willingness from the researchers to change the definition of efficacy and success in an intervention, based on what communities want and need. It will require looking at different disciplines and paradigms, beyond techno-solutionist paradigms and beyond well-trodden fields like psychometrics and developmental psychology (and yes, algorithmic "fairness"), and instead towards the voices of community organizers, social justice scholars, critical theorists, and others. This will require humility on the part of researchers and funders, a willingness to be part of a change that may leave them with less control at the end of the funding and research process than they had at the start.

The field of AI ethics more broadly is grappling with this issue as well. Despite dozens of value statements for ethical AI produced by large technology companies and government agencies (Jobin et al., 2019), AI systems continue to be developed that discriminate and perpetuate injustice. While there may be legitimate organizational reasons why AI practitioners have been unable to put these principles into practice (e.g. Holstein et al., 2018, Stark and Hoffmann,

2019, Madaio et al., 2020, Rakova et al., 2020), others have been sceptical of these companies' intentions. Some critics describe these AI ethical statements as "fairwashing" or "ethics-washing"—that is, developing principles for ethical AI while doing little to change the nature of such technology or the organizational processes that led to their design (Bietti, 2020), acting as a "smokescreen" for business as usual (Sloane, 2019). Thus, while it may be worthwhile to begin with efforts to support more diverse perspectives on educational AI teams and more participation from marginalized communities in those systems' design, this will not be enough to transform fundamentally unjust systems.

Equitable futures for AI in education

As we close, we ask what an alternative vision for a more equitable future for educational AI might entail. First, and most critically, we argue that educational AI researchers and designers should adopt a *design justice* approach to educational AI research. As proposed by Sasha Costanza-Chock (2020, p.23), design justice is a "framework for analysis of how design distributes benefits and burdens between various groups of people." This involves interrogating the values encoded into designed systems; meaningfully involving members of marginalized and impacted communities in the design of technology; and, more generally, critically interrogating the narratives, sites, and pedagogies around design—here, the design of educational AI systems. We have begun such efforts in this chapter by tracing socio-historical legacies of educational inequity through several categories of educational AI systems that may perpetuate unjust ideologies and structures of oppression, drawing on lenses from critical theory and structural justice to inform this work. To design more equitable educational AI, though, will require the learning science and technology community to learn, adopt, and promote theories and methods fields outside of what is considered to be a core research area for AI—approaches that may draw on design justice, critical theory, participatory design, and other areas.

But changing the direction and goals of a research community means not only that individuals should change their research and design practices, but that the field as a whole should interrogate and confront the ways in which systemic educational inequities may be reproduced in the design, research, and policy of educational AI. What does it mean to be a justice-oriented learning science researcher? How might the existing incentives of the field be changed to encourage researchers to interrogate ethical issues and centre justice-oriented decisions in their research practice? These incentives may include the grants and funding that learning scientists pursue; the collaborators they choose; the role of stakeholders in their research (including grappling with power hierarchies between and within communities of stakeholders); and researchers' ongoing engagement with the impact and potential inequities of their research after dissemination and deployment. Ideally, such an approach would entail a longer-term view of how research and development of educational AI (and educational technology more broadly) impacts learners' educational opportunities over the current, more incremental approaches. To what extent might values of justice and equity be adopted in conference and journal calls, review processes, and paper awards? In tenure and promotion reviews at universities? How might we avoid the co-optation of calls for equity that become neutered and narrowly scoped into neat technical fixes and ethics-washing?

We, along with others in AI more broadly (e.g. Benjamin 2019a), argue that the field of learning science and educational AI needs new, more radical visions for equitable learning futures. Visions for the kinds of technologies that can be built are shaped by what has been called "socio-technical imaginaries", or:

> The collectively held, institutionally stabilized, and publicly performed visions of desirable futures, animated by shared understandings of forms of social life and social order attainable through, and supportive of, advances in science and technology.
>
> (Jasanoff and Kim, 2015, p.4)

The socio-technical imaginaries of our current field of educational AI are shaped and circumscribed by the historical legacy of the matrix of domination in education and technology. But they can be remade. To do this, we are inspired by Keyes et al.'s (2019) call for *counterpower*, or what they call emancipatory autonomy in human–computer interaction, or, more simply, anarchist HCI. For them, counterpower involves fostering community-appropriate and community-determined research and design, both between researchers and stakeholders as well as within the research community itself (here, learning science and educational AI), akin to what Asad et al. (2019) have referred to as "academic accomplices"—scholars whose research is designed to support (rather than displace) the already ongoing justice work on communities. This move towards counterpower would involve everyone, not simply a privileged few, in taking control over the means to shape the forms of socio-technical educational systems.[33] What might such counterpower look like for learning science research, and how might it lead to new socio-technical imaginaries for educational AI?

For some research directions, it may be the case that the research should simply cease—where "the implication is *not* to design" (Baumer and Silberman, 2011, Barocas et al., 2020). Os Keyes (2019b) poses a similar challenge by arguing that data science's approach to quantification and classification is intrinsically at odds with—and a danger to—queer lives. Predictive policing presents another such case, where generations of racist policing practices means that algorithms trained on these data will inevitably reproduce and exacerbate these practices (Dixon-Román et al., 2019, Richardson et al., 2019). In such cases, injustices are inextricably embedded in the proposed technical solutions. For these types of tasks or methods, no amount of group fairness measurement or user experience (UX) optimization of a workflow will produce anything other than a reproduction and entrenchment of existing structures of oppression. Thus, in the absence of regulatory policy, the only recourse may be for people to organize to shut it down. In AI more broadly, public acts of resistance or refusal are becoming more common. For instance, communities have organized against computer vision used in public housing projects (Gilman, 2019), and the Stop LAPD Spying Coalition has successfully organized to ban predictive policing in Los Angeles, among other cities.[34] In education, one might look to the recent protests in the UK to "F*ck the algorithm" that predicted students' A-level grades or student resistance to automated proctoring systems (Cahn et al., 2020),[35] among others.[36] However, these examples are acts of resistance to and refusal of systems that are already designed, deployed, and causing harm in the world.

We thus call for a wider range of design methods and theories to envision more radical, equitable futures for the learning sciences and AI in education. The design of our modes of learning is too important to be left in the hands of a privileged few. Current rhetoric from AI corporations and researchers (Moreau et al., 2019) is full of calls to "democratize" AI, which mostly seems to refer to producing open-source tools for developing machine learning models (e.g. TensorFlow). In practice however, while platforms like Tensor-Flow may be freely available, simply giving more—often already privileged (West et al., 2019)—people access to them will do little to change the fundamentally inequitable systems and power structures underlying the social contexts in which they are developed and used. Indeed, many current calls for ethical approaches to educational AI lean heavily on modelling after existing pedagogical paradigms (cf. du Bouley, this volume), which, as we discussed earlier, may reproduce or exacerbate existing structures of oppression in schooling.

Instead, a more radical vision for democratizing data-driven learning technologies might reflect Paulo Freire's (1970) vision of a *liberatory* pedagogy that allows learners to propose and engage with the problems that are essential for their lives. There is a rich lineage of resistance to centralized hierarchies in education, including the critical theorist Ivan Illich (1973), who, among others, famously called for "deschooling society (see also Giroux, 2001, Freire, 1970, hooks, 1994, Meyerhoff, 2019). A full discussion of how the vision of Freire and Illich might be enacted in data-driven educational technology is beyond our scope here, but we are encouraged by recent work on the implications of a Freireian pedagogy for learning analytics (Broughan and Prinsloo, 2020). Such traditions suggest additional opportunities for learners to take control and ownership over educational AI systems.

The design approaches and theories that fit neatly into the existing body of learning science and technology research have resulted in reproductions of existing, inequitable bricks-and-mortar education systems. We have built algorithms that reflect back the inequities that are already in place. At best, educational AI researchers have conducted group-fairness comparisons for learners from different populations (e.g. Kizilcec and Lee, 2020, Gardner et al., 2019). While such efforts are promising steps toward mitigating fairness harms of existing systems, this retrenchment of existing algorithmic fairness paradigms will not lead to the creation of new socio-technical imaginaries, or to the design of more liberatory forms of education. As a field, we might instead look to methods from feminist speculative design (Martins, 2014) and critical design (Bardzell et al., 2012, Bardzell and Bardzell, 2013), which endeavour to provoke and problematize (Forlano and Mathew, 2014), and to have bold visions for designing more liberatory futures.

One source of these new socio-technical imaginaries may be queer theory. Scholars in queer theory have used the term "queer" as a verb, to describe a resistance to and deconstruction of binary and hierarchical categories and structures of oppression (Butler, 2011, Ahmed, 2006, Muñoz et al., 2019). Although it originated in resisting rigid categories of gender and sexuality, it has been used to problematize hierarchical relations of power more broadly, including in the field of HCI and technology design (Light, 2011) and data science (Keyes, 2019b). Inspired by this, we ask what it would take *to queer* learning technologies—to offer resistance to the dominant modes of thinking that reinforce systems of oppression in the learning sciences and educational AI. This might involve using critical design methods to provoke and problematize foundational assumptions in learning technologies, including what should be learned and what it means to have learned it—to challenge dominant ideologies of what a "good" learner is and resist the technologies that treat deviation from the norm as suspicious.

Additionally, Dixon-Román and others have argued that we might look to the field of Afrofuturism as another source of methods and theories to envision new socio-technical imaginaries and develop new visions for more liberatory futures (de Freitas and Dixon-Román, 2017, Benjamin, 2019a). That is to say, if particular socio-political processes of colonial and post-colonial violence never occurred, how might socio-technical systems be designed differently, have different purposes, and enable alternative forms of reasoning other-wise? Afrofuturism entails a critical examination of the historical conditions that led to current societal inequities while opening up a space for re-imagining alternative futures by asking the "what if" questions that centre an affirmative perspective of people of colour (Dixon-Román et al., 2019, Gaskins, 2019). Winchester (2018) has described how Afrofuturism might "place the often-disenfranchised Black voice central in the design narrative" and "plug the imagination gap" in technology design. For a vision of how Afrofuturism might be used to counteract the "racializing forces" of educational AI, see Dixon-Román et al. (2020).

All of this may require rethinking the standard AI research and design lifecycle to prioritize equity and justice, and to involve (and empower) stakeholders from marginalized communities throughout this lifecycle in ways that avoid reproducing existing power dynamics in their participatory design approaches. This may entail a radical transformation of the "institutionally stabilized" structures and incentives of the current funding and research landscape to create welcoming spaces for diverse voices to shape the socio-technical imaginaries of educational

AI and ed tech more broadly (Tuck and Yang, 2018, Jasanoff and Kim, 2015). It may require teaching learning science and educational AI students about the history and legacies of educational injustice, critical theory, and broader societal systems of oppression.

Conclusion

Educational policies and practices present visions of a particular type of learner, and attempt to prepare that learner for life in society—educational AI systems then instantiate these visions and values into algorithmic systems that may further entrench them. Whose visions are these? What type of learner is imagined, and what type of society are they being educated for? These are questions with critical consequences in a settler colonialist, white supremacist, patriarchal, cis heteronormative, ableist society. Paulo Freire and bell hooks, among other theorists and critics, have called for a more radical, liberatory form of education, where, rather than simply reproducing inequitable societal structures, the role of education is instead a provocation to rethink what is possible—to remake the world in a more radical, more just, and more equitable way.

This chapter interrogates issues of structural injustice in educational AI technologies through applying critical lenses to examining several forms of educational AI systems. The problems are complex and interwoven, and resist straightforward analyses and answers—including quick technical solutions and neat group-level evaluations of "AI fairness." What is needed are approaches to transforming the epistemology of educational AI, working towards justice and equity—both in educational AI technologies and in the socio-technical and socio-political milieu in which they are designed. We do not offer solutions to the core challenges we have presented. To offer neat solutions would be to undermine the argument we have been making.

What this historical moment, the crisis of the COVID-19 pandemic, has revealed is the potential for doing work outside the norms. We are in the midst of rapid and fundamental change to our educational system. We can use this as an opportunity to radically re-imagine what we want for our education systems—including educational algorithmic systems and socio-technical systems more broadly. Funding organizations and technology corporations are often the ones with the power and privilege to drive large-scale change. And yet, as a community of researchers and practitioners, there is much we can collectively do to transform the trajectory of the field. There is an enormous rethinking about the role of technology in education that is beginning to occur worldwide. We must take this as an opportunity to reshape the priorities of the educational research we do and the research we support, towards addressing structural injustice in educational AI.

Notes

1   https://www.worldbank.org/en/data/interactive/2020/03/24/world-bank-educa tion-and-covid-19.

2   In this chapter, we use the term AI to refer to data-driven algorithmic assemblages broadly construed. Data-driven algorithms have a lengthy history in education, from computer-aided instructional systems in the 1970s (Carbonell, 1970) to intelligent tutoring systems that provide feedback and instructions to learners on the basis of students' data (Pane et al., 2014), with more recent versions of such systems drawing on advances in machine learning (Piech et al., 2015) and natural language processing (Mayfield et al., 2019). Following Richardson's writing on algorithmic decision systems (2021), we use the term AI expansively, rather than narrowly scoped to refer only to systems that include technical components such as machine learning, given that many data-driven algorithmic systems may not strictly involve machine learning and are still often marketed under the label of—and conceptualized in the public consciousness as—AI; and, moreover, data-driven assemblages are susceptible to—and further contribute to—the same biases pervasive in AI more generally.

3   https://www.colorado.edu/today/ai-education.

4   https://www.theguardian.com/news/2020/may/13/naomi-klein-how-big-tech-pla ns-to-profit-from-coronavirus-pandemic.

5   https://www.de.ed.ac.uk/news/edtech-pandemic-shock-blog-ben-williamson-and-a nna-hogan.

6   We focus in this chapter on the US context, given the lived experiences of the authors. Further research should extend this lens to implications for educational AI in global contexts—as work such as Sambasivan et al. (2021), Ismail and Kumar (2021), and Mohamed et al. (2020) have done for AI more generally.

7   https://facctconference.org.

8   United States law specifically defines the following characteristics as protected: race, colour, religion, sex and gender identity, pregnancy, national origin, age, disability, veteran status, and genetic information. Internationally, specific protections differ by jurisdiction.

9   We write as researchers in the United States, but similar systemic forces shape social structures everywhere, in different ways.

10   More than 60 years after the US Supreme Court declared school segregation unconstitutional in their 1954 *Brown v. Board of Education* ruling, many American schools remain heavily segregated, and the legacy of historical racial oppression hovers over the entire American school system. In a recent Economic Policy Institute analysis of data from the National Assessment of Educational Progress, nearly 7 in 10 (69%) Black students attended a school where a majority of students were Black, Hispanic, Asian, or American Indian (García, 2020). In contrast, only 1 in 8 (13%) of white students attended a school where a majority of students were people of colour. Black and Hispanic students are also substantially more likely than white students to not complete high school, with 79% and 81% graduation rates, respectively, compared to 89.1% of white students (see US Department of Education, 2020 for 2017– 18 statistics, the latest year on record. Students with disabilities reported the lowest rates of school completion, with only 67.1% completing high school.

11   bell hooks chooses to have her pen name in lowercase to "shift attention from her identity to her ideas" https://www.nytimes.com/2019/02/28/books/bell-hooks-m in-jin-lee-aint-i-a-woman.html.

12   Although prior work has identified affective states that are purportedly positively associated with learning (e.g. Craig et al., 2004, Csikszentmihalyi, 1997), recent work has critiqued the racialized construction of such affective states in education (Zembylas, 2021).

13 https://www.classdojo.com/.
14 We use the term "disabled" following scholars in the field of critical disability studies (Mankoff et al., 2010, Spiel et al., 2020, Goodley et al., 2019).
15 While automated proctoring technologies (e.g. Proctorio, ProctorU, etc.) had been in use prior to COVID-19, the pandemic accelerated adoption of these platforms, with Proctorio reportedly administering "2.5 million exams—a 900 percent increase from the same period last year." https://www.vox.com/recode/2020/5/4/21241062/schools-cheating-proctorio-artificial-intelligence.
16 https://jeffreymoro.com/blog/2020-02-13-against-cop-shit/.
17 https://insidehighered.com/blogs/college-ready-writing/surveillance-state.
18 http://stpp.fordschool.umich.edu/sites/stpp.fordschool.umich.edu/files/file-assets/cameras_in_the_classroom_ful.
19 https://www.sixthtone.com/news/1003759/camera-above-the-classroom.
20 https://www.vox.com/recode/2020/1/25/21080749/surveillance-school-artificial-intelligence-facial-recognition.
21 https://www.the74million.org/article/as-covid-creeps-into-schools-surveillance-tech-follows/.
22 Although there are, of course, other logics at work here, such as the business models that motivate many educational technologies (cf. Williamson, 2020, Teräs et al., 2020).
23 These approaches follow what Eli Meyerhoff (2019) has described as a "romantic narrative" of educational progress—that learners advance through vertically arranged stages of educational progress, battling obstacles on the way to ascending to some imagined higher plane of existence after graduation.
24 https://eliterate.us/instructure-dig-and-student-early-warning-systems/.
25 There is a longer tradition of pathologizing students as, for instance, patients in need of inoculation, as in Illich (1973).
26 https://www.nytimes.com/2020/09/08/opinion/international-baccalaureate-algorithm-grades.html.
27 https://www.theguardian.com/education/2020/aug/13/almost-40-of-english-students-have-a-level-results-downgraded.
28 https://unherd.com/2020/08/how-ofqual-failed-the-algorithm-test/.
29 https://hbr.org/2020/10/to-build-less-biased-ai-hire-a-more-diverse-team.
30 https://www.fastcompany.com/90608471/timnit-gebru-google-ai-ethics-equitable-tech-movement.
31 https://participatoryml.github.io.
32 http://pdlak.utscic.edu.au/call.html.
33 One can see echoes of calls for liberatory approaches to technology more generally (e.g. Benjamin, 2019a, Winchester III, 2018, Tierney, 2019), and tensions in political traditions between participation and paternalism (e.g. Cooke and Kothari, 2001, Moir and Leyshon, 2013).
34 https://capp-pgh.com.
35 https://www.eff.org/deeplinks/2020/09/students-are-pushing-back-against-proctoring-surveillance-apps.
36 https://www.donnalanclos.com/listening-to-refusal-opening-keynote-for-aptconf-2019/.

References

Agarwal, A., Beygelzimer, A., Dudik, M., Langford, J., and Wallach, H. (2018). A reductions approach to fair classification. In *International Conference on Machine Learning*, pages 60–69.

Aguliera, E. and Nightengale-Lee, B. (2020). Emergency remote teaching across urban and rural contexts: Perspectives on educational equity. *Information and Learning Sciences*, 121(5–6):471–478.

Ahmad, N., Hussain, M., Riaz, N., Subhani, F., Haider, S., Alamgir, K. S., and Shinwari, F. (2013). Flood prediction and disaster risk analysis using GIS based wireless sensor networks: A review. *Journal of Basic and Applied Scientific Research*, 3(8):632–643.

Ahmed, S. (2006). *Queer phenomenology: Orientations, objects, others*. Duke University Press.

Ahuja, K., Kim, D., Xhakaj, F., Varga, V., Xie, A., Zhang, S., Townsend, J. E., Harrison, C., Ogan, A., and Agarwal, Y. (2019). Edusense: Practical classroom sensing at scale. *Proceedings of the ACM on Interactive, Mobile, Wearable and Ubiquitous Technologies*, 3(3):1–26.

Anastasi, A. (1961). Psychological tests: Uses and abuses. *Teachers College Record*, 62(5):1–5.

Angwin, J., Larson, J., Mattu, S., and Kirchner, L. (2016). Machine bias. *ProPublica*, May, 23.

Arnstein, S. R. (1969). A ladder of citizen participation. *Journal of the American Institute of Planners*, 35(4):216–224.

Asad, M., Dombrowski, L., Costanza-Chock, S., Erete, S., and Harrington, C. (2019). Academic accomplices: Practical strategies for research justice. In *Companion Publication of the 2019 on Designing Interactive Systems Conference 2019 Companion*, pages 353–356.

Athanasiadis, C., Hortal, E., Koutsoukos, D., Lens, C. Z., and Asteriadis, S. (2017). Personalized, affect and performance-driven computer-based learning. In *Proceedings of the 9th International Conference on Computer Supported Education CSEDU*, volume 1, pages 132–139.

Balls-Berry, J. E. and Acosta-Perez, E. (2017). The use of community engaged research principles to improve health: community academic partnerships for research. *Puerto Rico Health Sciences Journal*, 36(2):84.

Bardzell, J. and Bardzell, S. (2013). What is "critical" about critical design? In *Proceedings of the SIGCHI Conference on Human Factors in Computing Systems*, pages 3297–3306.

Bardzell, S., Bardzell, J., Forlizzi, J., Zimmerman, J., and Antanitis, J. (2012). Critical design and critical theory: The challenge of designing for provocation. In *Proceedings of the Designing Interactive Systems Conference*, pages 288–297.

Barocas, S., Biega, A. J., Fish, B., Niklas, J., and Stark, L. (2020). When not to design, build, or deploy. In *Proceedings of the 2020 Conference on Fairness, Accountability, and Transparency*, pages 695–695.

Barocas, S. and Selbst, A. D. (2016). Big data's disparate impact. *California Law Review*, 104:671–732.

Basch, C. A., Bruesewitz, B. J., Siegel, K., and Faith, P. (2000). Financial risk prediction systems and methods therefor. US Patent 6,119,103.

Baumer, E. P. and Silberman, M. S. (2011). When the implication is not to design (technology). In *Proceedings of the SIGCHI Conference on Human Factors in Computing Systems*, pages 2271–2274.

Beckett, L. (2019). Under digital surveillance: how American schools spy on millions of kids. *The Guardian*. https://bit.ly/3c6VTMg. (Accessed on 04/22/2020).

Benjamin, R. (2019a). *Captivating technology: Race, carceral technoscience, and liberatory imagination in everyday life*. Duke University Press.

Benjamin, R. (2019b). *Race after technology: abolitionist tools for the new Jim code*. John Wiley & Sons.

Bennett, C. L. and Keyes, O. (2019). *What is the point of fairness? Disability, AI, and the complexity of justice*. In Proceedings of the ASSETS Workshop on AI Fairness for People with Disabilities, Pittsburgh, PA.

Bietti, E. (2020). From ethics washing to ethics bashing: A view on tech ethics from within moral philosophy. In *Proceedings of the 2020 Conference on Fairness, Accountability, and Transparency*, pages 210–219.

Blodgett, S. L., Barocas, S., DauméIII, H., and Wallach, H. (2020). Language (technology) is power: A critical survey of "bias" in NLP. In *Proceedings of the Association for Computational Linguistics (ACL)*, pages 5454–5476.

Bolukbasi, T., Chang, K.-W., Zou, J. Y., Saligrama, V., and Kalai, A. T. (2016). Man is to computer programmer as woman is to homemaker? Debiasing word embeddings. In Lee, D. D., Sugiyama, M., Luxburg, U. V., Guyon, I., and Garnett, R. (eds), *Advances in neural information processing systems* 29, pages 4349–4357. Curran Associates.

Boser, U. (2012). *Race to the top: What have we learned from the states so far? A state-by-state evaluation of race to the top performance*. Center for American Progress.

Bottiani, J. H., Bradshaw, C. P., and Mendelson, T. (2017). A multilevel examination of racial disparities in high school discipline: Black and white adolescents' perceived equity, school belonging, and adjustment problems. *Journal of Educational Psychology*, 109(4):532–545.

Bourdieu, P. (1977). *Outline of a theory of practice*, volume 16. Cambridge University Press.

boyd, d. and Crawford, K. (2012). Critical questions for big data. *Information, Communication & Society*, 15(5):662–679.

Broughan, C. and Prinsloo, P. (2020). (Re)centring students in learning analytics: In conversation with Paulo Freire. *Assessment & Evaluation in Higher Education*, 45(4):617–628.

Brynjarsdottir, H., Håkansson, M., Pierce, J., Baumer, E., DiSalvo, C., and Sengers, P. (2012). Sustainably unpersuaded: How persuasion narrows our vision of sustainability. In *Proceedings of the SIGCHI Conference on Human Factors in Computing Systems*, pages 947–956.

Buolamwini, J. and Gebru, T. (2018). *Gender shades: Intersectional accuracy disparities in commercial gender classification*. In Conference on Fairness, Accountability and Transparency, pages 77–91.

Butler, J. (2011). *Gender trouble: Feminism and the subversion of identity*. Routledge.

Cahn, A. F., Magee, C., Manis, E., and Akyol, N. (2020). *Snooping where we sleep: The invasiveness and bias of remote proctoring systems*. Surveillance Technology Oversight Project.

Carbonell, J. R. (1970). AI in CAI: An artificial-intelligence approach to computer-assisted instruction. *IEEE Transactions on Man-Machine Systems*, 11(4):190–202.

Chang, C., Zhang, C., Chen, L., and Liu, Y. (2018). An ensemble model using face and body tracking for engagement detection. In *Proceedings of the 20th ACM International Conference on Multimodal Interaction*, pages 616–622.

Chouldechova, A. (2017). Fair prediction with disparate impact: A study of bias in recidivism prediction instruments. *Big Data*, 5(2):153–163.

Cifor, M., Garcia, P., Cowan, T., Rault, J., Sutherland, T., Chan, A. S., Rode, J., Hoffmann, A. L., Salehi, N., and Nakamura, L. (2019). Feminist data manifest-no. Institute for Research on Women and Gender.

Cleary, T. A. (1968). Test bias: Prediction of grades of negro and white students in integrated colleges. *Journal of Educational Measurement*, 5(2):115–124.

Collins, P. H. (1990). *Black feminist thought: Knowledge, consciousness, and the politics of empowerment*. Routledge.

Cooke, B. and Kothari, U. (2001). *Participation: The new tyranny?*Zed Books.

Corbett, E. and Le Dantec, C. A. (2018). The problem of community engagement: Disentangling the practices of municipal government. In *Proceedings of the 2018 CHI Conference on Human Factors in Computing Systems*, pages 1–13.

Corbett-Davies, S. and Goel, S. (2018). *The measure and mismeasure of fairness: A critical review of fair machine learning*. Synthesis of tutorial presented at ICML 2018.

Costanza-Chock, S. (2018). Design justice: Towards an intersectional feminist framework for design theory and practice. *Proceedings of the Design Research Society*. doi:10.21606/drs.2018.679.

Costanza-Chock, S. (2020). *Design justice: Community-led practices to build the worlds we need.* MIT Press.

Craig, S., Graesser, A., Sullins, J., and Gholson, B. (2004). Affect and learning: An exploratory look into the role of affect in learning with AutoTutor. *Journal of Educational Media*, 29(3):241–250.

Crawford, K. (2017). The trouble with bias, 2017. Invited talk by Kate Crawford at the Conference on Neural Information Processing Systems (NIPS). http://blog.revolutionanalytics.com/2017/12/the-trouble-withbias-by-kate-crawford. html.

Crenshaw, K. (1989). *Demarginalizing the intersection of race and sex: A Black feminist critique of antidiscrmination doctrine, feminist theory and antiracist politics*. University of Chicago Legal Forum.

Crenshaw, K. (1990). Mapping the margins: Intersectionality, identity politics, and violence against women of color. *Stanford Law Review*, 43:1241.

Csikszentmihalyi, M. (1997). *Flow and education. NAMTA Journal*, 22(2):2–35.

D'Mello, S. K. and Graesser, A. (2010). Multimodal semi-automated affect detection from conversational cues, gross body language, and facial features. *User Modeling and User-Adapted Interaction*, 20(2):147–187.

D'Mello, S. K., Olney, A. M., Blanchard, N., Samei, B., Sun, X., Ward, B., and Kelly, S. (2015). Multimodal capture of teacher-student interactions for automated dialogic analysis in live classrooms. In *Proceedings of the 2015 ACM on international conference on multimodal interaction*, pages 557–566.

Daggett, L. M. (2008). FERPA in the twenty-first century: Failure to effectively regulate privacy for all students. *Catholic University Law Review*, 58:59–112.

Davidson, T., Bhattacharya, D., and Weber, I. (2019). *Racial bias in hate speech and abusive language detection datasets*. In Proceedings of the Workshop on Abusive Language Online.

Davis, L. J. (1995). *Enforcing normalcy: Disability, deafness, and the body*. Verso.

de Freitas, E. and Dixon-Román, E. (2017). The computational turn in education research: Critical and creative perspectives on the digital data deluge. *Research in Education*, 98(1):3–13.

Delgado, R. and Stefancic, J. (2017). *Critical Race Theory: An Introduction* (3rd edn). New York University Press.

Dixon, L., Li, J., Sorensen, J., Thain, N., and Vasserman, L. (2018). *Measuring and mitigating unintended bias in text classification*. In Conference on Artificial Intelligence, Ethics, and Society, New Orleans, LA.

Dixon-Román, E., Nichols, T. P., and Nyame-Mensah, A. (2020). The racializing forces of/in AI educational technologies. *Learning, Media and Technology*, 45(3):236–250.

Dixon-Román, E., Nyame-Mensah, A., and Russell, A. R. (2019). Algorithmic legal reasoning as racializing assemblages. *Computational Culture*, 7:1–41.

Dixon-Román, E. J. (2017). *Inheriting possibility: Social reproduction and quantification in education*. University of Minnesota Press.

Donlon, T. F. (1981). The SAT in a diverse society: Fairness and sensitivity. *College Board Review*, 122:16–21, 30–32.

Dorn, E., Hancock, B., Sarakatsannis, J., and Viruleg, E. (2020). *Covid-19 and student learning in the United States: The hurt could last a lifetime*. McKinsey & Company.

Doroudi, S. and Brunskill, E. (2019). Fairer but not fair enough on the equitability of knowledge tracing. In *Proceedings of the 9th International Conference on Learning Analytics and Knowledge*, pages 335–339.

Dwork, C., Hardt, M., Pitassi, T., Reingold, O., and Zemel, R. (2012). Fairness through awareness. In *Proceedings of Innovations of Theoretical Computer Science*, pages 214–226.

Eubanks, V. (2018). *Automating inequality: How high-tech tools profile, police, and punish the poor.* St. Martin's Press.

Feagin, J. R. and Ducey, K. (2000). *Racist America: Roots, current realities, and future reparations.* Routledge.

Fessler, L. (2017). We tested bots like Siri and Alexa to see who would stand up to sexual harassment. *Quartz.* https://qz.com/911681/we-tested-apples-siri-amazon-echos-alexa -microsofts-cortana-and-googles-google-home-to-see-which-personal-assistant-bots-sta nd-up-for-themselves-in-the-face-of-sexual-harassment/.

Forlano, L. and Mathew, A. (2014). From design fiction to design friction: Speculative and participatory design of values-embedded urban technology. *Journal of Urban Technology*, 21(4):7–24.

Foucault, M. (1979). Right of death and power over life. In *The History of Sexuality*, volume 1 (trans. Hurley, R,). Allen Lane.

Fox, C., Waters, J., Fletcher, G., and Levin, D. (2012). *The broadband imperative: Recommendations to address K-12 education infrastructure needs.* State Educational Technology Directors Association.

Freire, P. (1970). *Pedagogy of the oppressed.* Bloomsbury.

Friedman, B. and Nissenbaum, H. (1996). Bias in computer systems. *ACM Transactions on Information Systems*, 14(3):330–347.

Gardner, J., Brooks, C., and Baker, R. (2019). Evaluating the fairness of predictive student models through slicing analysis. In *Proceedings of the 9th International Conference on Learning Analytics and Knowledge*, pages 225–234.

Gaskins, N. (2019). Techno-vernacular creativity and innovation across the African diaspora and global south. In Benjamin, R. (ed.), *Captivating technology: Race, carceral technoscience, and liberatory imagination in everyday life*. Duke University Press, pages 252–274.

Gillen, S., Jung, C., Kearns, M., and Roth, A. (2018). Online learning with an unknown fairness metric. In *Advances in Neural Information Processing Systems*, pages 2600–2609.

Gilman, M. (2019). Voices of the poor must be heard in the data privacy debate. *JURIST.* https://www.jurist.org/commentary/2019/05/voices-of-the-poor-must-be-heard-in-the-data-privacy-debate/. (Accessed on 05/01/2020).

Giroux, H. A. (2001). *Theory and resistance in education: Towards a pedagogy for the opposition.* Greenwood Publishing Group.

Glennen, R. E. and Baxley, D. M. (1985). Reduction of attrition through intrusive advising. *NASPA Journal*, 22(3):10–14.

Goodley, D., Lawthom, R., Liddiard, K., and Runswick-Cole, K. (2019). Provocations for critical disability studies. *Disability & Society*, 34(6):972–997.

Green, B. (2018). Data Science as political action: Grounding data science in a politics of justice. arXiv:1811.03435.

Greene, D. (2021). *The promise of access: Technology, inequality, and the political economy of hope.* MIT Press.

Gregory, A. and Fergus, E. (2017). Social and emotional learning and equity in school discipline. *Future of Children*, 27(1):117–136.

Hall, J., Roman, C., Jovel-Arias, C., and Young, C. (2020). Pre-service teachers examine digital equity amidst schools' COVID-19 responses. *Journal of Technology and Teacher Education*, 28(2):435–442.

Hanna, A., Denton, E., Smart, A., and Smith-Loud, J. (2020). *Towards a critical race methodology in algorithmic fairness*. In Conference on Fairness, Accountability and Transparency.

Hansen, J. D. and Reich, J. (2015). Democratizing education? Examining access and usage patterns in massive open online courses. *Science*, 350(6265):1245–1248.

Harrington, C., Erete, S., and Piper, A. M. (2019). Deconstructing community-based collaborative design: Towards more equitable participatory design engagements. *Proceedings of the ACM on Human-Computer Interaction*, 3(CSCW):1–25.

Heitzeg, N. A. (2009). Education or incarceration: Zero tolerance policies and the school to prison pipeline. *Forum on Public Policy Online*, 2009(2). ERIC EJ870076.

Henderson, N. L., Rowe, J. P., Mott, B. W., Brawner, K., Baker, R., and Lester, J. C. (2019). 4D affect detection: Improving frustration detection in game-based learning with posture-based temporal data fusion. In *Proceedings of the 20th International Conference on AIED*, pages 144–156.

Hoffman, S. (2014). Zero benefit: Estimating the effect of zero tolerance discipline polices on racial disparities in school discipline. *Educational Policy*, 28(1):69–95.

Hoffmann, A. L. (2019). Where fairness fails: Data, algorithms, and the limits of anti-discrimination discourse. *Information, Communication & Society*, 22(7):900–915.

Hoffmann, A. L. (2021). Terms of inclusion: Data, discourse, violence. *New Media & Society*, 23(12):3539–3556.

Holmes, W., Porayska-Pomsta, K., Holstein, K., Sutherland, E., Baker, T., Shum, S. B., Santos, O. C., Rodrigo, M. T., Cukurova, M., Bittencourt, I. I., *et al.* (2021). Ethics of AI in education: Towards a community-wide framework. *International Journal of Artificial Intelligence in Education*. doi:10.1007/s40593-021-00239-1.

Holstein, K., McLaren, B. M., and Aleven, V. (2019). *Designing for complementarity: Teacher and student needs for orchestration support in AI-enhanced classrooms*. In *Proceedings of the 2019 International Conference on AIED*, pages 157–171.

Holstein, K., Vaughan, J. W., DauméIII, H., Dudík, M., and Wallach, H. (2018). Improving fairness in machine learning systems: What do industry practitioners need? In *Proceedings of the 2019 CHI Conference on Human Factors in Computing Systems*.

hooks, b. (1994). *Teaching to transgress*. Routledge.

Hunt, D. E. (1966). Adolescence: Cultural deprivation, poverty, and the dropout. *Review of Educational Research*, 36(4):463–473.

Hutchinson, B. and Mitchell, M. (2019). 50 years of test (un)fairness: Lessons for machine learning. In *Proceedings of the Conference on Fairness, Accountability, and Transparency*, pages 49–58.

Hutt, S., Gardner, M., Duckworth, A. L., and D'Mello, S. K. (2019). *Evaluating fairness and generalizability in models predicting on-time graduation from college applications*. International Educational Data Mining Society.

Illich, I. (1973). *Deschooling society*. Penguin.

Ismail, A. and Kumar, N. (2021). Ai in global health: The view from the front lines. In *Proceedings of the 2021 CHI Conference on Human Factors in Computing Systems*, pages 1–21.

Jasanoff, S. and Kim, S.-H. (2015). *Dreamscapes of modernity: Sociotechnical imaginaries and the fabrication of power*. University of Chicago Press.

Jobin, A., Ienca, M., and Vayena, E. (2019). The global landscape of AI ethics guidelines. *Nature Machine Intelligence*, 1:389–399.

Kalluri, P. (2020). Don't ask if artificial intelligence is good or fair, ask how it shifts power. *Nature*, 583(7815):169–169.

Karabel, J. (2006). *The chosen: The hidden history of admission and exclusion at Harvard, Yale, and Princeton*. Mariner Books.

Keleher, T. (2000). Racial disparities related to school zero tolerance policies: Testimony to the US Commission on Civil Rights. https://files.eric.ed.gov/fulltext/ED454324.pdf.

Keyes, O. (2019a). Counting the countless: Why data science is a profound threat for queer people. *Real Life Magazine*, 8 April.

Keyes, O. (2019b). The bones we leave behind. *Real Life Magazine*, 7 October.

Keyes, O., Hoy, J., and Drouhard, M. (2019). Human-computer insurrection: Notes on an anarchist HCI. In *Proceedings of the 2019 CHI Conference on Human Factors in Computing Systems*, pages 1–13.

Kim, C. Y., Losen, D. J., and Hewitt, D. T. (2010). *The school-to-prison pipeline: Structuring legal reform*. New York University Press.

Kim, M., Reingold, O., and Rothblum, G. (2018). Fairness through computationally-bounded awareness. In *Advances in Neural Information Processing Systems*, pages 4842–4852.

Kizilcec, R. F. and Lee, H. (2020). Algorithmic fairness in education. arXiv:2007.05443.

Kizilcec, R. F., Chen, M., Jasinska, K. K., Madaio, M., and Ogan, A. (2021). Mobile learning during school disruptions´ in sub-Saharan Africa. *AERA Open*. doi:10.1177/23328584211014860.

Klein, N. (2007). *The shock doctrine: The rise of disaster capitalism*. Allen Lane.

Kleinberg, J., Mullainathan, S., and Raghavan, M. (2016). Inherent trade-offs in the fair determination of risk scores. arXiv:1609.05807.

Kosciw, J. G., Greytak, E. A., Zongrone, A. D., Clark, C. M., and Truong, N. L. (2018). The 2017 National School Climate Survey: The experiences of lesbian, gay, bisexual, transgender, and queer youth in our nation's schools. ERIC ED590243.

Kotsiantis, S. B., Zaharakis, I., and Pintelas, P. (2007). Supervised machine learning: A review of classification techniques. *Emerging Artificial Intelligence Applications in Computer Engineering*, 160(1):3–24.

Krafft, P., Young, M., Katell, M., Lee, J. E., Narayan, S., Epstein, M., Dailey, D., Herman, B., Tam, A., Guetler, V., *et al.* (2021). An action-oriented AI policy toolkit for technology audits by community advocates and activists. In *Proceedings of the 2021 ACM Conference on Fairness, Accountability, and Transparency*, pages 772–781.

Kulik, J. A. and Fletcher, J. (2016). Effectiveness of intelligent tutoring systems: a meta-analytic review. *Review of Educational Research*, 86(1):42–78.

Kumashiro, K. K. (2000). Toward a theory of anti-oppressive education. *Review of Educational Research*, 70(1):25–53.

Lando, D. (2009). Credit risk modeling. In Andersen, T., Davis, R., Kreiß, J.-P., and Mikosch, T. (eds), *Handbook of financial time series*, pages 787–798. Springer.

Lee, H. and Kizilcec, R. F. (2020). *Evaluation of fairness trade-offs in predicting student success*. arXiv:2007.00088.

Lemann, N. (2000). *The big test: The secret history of the American meritocracy*. Farrar, Straus and Giroux.

Li, M., Zhang, L., Ji, H., and Radke, R. J. (2019). Keep meeting summaries on topic: Abstractive multi-modal meeting summarization. In *Proceedings of the 57th Annual Meeting of the Association for Computational Linguistics*, pages 2190–2196.

Liang, J., Li, C., and Zheng, L. (2016). *Machine learning application in MOOCs: Dropout prediction*. In 11th International Conference on Computer Science and Education, pages 52–57.

Light, A. (2011). HCI as heterodoxy: Technologies of identity and the queering of interaction with computers. *Interacting with Computers*, 23(5):430–438.

Linn, R. L. (1973). Fair test use in selection. *Review of Educational Research*, 43(2):139–161.

Loukina, A., Madnani, N., and Zechner, K. (2019). The many dimensions of algorithmic fairness in educational applications. In *Proceedings of the 14th Workshop on Innovative Use of NLP for Building Educational Applications*, pages 1–10.

Lykourentzou, I., Giannoukos, I., Nikolopoulos, V., Mpardis, G., and Loumos, V. (2009). Dropout prediction in e-learning courses through the combination of machine learning techniques. *Computers & Education*, 53(3):950–965.

Madaio, M. A., Stark, L., Wortman Vaughan, J., and Wallach, H. (2020). Co-designing checklists to understand organizational challenges and opportunities around fairness in AI. In *Proceedings of the 2020 CHI Conference on Human Factors in Computing Systems*, pages 1–14.

Madnani, N., Loukina, A., von Davier, A., Burstein, J., and Cahill, A. (2017). Building better open-source tools to support fairness in automated scoring. In *Proceedings of the First ACL Workshop on Ethics in Natural Language Processing*, pages 41–52.

Mandalapu, V. and Gong, J. (2018). *Towards better affect detectors: Detecting changes rather than states*. In International Conference on Artificial Intelligence in Education, pages 199–203.

Mankoff, J., Hayes, G. R., and Kasnitz, D. (2010). Disability studies as a source of critical inquiry for the field of assistive technology. In *Proceedings of the 12th international ACM SIGACCESS Conference on Computers and Accessibility*, pages 3–10.

Márquez-Vera, C., Cano, A., Romero, C., Noaman, A. Y. M., Mousa Fardoun, H., and Ventura, S. (2016). Early dropout prediction using data mining: A case study with high school students. *Expert Systems*, 33(1):107–124.

Martinez-Maldonado, R., Mangaroska, K., Schulte, J., Elliott, D., Axisa, C., and Shum, S. B. (2020). Teacher tracking with integrity: What indoor positioning can reveal about instructional proxemics. *Proceedings of the ACM on Interactive, Mobile, Wearable and Ubiquitous Technologies*, 4(1):1–27.

Martins, L. P. de O. (2014). *Privilege and oppression: Towards a feminist speculative design*. In *Proceedings of DRS*, pages 980–990.

Massumi, B. (2015). *Ontopower: War, powers, and the state of perception*. Duke University Press.

Mayfield, E., Madaio, M., Prabhumoye, S., Gerritsen, D., McLaughlin, B., Dixon-Román, E., and Black, A. W. (2019). *Equity beyond bias in language technologies for education*. In Proceedings of the Fourteenth Workshop on Innovative Use of NLP for Building Educational Applications, pages 444–460.

Meyerhoff, E. (2019). *Beyond education: Radical studying for another world*. University of Minnesota Press.

Mohamed, S., Png, M.-T., and Isaac, W. (2020). Decolonial AI: Decolonial theory as sociotechnical foresight in artificial intelligence. *Philosophy & Technology*, 33(4):659–684.

Moir, E. and Leyshon, M. (2013). The design of decision-making: Participatory budgeting and the production of localism. *Local Environment*, 18(9):1002–1023.

Moore, S. D. M., Jayme, B. D. O., and Black, J. (2021). Disaster capitalism, rampant EdTech opportunism, and the advancement of online learning in the era of COVID-19. *Critical Education*, 12(2). doi:10.14288/ce.v12i2.186587.

Moreau, E., Vogel, C., and Barry, M. (2019). A paradigm for democratizing artificial intelligence research. In Esposito, A., Esposito, A. M., and Jain L. C. (eds), *Innovations in Big Data Mining and Embedded Knowledge*, pages 137–166. Springer.

Morozov, E. (2013). *To save everything, click here: The folly of technological solutionism*. Public Affairs.

Muller, M. J. (2007). Participatory design: The third space in HCI. In Sears, A. and Jacko, J. (eds), *The human–computer interaction handbook*, pages 1087–1108. CRC Press.

Muñoz, J. E., Chambers-Letson, J., Nyong'o, T., and Pellegrini, A. (2019). *Cruising utopia: The then and there of queer futurity*. New York University Press.

Nam, S. and Samson, P. (2019). *Integrating students' behavioral signals and academic profiles in early warning system*. In International Conference on Artificial Intelligence in Education, pages 345–357. Springer.

Noble, S. U. (2018). *Algorithms of oppression: How search engines reinforce racism*. New York University Press.

North, C. E. (2006). More than words? Delving into the substantive meaning(s) of "social justice" in education. *Review of Educational Research*, 76(4):507–535.

Nur, N., Park, N., Dorodchi, M., Dou, W., Mahzoon, M. J., Niu, X., and Maher, M. L. (2019). *Student network analysis: A novel way to predict delayed graduation in higher education*. In International Conference on AIED, pages 370–382. Springer.

Obermeyer, Z., Powers, B., Vogeli, C., and Mullainathan, S. (2019). Dissecting racial bias in an algorithm used to manage the health of populations. *Science*, 366 (6464):447–453.

Ocumpaugh, J., Baker, R., Gowda, S., Heffernan, N., and Heffernan, C. (2014). Population validity for educational data mining models: A case study in affect detection. *British Journal of Educational Technology*, 45(3):487–501.

Ogan, A. (2019). Reframing classroom sensing: Promise and peril. *Interactions*, 26(6):26–32.

Okur, E., Alyuz, N., Aslan, S., Genc, U., Tanriover, C., and Esme, A. A. (2017). *Behavioral engagement detection of students in the wild*. In International Conference on Artificial Intelligence in Education, pages 250–261. Springer.

Palmer, N. A., Greytak, E. A., and Kosciw, J. (2016). *Educational exclusion: Drop out, push out, and the school-to-prison pipeline among LGBTQ youth*. GLSEN.

Pane, J. F., Griffin, B. A., McCaffrey, D. F., and Karam, R. (2014). Effectiveness of cognitive tutor Algebra I at scale. *Educational Evaluation and Policy Analysis*, 36(2):127–144.

Papageorge, N. W., Gershenson, S., and Kang, K. M. (2020). Teacher expectations matter. *Review of Economics and Statistics*, 102(2):234–251.

Parisi, L. and Dixon-Román, E. (2020). Data capitalism, sociogenic prediction and recursive indeterminacies. In Mörtenböck, P. and Mooshammer, H. (eds), *Data determinacy: Public plurality in an era of data determinacy*. Routledge.

Passi, S. and Barocas, S. (2019). *Problem formulation and fairness*. In Conference on Fairness, Accountability and Transparency.

Pedro, M. O., Baker, R., Bowers, A., and Heffernan, N. (2013). Predicting college enrollment from student interaction with an intelligent tutoring system in middle school. In *Proceedings of the 6th International Conference on Educational Data Mining*.

Pei, L. and Crooks, R. (2020). Attenuated access: Accounting for startup, maintenance, and affective costs in resource constrained communities. In *Proceedings of the 2020 CHI Conference on Human Factors in Computing Systems*, pages 1–15.

Picard, R. W. (2000). *Affective computing*. MIT Press.

Piech, C., Bassen, J., Huang, J., Ganguli, S., Sahami, M., Guibas, L. J., and Sohl-Dickstein, J. (2015). Deep knowledge tracing. *Advances in Neural Information Processing Systems*, 28:505–513.

Pierre, J., Crooks, R., Currie, M., Paris, B., and Pasquetto, I. (2021). Getting ourselves together: Data-centered participatory design research & epistemic burden. In *Proceedings of the 2021 CHI Conference on Human Factors in Computing Systems*, pages 1–11.

Prinsloo, P. and Slade, S. (2014). Educational triage in open distance learning: Walking a moral tightrope. *International Review of Research in Open and Distributed Learning*, 15 (4):306–331.

Raghavan, M., Barocas, S., Kleinberg, J., and Levy, K. (2020). Mitigating bias in algorithmic hiring: Evaluating claims and practices. In *Proceedings of the 2020 Conference on Fairness, Accountability, and Transparency*, pages 469–481.

Rakova, B., Yang, J., Cramer, H., and Chowdhury, R. (2020). Where responsible AI meets reality: Practitioner perspectives on enablers for shifting organizational practices. arXiv:2006.12358.

Reich, J., Buttimer, C. J., Fang, A., Hillaire, G., Hirsch, K., Larke, L., Littenberg-Tobias, J., Moussapour, R. M., Napier, A., and Thompson, M. (2020). Remote learning guidance from state education agencies during the COVID-19 pandemic: A first look. doi:10.35542/osf.io/437e2.

Richardson, R. (2021). Defining and demystifying automated decision systems. *Maryland Law Review*. https://ssrn.com/abstract=3811708.

Richardson, R., Schultz, J., and Crawford, K. (2019). Dirty data, bad predictions: How civil rights violations impact police data, predictive policing systems, and justice. *New York University Law Review Online*, 94:192–233. https://ssrn.com/abstract=3333423.

Robertson, S. and Salehi, N. (2020). What if i don't like any of the choices? The limits of preference elicitation for participatory algorithm design. arXiv:2007.06718.

Rosa, J. and Flores, N. (2017). Unsettling race and language: Toward a racio-linguistic perspective. *Language in Society*, 46:621–647.

Roschelle, J., Lester, J., and Fusco, J. (2020). *AI and the future of learning: Expert panel report.* Technical report, Digital Promise.

Sambasivan, N., Arnesen, E., Hutchinson, B., Doshi, T., and Prabhakaran, V. (2021). Re-imagining algorithmic fairness in India and beyond. In *Proceedings of the 2021 ACM Conference on Fairness, Accountability, and Transparency*, pages 315–328.

Sap, M., Card, D., Gabriel, S., Choi, Y., and Smith, N. A. (2019). The risk of racial bias in hate speech detection. In *Proceedings of the Association for Computational Linguistics (ACL)*.

Scholes, V. (2016). The ethics of using learning analytics to categorize students on risk. *Educational Technology Research and Development*, 64(5):939–955.

Schmitt, A. P. and Dorans, N. J. (1990). Differential item functioning for minority examinees on the SAT. *Journal of Educational Measurement*, 27(1):67–81.

Selbst, A. D., Boyd, D., Friedler, S. A., Venkatasubramanian, S., and Vertesi, J. (2019). Fairness and abstraction in sociotechnical systems. In *Proceedings of the Conference on Fairness, Accountability, and Transparency*, pages 59–68. ACM.

Simonite, T. (2018). When it comes to gorillas, google photos remains blind. *Wired*, 11 January.

Slade, S. and Prinsloo, P. (2013). Learning analytics: Ethical issues and dilemmas. *American Behavioral Scientist*, 57(10):1510–1529.

Sloane, M. (2019). *Inequality is the name of the game: Thoughts on the emerging field of technology, Ethics and Social Justice.* In Weizenbaum Conference 2019 "Challenges of Digital Inequality: Digital Education, Digital Work, Digital Life".

Sloane, M., Moss, E., Awomolo, O., and Forlano, L. (2020). Participation is not a design fix for machine learning. arXiv:2007.02423.

Spiel, K., Gerling, K., Bennett, C. L., Brulé, E., Williams, R. M., Rode, J., and Mankoff, J. (2020). Nothing about us without us: Investigating the role of critical disability studies in HCI. In *Extended Abstracts of the 2020 CHI Conference on Human Factors in Computing Systems*, pages 1–8.

Stark, L. and Hoffmann, A. L. (2019). Data is the new what? Popular metaphors & professional ethics in emerging data culture. *Journal of Cultural Analytics*, 4(1). doi:10.22148/16.036.

Swauger, S. (2020). Our bodies encoded: algorithmic test proctoring in higher education. In Stommel, J., Chris Friend, C., and Morris, S. (eds), *Critical digital pedagogy*. Hybrid Pedagogy.

Tang, C., Ouyang, Y., Rong, W., Zhang, J., and Xiong, Z. (2018). *Time series model for predicting dropout in massive open online courses*. In International Conference on Artificial Intelligence in Education, pages 353–357. Springer.

Teräs, M., Suoranta, J., Teräs, H., and Curcher, M. (2020). Post-COVID-19 education and education technology "solutionism": A seller's market. *Postdigital Science and Education*, 2:863–878.

Thorndike, R. L. (1971). Concepts of culture-fairness. *Journal of Educational Measurement*, 8(2):63–70.

Tierney, M. (2019). *Dismantlings: Words against machines in the American long seventies*. Cornell University Press.

Tsatsou, D., Pomazanskyi, A., Hortal, E., Spyrou, E., Leligou, H. C., Asteriadis, S., Vretos, N., and Daras, P. (2018). *Adaptive learning based on affect sensing*. In International Conference on Artificial Intelligence in Education, pages 475–479. Springer.

Tuck, E. and Yang, K. W. (2018). *Toward what justice? Describing diverse dreams of justice in education*. Routledge.

Varney, J. (2012). Proactive (intrusive) advising. *Academic Advising Today*, 35(3):1–3.

US Department of Education (2020). Edfacts data files: U.S. https://bit.ly/3d4yRWE. (Accessed on 04/17/2020).

Warschauer, M. and Matuchniak, T. (2010). New technology and digital worlds: Analyzing evidence of equity in access, use, and outcomes. *Review of Research in Education*, 34(1):179–225.

Weinstein, M. (2020). School surveillance: The students' rights implications of artificial intelligence as K-12 school security. *North Carolina Law Review*, 98(2):438.

Weiss, J. (1987). The golden rule bias reduction principle: A practical reform. *Educational Measurement: Issues and Practice*, 6(2):23–25.

West, S. M., Whittaker, M., and Crawford, K. (2019). *Discriminating systems: Gender, race and power in AI*. AI Now Institute.

Williamson, B. (2017). Decoding ClassDojo: Psycho-policy, social-emotional learning and persuasive educational technologies. *Learning, Media and Technology*, 42(4):440–453.

Williamson, B. (2020). Re-engineering education. *Code acts in education*, 14 February.

WinchesterIII, W. W. (2018). Afrofuturism, inclusion, and the design imagination. *Interactions*, 25(2):41–45.

Winner, L. (1980). Do artifacts have politics? *Daedalus*, 109(1):121–136.

Winograd, T., Flores, F., and Flores, F. F. (1986). *Understanding computers and cognition: A new foundation for design*. Intellect Books.

Young, I. M. (1990). *Justice and the politics of difference*. Princeton University Press.

Zeide, E. (2015). Student privacy principles for the age of big data: Moving beyond FERPA and FIPPS. *Drexel Law Review*, 8:339.

Zembylas, M. (2021). Sylvia Wynter, racialized affects, and minor feelings: Unsettling the coloniality of the affects in curriculum and pedagogy. *Journal of Curriculum Studies*, 1–15.

Zhao, Z., Pan, H., Fan, C., Liu, Y., Li, L., Yang, M., and Cai, D. (2019). *Abstractive meeting summarization via hierarchical adaptive segmental network learning*. In The World Wide Web Conference, pages 3455–3461.

9 The overlapping ethical imperatives of human teachers and their Artificially Intelligent assistants

Benedict du Boulay

Introduction

Intelligent Tutoring Systems (ITSs) and Intelligent Learning Environments (ILEs) have been developed and evaluated over the last 40 years. In this chapter I conflate these types of systems under the more general title of Artificial Intelligence in Education (AIED) systems. Recent meta-analyses show that AIED systems perform well enough to act as effective classroom assistants under the guidance of a human teacher (for a review, see du Boulay, 2016, p.115). However, despite these successes, they have been caught up in broader controversies about their pedagogy, the role of Artificial Intelligence in society, and about the entry of big data companies into the education market and the harvesting of learner data (see, e.g. Watters, 2015; Williamson, 2018b).

Recent Criticism of AIED Systems

There has been ongoing criticism of AIED systems as operating only in the pedagogical mode of the earliest ITSs with consequently limited learner-agency (Herold, 2017; Watters, 2015, 2017; Wilson & Scott, 2017). The pedagogical expertise of AIED systems has much expanded since those days, and in addition the role of the human teacher in orchestrating how such systems are used in time and across groups of learners is now better understood (see e.g. Kessler et al., 2019) and supported (see e.g. Heffernan & Heffernan, 2014; Holstein et al., 2018). For a more elaborated version of this argument, see for example, du Boulay (2019).

In ethical terms, Williamson (2018a, 2018b, 2019) has criticized the entry of big data companies into the field of education on two grounds. First, their expertise is not centrally educational and can lead to a very poor educational experience.[1] Second, their motivation is suspect in terms of how they might use the data that they "harvest" from interactions with learners. The poor quality of the learning experience violates the general principle of "doing one's best". The use of this data for anything other than educational reasons violates the general principle of "exploiting their position".

DOI: 10.4324/9780429329067-12

In a recent paper I tried to deal with what are generally misplaced criticisms of the pedagogy of AIED systems, in particular that their pedagogy was no better than a "Skinner Box":

> This paper concentrates on rebutting the criticisms of the pedagogy of ITSs and ILEs. It offers examples of how a much wider range of pedagogies are available than their critics claim. These wider pedagogies operate at both the screen level of individual systems, as well as at the classroom level within which the systems are orchestrated by the teacher. It argues that there are many ways that such systems can be integrated by the teacher into the overall experience of a class. Taken together, the screen-level and orchestration-level dramatically enlarge the range of pedagogies beyond what was possible with the "Skinner Box".
>
> (du Boulay, 2019, p.2902)

The present chapter briefly examines some of the ethical issues underpinning these criticisms as well as other ethical issues inherent in teaching. For example, when one observes the behaviour of human teachers and some AIED systems, one finds that they sometimes deliberately set out to cause short-term discomfort to students as a means to increase learning in the longer term, not unlike doctors causing pain or damage in a treatment that will eventually cure the patient. This chapter examines some of these means *vs.* ends dilemmas.

The chapter is organized as follows. First, there is a general discussion of the professional ethics of human teaching, followed by their application to AIED systems. Next there is a discussion of recent criticisms of AIED systems from an ethical standpoint. Finally, there is a discussion of the means *vs.* ends dilemmas where a teacher or an AIED system may challenge, discomfort, confuse or provide false feedback in the expectation of increasing learning.

The Ethics of Human Teaching

A good place to start in considering the ethical implications of AIED is by considering ethical implications as they apply to human teachers. By "ethical implication" I mean specifically the *professional* ethical implications as opposed to any broader moral guidelines. By "teachers" I include all kinds of teachers, tutors, and lecturers in formal educational establishments. Some of the theoretical complexities of disentangling the moral *vs.* the professional in ethics and then trying to create a professional code for teachers are set out by Campbell (2000). She argues that "Such principles as trust, integrity, honesty, justice and care form the values fundamental to professional accountability and they are firmly rooted in the practice of teaching." Thus, a teacher promising to help a learner and then omitting to do so, a teacher having a favourite who gets much more attention than other students, or a teacher telling a parent that her son is doing really well when he is not violate the moral principles that underpin professional ethics. Campbell also identifies six kinds of stakeholder:

students, other teachers, the headteacher and other administrators, the school board of governors, the parents, and the wider community. This chapter concentrates on professional teaching ethics with respect to students.

As an example of a specific code of conduct, the General Teaching Council of Scotland (2012) set out its Code of Professionalism and Conduct (CoPAC). This code covers all the stakeholders mentioned above. With respect to learners, it identifies the following seven individual guidelines, as well as identifying two guidelines around the professional expertise of teachers qua teaching (Table 9.1. The underlying principle of doing one's best as a teacher is covered in 2.3, 2.5, 2.7, 3.1, and 3.2. Not exploiting a position of authority is covered in 2.1, 2.2, 2.4, 2.6, and 3.1.

The above ethical guidelines hardly touch on the impact of contemporary educational technology on the role of the teacher. For example, if a school purchases some educational technology, how is an individual teacher to monitor the acquisition of data about a pupil by the system's vendor (as per Guideline 2.1)?

The Ethics of AIED Systems

Within the AIED community there are the beginnings of the development of a code of professional ethics. The Institute of Ethical AI and Machine Learning, founded in 2018, has set out eight pledges relating to professional good conduct. These concern the design, development, and deployment of educational (and more broadly AI) systems that contain some element of machine learning and/or prediction, but do not specifically relate to professionalism around pedagogic interactions, for example *"Trust by privacy*: I commit to build and communicate processes that protect and handle data with stakeholders that may interact with the system directly and/or indirectly."[2] More broadly within AI in general there is a plethora of guidelines and checklists designed to guide the design, development, and auditing of AI-based systems (for a review, see e.g. Morley et al., 2019).

The ethical dimension of designing AIED systems requires that the designers of such systems have some training in ethics. In Chapter 10 of this volume, Howley, Mir, and Peck explore the issue of training computer science students in ethics, not least as some of them will become the designers of AIED systems, as well as building other systems that we all use. For accounts of ethical guidelines as they apply in other parts of the educational ecosystem, see Chapters 2 and 5 in this volume.

The Changing Role of the Teacher Deploying AIED Systems

The earliest examples of artificially intelligent tutoring systems were very much rooted in the idea that there would be a one-to-one interaction between the learner and the system. The role of the human teacher was largely to introduce the system to the learner and then leave them to it. For example,

Table 9.1 CoPac ethical guidelines

Towards the Learner	Professional Standing
2.1 You must treat sensitive, personal information about pupils with respect and confidentiality and not disclose it unless required to do so by your employer or by law	3.1 You should maintain and develop your professional practice to ensure you continue to meet the requirements of the Standard for Full Registration which comprise: • Professional knowledge and understanding; • Professional skills and abilities; • Professional values and personal commitment
2.2 You must be truthful, honest, and fair in relation to information you provide about pupils	3.2 You should refresh and develop your knowledge and skills through Continuing Professional Development and maintenance of reflective good practice
2.3 You should aim to be a positive role model to pupils and motivate and inspire them to realize their full potential	
2.4 You must maintain an up-to-date knowledge and understanding of, implement, and comply with, child and protected adult procedures as they may currently apply in your workplace	
2.5 As a member of the children's workforce in Scotland, you should recognize your role as a professional in delivering better outcomes for children and young people	
2.6 You must raise any concerns that you may have about the behaviour of any colleague in connection with a child or protected adult, using the appropriate procedures in place	
2.7 You should be aware of the general principles of the UN Convention on the Rights of the Child regarding equal treatment, the child's best interests, and giving appropriate weight to the views of the child	

Adapted from General Teaching Council Scotland (2012).

the SOPHIE system helped an individual learner debug an electronic circuit by providing an exploratory environment in which various hypotheses about a bug in the displayed circuit could be tested and possibly fixed (Brown et al., 1975). At that time any ethical issue about teaching or about the collection of learner data was not uppermost in the minds of the developers of the system. They were mostly concerned to see whether such a system could be built at all as an example of the use of Artificial Intelligence in Education. The implicit ethical aspect of the work was the desire to build a system that could provide an educational interaction as good as, or even better than, that available from a skilled human tutor working one-to-one with the learner, thus opening the possibility that many more learners could be helped than those with the means to hire a personal, skilled tutor.

As with human tutors, the implicit ethical dimension is that artificial tutors will not just teach to the best of their ability, but will also teach "the truth" as their designers see it and help develop the learners' skills in a productive rather than unproductive direction. In addition, there is an expectation that tutors will not use their skills as tutors to help learners acquire antisocial, illegal, or immoral skills, behaviour, and attitudes. So, in the case of SOPHIE it would have been unethical if, for example, the tutor had taught incorrect debugging skills, taught ways to hack into other people's online accounts (say) rather than debugging electronic circuits, or had deliberately just taught badly. Of course, this raises the issue of who should be held to account for any unethical behaviour: the designer of the system, the human teacher who makes use of it in her class, or the school governors or headteacher who mandates its use. Clearly also, all of the above is rooted in the cultural and ethical norms of the society within which the tutoring is taking place.

As AIED systems came to be more widely used and sold commercially, the issue arose as to what advice should be given to teachers whose educational establishment had purchased them. An early example of careful attention to these "user instructions" was the method of deployment of the family of Cognitive Tutors (see, e.g. Koedinger et al., 1997). Reflecting on the deployment of the Cognitive Tutor for Algebra (CTAI) in Pittsburgh (the "big city"), Koedinger noted:

> Another core challenge was figuring out how to embed this new technology into the existing social context of schools, that is, into the instructional practices teachers were already using. A big theme of the Algebra tutor curriculum for the Pittsburgh Urban Mathematics Project, PUMP, as it was called at the time, was to work with teachers to understand how to integrate technology with classroom instruction. We took the strong position that we would redesign the whole course from the bottom up including replacements for the textbook, new kinds of assessments, use of collaborative learning in the classroom portion of the curriculum, and new teaching approaches. We evolved to the point where we recommended use of non-technology text materials (on paper and unbound) and practices in the regular classroom for 3 days a week and use of the tutor in the computer lab during the other 2 days a week. We did not have quite enough tutor material to reach this goal in this first study, but it was soon to come. Integration of the tutor technology with other teaching practices was an important goal of this study.
>
> (Koedinger & Aleven, 2016, page 15)

An example of a large and expensive evaluation of a much later version of the CTAI, where the above guidelines for teachers about the integration of the technology were not fully followed, is described in Karam et al. (2017) and Pane et al. (2014). Although there was some training of the teachers in the effective use of the Tutor, it clearly was not enough:

> None of the CTAI components were implemented fully as recommended by the developer. Further, no individual teacher implemented fully (score of 1) all the components of the curriculum as intended by the developer. Overall, scores for teacher implementation of CTAI components ranged from 0.51 to 0.86. Teachers, in general, had greatest adherence to the CTAI's prescribed practices in student grouping and software use, and lowest adherence to prescribed practices in curriculum structure and materials, curriculum content, and assessment.
>
> (Karam et al., 2017, page 408)

Within AIED the importance of the role of the human teacher is re-emerging as the "orchestrator" of multiple educational resources in the classroom, including AIED systems (Dillenbourg, 2013). Indeed, systems have been developed to help the human teacher manage the extra complexity of off-loading some of her tasks on to AIED systems and also guide her towards helping those students who most require her personal help (see e.g. Holstein et al., 2018).

A further potential change in the AIED ethical landscape is the rise of systems that track and attempt to manipulate the affective and motivational states of learners (see, e.g. Arroyo et al., 2014). Clearly, the objective of such systems is to assist the learner out of unproductive affective states such as boredom or frustration and help them stay in productive states such as hopeful and committedly hard-working. However, in dealing with students in both cognitive and affective terms there is scope for bad practice, such as misidentifying the affective state of the students, leading them to doubt their own meta-affective capability – a kind of technically augmented "gaslighting".

The extra complexity in the number of stakeholders involved in deploying an AIED system in the classroom and the use of machine learning to derive (potentially biased) patterns in learner data have opened further ethical issues for AIED. These topics are explored in detail elsewhere in this volume; see Holstein and Doroudi (Chapter 6) and Kizilcec and Lee (Chapter 7).

Some Dilemmas around Means *vs* Ends Trade-offs

While misappropriating learner data or offering poor-quality educational experiences are clearly not in line with the professional ethics of teaching, there are other practices that are ethically more nuanced. This section identifies a number of ethical dilemmas in the general area of "doing one's best" for students. As already indicated, there are ethical dilemmas around the gathering and use of learner data, but these are not addressed in this chapter. In their different ways the pedagogic tactics described below adopt a method that causes short-term negative affective states in students as a way to help them in the longer term to learn more or better than they might otherwise have done without this extra impulse.

The Hippocratic Oath

In some ways the medical profession can provide insights into some of the ethical issues faced by teachers. The following is an excerpt from the version of the Hippocratic Oath sworn by American practitioners, adapted from Tyson (2001):

- I will remember that there is art to medicine as well as science, and that warmth, sympathy, and understanding may outweigh the surgeon's knife or the chemist's drug.
- I will respect the privacy of my patients, for their problems are not disclosed to me that the world may know. Most especially must I tread with care in matters of life and death. If it is given to me to save a life, all thanks. But it may also be within my power to take a life; this awesome responsibility must be faced with great humbleness and awareness of my own frailty. Above all, I must not play at God.
- I will remember that I do not treat a fever chart, a cancerous growth, but a sick human being, whose illness may affect the person's family and economic stability. My responsibility includes these related problems, if I am to care adequately for the sick.
- I will remember that I remain a member of society, with special obligations to all my fellow human beings, those sound of mind and body as well as the infirm.

The shorter form of the Hippocratic Oath can be summarized as "Practise two things in your dealings with disease: either help or do not harm the patient."

Of course, there are many differences between the practice of doctors and that of teachers. First, these include largely one-to-one interactions between doctor and patient (though in hospital it's common that teams rather than individuals will make treatment decisions) *vs.* typically one-to-many interactions between teacher and students (though there will be many one-to-one interactions too). Second, there is the doctor's possibility to offer no treatment *vs.* the lack of such a possibility in most teaching situations. However, the underlying imperative underpinning both professions is similar, whether working alone or in a team – do one's best to be helpful and try to do no harm.

The introduction of educational technology into teaching adds a third player, namely the designer of that technology. For them there is no equivalent of the Hippocratic Oath or the Professional Guidelines for Teachers, though we see the beginnings of such guidelines in the creation of the Institute of Ethical AI and Machine Learning, mentioned earlier. In addition, the educational technology adds an extra layer of ethical responsibility on the teacher to ensure that the use of this technology itself is helpful and does no harm. This is especially important with respect to AIED systems because of their ability to come to decisions about students interacting with them in an unsupervised manner. For teachers to be able to discharge this responsibility they need to be trained in AIED in general, and by the designers of the system (or their agents), as to the best and safest ways to use the system.

In medicine, treating a disease may involve short-term pain, danger, or discomfort for the patient in order to secure better health in the longer term. Chemotherapy is a classic example, not least in that the pain and discomfort of this treatment is likely to be much worse than the pain and discomfort of the cancer in its earlier stages that it is there to treat. Thus, medicine daily balances the issue of means *vs.* ends. As patients, we generally trust doctors and accept that their suggestions for unpleasant or even dangerous medical interventions are made in our own best interests

In their look at the future of AIED, and in particular its use of pedagogical agents, Walker and Ogan (2016, page 713) argue that:

> We envision a future in which AIED systems adaptively create social relationships with their learners in addition to modelling student learning and providing adaptive cognitive support. By deliberate design of the relationships between learners and systems, the systems can have maximal impact on student learning and engagement.

An important component of such pedagogical social relationships, as with doctors, is the issue of trust. Learners, like patients, are potentially vulnerable, and the social aspects of the interaction between teachers and learners can be misused. A learner needs to feel that any short-term discomfort in learning provoked by the teacher is part of a journey to better learning outcomes in the end (for an early example of this issue, see Self, 1999). And the teacher needs to feel that the balance between the likely initial discomfort and the helpful value of the overall objectives is warranted.

In the following subsections we briefly examine four means *vs.* ends dilemmas in pedagogic tactics, namely (i) the use of disruption and confrontation, (ii) the refusal to offer help when requested by the student, (iii) the deliberate fostering of confusion in the student, and (iv) the provision of false feedback to the student.

Disruption and Confrontation

Many AIED systems have incorporated embodied pedagogical agents on the screen, typically a teacher and/or a peer. The role of peers can vary from simply being congenial companions to being more able partners in the learning process, through to being fellow learners whom the human student should teach (for a review of agent roles, see, e.g. Haake & Gulz, 2009). Most of the roles are directly and clearly supportive, but Haake and Gulz list two others that are only indirectly supportive, and may even be counter-productive – namely the "troublemaker" (see, e.g. Aimeur & Frasson, 1996) and the critic, the criticizing co-learner (e.g. Hietala & Niemirepo, 1998).

> we propose a new learning strategy (called learning by disturbing) derived from the learning companion and in which the companion is a trouble-maker who sometimes gives good advice to the learner but also gives wrong recommendations. The goal of this particular companion is to provoke the reaction of the learner.
>
> (Aimeur & Frasson, 1996, page 115)

More recently, Silvervarg and colleagues developed these ideas into a Challenger Teachable Agent (CTA) and explored how "how students respond when the CTA disagrees and questions their suggestions, and how groups of students, differing in response behavior and in self-efficacy, experience the CTA" (2014, page 411)

Clearly having an online peer criticize, challenge, or offer unhelpful recommendations has the possibility to overly disconcert the human learner, even if in the end this "disturbance" leads to learning. This kind of "disruptive" pedagogical tactic is also used by human teachers. For example, Christina Schwabenland (2009), who teaches courses in Higher Education on managing diversity, describes her use of disruption as a pedagogic intervention. The very nature of her teaching material means that she necessarily provokes disequilibrium amongst some of her students because the material will necessarily challenge their preconceptions and deeply held beliefs. Luckily most science, technology, engineering, and mathematics (STEM) subjects, typically where AIED systems operate, are largely able to avoid this kind of ethical dilemma; but one can imagine a teacher deploying an AIED attempting to teach Evolution (say) in a culture that is strongly wedded to Creationism. Given Schwabenland's subject, she found a further, more personal ethical dilemma surrounding the very authority vested in her as a teacher:

> Any teacher who is committed to social change has to struggle with two paradoxes; firstly, his/her simultaneous location as both the active representative of a system that reproduces structural inequalities and also its challenger; and, secondly, the primacy he/she accords to her own beliefs and values, however desirable and potentially liberatory he/she finds them to be. He/she cannot but privilege some positions over others.
>
> (Schwabenland, 2009, page 303)

Other stances, less disruptive towards teaching "challenging" topics, are also possible. For example, Rosiek (2003) described ways that such topics can be approached more obliquely so as to reduce the students' sense of being directly challenged and thus remain receptive to the material.

Acting Like a Human Tutor and the "Assistance Dilemma"

Related to the authority and social status of a human teacher is the issue of the degree to which it is socially acceptable and/or pedagogically effective for an AIED system to adopt strategies that are effectively used by human teachers, and *vice versa*. For example, Graesser, in recounting the design history of AutoTutor, argued that human tutors are not always the gold standard:

> For example, [human] tutors are prone to give a summary recap of a solution to a problem, or answer to a difficult question, that requires many conversational turns. It would be better to sometimes have the student give the summary recap in order to promote active student learning, to encourage the student to practice articulating the information, or to allow the tutor to diagnose remaining deficits. As another example, tutors often assume that the student understands what the tutor expresses in an exchange whereas students often do not understand, even partially. Indeed, there often is a large gulf between the knowledge of the student and that of the tutor. It sometimes would be better for the tutor to ask follow up questions to verify the extent to which the student understands what the tutor is attempting to communicate. Ideal tutoring strategies are needed to augment or replace some of the typical conversation patterns in human tutoring.
>
> (Graesser, 2016, page 127)

A practice often used by human tutors and AIED systems is the refusal to offer help when requested by the learner because it is believed that the learner can progress without that help, and indeed *should* attempt to progress without that help (du Boulay et al., 1999). This issue of the "assistance dilemma" has been explored by Rummel and colleagues, largely as a practical rather than an ethical issue:

> For instance, the timing of support dimension taps into the so-called assistance dilemma … which poses the fundamental question of how to balance the giving and withholding of assistance to achieve optimal student learning. Whereas in some cases providing immediate assistance may serve as a scaffold, in other cases it may be a crutch that prevents students from engaging in sense-making activities on their own and acquiring deep knowledge. Whereas withholding assistance might in some cases lead students to struggle and experience extraneous cognitive load, in other cases it may create desirable difficulties that enable students to learn by overcoming challenges.
>
> (Rummel et al., 2016, page 791; citations omitted)

Inducing Confusion

If Schwabenland advocated the pedagogy of disruption, Lehman et al. explored the pedagogy of induced confusion. In their work they addressed:

the possibility of confusion induction in a study where learners engaged in trialogues on research methods concepts with animated tutor and student agents. Confusion was induced by staging disagreements and contradictions between the animated agents, and then inviting the (human) learners to provide their opinions.

(Lehman et al., 2013, page 85)

While there was some short-term confusion for all students, those students who resolved the contradictions showed better learning gains than those who had not been induced to be confused.

In a more low-key way, Vizcaino (2005) deployed a pedagogical agent as a participant in a group exercise to solve programming problems. The students and the pedagogical agent were operating remotely and communicated via a textual chat interface without any visible presence, with the agent pretending to be another student. The agent would encourage students who were not participating fully to speak up, and those who were dominating to pipe down. One of the agent's interventions was triggered when the group seemed to be getting towards the correct answer to the problem too quickly and easily. It would then interject with a suggestion that another, *deliberately misleading*, path should be followed in order to try to get the students to reflect more deeply on the quality of their initially chosen solution.

Providing False Feedback

It is common practice for teachers and AIED systems to falsely praise the effort and even the performance of students who are not doing well in the hope that this will motivate them.

In an interesting experiment, Strain and colleagues tested the effects of providing learners with false audio feedback of their heartbeats: accelerated, as might occur in challenging or distressing situations, baseline, or no feedback. They found that:

In general, learners experienced more positive/activating affective states, made more confident metacognitive judgments, and achieved higher learning when they received accelerated or baseline biofeedback while answering a challenging inference question, irrespective of the perceived source of the biofeedback.

(Strain et al., 2013, page 22)

So, fooling students into thinking they were well involved in tackling a challenging problem, because their heartbeat (apparently) told them so, was actually helpful, not least because the students did not interpret the accelerated heartbeat as a sign of their distress.

Conclusions

This chapter has explored some of the ethical dilemmas associated with the deployment of AIED systems. It considered the professional ethics of teachers to suggest two underlying principles: (i) doing one's best as a teacher, and (ii) not exploiting one's position as a teacher. It then looked at recent criticisms of AIED systems to see that some deployments had indeed involved neither doing their best nor taking a disinterested position.

Following this, there was a brief discussion about less dramatic ethical dilemmas involving means/ends trade-offs in teaching, whether by human or AIED system. These covered such areas as provoking disruption, withholding help, deliberately causing confusion, and providing false feedback.

Arising from this, there are lessons for the design and deployment of AIED systems that include the following four broad guidelines:

1   Systems should be designed via an iterative co-design process that involves the immediate stakeholders, typically teachers and students, but also possibly parents and others. This will increase the chances that the system helps solve an educational problem of concern to them and in a way that works for them in the context in which it is to be used.
2   Users of systems need training not just in how to use the system (e.g. which button does what) but also in how the system should be used to produce the greatest pedagogic value.
3   Teachers need training not just in how to get the best from the system but also in how to integrate the system into the wider context of their work with students: in other words, good practice in orchestration. This will be especially important if the system deploys pedagogical tactics such as provoking disruption, withholding help, deliberately causing confusion, and providing false feedback as the human teacher may need to explain this behaviour to a student who does not find it at all helpful.
4   All stakeholders should have clarity of what kinds of data the system extracts and creates, what data is stored and/or transmitted, and who has what rights over that data.

Notes

1   See, for example, https://twitter.com/AGavrielatos/status/1121704316069236739 and https://twitter.com/hashtag/TellPearson?src=hash.
2   https://ethical.institute/principles.html.

References

Aimeur, E. & Frasson, C. (1996). Analyzing a new learning strategy according to different knowledge levels. *Computers & Education*, 27(2), 115–127.
Arroyo, I., Woolf, B. P., Burleson, W., Muldner, K., Rai, D. & Tai, M. (2014). A multimedia adaptive tutoring system for mathematics that addresses cognition,

metacognition and affect. *International Journal of Artificial Intelligence in Education*, 24(4), 387–426.

Brown, J. S., Burton, R. R. & Bell, A. G. (1975). SOPHIE: A step towards a reactive learning environment. *International Journal of Man Machine Studies*, 7, 675–696.

Campbell, E. (2000). Professional ethics in teaching: Towards the development of a code of practice. *Cambridge Journal of Education*, 30(2), 203–221. doi:10.1080/03057640050075198.

Dillenbourg, P. (2013). Design for classroom orchestration. *Computers & Education*, 69, 485–492. doi:10.1016/j.compedu.2013.04.013.

du Boulay, B. (2016). Artificial Intelligence as an effective classroom assistant. *IEEE Intelligent Systems*, 31(6), 76–81. Retrieved from http://online.qmags.com/INTS1116/default.aspx?sessionID=8BB8302BBF05B82EF251C8204&cid=3461801&eid=20075&pg=79&mode=2#pg79&mode2.

du Boulay, B. (2019). Escape from the Skinner Box: The case for contemporary intelligent learning environments. *British Journal of Educational Technology*. doi:10.1111/bjet.12860.

du Boulay, B., Luckin, R. & del Soldato, T. (1999, Jul 19–23). *The plausibility problem: Human teaching tactics in the 'hands' of a machine.* Paper presented at the 9th International Conference on Artificial Intelligence in Education (AI-ED 99), Le Mans, France.

General Teaching Council Scotland. (2012). Code of professionalism and conduct. Retrieved from https://www.gtcs.org.uk/regulation/copac.aspx.

Graesser, A. C. (2016). Conversations with AutoTutor help students learn. *International Journal of Artificial Intelligence in Education*, 26(1), 124–132. doi:10.1007/s40593-015-0086-4.

Haake, M. & Gulz, A. (2009). A look at the roles of look and roles in embodied pedagogical agents: A user preference perspective. *International Journal of Artificial Intelligence in Education*, 19(1), 39–71.

Heffernan, N. T. & Heffernan, C. L. (2014). The ASSISTments ecosystem: Building a platform that brings scientists and teachers together for minimally invasive research on human learning and teaching. *International Journal of Artificial Intelligence in Education*, 24(4), 470–497. doi:10.1007/s40593-014-0024-x.

Herold, B. (2017). The case(s) against personalized learning. *Education Week*, 37(12), 4–5. Retrieved from https://www.edweek.org/ew/articles/2017/11/08/the-cases-against-personalized-learning.html.

Hietala, P. & Niemirepo, T. (1998). The competence of learning companion agents. *International Journal of Artificial Intelligence in Education*, 9, 178–192.

Holstein, K., McLaren, B. M. & Aleven, V. (2018). Student learning benefits of a mixed-reality teacher awareness tool in AI-enhanced classrooms. In C. P. Rosé, R. Martínez-Maldonado, H. U. Hoppe, R. Luckin, M. Mavrikis, K. Porayska-Pomsta, B. McLaren & B. du Boulay (Eds.), *Artificial Intelligence in Education: 19th International Conference, AIED 2018, London, UK, June 27–30, 2018 Proceedings, Part I* (pp. 154–168). Cham: Springer.

Karam, R., Pane, J. F., Griffin, B. A., Robyn, A., Phillips, A. & Daugherty, L. (2017). Examining the implementation of technology-based blended algebra I curriculum at scale. *Educational Technology Research & Development*, 65, 399–425. doi:10.1007/s11423-016-9498-6.

Kessler, A., Boston, M. & Stein, M. K. (2019). Exploring how teachers support students' mathematical learning in computer-directed learning environments. *Information and Learning Sciences* 121(1–2), 52–78. doi:10.1108/ILS-07-2019-0075.

Koedinger, K. R. & Aleven, V. (2016). An interview reflection on "intelligent tutoring goes to school in the big city". *International Journal of Artificial Intelligence in Education*, 16(1), 13–24. doi:10.1007/s40593-015-0082-8.

Koedinger, K. R., Anderson, J. R., Hadley, W. H. & Mark, M. A. (1997). Intelligent tutoring goes to school in the big city. *International Journal of Artificial Intelligence in Education*, 8(1), 30–43.

Lehman, B., D'Mello, S., Strain, A., Mills, C., Gross, M., Dobbins, A., … Graesser, A. C. (2013). Inducing and tracking confusion with contradictions during complex learning. *International Journal of Artificial Intelligence in Education*, 22(1–2),85–105.

Morley, J., Floridi, L., Kinsey, L. & Elhalal, A. (2019). From what to how: An initial review of publicly available AI ethics tools. *Methods and Research to Translate Principles into Practices*. Retrieved from https://arxiv.org/abs/1905.06876.

Pane, J. F., Griffin, B. A., McCaffrey, D. F. & Karam, R. (2014). Effectiveness of Cognitive Tutor Algebra I at scale. *Educational Evaluation and Policy Analysis*, 36(2), 127–144. doi:10.3102/0162373713507480.

Rosiek, J. (2003). Emotional scaffolding: An exploration of the teacher knowledge at the intersection of student emotion and the subject matter. *Journal of Teacher Education*, 54(4), 399–412.

Rummel, N., Walker, E. & Aleven, V. (2016). Different futures of adaptive collaborative learning support. *International Journal of Artificial Intelligence in Education*, 26(2), 784–795. doi:10.1007/s40593-016-0102-3.

Schwabenland, C. (2009). An exploration of the use of disruption as a pedagogic intervention. *Educational Action Research*, 17(2), 293–309. doi:10.1080/09650790902914258.

Self, J. (1999). The defining characteristics of intelligent tutoring systems research: ITSs care, precisely. *International Journal of Artificial Intelligence in Education*, 10, 350–364.

Silvervarg, A., Kirkegaard, C., Nirme, J., Haake, M. & Gulz, A. (2014). Steps towards a Challenging Teachable Agent. In T. Bickmore, S. Marsella & C. Sidner (Eds.), *Proceedings of Intelligent Virtual Agents. IVA 2014* (pp. 410–419). Cham: Springer.

Strain, A. C., Azevedo, R. & D'Mello, S. K. (2013). Using a false biofeedback methodology to explore relationships between learners' affect, metacognition, and performance. *Contemporary Educational Psychology*, 38(1), 22–39. doi:10.1016/j.cedpsych.2012.08.001.

Tyson, P. (2001). The Hippocratic Oath today. *Nova*. Retrieved from https://www.pbs.org/wgbh/nova/article/hippocratic-oath-today/.

Vizcaino, A. (2005). A simulated student can improve collaborative learning. *International Journal of Artificial Intelligence in Education*, 15(1), 3–40.

Walker, E. & Ogan, A. (2016). We're in this together: Intentional design of social relationships with AIED systems. *International Journal of Artificial Intelligence in Education*, 26(2), 713–729.

Watters, A. (2015). Education technology and Skinner's Box. Retrieved from http://hackeducation.com/2015/02/10/skinners-box.

Watters, A. (2017). Dunce's app: How Silicon Valley's brand of behaviorism has entered the classroom. *The Baffler*. Retrieved from https://thebaffler.com/latest/behaviorism-education-watters.

Williamson, B. (2018a). Learning lessons from data controversies. Retrieved from https://codeactsineducation.wordpress.com/2018/12/18/learning-lessons-from-data-controversies/.

Williamson, B. (2018b). The tech elite is making a power-grab for public education. Retrieved from https://codeactsineducation.wordpress.com/2018/09/14/new-tech-power-elite-education/.

Williamson, B. (2019). Policy networks, performance metrics and platform markets: Charting the expanding data infrastructure of higher education. *British Journal of Educational Technology*, 50(6), 2794–2809. doi:10.1111/bjet.12849.

Wilson, C. & Scott, B. (2017). Adaptive systems in education: A review and conceptual unification. *International Journal of Information and Learning Technology*, 34(1), 2–19. doi:10.1108/IJILT-09-2016-0040.

10 Integrating AI ethics across the computing curriculum

Iris Howley, Darakhshan Mir and Evan Peck

Introduction

Kate Crawford's 2018 talk on "You and AI: The Politics of AI" at the Royal Society describes a common story of machine learning researchers presenting their predictive policing model, built on datasets from police departments which include such disconcerting issues as labelling infants as identified gang members and the inability of people in the dataset to correct how they are classified within.[1] When asked about these issues, one of the presenters replied, "Well, I'm just an engineer." However, as AI and machine learning technologies scale and deploy to impact thousands (if not millions) of people, refusing responsibility for biased and problematic AI models is no longer affordable from a societal perspective. As the impact of Artificial Intelligence on humanity grows, so does the need for broader ethics training for the future developers of those technologies.

As computer science (CS) educators, it is our responsibility to provide students with the tools to be successful citizens of the world, including habits of critical reflection that weigh the intended and unanticipated consequences of developing software, as well as the larger structural and socio-political conditions in which such software will be embedded. Much has changed since the classic computer ethics courses were created. While they often lean on examples of rocket explosions and radiation overdoses that derive from software malfunctions, new cases must now involve AI algorithms' unanticipated consequences that impact our social and mental well-being, issues of equity, justice, and bias in our societies, as well as physical safety. At the same time, there is a growing recognition within and outside the computing profession that AI-based (or other data-based) decision-making processes are inherently political in that they serve and support certain power configurations over others (Green, 2018; Rogaway, 2015). While it is necessary to update the content of computer ethics courses with these new and emerging issues introduced by AI, it is also time to free computer ethics from its isolation within a single, siloed course. Distributing AI ethics topics through the computer science curriculum better reflects ethics' centrality and importance to the development of technology, and helps centre human values throughout this process. In this chapter, we discuss various use cases from the perspective of

DOI: 10.4324/9780429329067-13

pedagogical practitioners integrating AI ethics across the higher education computer science curriculum. We include examples and approaches for introducing students to AI ethics in the very earliest computer science courses, extending through students' academic careers into upper-level courses. We also present a brief reflection on the challenges and affordances of getting students to think about larger structural conditions in addition to the individual intent of technologists.

When we open the details of our daily lives to technology, we also open up the opportunity for our daily lives to be processed, digested, and analysed by algorithms to extrapolate meaning from the minutiae. Or if we ourselves do not willingly surrender our data, our data and preferred outcomes are being formalized as complex algorithms anyway, assisting officials in determining the level of healthcare we are owed (Lecher, 2018), whether our résumé makes it to the interview stage (Dastin, 2018), and determining who is deserving of parole (Angwin et al., 2016), among other decision-assisting contexts. These algorithms are developed in the hands of software engineers and computer scientists, professionals who, having passed through the hoops of computer science training, are promoted to these positions of power, implementing algorithms – thereby making decisions that impact the daily lives of ourselves, our family, and our communities. However, prior to this professional laurelling, these algorithm-defining experts are students – one student of many in our classrooms, learning their first sorting algorithm and how to swap the values of two variables. As educators, we must ensure our students are equipped with the skills necessary to critically consider the algorithms they implement in their future careers, how their software design decisions can impact human lives, and whose interests these algorithms serve. Today's students will be tomorrow's algorithm engineers; and, through their everyday practice (whether or not they are aware of it), they will weigh efficiency and profit against public safety, justice, fairness, and good for humanity. This path of value negotiation is not straightforward and cannot be explicitly taught with a brief review of a code of ethics.

This concept of computer ethics is often relegated to its own separate course fully dedicated to the topic, especially at larger institutions of learning. While this arrangement does provide opportunity for significant breadth and depth into the consequences of developing computational technology, it also signifies that ethics is a separate topic, often further emphasized by housing the course in a department separate from the computer sciences. In a related context, that of engineering education, Leydens and Lucena emphasize the importance of inculcating *sociotechnical thinking*, which involves "non-bifurcated reasoning in which the social and technical dimensions are not seen as occupying separate realms" (2017, p. 5). Instead, engineers intentionally learn to reflect on the social, political, and associated factors that both shape and are shaped by technical solutions and decision-making processes they are developing. Viewing sociotechnical thinking through the lens of justice, Leydens and Lucena remark on the insufficiency of relegating ethical thinking to isolated ethics courses, noting that this leads to the marginalization of socio-technical thinking in the engineering curriculum. Instead, they advocate for approaches that integrate the social and technical aspects of "problem definition and solution" at multiple junctures throughout the engineering curriculum. In this chapter, we propose distributing computational ethics topics throughout the computing curriculum, emphasizing the central role that critical algorithmic design plays in computer science's impact on society. We also provide some exemplary case studies to illustrate some initial approaches for realizing ethics as a central core to computer science.

Computing Ethics Pedagogical Approaches Overview

Incorporating ethics as a concept into computer science is not a new approach itself as computer code and organizational structure have collided for decades, with occasional dire consequences accompanied by extensive post-mortem accident reports. Whether it be the Ariane-5 rocket exploding in mid-air due to an overflow error (Gleick, 1996) or the Therac-25 radiation machine overdosing six patients with radiation poisoning due to complex interactions with poor user interface design, race conditions, organizational hierarchy, and lax government regulation (Huff & Brown, 2004), there is existing curricular support for investigating these classic use cases. However, with the increasing reliance on Artificial Intelligence for algorithmic decision-making in society at large, there are new case studies that should be included in computer ethics; and here we outline some of the newest published pedagogical work to do so. We will summarize many of the techniques currently employed today, which includes interdisciplinary support for ethics topics, incorporating AI ethics into introductory courses, and providing AI ethics modules in computer science electives.

Integrated computer ethics with philosophy teaching assistants

Harvard University recently implemented a program to integrate ethical issues in computer science, which they named "Embedded EthiCS" (Grosz et al., 2019). Through this plan, they distribute ethical reasoning pedagogy throughout the standard computer science curriculum, embedding these new concepts into existing courses. In each Embedded EthiCS course taught by a computer science faculty member there is also an advanced PhD student or postdoctoral fellow in philosophy assisting. In close collaboration with the course instructor, the teaching assistant develops modules relevant to the course content and leads one or two class sessions on the issue, accompanied by a cumulative assignment. Each module is designed to focus on three core ethical reasoning skills: identifying and anticipating ethical problems in the development and use of computing technologies; reasoning, both alone and in collaboration with others, about those problems and solutions, using concepts and principles from moral philosophy; and communicating their understanding of how to address those problems.

The Embedded EthiCS program was piloted in the 2017 and 2018 academic years across 14 different courses (Grosz et al., 2019). These courses included primarily undergraduate courses covering topics such as introductory programming, theory, networks, programming languages, human–computer interaction, and Artificial Intelligence. Student responses to the ethics pilot were overwhelmingly positive, and informal feedback from faculty was also supportive. The authors found the modules were most successful when the problems covered connected technical material to ethical issues already important to students, such as race and gender bias in automated hiring/interviewing systems. Modules incorporated topics such as the value of privacy and whether it is a right, design requirements for moral or ethical specification, and censorship and fake news, among other ethical issues.

For larger computer science courses with graduate students and teaching staff in philosophy departments, the Embedded EthiCS approach may work well. It effectively removes the burden of being an ethics expert from the computer science faculty, and incorporates experts from other fields, providing opportunities for all instructors to contribute to the interdisciplinary learning of students. At institutions where this level of collaboration is not possible, the burden may fall on the computer science instructors to create their own modules, which may require extensive additional effort to increase ethics expertise.

Integrated computer ethics without teaching assistants

Davis and Walker (2011) present practical approaches to incorporating social issues of computing into smaller institutions, using their liberal arts college, Grinnell College, as the running example. At these smaller programs, students often spend 40% of their coursework on their major, compared to the 60% or more in a typical Bachelor of Science or Engineering course. And so, one of the goals for this approach is to integrate social issues across the computer science curriculum due to practical logistics issues such as limits on student course-taking. At Grinnell, there are modules on computational social ethics for non-majors via the Digital Age course, and first-year tutorials. These classes can include timely topics such as the role of social media in protests and government upheaval, or topics from the computer ethics textbook *A Gift of Fire* (Baase, 2012). For computer science majors, instructors include discussion prompts to consider ethical issues throughout the curriculum, including courses on databases, Artificial Intelligence, and theory of computation. In some courses, such as Software Design, students may be asked to research and present incidents such as Therac-25; or, in Computer Networks, students may read research papers on socially minded network protocols such as onion routing, which is designed for Internet anonymity. Human–Computer Interaction at Grinnell naturally lends itself to projects systematically considering a wide array of design stakeholders as well as ethical treatment of human subjects. Advanced projects, reading groups, and other informal learning opportunities are also leveraged to distribute exposure and hands-on learning with ethics issues in computing.

As in the Harvard Embedded EthiCS program, Davis and Walker also stress the importance of simply mentioning social issues in all computer science courses. For many instructors new to computing ethics, this may be a very practical and doable step towards incorporating more ethics awareness into the computer science curriculum.

Computer Ethics Modules in Human–Computer Interaction

While the previous two approaches discuss distributing ethics coursework across the computing curriculum at a high level, there is also significant recent work that dives deeper into a specific course. Skirpan et al. (2018) describes multiple ethics interventions intended for a Human-Centred Computing course. The authors used a novel "spectrogram" exercise to elicit initial student beliefs: students were asked to stand in a line and were then asked a question with two polar extremes. Students then rearranged their position in the line to represent where in the continuum between the extremes their opinion belonged. Polarizing questions included:

- Do you believe Facebook is good or bad for society?
- Do you believe face recognition technology is good or bad for society?
- Do you think it is good or bad for Facebook to use face recognition technology to identify the faces of untagged people?

(Skirpan et al., 2018)

In other in-class workshops, students were asked to complete tasks such as develop a "wealth index" using Facebook profile data, which was then followed by a talk back where the class discussed biases and concepts of data fairness. Class workshops were preceded by guest lecturers who were experts on that day's topic: a privacy lawyer, researchers focusing on cooperative ownership of data, a typography artist, a senior computer scientist with 50 years' observation of technology transition, etc. Concepts from the ethics sessions were incorporated into the semester-long group project by modifying the project design and including reflections. For instance, the privacy lawyer discussed the European Union's General Data Protection Regulation (GDPR) and students were asked to review their designs, identifying conflicts under the new regulations.

We note that many of the classroom ethics topics considered by Skirpan et al. focus on data ethics, providing an opportunity to naturally integrate them in relevant computer science courses such as Data Structures, Algorithms, Computer Security, Data Mining, Design and Management of Databases, and Machine Learning.

Artificial Intelligence Education for Middle School

While the bulk of the overview in this section highlights pedagogical approaches to AI ethics in higher education, these discussions can begin earlier. The Massachusetts Institute of Technology (MIT) Media Lab's Personal Robots Group has recently released materials for "An Ethics of Artificial Intelligence Curriculum for Middle School Students."[2] Students encounter a series of technical topics, such as building a machine learning classifier or determining what data a YouTube recommendation algorithm is using to make predictions. These concepts are then accompanied by various activities, such as through bingo cards or interface redesigns, to help students reflect on the ethical implications of the technology.

In the unit on "Introduction to Algorithms as Opinions" the authors redesign the "peanut butter sandwich making task," which is often used as a fun activity for introductory computer science students to hint at the level of specificity to design an algorithm for a computer. The instructor has the ingredients to make a peanut butter sandwich (bread, a jar of peanut butter, a knife, a plate, etc.), and asks the students to provide computer instructions to create the sandwich. Students will typically start out with commands such as "get a piece of bread from the bag," and the instructor may rip the bag apart to retrieve the slice of bread, may grab just a small piece of a slice of bread, etc. In the open-source curriculum "An Ethics of Artificial Intelligence Curriculum for Middle School Students" this activity is modified to illustrate that algorithms prioritize certain preferences, and that there is often no universal definition of "best." Students share their instructions with a partner and discuss as a class whether they are optimizing for tidiness (i.e. inclusion of instructions to clean up), optimizing for fun (i.e. cutting the sandwich into playful shapes), and other types of possible sandwich-optimizations. These sandwich-preferences are then tied into technology, which is illustrated by a Google search result on two different accounts returning different results.

Computer Ethics Questioning Framework in Machine Learning

The previously summarized articles contained activities that could be integrated into discussions of Artificial Intelligence ethics, although that was not necessarily how the activities were implemented. Saltz et al. (2019) is a recent systematic literature review examining current machine learning scholarship that addresses ethics in some way. The review identified three areas of focus on the topic of ethics in machine learning – Oversight Challenges, Data Challenges, and Model Related Challenges – accompanied by the guiding questions shown in Table 10.1.

These questions were then provided to students for an assignment in which they analysed two publicly described machine learning projects to identify the top three ethical issues of the project. For example, question 9 on model transparency would likely result in a flag being raised on most neural networks projects, as transparency/explainability is difficult to achieve with the multiple middle layers of these network models. This assignment was accompanied by a general discussion of machine learning ethics, and identifying ethics issues in a sample machine learning project. The authors then conclude by proposing additional relevant ethics questions for three modules in machine learning on the topics of logistic regression, random forest classifiers, and multi-models.

Table 10.1 Three areas of focus on the topic of ethics in machine learning (Saltz et al., 2019)

Challenge	Theme	Questions
Oversight	Accountability and Responsibility	1. Which laws and regulations are applicable?
		2. How is ethical accountability achieved?
Data	Data Privacy and Anonymity	3. How are the legal rights of organizations and individuals impinged by our use of the data?
		4. How are an individual's privacy and anonymity impinged via aggregation and linking of the data?
	Data Availability and Validity	5. How do you know the data is ethically available for its intended use?
		6. How do you know the data is valid for its intended use?
Model	Model and Modeller Bias	7. How have you identified and minimized bias in the data or model?
		8. How was any potential modeller bias identified and mitigated?
	Model Transparency and Interpretation	9. How transparent does the model need to be, and how is that transparency achieved?
		10. What are likely misinterpretations of the results, and what can be done to prevent those?

The case studies presented above illustrate the opportunities already present in a typical CS curriculum to foster ethical and sociotechnical thinking among CS students in a diverse set of institutions. We advocate for distributing ethical thinking through various stages of the CS curriculum, integrating it with core computing concepts when possible, for two reasons. First, ethical and sociotechnical dimensions of computing are frequently made visible in the CS curriculum, indicating that ethics are an integral part of being a computer scientist. The second reason, as Leydens and Lucena (2017) articulate, is to develop CS students' capacities as "problem definers" in addition to "problem solvers" who are capable of considering the deployment of solutions within the larger societal contexts from which these problems arise. To explore these opportunities, the authors of this chapter, in collaboration with colleagues at other institutions, organized a workshop of CS faculty interested in such an integrative approach.

Workshop on Distributed CS Ethics Module Creation

The authors of this chapter ran a workshop at the Association for Computing Machinery Special Interest Group on Computer Science Education conference in 2019 titled "Make and Take an Ethics Module: Ethics Across the CS Curriculum," along with Janet Davis of Whitman College and Michael Stewart of James Madison University (Mir et al., 2019).

Twenty-four computer science educators participated in a three-hour collaborative workshop to create modules on ethical thinking in a CS course. In groups, participants chose an existing course in the typical CS curriculum, and coalesced around common themes to collaboratively create a module that *integrates* critical reflection on ethical choices and societal impact of computing with the practice of computing. Participants worked in five groups and developed sketches of five modules consisting of topics in web development, data science, Object-Oriented Programming, and data structures. Each group was tasked with identifying a target course, a technical topic within the course, and the associated ethical concerns and issues. The groups outlined the learning goals of the module, whether the module would involve in-class work and/or homework, whether it would be individual or collaborative, what artefacts the students would submit, and how they would be assessed.

We illustrate the process that the groups went through using the web development module as an example. After identifying the CS course they were designing for, group members outlined technical and ethical dimensions of the learning goals of their module. The technical aspects involved elements of HTML5 (such as forms and various elements), CSS, JavaScript (such as POST requests), the JSON format, and form validation with HTML5, CSS, and JavaScript. The ethical components involved thinking through: bias (such as gender bias present in the assumptions of cisgenderism, and geographical bias with the assumption of a US residential address); discrimination (such as requiring a last name, which discriminates against cultures that do not use a last name, and requiring the use of English); inclusion and exclusion; accessibility; legal aspects; privacy in the default solutions; and how potential solutions could be modified to be more attuned to these biases. Group members designed an assignment that required students to develop an online application for a specific scenario that would employ decision-making logic (such as a restaurant order, or a college or job application). Technical concepts would include the use of form elements, checkboxes, radio buttons, dropdown menus, input validation, default options, collection of data from the user, encoding of action based on the data collected, and the use of test data. Associated ethical components of the assignment would include a written report on viewing their designed application from the perspective of users with different needs and preferences, keeping in mind ethical considerations (such as bias and discrimination) outlined above. Furthermore, students would reflect on the need for additional test data, and how the use of test data encodes which kind of user is deemed to be "normal." The module illustrates that integrating *sociotechnical thinking* with *technical practice* can begin with smaller-level assignments. If modules such as these become pervasive in the CS curriculum, students will have the opportunity to see that the social contexts are never divorced from technical decisions and solutions. The next section discusses how one of the authors has used this approach in designing a module for an introductory course in computer science.

Integrating Ethics across the Computing Curricula

Case study: Ethics in CS 1

CS 1 offers an important space to calibrate students to programming habits and values that will follow them deep into their careers. Many introductory courses lean on technical problems with purely technical solutions. Reorienting the course towards the *sociotechnical* problems not only mirrors the muddy issues that computer scientists are likely to encounter in their careers, but also aligns with the motivations and values of many incoming students.

The Introduction to Computer Science course at Bucknell University, Pennsylvania, infuses ethical thinking into the curriculum in three important ways:

1   By tightly integrating it directly with *technical* content throughout the semester rather than isolating ethics to a single lecture or assignment.
2   Situating lab or homework problems in sociotechnical contexts where technical solutions without an understanding of people or places are likely to fail.
3   By requiring students to externalize their values with code.

Here, we describe one activity (in a larger sequence) that is completed within a two-hour collaborative laboratory setting.

Housing assignments: algorithms as decision-makers

Just one week into their CS 1 course designed by Evan Peck of Bucknell University, students at the university are presented with a sociotechnical problem that raises issues of transparency and fairness (Parlante et al., 2020). At this moment in the traditional CS 1 curriculum, students learn conditional statements for the first time (if/else), and typically complete small, game-like scenarios in a laboratory setting (such as rock, paper, scissors). While effective in teaching technical skills, there is a consequence to these trivial exercises. Students learn purely technical solutions to purely technical problems, reinforcing early notions that technical solutions are king of the values hierarchy of their CS education.

But many real-world AI problems are messier, requiring careful reflection to navigate decisions with complex human trade-offs. How can we reinforce these ethical decision-making habits alongside the development of their technical skills? In our case, we shift the domain. Instead of applying conditional statements to *rock, paper, scissors*, students are presented with a housing prioritization scenario.

When we say the word "algorithm" we tend to ascribe agency to the computer. It is deciding things for us. But the reality is that there is no magic. There are software developers like you and me who design and create sets

> These algorithms are all around us, and they are constantly making decisions.
>
> The decisions we make in code impact the lives of real people. For example, the *Silicon Valley Triage Tool* is an algorithm that identifies homeless people for whom provision of housing would cost the public less than keeping them homeless. So, even as we learn the simple structures of code, we need to think about how we can make *good* decisions? When the livelihood of people depends on us, how can we be fair?
>
> We are going to explore this idea in a more familiar context to you – *university housing*. Universities like Bucknell select methods that determine the order in which students can choose their housing. You might not think of it as one, but this method is *an algorithm*. In this studio, you will have the opportunity to design your own algorithm and make sure that *the decisions we make are never untethered from the people we impact.*

While still focused on rehearsing conditional statements, students are guided through an iterative design process to program a command-line interface that assigns housing priority at the university.

- **Assessing needs:** "You should not create a program that serves people without talking to people. Talk to other students in class. Ask them about their needs. What unique factors may be important in deciding who should choose housing first?"
- **Prototype an algorithm:** "Now it is time to translate our student needs into a concrete algorithm. Our program will: (1) ask students questions (like *What class year are you?*); (2) assign points based on their answers (like *4 points for senior*); (3) accumulate their total points across all answers (like *You have 23 housing points*)."
- **Test with real users:** "You should not create a program that serves people without testing it on people. At a minimum, you should test it with a couple of people around you. Were the results what you expected? Did you discover any cases which you haven't accounted for previously?"
- **Code:** "Translate your algorithm into code."

At each step in their process, students must confront their assumptions – about their own values and the values of the people who will be impacted by their software. Through this activity, students develop diverse, and sometimes competing, prioritizations regarding housing. Exactly how students value the impact of disability, participation in athletics, age, health concerns, or off-campus commitments in the housing process is explicitly represented in their code (Figure 10.1). This explicit representation not only forces students to reckon with the formal representation of their own beliefs, but also provides a concrete platform to base further discussions on the topic.

```
----------------------------
  HOUSING SCORE CALCULATOR
----------------------------
How many credits do you have?: 20
Do you have a job on campus? (Y/N): N
Are you a student athlete? (Y/N): Y
Do you require accommodations through the office of Accessibility Resources? (Y/N): N
Have you been on probation in your time at Bucknell? (Y/N): N

----YOUR HOUSING SCORE--------
Your housing points score is 3
----------------------------
> █
```

Figure 10.1 A sample program that considers academic standing, off-campus commitments, and accessibility

At the conclusion of their program, students are encouraged to leave the classroom and find additional people to test their code, recording the feedback they receive. In particular, students are asked to reflect on the questions: *Which students are most likely to benefit from your algorithm?* and *Which students are most likely to be forgotten by your algorithm?*

After the assignment

While the activity is technically simple, it introduces reflective habits that are important in the development of responsible computer scientists. At this point, the long-term effects of such interventions are anecdotal, but there are encouraging short-term signals. For example, following the activity, students are required to fill out a questionnaire prompting them to reflect on what conceptual questions they might have about the topic. In past iterations of the course, those questions focused entirely on technical content (e.g. conditional statements or variables). However, after completing the housing assignments, the questions also touched on topics of algorithmic fairness – questioning strategies to understand groups that do not mirror their own needs. We hope that this subtle shift in questions represents an important shift in mindset – questions about making socially responsible decisions are pushed as far to the front of student attention in the course as more traditional technical topics in CS 1.

Subsequent class discussion also led to lively discussions surrounding algorithmic transparency after the following prompt: *Your program doesn't show point values along the way … should it?* Student debates echoed those who argue for and against black box models in machine learning.

It's important to note that this activity does not live in isolation. Subsequent labs explore similar themes of representation, transparency, and automated decision-making. Three additional examples:

- **Learning functions and data types:** Students write input validation code for an online form – deciding how to capture personal information from diverse audiences that are difficult to distil in a single template (for example, name conventions, phone number conventions, gender representation).

- **Learning loops:** Students design an algorithm that filters job applications based entirely on student Grade Point Average (GPA). In this process, they wrestle with writing neutral decision-making algorithms that do not disadvantage various groups of students.
- **Learning 2D arrays:** Students write a program that outputs an average image of several human faces. This activity prompts questions of representation in training data sets, and discussions surrounding face recognition software.

We see continued reinforcement of ethical reflection to be a key component of helping mould more ethical technologists in AI.

Case study: Contextualizing the moral machine

MIT's Moral Machine provides a self-driving car version of the trolley dilemma (Awad et al., 2018).[3] That is, it presents the viewer with a series of hypothetical situations in which they must make a decision for the self-driving car algorithm: save the passengers in the vehicle or the pedestrians on the street? Will the viewer's decision change if there are more women in the car or on the crosswalk? Will it change if the pedestrians are elderly? Overweight? Jaywalking? Walking dogs? Carrying infants? Unemployed? What if you have the option to swerve versus continuing straight, and the different pedestrian groups have different demographics?

Educators often use the Moral Machine as a means to introduce students to the ethics of sociotechnical systems. For students who have never thought about their roles in this complex sociotechnical system, the Moral Machine may present a simple enough introduction to the power society provides to technology and, in turn, to designers of that technology. While this is possibly an appropriate entry point for new thinkers in this area, the activity is not free from critique. In particular, the development of an ethical mindset demands a multi-disciplinary approach with a particular emphasis on power and history. Part of what the Moral Machine simplifies away in order to achieve this accessibility is one of the most important aspects of developing an ethical frame: the history of power. The technology designer does not make decisions about self-driving car algorithms independently; those decisions are informed by myriad biases inherited from society, organizational culture, and the surrounding communities whose historical biases developed over centuries. Future self-driving cars will not be explicitly programmed to "avoid injuring infants and dogs at all costs"; but, through the development of a complex series of algorithmic decisions, such priorities will reflect the existing priorities of the societies producing the self-driving car.

For those practitioners encountering the edges of the Moral Machine's utility, the researchers who developed the application discuss it as a way to investigate cross-cultural moral preferences (Awad et al., 2018). The value in stepping through the over-simplified questions of the Moral Machine as a class may be to not only reflect on one's own values, but also to see how there is no universal set of values. The Moral Machine's developers identify what kinds of morals were codified in the restricted decision-making environment of their application, and identify clusters of countries and demographics whose decisions align. Participating in the Moral Machine activity, guiding student critique of the game mechanics, verbalizing take-aways, and discussing the developers' research results provides students with a more nuanced landscape of the purpose of this activity.

In the Human–Computer Interaction course led by Iris Howley at Williams College, Massachusetts, this contextualized Moral Machine activity is not the students' first encounter with considering and critiquing perspectives of power in design. The course is an upper-level elective in computer science, but often has a small sampling of second-year students and non-majors. Class sessions regularly begin with a discussion of news articles or conversations occurring in user-experience professional communities, and provide opportunities for students to discuss current issues. A simple example is a discussion of why there is push-back against user personas in user research due to its potential slippery slope into stereotyping users (Turner & Turner, 2011). These critiques are distributed throughout the semester so that, when the unit on data-driven design occurs, the class is already accustomed to questioning the validity of existing practices. It is at this point that the Moral Machine activity occurs, accompanied by a sampling of articles from the popular media about the consequences of collecting personally identifiable information, the gig economy, deception in technology, and algorithmic decision-making, among other issues.

What is missing from the weeks of priming students to critique the status quo in technology development, and also easily missed in an exploration of the Moral Machine, is a path forward for the students. It is absolutely essential to provide students an outlook on current tech events and scandals that helps them understand how they can be agents of change. Forgetting this crucial step may result in a shift in student dispositions toward learned helplessness. Introducing the class to just a few current responses to ethical dilemmas provides inspiration for students as they pursue the next stage of their career. Iris Howley's approach to this is essentially a survey of recent articles where tech companies have been inspired to change their behaviour. This includes coverage of government regulation, such as the EU's General Data Protection Regulation, and the work of citizens to hold companies accountable to the GDPR through lawsuits (Veale, 2019). There is a brief overview of worker-led protests and walkouts, such as Google employees' letter of protest with regard to working with the United States Pentagon (Shane & Wakabayashi, 2018) or their walkout to oppose the company's support of censored search in China (Gallagher, 2018), among others. Whistle-blowers are also included, particularly Susan Fowler's blog post that eventually led to Uber CEO Travis Kalanick's resignation (Bariso, 2017). The class coverage of these events and responses changes from year to year, depending on the uncovered issues from the tech industry.

By the end of the semester, students produce a design manifesto detailing five of the most important components of their design philosophy, of which personal consideration of ethics is one component. This allows students to focus on all the ethical implication conversations distributed throughout the semester and consider how those conversations inform their own perceptions of their role as a developer of technology. Students' personal codes of ethics within the design manifesto typically span everything from a set of expectations and limits of themselves and future employers, to a commitment to more thorough identification of stakeholders, to replacing the goal of "being cool" with "don't be evil."

Discussion

The integration of computing technology into the daily lives of people requires a re-examination of how we teach new generations about algorithms and Artificial Intelligence – not just as consumers of technology but also as designers of technology. Integrating AI ethics across the curriculum reflects not only the distributed nature of ethics in computing but also its importance in human lives. In this chapter we provide a high-level overview of many existing approaches to teaching the ethics of Artificial Intelligence across the computing curriculum, to a variety of age groups, with a variety of resources, in a variety of teaching styles. While no one approach described here will fit every instructor's needs, many of these activities can be adapted to fit the varying learning trajectories of students in a diversity of classrooms.

There is also a wide variety of resources available to computer science educators for investigating the ethics of Artificial Intelligence; but this information is distributed and can often be found buried in non-AI based ethics curricula. Casey Fiesler's "Tech Ethics Curricula: A Collection of Syllabi" is one such source that corrals a large quantity of resources on the topic of tech ethics; but the individual practitioner may need to wade through over 200 course syllabi which may or may not have an Artificial Intelligence focus.[4] We hope that this chapter has provided some initial pointers to foundational resources to ease the burden of discovering additional AI ethics pedagogical content. More and more pedagogical resources for the teaching of AI ethics become available as instructors recognize the importance of developing ethical skills and iteratively design activities, and then releasing their materials via research publications and open education resources. This chapter summarized a wide sampling of some of the latest techniques, including our own; but the AI ethics teaching frontier is rapidly advancing, and we recommend the reader investigate what new resources were shared since the finalizing of this chapter.

Notes

1 https://www.youtube.com/watch?v=HPopJb5aDyA.
2 https://www.media.mit.edu/projects/ai-ethics-for-middle-school/overview/.
3 http://moralmachine.mit.edu/.
4 https://medium.com/@cfiesler/tech-ethics-curricula-a-collection-of-syllabi-3eedfb76be18.

References

Angwin, J., Larson, J., Mattu, S. & Kirchner, L. (2016, May 23). Machine bias: there's software used across the country to predict future criminals. And it's biased against blacks. *ProPublica*. https://www.propublica.org/article/machine-bias-risk-assessm ents-in-criminal-sentencing.

Awad, E., Dsouza, S., Kim, R., Schulz, J., Henrich, J., Shariff, A., ... & Rahwan, I. (2018). The moral machine experiment. *Nature*, 563(7729), 59.

Baase, S. (2012). *A gift of fire*. Pearson.

Bariso, J. (2017, June 21). How a single, courageous voice led Uber's CEO to resign. *Inc.* Retrieved from https://theintercept.com.

Dastin, J. (2018). Amazon scraps secret AI recruiting tool that showed bias against women. *Reuters*. Retrieved from https://www.reuters.com/article/us-amazon-com -jobs-automation-insight-idUSKCN1MK08G.

Davis, J. & Walker, H. M. (2011, March). Incorporating social issues of computing in a small, liberal arts college: A case study. In *Proceedings of the 42nd ACM technical symposium on Computer science education* (pp. 69–74). ACM.

Gallagher, R. (2018, November 27). Hundreds of Google employees tell bosses to cancel censored search amid worldwide protests. *The Intercept*. Retrieved from https://theintercep t.com.

Gleick, J. (1996, December 1). A bug and a crash: sometimes a bug is more than a nuisance. *New York Times Magazine*.

Green, B. (2018). Data science as political action: Grounding data science in a politics of justice. ArXiv:1811.03435.

Grosz, B. J., Grant, D. G., Vredenburgh, K., Behrends, J., Hu, L., Simmons, A. & Waldo, J. (2019). Embedded EthiCS: Integrating ethics across CS education. *Communications of the ACM*, 62(8), 54–61.

Huff, C. W. & Brown, R. (2004). Integrating ethics into a computing curriculum: A case study of the Therac-25. In A. Akera & W. Aspray (Eds.), *Using history to teach computer science and related disciplines* (pp. 255–277). Computer Research Association.

Lecher, C. (2018, March 21). What happens when an algorithm cuts your health care. *The Verge*.

Leydens, J. A. & Lucena, J. C. (2017). *Engineering justice: Transforming engineering education and practice*. John Wiley & Sons.

Mir, D., Howley, I., Davis, J., Peck, E. & Tatar, D. (2019, February). Make and take an ethics module: Ethics across the CS curriculum. In *Proceedings of the 50th ACM Technical Symposium on Computer Science Education* (pp. 1239–1239). ACM.

Parlante, N., Zelenski, J., DeNero, J., Allsman, C., Perumpail, T., Arya, R., Gupta, K., Cang, C., Bitutsky, P., Moughan, R., Malan, D.J., Yu, B., Peck, E.M., Albing, C., Wayne, K., Schwarz, K. (2020, February). Nifty assignments. In *Proceedings of the 51st*

ACM Technical Symposium on Computer Science Education (SIGCSE '20) (pp. 1270–1271). ACM. doi:10.1145/3328778.3372574.

Rogaway, P. (2015). The moral character of cryptographic work. *Lecture Notes in Computer Science*, 9452.

Saltz, J., Skirpan, M., Fiesler, C., Gorelick, M., Yeh, T., Heckman, R., ... & Beard, N. (2019). Integrating ethics within machine-learning courses. *ACM Transactions on Computing Education (TOCE)*, 19(4), 32.

Shane, S. & Wakabayashi, D. (2018, April 4). "The business of war": Google employees protest work for the Pentagon. *New York Times*.

Skirpan, M., Beard, N., Bhaduri, S., Fiesler, C. & Yeh, T. (2018, February). Ethics education in context: A case study of novel ethics activities for the CS classroom. In *Proceedings of the 49th ACM Technical Symposium on Computer Science Education* (pp. 940–945). ACM.

Turner, P. & Turner, S. (2011). Is stereotyping inevitable when designing with personas? *Design Studies*, 32(1), 30–44.

Veale, M. (2019). *Governing Machine Learning that Matters* (Doctoral dissertation, University College London).

Conclusions
Toward ethical AIED

Kaśka Porayska-Pomsta and Wayne Holmes

In 1960, Norbert Wiener discussed "Some Moral and Technical Consequences of Automation" (Wiener, 1960). A pioneer of cybernetics, often credited with an early formulation of intelligent behaviour (of living things and machines) as a feedback mechanism, Wiener made two related observations which are not only pertinent to this day, but whose implications have since acquired a somewhat prophetic quality.

The first observation relates to learning and adaptive capabilities as prerequisites of human-like 'intelligent' computers – whereby, to be considered artificially intelligent, a machine must be able to learn from and to act on the environment in ways that maximise the probability of it achieving some pre-specified objective. This first point has been well rehearsed and refined over the past 60 years (see e.g. Legg and Hutter, 2007; Russell and Norvig, 1995; Russell, 2019) in what has subsequently become known as the field of Artificial Intelligence. The outcomes and implications of these rehearsals continue to emerge in diverse forms of AI innovations and applications, including in the context that is central to this book, namely AI in education. One implication, for better or worse, that relates to Wiener's first observation is the ever-growing 'smartness' of technology, which often transcends some human capabilities – *nota bene* the technology's capacity to track and harness at speed a growing number of pasts in some specific contexts to predict many possible futures in those same contexts (e.g. Russell, 2019).

The significance of Wiener's second observation, which links directly to the implication stated above, remained largely obscured to AI practitioners until the recent advances in AI (*sic* machine learning) and the shift of AI from research laboratories into mainstream usage. This second point concerns the idea that, as machine capabilities grow and as technologies become smarter, our ability to keep pace with and to understand their operations decreases. This gap between the increasing machine smartness and our ability to keep up with it is time-constant in the sense that, while machine performance accelerates both in speed and accuracy on specific tasks, human abilities remain comparatively unchanged and slow. Put together, the two observations highlight a real possibility of an event horizon for humans (a singularity) whereby, in Wiener's own words: "by the time we are able to react to information

DOI: 10.4324/9780429329067-14

conveyed by our senses and stop the car we are driving, it may already have run head on into a wall" (p. 81). Wiener's profound and to date largely disregarded take-home caution here is that:

> *If we use, to achieve our purposes, a mechanical agency with whose operation we cannot interfere once we have started it,* because the action is so fast and irrevocable that we have not the data to intervene before the action is complete, *then we had better be quite sure that the purpose put into the machine is the purpose which we really desire* and not merely a colourful imitation of it.
>
> (Wiener, 1960, p. 1358; emphasis added)

While it might be tempting to interpret Wiener's caution as a doomsday exaggeration, given the increasingly well-documented concerns about AI's operation and the impact thereof in diverse contexts, it is difficult to ignore the palpability of the situation it refers to. At a general level, there are multiple questions that arise from this caution. One such question is philosophical in nature, as it relates to what we consider the desired purpose (or purposes) to be. To address this question demands a continuous (re-)interrogation of our values from different epistemological perspectives (moral, social, economic, individual, collective, etc.) and at different levels of granularity – from high-level aspirations for society down to low-level tangible outcomes for individuals. As has been discussed throughout this book, such questioning is non-trivial, for the answers will depend on who is formulating and addressing the questions, when, and why (Chapter 6). Such questioning is also likely impossible to lead to conclusive answers, or to solutions that simultaneously or permanently satisfy all concerns and all concerned (Chapter 7).

Another important question that arises from Wiener's reflections is of a civil engineering nature, as it interrogates what AI technologies we design and how we ensure that they are fit for our purpose (assuming that the purpose is known). Indeed, the question relates to whether and how we build AI tools to address human challenges in ways that are beneficial not merely by intention but by their design, operation, and, critically, by the feedback that comes from their actual usage.

In his recent work, Stuart Russell returned to Wiener's observations, both to debunk the popular notion of AI as a human mirroring artefact and to question the fundamental assumptions of the field as a whole (see for example Russell, 2019; ATI lecture).[1] In doing so, Russell draws a precise link between those fundamental assumptions (which he declares mistaken) and the moral and ethical challenges related to AI technologies. Specifically, he emphasises and reiterates Wiener's second observation by stating that while AI already exceeds some human capabilities, and at some point in the future it may exceed them all – although currently there is scant evidence of that (Vallor, 2021) – there will never be a time when human and AI capabilities will be comparable. Where AI is growing computationally powerful, humans remain computationally limited; where AI remains rigid in its preferences, human preferences have high plasticity; where human preferences and inferences are hierarchically structured, those of AI are often not, and so on.

To try to compare AI and humans is not only misguided; it also fuels an unwanted division between AI, the ethics of AI, and the ethics of the broader socio-economic systems (including the educational system) within which AI operates. This is because such comparison diverts us from the fact that much human activity, including the technological inventions that are used to aid or enhance such activity, is based on the same standard model – namely one that involves setting an objective and devising means that single-mindedly maximise the achievement of that objective. The standard model we use in AI is rooted deeply within the economics of our existence, where success is evaluated against discrete and measurable benefits and utilitarian values (typically using economic values of cost, loss, utility, etc.) that are fixed into the way we define and go about achieving our objectives in society more generally. As Russell explains, the issue with this standard model being applied in AI lies in its rigid insistence on solving problems within local optima of the limited contexts within which AI operates. It also lies in human fallibility in specifying the objectives that can be guaranteed to be ethical and beneficial to all possible stakeholders at all times, or that can extend towards pursuing global optima that are native to the complex nature of human environments and activities (see also Chapter 1).

There are many examples in AI, and indeed in other domains, that demonstrate these issues. In AI, this has become manifest through some more obvious examples of the choices of problems with which AI has been tasked, that are ethically questionable at their base – such as the infamous example of using face recognition to predict criminality. Some less obvious examples include defining the objective function to maximise click-throughs, for example on social media. Far from having innocent consequences, this has led to a marked proliferation of divisions between people, and an entrenchment of people's prejudices, by the sheer fact that by feeding people content that they are likely to click on, their pre-existent biases tend to be reinforced. Here, Russell draws our attention to how the standard model of AI lies at the core of even the simplest machine learning algorithms, making people more uniform and predictable. Instead of merely pushing content that the users want, the machine learning algorithms that underpin these kinds of applications fundamentally modify people's views towards more predictable and eventually towards more extreme positions, hence creating a much easier environment for AI to classify and to achieve its objectives.

Given that within the standard model, the sole true objective of AI is to optimise the local environment to maximise the chances of success therein, it stands to reason that, if the objective we assign to the AI is wrong or harmful to us (or some of us) by some definition, then the smarter the AI and the worse the outcomes will be for us. Linking back to Wiener's car crash metaphor, given human neuro-cognitive make-up that predisposes us to act on first impressions and automating habitual processes such as the way we interpret our environment and make decisions (see e.g. Houdé et al., 2000), we may not realise in time how we are being changed by this standard optimisation model being enacted on us. In this context, one blind-spot in how we study the benefits and pitfalls of our relationship with AI seems to lie in our lack of understanding of and available research on how AI interacts with human psychology – a point alluded to by Holstein and Doroudi in Chapter 6.

As has been discussed and examined throughout this book, AI in education is not immune to the concerns raised by Wiener and Russell. Furthermore, it represents one of the very high-stakes areas in which these concerns must be examined and addressed urgently, given that education not only shapes life-long thinking and action of individuals from a young age, but also that it is an obligatory element of every person's development, and a fundamental human right. Jutta Treviranus' eloquent discussion in Chapter 1 speaks of the over-arching ethical concerns for AI in education deriving from its unexceptional position within the broader AI domain insofar as its dominant investment in developing tools such as tutoring systems that optimise "the path to the dead-end of the local optima". Such local optima are defined by the demands of the pre-existent socio-economic contexts, of which education forms an integral part. Her commentary seems not so much about tutoring systems being wrong or unethical in themselves; rather, it is about the lack of recognition (mainly outside the AIED community) that they are limited in terms of their pedagogies and their target domains and target users.

AIED: A solution and/or applied philosophy?

Intelligent tutoring systems represent a *low hanging fruit* for the EdTech industry and business-driven educational policies, as they easily fit into the established interpretation of what learning is in terms of drill and practice mastery learning towards exams. Intelligent tutoring systems do not challenge the status quo of the educational system, and thus their offering is relatively easily monetised. And yet, as is clear from du Boulay's defence in Chapter 9 of the AIED pedagogies and his discussion of the related ethical dimensions, the pedagogies employed in intelligent tutoring systems represent only one example researched and designed for in the field. Other forms of pedagogies include exploratory learning, collaborative learning, enquiry learning, learning by teaching, etc. (see also the Introduction to this volume) – each involving diverse and often nuanced pedagogical strategies and tactics. These pedagogies also recruit tools such as open learner models (e.g. Bull and Kay, 2016), learning by teaching (Biswas et al., 2005), or nuanced help-seeking approaches (Aleven et al., 2016), that aim to foster in students critical thinking through reflection, self-monitoring, and self-regulation – albeit that few of these have graduated from the lab to become commercial or widely available tools. Thus, as du Boulay explains, the last 20 years have seen a growing diversification of AIED pedagogies, with AIED researchers investing greatly both in understanding what best pedagogical practices are in different contexts and in trying to define and support what Seymour Papert called the *art of learning*, which involves active construction of knowledge, discovery, learning from mistakes, and metacognitive competencies. This investment stands in contrast with many commercial EdTech practices and claims, which, as Paulo Blikstein highlighted in his invited talk at the International Conference on Artificial Intelligence in Education in 2018, reflect the industry's push to seize on the seductive allure of AI as a commercial highlight to deliver half-baked and educationally questionable quack 'solutions'. In his chapter, du Boulay channels growing calls for the need to establish auditing processes for AIED to monitor the quality of the educational offerings from the EdTech industry and AIED research community.

One question that arises from du Boulay's discussion relates to what should be the role of AIED research, if any, in establishing best AIED practices and related ethics auditing processes? How should the AIED research community position its contribution with respect to the growing appetite of a money-making industry and stop-gap fixes by governments to introduce evidence- and knowledge-poor, self-proclaimed miracle cures to the challenges and ailments of the educational systems? These questions are not intended to dismiss the potential of the EdTech industry or AI-related education policies. Instead, in line with Blikstein's reflections, they aim to help us pause and consider what we want and need respectively from policy, from the EdTech, and from the AIED research community. While policy tends to be an enabling force for change in the real-world contexts – and while EdTech may have better financial resources to deliver at speed AIED applications that work in the real world – AIED research allows us to consider fundamental questions about how humans learn and develop; how we can support learning and development of students across different ages and in different domains; what constitute best pedagogical practices and contexts that are conducive to learning; how AI tools might be designed specifically to support teachers rather than to undertake teacher tasks, and so on. For examples of this see Aleven et al. (2016). In asking such questions, AIED's identity emerges not merely as a design science where interventions are being developed to improve educational outcomes, but as a form of applied philosophy where challenges are being identified and positioned in wider human contexts, and fundamental theory is being developed.

The view of AIED as an applied philosophy aligns with Smuha's discussion in Chapter 5 and with Treviranus' suggestion in Chapter 1 that the way out of the dead-end of the local optima is to diversify our perspectives – to be willing to fail, to change paths and strategies to collaborate across differences, and to find the courage and means to extend our thinking beyond the categorical – so that we can embrace human difference as a strength and as a welcome catalyst for innovation and cultural progress rather than as a hindrance (see also Porayska-Pomsta and Rajendran, 2019; Mau, 2019). Treviranus' manifesto for the future of AI in education involves key questions such as: what do we want to automate, accelerate, and optimise in education; what are we willing to remove from the current practices; and how will the purposes we put into the teaching machines ultimately shape who we are and how we function individually and collectively? Through this she draws attention to the fact that the way we design and deploy AI in education and what ethical questions we interrogate in this context are not separate from the questions about the values and moral drivers that we must ask of the educational system itself in order to then inform how such systems might be served by the AI power tools.

The call for change in the way that we think about the role and designs of AI in education systems in either amplifying or alleviating broader socio-technical and economic inequalities and exclusive practices is a running theme throughout this book. Each chapter offers an important contribution towards developing a clear, transdisciplinary understanding of what it is that AI does and may still contribute to the context of supporting human learning and development. Crucially, each chapter rehearses distinct questions about AI in education within the broader socio-economic context, spotlighting key issues from different standpoints. From these different perspectives, we can begin to piece together an initial sketch of AI in education's strengths and weaknesses, considered common across the different perspectives, and we can identify the blind-spots for the field with respect to ethics.

In Chapter 6, Holstein and Doroudi provide a detailed map of the perspectives of stakeholders whose voices are crucial to our gaining a better view on the questions we may need to ask of AI in education as operating in much larger socio-technical settings. In this, they implicitly highlight the diverse nature of the pronoun 'we' that is routinely used in calls to action (also prevalent in this book) in AI in education. Their discussion and the roadmap towards fairer AIED highlight the need for transparency and precision in declaring whose perspective is being emphasised, in pointing out that each perspective employs different methods that may lead to very different conclusions. Treviranus (Chapter 1), Brossi, Castillo and Cortesi (Chapter 4), and Madaio, Blodgett, Mayfield and Dixon-Román (Chapter 8) all apply different magnifying glasses to explicate that too often the perspectives and the diverse needs of the key intended beneficiaries, namely learners, are invisible to the designers of curricula – and, by extension, to the designers of AI systems who implement those curricula. Brossi and colleagues focus on the need for the active participation of young people in the design, deployment, and evaluation of AI systems that they are asked to use; but they point out that the lack of such participation reflects established 'adults-know-best' assumptions within the pre-existent systems that all too often lead to young people being disenfranchised from their own educational experiences. Madaio et al. talk about the frequent erasure of learners from minority groups by the sheer fact that mainstream curricula are designed typically by dominant groups for the dominant populations (typically white middle classes), which often hinders the cultural accessibility of the established curricula and related pedagogies to learners from minority groups. Treviranus delivers another example of the exclusive nature of the mainstream educational system which de facto marginalises neurodiverse learners because it is in essence designed to cater for neurotypical learners, whereby any marked divergence from the so-called 'norm' is understood as a form of deficit and deviation (leading to, but all too often not being recognised as, harms of ex-nomination). The issues raised within those chapters are not exclusive to AIED; rather, they highlight issues that pervade the educational and other domains of the socio-economic system. As such, the discussions within this book reveal how technology designs mirror the established system and how technology serves as an amplifier of this system. Thus, while AI may not mirror us, it has certainly proven to be able to offer a clear mirror on ourselves and our practices.

AIED: A research methodology

Many of the examples described in this book document biases that are prevalent in educational contexts. Such biases tend to lead to a multitude of consequences related to both harms of allocation (i.e. the inability of some people to access key resources) and harms of representation (i.e. some people's identities and associated needs not being represented, or being over-represented to the point of stigma), as already outlined in the Introduction to this volume. Such biases also solidify particular research foci within the AIED field, as well as the assumption of cultural and neuro-cognitive uniformity of student populations. As is demonstrated throughout this book, a precise contextualisation of these biases is necessary to allow us to question systematically who the different AIED systems serve and how; how they may serve as enablers to some and disablers to others; and who benefits and who loses out, and why, as a consequence of the particular AIED designs and modes of deployment. In turn, such questioning is necessary to improve, update, and de-bias our research practices and methods (Fox, Chapter 2; Madaio et al., Chapter 8). It is also important to our being able to diversify AIED's research and design methodologies; to facilitate a greater transparency with respect to the strengths and weaknesses of the tools we build to then inform our policies with respect to AIED (see especially Bartoletti's discussion in Chapter 3); and, as Howley, Mir and Peck explain in Chapter 10, to educate AI practitioners for whom ethical considerations of the AIED systems are as critical as the programming languages they use to develop such systems.

One important characteristic of AIED that is rarely recognised outside of the immediate AIED community is that it relies on AI models not just to build intelligent learning environments to deliver educational solutions, but also (and in many respects primarily) to address the fundamental questions (philosophical, theoretical, and practical) raised within the field. This methodological aspect of AIED (*AIED as a methodology*; see also Porayska-Pomsta, 2016) is clearly illustrated through Kizilcec and Lee's painstaking examination in Chapter 7 of the assumptions related to fairness and equity in education, and AIED more specifically, as encoded in algorithms. Through examining different models of fairness, they draw attention to the types of assumptions and methodologies that impact on the quality of data and algorithms in AI applications for education. They use this examination to elaborate on the challenges identified in the broader AI context with respect to fairness, specifically highlighting and demonstrating mathematically that equity and equality are two somewhat contradictory central notions related to fairness in education. The contradictions they reveal raise questions about the disparities between how AIED's diverse users are treated and how they are impacted by algorithmic interventions. While equality may be achieved through innovation if all individuals benefit the same amount regardless of their pre-existing capabilities, to achieve equity (e.g. closing the achievement gaps between learners from different socio-economic backgrounds) the impact of innovation must be positively greater for those with lower outcomes. This positioning presents a set of questions, likely some dilemmas, and further obligation of transparency for AIED designers with respect to both the form of algorithmic fairness they choose to furnish their systems with and the claims they can make about the generalisability of their applications to diverse users and contexts of use. When used as a research methodology AI can offer a means for systematic experimentation and interrogation in this context.

Concluding remarks

Every domain of AI's potential application reflects the overarching ethical concerns discussed across the ethical AI literature (e.g., Floridi and Cowles, 2019). However, each domain also brings very specific challenges that require not only close and contextualised examinations but also actionable 'so whats' that can lead us out of the inertia fuelled by the rhetoric of the futility of any resistance against 'AI happening to us' into active explorations of the possible answers that illuminate, confront, and allow us to change the status quo. Equally, we do not want to resist for the sake of resistance. Instead, we are after a systematic and considered understanding of the risks as well as the benefits of AI that can be used as a basis for informed debate, decision-making, and refinement of our practices.

Throughout this book, there is a consistency with respect to the kinds of ethical challenges that the field of AIED faces; and a set of proposals from across different perspectives for how we need to go about questioning what AIED is, what role it plays and might need to play in society, and how it can become a more defined and accountable discipline. There is a concerted call for questioning the assumptions on which AIED is based and for continuous involvement of multiple, diverse stakeholders in the design and auditing of AIED systems as well as the research methods and outcomes thereof that are employed within the field. No contribution in this book offers definitive answers. Instead, each chapter poses a series of critical questions for the AIED field. Sometimes these questions pertain to the kind of educational tools that AIED produces and their role in amplifying or ameliorating social inequities. In other instances the questions focus on the ethical value of the assumptions we make in both how we design AIED systems and why, whereas in other cases the authors pose fundamental philosophical questions about what role AIED plays in shaping the way we educate the new generations. The totality of the contributions presented in this book leads to a picture of AI in education as a multifaceted discipline (as illustrated in Figure 11.1) which can act as a form of applied philosophy, a methodology for studying questions about learning and pedagogy, and as a form of civil engineering concerned with addressing immediate education-related challenges within society at large.

In the Introduction to this book, we suggested that a wider foundational perspective may need to be adopted by the AIED practitioners to engage actively in establishing the purpose of the AIED field (Holmes et al., 2018; Kay, 2012). As has been illustrated through all of the contributions herein, the community is ready to step up its engagement with the broader societal contexts which it has always claimed to serve to ensure that it is both *doing things ethically* and *doing ethical things* (Holmes et al., 2021), and that its research and practices are able to stand up to scrutiny within those wider contexts.

If, as AIED practitioners often claim, such a grand ambition is to help make education and access to it fair and equitable, then a number of conditions, derived from the discussions throughout this book, need to be met (documented in the bottom-right corner of Figure 11.1). First, individual AIED systems need to be built for **transparency** to allow for inspection by different stakeholders of a multitude of assumptions on which they are based. These include pedagogical assumptions (i.e. the pedagogical approaches that they encode): data on which their models have been constructed; biases both in terms of their representational quality, such as a declaration of the exact intended users; and the exact socio-cultural orientation of their curricular, pedagogical, and communication models.

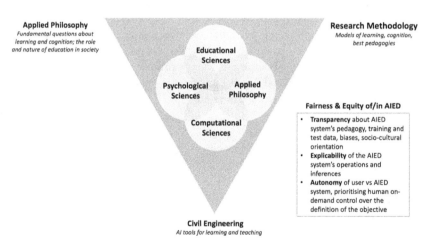

Figure 11.1 Multifaceted nature of the AIED field, affording a flexible transdisciplinary approach to designing for and auditing fairness and equity of and in AIED systems

Second, the systems need to be built for **explicability** with respect to their operations. This includes: explaining how the algorithms that underpin their models make inferences; what objective function or measure of success they follow; and what their known inferential blind-spots are (e.g. generalisability across different students in different learning scenarios, levels of analytic granularity, etc.).

Third, the systems need to be built for human **autonomy**, giving different users the ability to modify or to stop the operation of the system. How this is achieved exactly will be determined by who the user is and, indeed, what standard model remains at the base of such systems. In this respect, AIED stands at the forefront of developments in the broader AI field, offering examples of AI-enabled approaches such as the open learner models and the teachable agents that challenge the standard model, at least of education, and where users are given different levels of control over their data and the systems' inferences. This last dimension relates directly to Russell's call for the need to challenge the standard model on which our AI designs are based (discussed earlier) by removing the assumption of a perfectly known objective from the design of AI systems, and instead relying on the interaction between the human and the AI to negotiate the objectives for the individual users, with AI taking actions that expand rather than dictate human choice.

As such, we are optimistic that AIED can serve to examine grand questions about the meaning and purpose of education, and about its own role in helping shape that purpose. Through the process of defining such a purpose AIED can help formulate research questions about human cognition and development. For example, to spotlight the strengths and weaknesses of particular pedagogical supports in particular educational settings and specific types of learners, it can help address practical questions about what tools we can design, at whom they are targeted (students directly or teachers to help them teach more effectively), and how we can deploy them to help our (transdisciplinary and multi-stakeholder) grand ambitions come to fruition. With a mindset of ethical AIED, we are also optimistic about the community's ability and willingness to offer knowledge (rather than opinion) about where true opportunities for AI enhancement or change of human educational practices exist, and provide scientific evidence of where caution or even opposition is needed.

Note

1 https://www.youtube.com/watch?v=_H87qqT8pdY&t=1s.

References

Aleven, V., Roll, I., MacLaren, B. M., & Koedinger, K. R. (2016). Help helps, but only so much: Research on help seeking with intelligent tutoring systems. *International Journal of Artificial Intelligence in Education*, 26, 205–223, doi:10.1007/s40593-015-0089-1.

Biswas, G., Leelawong, K., Schwartz, D., Vye, N., & the Teachable Agents Group at Venderbilt (2005). Learning by teaching: A new paradigm for educational software.

International Journal of Applied Artificial Intelligence, 19(3–4), 363–392. doi:10.1080/08839510590910200.

Bull, S. & Kay, J. (2016). SMILI⊠: A framework for interfaces to learning data in open learner models, learning analytics and related fields. *International Journal of Artificial Intelligence in Education,* 26(1), 293–331. doi:10.1007/s40593-015-0090-8.

Floridi, L. & Cowls, J. (2019). A unified framework of five principles for AI in society. *Harvard Data Science Review,* 1(1).

Holmes, W., Anastopoulou, S., Schaumburg, H., & Mavrikis, M. (2018). *Technology-enhanced personalised learning: Untangling the evidence.* Robert Bosch Stiftung. https://www.bosch-stiftung.de/sites/default/files/publications/pdf/2018-08/Study_Technology-enhanced%20Personalised%20Learning.pdf.

Holmes, W., Porayska-Pomsta, K., Holstein, K., Sutherland, E., Baker, T., Shum, B. S., Santos, O. C., Rodrigo, M. M. T., Cukorova, M., Bittencourt, I. I., & Koedinger, K. (2021). Ethics of AI in education: Towards a community-wide framework. *International Journal of Artificial Intelligence in Education.* doi:10.1007/s40593-021-00239-1.

Houdé, O., Zago, L., Mellet, E., Moutier, S., Pineau, A., Mazoyer, B., & Tzourio-Mazoyer, N. (2000). Shifting from the perceptual brain to the local brain: The neural impact of cognitive inhibition training. *Journal of Cognitive Neuroscience,* 12(5), 721–728.

Kay, J. (2012). AI and education: Grand challenges. *IEEE Intelligent Systems,* 27(5), 66–69. doi:10.1109/MIS.2012.92.

Legg, S. & Hutter, M. (2007). Universal intelligence: A definition of machine intelligence. *Minds & Machines,* 17, 391–444. doi:10.1007/s11023-007-9079-x.

Mau, S. (2019). *The metric society: On the quantification of the social.* Wiley.

Porayska-Pomsta, K. (2016). AI as a methodology for supporting educational praxis and teacher metacognition. *International Journal of Artificial Intelligence in Education,* 26, 679–700. doi:10.1007/s40593-016-0101-4.

Porayska-Pomsta, K. & Rajendran, G. (2019). Accountability in human and artificial decision-making as the basis for diversity and educational inclusion. In J. Knox, Y. Wang & M. Gallagher (eds), *Speculative futures for artificial intelligence and educational inclusion.* (pp. 39–59). Springer.

Russell, S. (2019). *Human compatible: Artificial intelligence and the problem of control.* Penguin.

Russell, S. & Norvig, P. (1995). *Artificial intelligence: A modern approach.* Prentice Hall.

Wiener, N. (1960). Some moral and technical consequences of automation. *Science,* 131, 1355–1358.

Vallor, S. (2021). The thoughts the civilized keep. *Noēma.* https://www.noemamag.com/the-thoughts-the-civilized-keep.

References

Aiken, R. M. & Epstein, R. G. (2000). Ethical Guidelines for AI in Education: Starting a Conversation, *International Journal of Artificial Intelligence in Education,* 11, pp. 163–176.

Floridi, L. & Cowles, J. (2019). A Unified Framework of Five Principles for AI in Society, *Harvard Data Science Review,* 1(1). doi:10.1162/99608f92.8cd550d1.

Holmes, W., Porayska-Pomsta, K., Holstein, K., Sutherland, E., Baker, T., Shum, S. B., Santos, O. C., Rodrigo, M. T., Cukurova, M., Bittencourt, I. I., & Koedinger, K. R. (2021). Ethics of AI in Education: Towards a Community-Wide Framework. *International Journal of Artificial Intelligence in Education.* doi:10.1007/s40593-021-00239-1.

Index

Locators in *italics* refer to figures and those in **bold** to tables. The acronym AI is used for Artificial Intelligence.